**Conservation**

*Conservation* by Clive Hambler is the latest addition to the popular Studies in **Biology** series of undergraduate textbooks. The book gives an overview of all aspects of this rapidly changing and controversial field. With the decline of species and our encroachment upon natural habitats, conservation is increasingly in the public eye. Maintaining the diversity of life on this planet and using our natural resources in a sustainable manner is important to protect the options of future generations. An understanding of conservation biology is essential to debates and action on the environment. As with all books in the series, *Conservation* will act as an aid to learning and to field work. It is meant to be used as an introductory text and as a study aid for examinations.

CLIVE HAMBLER is a lecturer in biological and human sciences at Hertford College and the Department of Zoology, University of Oxford, UK.

**Studies in Biology** series is published in association with the Institute of Biology (London, UK). The series provides short, affordable and very readable textbooks, aimed primarily at undergraduate biology students. Each book offers either an introduction to a broad area of biology (e.g. *Introductory Microbiology*), or a more in-depth treatment of a particular system or specific topic (e.g. *Photosynthesis*). All of the subjects and systems covered are selected on the basis that all undergraduate students will study them at some point during their biology degree courses.

## Titles available in this series

# Conservation

Clive Hambler

Department of Zoology, University of Oxford

CAMBRIDGE
UNIVERSITY PRESS

PUBLISHED BY THE PRESS SYNDICATE OF THE UNIVERSITY OF CAMBRIDGE
The Pitt Building, Trumpington Street, Cambridge, United Kingdom

CAMBRIDGE UNIVERSITY PRESS
The Edinburgh Building, Cambridge, CB2 2RU, UK
40 West 20th Street, New York, NY 10011–4211, USA
477 Williamstown Road, Port Melbourne, VIC 3207, Australia
Ruiz de Alarcón 13, 28014 Madrid, Spain
Dock House, The Waterfront, Cape Town 8001, South Africa

http://www.cambridge.org

First published 2004

Printed in the United Kingdom at the University Press, Cambridge

*Typefaces* Adobe Garamond 11/13 pt. and Frutiger    *System* LATEX $2_\varepsilon$   [TB]

*A catalogue record for this book is available from the British Library*

*Library of Congress Cataloguing in Publication Data*
Hambler, Clive, 1960 –
Conservation / Clive Hambler.
   p.   cm. – (Studies in biology)
Includes bibliographical references (p. ).
ISBN 0 521 80190 7 (hardback) – ISBN 0 521 00038 6 (paperback)
1. Conservation biology.   I. Title.   II. Series.
QH75.H3626    2003
333.95′16 – dc21      2003055316

ISBN 0 521 80190 7 hardback
ISBN 0 521 00038 6 paperback

# Contents

# Preface

Conservation is at the core of environmental science. Maintenance of the diversity of species and habitats, and the sustainable use of resources, are important to protect the options of future generations. Many would argue it is also a moral imperative that humanity does not needlessly destroy other inhabitants of this planet.

No single book can cover in depth the full range of the science and practice of conservation. I hope that this small guide can at least give an overview of the scope of the subject. It is intended to serve both as an introduction to those new to the field, and as a modern synthesis to demonstrate links between the many specialisms required in conservation. It focuses on generalities, which are illustrated by examples and supported by evidence from the field and from theory. It is intended as an aid for coursework, fieldwork, and management. Technical terms have been kept to a minimum. Instead of a glossary, a definition is given at the first use of specialist terms and phrases (which can be found via the index). There is slight overlap between some sections, to make each more self-explanatory. A huge amount is being written about conservation, and this book should help to guide readers towards the most influential specialist sources.

Environmental sciences are advancing rapidly, against a cultural and policy background that is changing even faster. There have been many developments in conservation biology in recent years, such as the recognition of the general importance of edges in habitat fragmentation, or concerns about introduced genes repeating the unpleasant surprises caused by introduced species. There have been rapid developments in the technology of management of captive populations and the re-introduction of species. The potential and limitations of restoration ecology are becoming clearer. Climate change is bleaching reefs and disrupting biogeographical zones. Gaia has achieved a scientific respectability. 'Sustainability' has become a buzzword – yet is it an illusion caused by a narrow, human-orientated vision of the world and resources? This book surveys these developments and debates, and places them in the matrix of classical ecology.

My measure of the success of this book will be how much it helps those of us who care about our own and other species to become more effective conservationists.

I thank the very many people with whom I have debated these issues over the years. I cannot thank them all individually, but they include: Susan Canney, Malcolm Coe, Nigel Collar, Charlie Gibson, Peter Henderson, Paul Johnson, David Macdonald, Jeanne Mortimer, Norman Myers, Jenny Newing, Chris Perrins, Mark Seaward, Sir Richard Southwood, Martin Speight, Phil Sterling, Graham Wragg, and Nobuyuki Yamaguchi – who also drew several of the figures. The opinions expressed are my own, and may be controversial. Any errors are also my own. Several publishers and authors very kindly gave permission to reproduce illustrations, as noted in the captions. An anonymous reviewer provided very helpful comments. In Oxford, the Department of Zoology, Hertford College, and my students and colleagues provided a stimulating environment. Cambridge University Press, and particularly Ward Cooper, Carol Miller and Beverley Lawrence, eased me through the project. I thank my family, for encouraging my biophilia. The book is dedicated to the natural world.

# 1

# Introduction to conservation

## 1.1 General introduction

Conservation is perhaps one of the most important subjects to understand. Are we devoting too much effort to it, or too little? Future generations will discover the answer, and they will judge us in the way we judge those who wiped out the dodo or fought over diminishing resources on remote islands. Conservation means different things to different people. In this book I aim to show the broad scope of the subject, and the need to be aware of the inter-linkage of many disciplines in theory and in practice. The subject includes fields as diverse as biology, philosophy, economics, chemistry, welfare and human rights. Conservation deals with issues that are very urgent – and, as we will see, often very controversial.

It should always be remembered that there are many personal and subjective opinions in conservation, as well as opinions supported by strong scientific consensus. The reader should see any book on conservation as an introduction to the debates, rather than a statement of universally agreed facts and solutions. It is important that people think for themselves about the issues, and decide what they feel are the strongest arguments supported by the best evidence.

This chapter examines the meaning of conservation, and how it has grown as a field. It also asks if we need conservation, and how much biodiversity there is. The second considers the general threats to biodiversity, and the third discusses the way priorities are set. We will then move in Chapter 4 to methods for monitoring and for Environmental Impact Assessment. Having selected sites and species to conserve, we may need to manage them as described in

Chapters 5 and 6. In Chapter 7 we examine the question of sustainability. Chapter 8 outlines the growing field of restoration ecology and the potential for repairing habitats. In Chapter 9 the role of social factors, such as economics, law and education, are presented briefly, to place biological conservation in context. The book concludes in Chapter 10 with an overview of the prospects for conservation.

Conservation has emerged as a mix of disciplines linked by a common philosophy. The basic and central aim of conservation is to prevent irreversible loss of the life on this planet. We may achieve this through management, which influences species, or habitats, or both. Through conservation we will certainly influence present generations, but we very much hope to leave the world a better place for future generations. This book will present the arguments which suggest that causing substantial and irreversible change to the living world will be severely detrimental to the welfare and prospects of huge numbers of people. Fortunately, we still have time to make a big difference.

## 1.1.1 Origins and meaning of conservation

Conservation did not develop suddenly as a subject, and it is older than many people believe. The idea has developed over thousands of years, in a variety of different forms and in many parts of the world. The word has been used in connection with nature for about a hundred years, after Theodore Roosevelt popularised its use in the USA as 'the wise use of the Earth and its resources'.

It is hard to find a definition of conservation which suits everybody. The World Conservation Strategy of 1980 defines it as: 'The management of human use of the biosphere so that it may yield the greatest sustainable benefit to the present generation while maintaining its potential to meet the needs and aspirations of future generations'. The three main aims of the Strategy are: to maintain essential ecological processes and life-support systems; to preserve genetic diversity; and to ensure the sustainable utilisation of species and ecosystems. This definition has been criticised by many conservationists because it is centred on the usefulness of nature to humans, rather than on protecting nature for its own sake. The distinction between the 'use value' and the 'intrinsic value' of nature is considered in Section 9.1.

I suggest a broader definition: 'Conservation is the protection of wildlife from irreversible harm'. Wildlife includes all non-domestic species and populations of plants, micro-organisms and animals. By 'irreversible' I mean changes that are not reversible within a human generation. By 'harm' I mean damage or declines due to people. As well as protecting species of no use, and the habitats required by populations, this will reduce the effects of one human generation on future generations (Section 1.3.1).

The main themes in the history of conservation have been the protection of spiritual and aesthetic features, preservation of game, maintenance of forest resources, protection of soils and water supplies, animal welfare and, more recently, concerns for genetic resources and the atmosphere. Conservation can be taken to include protection of geological features and soils (which often have relevance to the study of life and the environment), and archaeological features (which may yield information regarding past environments).

Although it may appear a boring exercise, it is very important and sobering that we begin by considering the long history of conservation. The words of early conservationists are often astonishingly similar to those of today. Yet despite such long-standing concern, and indeed action, many problems such as loss of forests, game and soil have often proved unstoppable, and the warnings of many farsighted leaders, authors and philosophers have proved correct. A summary of events which I suggest have been particularly significant in the development of international conservation is given in Table 1.1.

Philosophies and activities that are recognisable as conservation can be found in early writings in many parts of the world. About 2550 years ago, the prophet Jeremiah noted '. . . the whole land is made desolate because no man layette it to heart.' Some 2450 years ago, Artaxerxes I tried to control the felling of Lebanese cedar. About 2400 years ago, in Ancient Greece, Plato lamented the loss of attractive forest and the subsequent soil erosion, which he saw as a consequence of population growth. Some 2000 years ago, Pliny the Elder was concerned that the Romans were desertifying the Mediterranean area through deforestation, and Varro noted that overgrazing by goats was destroying vegetation.

Many religious practices have led incidentally or deliberately to conservation. Belief in the presence of spirits in particular areas, or in trees and rocks, has often helped to protect nature. Mediterranean peoples believed gods inhabited hill crests and mountains – which were consequently cherished. In the Middle East, groves of trees were protected because they were the residences of gods, and sacred groves were protected by the Greeks and Romans; these were often the only woodlands to survive in a region. In Africa, Madagascar and India, forests were set aside for spiritual reasons, including the presence of ancestral spirits. Monasteries in ancient China protected relicts of oak and cedar forests, and some Buddhist and Taoist shaman protected groves in which to meditate – an early expression of Transcendentalism (Section 1.3.1). In North America, tribes revered the spirits of many animal species, and chose not to hunt some of them. Some 800 years ago, St Francis of Assisi departed from

Table 1.1 *Some pivotal dates in the development of conservation*

| | |
|---|---|
| 1803 | Thomas Malthus publishes essay on limits to population growth |
| 1886 | Audubon Society founded in USA in response to slaughter of bird species and plumage trade |
| 1892 | Sierra Club founded by John Muir and others in USA to 'enjoy, explore and protect' wild places |
| 1899 | Royal Society for the Protection of Birds founded in Britain, in response to the fur and plumage trade |
| 1902 | International Council for Bird Preservation conceived (became ICBP, then BirdLife International) |
| 1903 | Society for the Preservation of the Fauna of the Empire founded (became Fauna and Flora Preservation Society, then Fauna and Flora International, FFI) |
| 1913 | John Muir and others protest against Hetch Hetchy Dam in California (subsequently built) |
| 1921 | State Committee for the Conservation of Nature formed in the USSR |
| 1924 | All-Russian Society for the Conservation of Nature founded |
| 1934 | Office International pour la Protection de la Nature founded (became IUCN, the World Conservation Union) |
| 1945 | United Nations Educational, Scientific and Cultural Organisation (UNESCO) founded |
| 1948 | Inter-American Conference on Conservation of Renewable Natural Resources |
| 1949 | Red Data Lists of threatened species initiated (became the Red Data Books of IUCN) |
| 1961 | World Wildlife Fund founded to raise money for IUCN (now the World Wide Fund for Nature, WWF) |
| 1962 | *Silent Spring* published, written by Rachel Carson – warning of pollution |
| 1968 | *The Population Bomb* written by Paul Ehrlich |
| 1968 | *Biological Conservation* launched – the first academic journal of conservation |
| 1960s | First photographs of the Earth from space by Apollo missions illustrate limits of the planet |
| 1970 | European Conservation Year |
| 1970 | First international meeting on conservation biology, organised by British Ecological Society |

| | |
|---|---|
| 1970 | Man and the Biosphere programme (MAB) launched by UNESCO to foster sustainable use |
| 1971 | Friends of the Earth founded – an early lobbying and fundraising group |
| 1972 | World Heritage Convention adopted |
| 1972 | UN Conference on the Human Environment, Stockholm – stimulated initiatives, e.g. UNEP |
| 1975 | Greenpeace – the first direct-action group – sails to 'save the whales' |
| 1976 | Wilderness Society founded in Australia |
| 1979 | Publication of *The Sinking Ark* by Norman Myers – the first synthesis of modern conservation |
| 1980 | World Conservation Strategy launched by IUCN, UNEP and WWF |
| 1982 | World Charter for Nature adopted by UN General Assembly |
| 1983 | Franklin Dam protest – David Bellamy arrested |
| 1985 | Society for Conservation Biology launched in the USA |
| 1987 | World Commission on Environment and Development reports on the state of the environment (*The Brundtland Report*) |
| 1987 | *Conservation Biology* launched – the third academic journal of conservation |
| 1987 | Montreal Protocol adopted to protect the ozone layer |
| 1989 | Thailand bans all logging in its forests |
| 1992 | United Nations Conference on Environment and Development (the Earth Summit) and Rio Declaration |
| 2001 | President Clinton of the USA signs an Executive Order protecting roadless Federal forests from logging and roads |
| 2002 | World Summit on Sustainable Development, Johannesburg, aims – where possible – to protect and restore marine fisheries, using protected areas and Maximum Sustainable Yields. Commitment to significantly reduce the loss of biodiversity by 2010 |

a traditional perspective focused on humans, and praised non-human life – as well as the Moon, Sun and stars. Many shamanic healing practices require respect for particular places and medicinal species.

Many ancient cultures, having recognised overuse of resources, took action to try to conserve forests, soils or game. In Ancient China 2600 years ago, rulers enclosed forested lands for protection of selected species from overhunting, and protected some individual species by laws. In Britain and France in the Middle Ages, many poachers were trapped in man-traps, or executed. In

1060, King Edward ordered the removal of fishing weirs on the Thames, Trent and Severn rivers in Britain. Legislation has regulated salmon fishing in Scotland since the fifteenth century. In Russia, laws protecting game were signed in the eleventh century; in seventeenth century Russia, 67 hunting laws were enacted, felling of trees was forbidden in Siberia (to protect the sable), and forests were protected to conserve individual tree species or to reduce flooding. In Germany in the sixteenth century, several princes revoked community land rights which were leading to forest destruction. Some 200 years ago, King Andrianampoinimerina of Madagascar punished people who wilfully destroyed forests.

What might be described as a *scientific* effort to manage forest resources for the long term, with protection or re-planting, was evident in Sweden by 1752. An awareness of environmental consequences of deforestation developed in numerous places. A link between deforestation, reduced rainfall, and increased erosion was suggested on British colonies in the Caribbean, and in 1776 an Ordinance was signed to protect the Tobago Forest Reserve '. . . for the purpose of attracting frequent Showers of Rain upon which the Fertility of Lands in these Climates doth entirely depend'. This is an example of conserving what we today call the 'ecosystem services' of water supply and soil-binding (Section 1.3.3).

The early history of awareness of the need for *global* conservation is dom-inated by Britain and the USA. These countries have motivated or served as models for many conservation initiatives around the world, although their prominence in this section of the book should not be taken to imply that mod-ern conservation is dominated by these nations. The British Empire, covering a quarter of the Earth's land in the nineteenth century, suffered many environ-mental problems which came to the attention of both colonists and govern-ment in Britain. In an early example of international conservation, colonists persuaded the government to protect forests in Madras, India, through a law in 1847, whilst aesthetic and scientific concern over the loss of the soils and vegetation of the Cape of South Africa led to protective legislation from 1846. In 1873, the American Association for the Advancement of Science presented Congress with a petition calling on the Federal Government to take some action to conserve natural resources. In the USA, the conspicuous loss of populations of species such as the bison, redwood, Carolina parakeet and the passenger pigeon, combined with the fragmentation of the once huge wilder-ness and the decline of game species, led to an ethic of protection of species and land on a large scale. In the USSR, the Geographical Society formed a Nature Conservancy Committee in 1907, which initiated legislation for nature reserves.

I suggest that the dawn of today's scientific conservation biology was linked to the dawn of understanding of evolution. The founders of modern biology – Charles Darwin, Thomas Huxley and others – gained the background to conservation by their observations on their travels, by their wonder at extinct fossil forms, and by their realisation that the world is a very changeable place. For example, Darwin and colleagues noted with concern the overhunting of the giant tortoises on Aldabra, in the Indian Ocean, which held the last wild population in the region: in 1874 they wrote to the Governor of Mauritius, expressing their concern over '. . . the imminent extinction of the Gigantic land Tortoises of the Mascarenes in the only locality where the last remains of this animal form are known to exist in a state of nature . . .'. They continued: 'The rescue and protection of these animals is recommended less on account of their utility . . . than on account of the great scientific interest attached to them. With the exception of a similar tortoise on the Galapagos Islands (now also fast disappearing), that of the Mascarenes is the only surviving link reminding us of those still more gigantic forms which once inhabited the continent of India in a past geological age . . . It flourished with the Dodo and Solitaire, and while it is a matter of lasting regret that not even a few individuals of these curious birds should have had the chance of surviving the lawless and disturbed conditions of past centuries, it is confidently hoped that the present Government and people . . . will find a means of saving the last examples of [their] contemporary'.

This quote illustrates that, by the end of the nineteenth century, some people were already aware of the utilitarian, scientific and moral importance of saving distinctive species – and indeed these remain the major themes in modern conservation.

Scientific education in conservation was evident by 1914 when W. Hordenay wrote the book *Wildlife Conservation in Theory and Practice* based on his lectures in Yale University; this title is echoed in several modern textbooks. However, conservation has very many elements other than science. The philosophical and aesthetic basis of conservation varies amongst cultures, places and times, and will be discussed in Section 1.3.

Animal welfare philosophies and sentiments have been entangled with wildlife conservation for some time. Although conservationists are more likely than most to be sensitive to animal suffering, the two issues are separable, and indeed animal suffering may happen as a result of conserving as well as not conserving. It is ironic that this early force for conservation sometimes leads to problems in modern conservation management, for example in control of exotic species, in game-hunting for revenue in reserves, and in culling to prevent overpopulation.

One British hunter operating in North America in the 1920s became sensitised to the decline of his prey (such as beaver and lynx) and to the suffering inflicted by traps. The concerns of his Native American wife for animal welfare helped convert him from killing animals to protecting them. The trapper then claimed he was a Native American, and called himself Grey Owl. His lecture tours and books were highly popular, and encouraged the British royalty to take an interest in conservation. He was the first popular ecowarrior. Animal welfare grew to be a highly conspicuous driving force for conservation in the 1970s. Some of the earliest public campaigns for conservation, and the first high-profile 'direct-action', came after television pictures of the cruelty of whaling. These led to the initial popularity of Greenpeace, who placed their boats between harpoon gunners and whales.

Pressure from sport hunters (concerned mainly with the loss of their prey, rather than welfare), led to many early game parks and national parks. Although some would deny it, this pressure has saved many species. The word 'park' comes from the Norman hunting 'parcs'. In Europe, as with America, hunting was – and is – part of the reason for protection of many private lands that remain relatively rich in wildlife. In Britain, these include upland moors that are protected and managed for shooting grouse, farm woodlands kept for introduced pheasants, and field margins for grey partridge. The best preserved forest in Europe is Bialoweiza, in Poland: this reserve was established in 1564 to attempt to save aurochs (wild cattle), and was protected from the stripping of forests for timber in the World Wars because the German leaders intended it to become their hunting preserve. By 1900, there were some 500 game parks in the USA, mostly maintained as private hunting clubs, and from 1900 colonial powers in Africa and India established many game reserves. The origins of conservation of freshwater and marine systems are also generally linked to the hunting and fishing lobby. Concern about declining fish stocks, such as the salmon in Britain, prompted legislation to keep rivers clean, whilst concern about the loss of game fish such as marlin and sailfish has recently led to outlawing of long-line fishing in some oceanic areas.

The first recognisable modern 'national parks', which were set up partly for protection of landscape heritage for the public good, rather than just for hunting, were in the USA, USSR and Britain. Aesthetic concerns for wilderness are evident in the writings of the Romantic poet William Wordsworth, who was inspired by the beauty of the English Lake District. Wordsworth wrote in 1810 of the need to protect the Lakes as 'national property' for all to enjoy, and this ideal of national heritage was echoed when Judge Cornelius Hedges opposed private ownership and development in the Yellowstone area of America. There was concern in America in the late 1800s about many of the Federal lands being lost through theft, or destroyed through overuse. Yellowstone Park was created by an Act in 1872, to be 'dedicated and set apart as a public park or pleasuring ground for the benefit and enjoyment of the people; and all persons who shall locate or settle upon or occupy [it] shall be considered trespassers and removed therefrom'. The impetus for this park came primarily from the eastern sports enthusiasts and from an idealist intent to save the interesting and beautiful scenery of the region, including the geysers. National Parks were also seen as refuges from hunting from which game animals would spread into adjacent lands. Hunting, fishing and trapping were permitted only for recreation and use by residents and visitors, so wildlife was theoretically protected from wanton destruction of game and timber and from exploitation for profit; however, following overhunting, it took until 1883 to prohibit all hunting and killing of game in Yellowstone Park, and to provide policing by the military. By 1900 there were 14 National Parks in the USA, and these served as models for other nations.

In 1916, the National Park Service Act created America's National Parks Service 'to conserve the scenery and the natural and historic objects and the wildlife therein and to provide for the enjoyment of the same in such manner and by such means as will leave them unimpaired for the enjoyment of future generations'. Scientific research into wildlife in the Parks began in earnest in 1921, with the Roosevelt Wild Life Experiment Station.

In the USSR, Lenin created a number of nature reserves by decree, such as the VI Lenin Nature Reserve, which was founded in 1919 to protect waterfowl and spawning grounds of commercial fish in the Volga Delta. The Soviets protected very large areas for genetic resources, protection of unique landscapes, and the study of processes in completely natural communities. Britain set up government agencies to select natural sites for protection, and designated its first National Parks (including the Lake District and Snowdonia) in 1951. Both the British and American parks reflect the widespread desire for a 'wilderness experience' (Section 1.3.2). However, whilst America still has some large areas which at least appear wild, the British Isles is more densely populated, and so the focus in Britain was on amenity and 'quiet enjoyment'. The British parks are unusual compared with those in many other countries because they were created in a landscape that was already very highly managed for agriculture. The agricultural and residential use of British parks surprises many foreign visitors expecting wilderness. This is particularly evident in the new South Downs National Park.

Societies dedicated to conservation grew from the middle of the nineteenth century. In Britain, the Commons, Open Spaces and Footpaths Preservation Society was founded in 1865, and developed by 1895 into the National Trust for places of Historic Interest or Natural Beauty. By 1900, there were numerous private nature reserves in Britain. The first private nature reserve in the USSR (Askania-Nova) was founded in 1874, to protect virgin steppe habitat, and became a State reserve in 1921. The plight of birds, with their exceptional beauty and fascination, led to the formation in the USA of the Audubon Society in 1886 and Sierra Club in 1892. Their members were outraged by the slaughter of birds such as the passenger pigeon, and various species of egret which were being overexploited for their fashionable feathers. In Britain, The Royal Society for the Protection of Birds (RSPB) grew for similar reasons from the Fur and Feather Group, which was founded in 1889, and became the first conservation society to act internationally. The Society for the Preservation of the Fauna of the Empire was also among the first international conservation organisations, and is now called Fauna and Flora International (FFI). The members' journals of the FFI and RSPB, *Oryx* and *Birds,* were amongst the first periodicals to promote and discuss conservation.

International organisations now dominate the conservation movement – as befits the global nature of the problem. The International Union for the Conservation of Nature and Natural Resources (IUCN, now the World Conservation Union) was founded in 1948 '. . . to promote or support action which will ensure the perpetuation of wild nature and natural resources on a world-wide basis, not only for their intrinsic cultural or scientific values but for the long-time economic and social welfare of Mankind'. The World Wildlife Fund (now the World Wide Fund for Nature, WWF) was established in 1961, partly to help raise funds for IUCN.

Conservation biology had become a distinctive discipline by 1968, when the multidisciplinary journal *Biological Conservation* was launched as 'The international Quarterly Journal devoted to scientific protection of plant and animal wildlife and to the Conservation or rational use of the biotic and allied resources of the land and fresh waters, sea and air, for the lasting cultural and economic welfare of Mankind'. Another journal on conservation, *Environmental Conservation*, commenced in 1974.

Major conferences began to draw nations together in conservation. In 1948, there was a multidisiplinary Inter-American Conference on Conservation of Renewable Natural Resources, which met at Denver, Colorado, '. . . to discuss one of the greatest of all problems of our times' and noted 'the goal of conservation is always permanence and plenty. People who do not believe in their future do not concern themselves with the conservation of their resources . . .'. In 1970, an international conference dedicated to conservation biology was organised by the British Ecological Society, which led to the classic book *The Scientific Management of Animal and Plant Communities for Conservation,* edited by two pioneers of conservation biology, Eric Duffey and A. S. Watt. A similar meeting in America in 1985 founded the Society for Conservation Biology, and its journal *Conservation Biology* commenced in 1987.

Conservation has become a mainstream political issue since the publication of the World Commission on Environment and Development (*The Brundtland Report*) in 1987, and the United Nations Conference on Environment and Development (UNCED or 'Earth Summit') in Rio in 1992. Various international and national mechanisms and treaties have been set up (Section 9.2). There has been a great rise in public discussion of the issues, and new terms such as 'biodiversity' and 'sustainability' have become buzzwords, displacing older ones such as 'wildlife' and 'preservation'. However, although the surge of global interest is recent, we should always remember that conservation has a *very* long history. Unfortunately, despite many of the ideas having been around for thousands of years, species have become extinct at a gathering pace.

As we have seen, conservation began in many places as a method for protecting species for various human uses – essentially to maintain a yield. To some, it was synonymous with 'preservation' – prevention of any changes induced by people. For thousands of years, there have been conservationists championing the idea of sustainable use, and the idea of protection of other species for their own sakes. These aims will be discussed in Section 1.3, after considering what diversity there is that may need conservation, and what pressures gave rise to the growth in concern.

## 1.2    Introduction to biodiversity

Biodiversity is the variety of life on Earth. A fuller definition is given in the *Convention on Biological Diversity* (CBD) from the 1992 Earth Summit: 'the variability among living organisms from all sources, including, amongst others, terrestrial, marine and other aquatic ecosystems and the ecological complexes of which they are a part; this includes diversity within species, between species and of ecosystems'. The diversity of indigenous human cultures is sometimes included, and most certainly needs urgent attention. However, it is not helpful to make the definition of biodiversity so inclusive, because culture can change very fast and because, as we shall see in Chapters 2 and 9, the protection of culture and the protection of non-human species may sometimes be in conflict.

Measurement of biodiversity is one of the greatest scientific challenges of our time. It is also one of the most urgent, because, unlike the exploration of subatomic particles or the cosmos, we must address the problem soon or we will lose the chance forever. With many species becoming extinct without trace, we may never know, even roughly, how many species there were on the planet when humans first evolved about two million years ago. The longer we delay an attempt to answer this question, the less accurate our answer will be. We will almost certainly leave this unanswered question as a legacy to our descendants – who will therefore never be able to gain a detailed understanding of their planet.

## 1.2.1  Diversity of species

Does it matter whether or not we know the number of species on the planet? It would certainly be helpful and interesting, but fortunately it is not a fact that is essential to conservation. Many of the processes which conservation seeks to protect depend on an unknown or changing number of species. Since we do not know the consequences of losing any one of these species, we should act with caution and assume that protecting most of them is sensible. However, we might want to know the number of species in an area to help us assess extinction rates, or to guess the value of sites for pharmaceuticals – diverse sites might have a longer potential list of medicinal species.

The diversity of species, or 'species richness' is the simplest aspect of bio-diversity to understand and quantify – but even this is in fact far from easy to measure, because biologists have long debated what a 'species' actually is. Ideally, a species is a group of organisms which can interbreed to produce fertile offspring, and which are reproductively isolated from other species. However, this situation is complicated by those species that reproduce asexu-ally, by groups such as the ducks, dogs and cats, which can hybridise amongst the 'species', and by micro-organisms such as bacteria and viruses, which can exchange genetic material between very distantly related forms. There is a spectrum of ability to hybridise, ranging through races and subspecies, and the distinctions are often subjective. Some biologists believe 'Evolutionary Significant Units' should replace the concept of species.

A diversity of species may approximate to a diversity of genes, and genes are the most fundamental unit of both biodiversity and evolution. Genes are even harder to count than species, and in Section 3.2.3 we will examine how to measure 'phylogenetic diversity' in order to protect genetic diversity for posterity.

One of the main problems in estimating the richness of species on Earth is knowing how many species of microbe there are – if indeed the term can be applied to them. Microbes occur in enormous abundance in most habitats – from volcanic hotsprings to oil seams kilometres below the Earth's surface. In a gram of soil, there may be more than 10 000 species of bacteria, but because most of them are too specialised to grow in culture, we know of their existence only through genetic probes. Crucially, it is not at all clear how widespread a typical microbial species is: do the same ones occur in soil in New Zealand, Europe and the Amazon? The great distance some microbes can disperse (as they float or are blown around the world) suggests such species might be widespread; alternatively, rapid evolution amongst microbes may lead to many distinctive local populations or species. In the marine environment, which was once thought to be a relatively sterile medium, it is now known there can be about a million microbes (including viruses) per cubic centimetre of water – but it is not known how widespread each type is.

In addition to the free-living microbes, it is possible that there are specialist microbial organisms parasitic in, or symbiotic with, every multicellular organism. Each relatively big species (such as an insect, plant or mammal) may support unique viruses, protists, fungi and bacteria – on or in its body.

The number of species of microbe may one day become clearer using 'molecular taxonomy', which compares the genetic material (DNA or RNA) of the organisms. The diversity of microbes may not seem to be an important conservation issue, but in fact they are very important for a variety of reasons – they are fundamental to ecosystem services, to disease and to the stability of ecosystems, and are the sources of numerous medicines such as antibiotics.

Despite the possibly overwhelming diversity of microscopic life, including fungi and protists, the estimates of the Earth's species richness have so far focused on the larger terrestrial invertebrates, and particularly the insects. There are several reasons for this. Invertebrates far outnumber the vertebrates and plants in richness. Their taxonomy is relatively easy, and enthusiasts have been working out the differences between species within groups such as the beetles and spiders for hundreds of years. We have a crude working knowledge of the relationship between morphological differences and the distinctiveness of species – for example, the genitalia of different species are usually physically distinctive (which isolates them from reproduction with other species). Even so, numerous species are being discovered each year, as new subtle differences are found. Indeed, the diversity of the nematodes and mites, which are often hugely abundant but morphologically similar, may one day be found (through molecular taxonomy) to far exceed the better-known groups.

The insects are conspicuous, clearly diverse and easy to separate as species. However, there are far too many individuals and species of insect for the current number of taxonomists to deal with. As a short-cut to an estimate of richness, various methods have been used that do not depend on identifying all the species, and some of these are discussed in Section 4.4.

During the 1970s, estimates of the number of species were of the order of a few million. Then, in 1980, Terry L. Erwin of the Smithsonian Institution caused great controversy when he suggested an estimate a factor of ten higher: possibly 30 million insects. Since then, the assumptions in his estimate (based on extrapolation from the herbivorous beetles in the canopy of a single tree species in one site in Panama) have been debated, yet Erwin continues to argue for large numbers of species. He argues there may be many species in small habitats (such as bark, or litter up trees, or tree-holes), and that specialist species will not be shared between such habitats.

On land the tropical forests often appear to be the most species-rich habitats, but the richness of tropical savannahs may also be high, and G. C. McGavin has shown this has been somewhat neglected. Similarly, in the oceans the coral reefs appear the richest sites – at least on superficial inspection. However, one of the greatest uncertainties in estimating the richness of the Earth is the richness of the oceans – and particularly the deep ocean floor, which is largely unexplored. According to P. J. D. Lambshead, there may be up to 100 million species of deep ocean nematodes! Similarly, P. Bouchet has found numerous species of tiny mollusc unique to individual submarine ridges, which could add up to large numbers of species. We do not know how homogenous the ocean floor is physically and chemically, how isolated and distinctive different regions of the floor are, and how well many marine organisms can disperse. We therefore cannot know the richness of species on Earth – even within a factor of ten!

There is a strong line of argument which suggests that global species richness is not as high as some scientists claim. Robert M. May argues that if we have only identified a tiny fraction of the species on the planet, then most of the species in a random sample from the ocean floor, or from a coral reef, or a rainforest canopy, should be new to science. Yet usually taxonomists find they can already identify a few percent of them – suggesting we are getting to grips with diversity.

As yet, only some 1.5–1.8 million species have been described by taxonomists (some more than once – a problem known as 'synonomy'). Even this figure is uncertain, because there is no central database of species which have been described. New species are being described at about 10000 per year. The estimated total richness on Earth varies from 3 million to over 100 million species, and a review by May reveals many experts suggest a figure in the range of 5–15 million. Based on the number of fossil families, some believe more species presently exist on Earth than ever before in its history.

## 1.2.2   Diversity of habitats

Whilst many people like the idea of 'habitat diversity', habitats are even more difficult to define and distinguish than species. In Section 3.2.3 we will see how the diversity of habitats may add to, but also detract from, the conservation value of a site. Here we consider what habitat diversity means.

Habitats are usually subjectively defined by the dominant vegetation or physical substrate, and by the climate of an area. We speak of habitats such as deserts, woodlands, and seagrass. On a smaller scale, habitats may be divided into 'micro-habitats', such as the forest canopy, tree-holes, bark, or rotting wood. Many species may use only one or a few of these, yet depend on the wider habitat to maintain the micro-habitat. The term 'habitat' is often used to describe where a species lives, or what it needs.

The use of the dominant vegetation and climate to label and map habitats is a convenience based on our own body size and sensory methods – and we should always remember that other organisms may partition the world in very different ways from us. Organisms may need more than one 'habitat'. For example, a great crested newt needs a pond to breed in, and grassland or woodland to grow and hibernate in – yet we would generally list and map these three as separate habitats. Similarly, to a protist, the edge of the pond may not be where the human eye sees it, but may be in what we call soil.

A number of other terms are used rather loosely when describing the combination of species in an area, and some of these may be interchanged with the word 'habitat'. The 'ecosphere' (or 'biosphere') is the entire ecosystem on the planet. 'Ecosystems' are generally seen as large areas, in which energy from the Sun or a geochemical source is dissipated as heat as it moves through a relatively self-contained food chain. However, some material and energy will leak into other ecosystems. People sometimes talk of relatively isolated small areas, such as ponds or tree-holes, as ecosystems. 'Biomes' are very large areas (often belts around the globe), with a broadly similar habitat, which some scientists divide into 'ecoregions'. An 'assemblage' is a neutral term, meaning the mix of species found in an area (without assuming strong interactions between them). A 'community' is a group of species in an area, many of which interact with each other – for example through mutualism, parasitism or predation.

In all these forms, habitats seldom have clear edges, and often share species. As will be seen in Section 4.2.1, there are statistical methods for 'community analysis' which can identify clusters of species, and physical and chemical features, that tend to occur together. Such 'natural' subdivision of the biosphere helps to simplify our description of it. Evolution may have linked species together ('co-evolution') as specialist pollinators, herbivores or predators – and so knowing that one species (such as oak, or redwood, or pampas grass) is present may help us guess which other species are likely to be present.

Habitat diversity is often important to conservationists because it is probably one of the main factors promoting a diversity of species in an area. Conservation of *natural* habitat diversity might therefore help us to reduce the extinction rate.

## 1.2.3   Extinction rates

Extinctions are doubtless going on all the time, but we witness very few of them – mainly the loss of conspicuous species like passenger pigeons and the dodo. Most extinctions are likely to be amongst little-studied, but species-rich, groups such as the invertebrates and microbes. Since few species leave fossils, most of these extinctions will happen without our ever knowing. If we do not know the number of species, then we cannot know the actual (*absolute*) number that are going extinct each year. However, we can make crude estimates of the *proportion* of species in a group or area that are becoming extinct, based on a number of ecological generalisations.

One important generalisation derives from the observation that a remote oceanic island which is one tenth the size of another is likely to contain about half the number of species of the larger island. This also holds, broadly, for isolated mountains, isolated lakes, etc. This 'species–area relationship' is one of the most powerful (and puzzling) patterns in nature, and various explanations have been put forward for it (Section 5.4.1). Fortunately, to examine extinction rates, it is the relationship that is important, not the cause of the relationship.

So, if a habitat is reduced to a tenth its former area by disturbance such as clear-felling or drainage, will it come to support half the species that it once held? In other words, are fragments of habitats sufficiently similar to islands for the species–area relationship to hold? And how long will the drop in richness to the new lower level (a process known as 'relaxation') take? These important questions remain unanswered, and different habitats may respond differently to fragmentation. Some studies of highly fragmented habitats (such as the Atlantic forests of Brazil, of which less than 10% remain) at first suggested fewer extinctions were occurring than predicted. However, T. Brooks and A. Balmford have estimated the number of species which will soon become extinct in these forests, using the list of threatened bird species (Section 3.1.3). If these threatened species (the 'living dead') do become extinct over several decades, the richness of the total area of the fragments will indeed fall to close to the predicted lower number of species. There is in effect an 'extinction debt'. As John R. Lawton has put it, some species are extinct but they don't yet know it.

Using the species–area relationship, we can predict the fraction of species which will probably *eventually* be lost from a habitat after a particular fraction of habitat loss (Fig. 5.10). For example, if we lose 90% of the Amazonian rainforest, we may eventually lose half its species – and so possibly a substantial fraction of the Earth's total. If we have good base-line data on the richness before fragmentation, we can also estimate the actual number of species of a group of organisms (such as birds or flowering plants) that will become extinct when a given fraction of the habitat is lost. However, the timescale over which this loss will occur will be much less certain. It is possible that fragments on continents will have rather lower extinction rates than predicted if there are more generalist species than on islands, but conversely they may have higher rates if there are more species prone to adverse edge effects from surrounding habitats (Section 5.4.2).

Species have of course naturally become extinct since the origin of life. Perhaps 95–99% of species that have ever existed are extinct. We can get some idea of the background rate of extinctions from the fossil record. There are notable natural periods of extinction which were so severe that the balance of fossils changed, and thus the type of rock that they formed changed. Indeed these events help define the different geological strata. The Permian–Triassic border, for example, may represent the loss of 95% of marine species, whilst the demise of the dinosaurs and their contemporaries at the end of the Cretaceous is more famous, if less severe, with about 75% loss.

Between these mass extinctions, the background rate of extinction of fossil forms suggests that the average lifetime of a vertebrate species is in the order of 1–2 million years. R. M. May and his colleagues have compared this with the rate of loss of large vertebrate species over the past 100 years, and note that the lifetime has dropped to some 10 000 years. Species lifetimes are predicted to drop to 200–400 years this century. This suggests that the rate of extinction is now about 100–1000 times the natural background (pre-historic) level, and it may rise in this century to 10 000 times the background level. The extermination of about half the species that were present on Earth when *Homo sapiens* first appeared will have taken only a few centuries: this is the sixth mass extinction.

The estimated extinction rates for different groups of organism in the past 400 years are shown in Table 1.2. Some groups, such as the fish, have very low rates of *recorded* extinction – but this is presumably because they are so poorly known. For example, the freshwaters of Malaysia were surveyed, and

Table 1.2 *Recorded global extinction rates in recent times*

| | No. of species certified extinct 1500–2000 | No. species threatened (2000) | Approx. total of recorded species | Approx. % recorded extinct | Approx. % recorded threatened |
|---|---|---|---|---|---|
| Molluscs | 239 | 938 | 70 000 | 0.3 | 1 |
| Crustaceans | 8 | 408 | 40 000 | 0.02 | 1 |
| Insects | 4 | 555 | 950 000 | 0.0004 | 0.06 |
| Other invertebrates | 4 | 27 | 130 000 | 0.003 | 0.02 |
| Fishes | 81 | 752 | 25 000 | 0.3 | 3 |
| Amphibians | 5 | 146 | 5000 | 0.1 | 3 |
| Reptiles | 21 | 296 | 8000 | 0.3 | 4 |
| Birds | 128 | 1183 | 9950 | 1.3 | 12 |
| Mammals | 83 | 1130 | 4860 | 1.7 | 24 |
| Gymnosperms | 0 | 141 | 880 | 0 | 16 |
| Dicotyledons | 69 | 5099 | 194 000 | 0.04 | 3 |
| Monocotyledons | 1 | 291 | 56 000 | 0.002 | 0.5 |
| Mosses | 3 | 80 | 15 000 | 0.02 | 0.5 |

*Notes:* (a) Only the birds, mammals and gymnosperms are sufficiently well recorded to be reliable, and the table illustrates the likely serious under-recording of extinctions and threats in other taxa.
(b) Totals for recorded species include species extinct since 1500. Inclusion of Polynesian induced extinctions might raise the total losses for birds to about 20% over the past 30 000 years (Section 2.1).
*Source:* Modified from Hilton-Taylor, C. (compiler) *2000 IUCN Red List of Threatened Species.* (IUCN Gland, 2000).

then re-surveyed 100 years later. The second survey found only 122 of the original 266 fish species – the rest are quite likely extinct or highly threatened. Extinctions are often not discovered for years after they have happened, and species are often not officially declared extinct for some years or decades after the last sighting. Occasionally, species which have been thought extinct are re-discovered – but usually at a very low population size. The 'Committee on Recently Extinct Organisms' (CREO) helps declare extinctions. A major review of the USA by L. L. Master and colleagues found that a third of its 15 300 native flowering plants are threatened with extinction. This is disturbing because the USA is relatively well recorded and well protected. Globally, well over 34 000 vascular plant species (12% of the known total), and some 1200 bird species (c. 12% of the total), are threatened (Chapter 2).

The extinction rates of invertebrates and microbes, if known, would dominate the total number of extinctions per century. Britain is one of the best places to examine the extinction rate of invertebrates because there has been relatively intensive recording and collecting of its species by amateur and professional entomologists for several hundred years. The Red Data Book of British invertebrates can be used to estimate the extinction rate. At 1–5% per century, this is of the same order of magnitude as for some better-known groups in Britain and internationally. Applying this rate to conservative estimates of 5–15 million species would suggest the actual number of species becoming extinct per century may be between 50 000 and 750 000. This is roughly 500–7500 per year, and 1–20 species per day. However, whilst such crude estimates are thought-provoking, they are *very* likely to prove wrong, owing to the uncertainties in the generality of the rate across taxa and biomes and in the estimate of the total number of species. It is safer to accept that we don't know.

## 1.3   The philosophy and ethics of conservation: why conserve?

Why worry about conservation? There are two main types of answer: 'utilitarian' and 'non-utilitarian'. These correspond to 'use' and 'non-use' values in Fig. 1.1. The utilitarian arguments suggest that biodiversity (from genes to ecosystems) should be saved because it has value to people through a range of products and services. The non-utilitarian argument is that species and populations have an intrinsic right to existence, so humans should respect and protect them. The utilitarian arguments can often be translated into economic arguments, whereas the intrinsic-value arguments depend on ethical ideals which are more difficult to include in conventional economics.

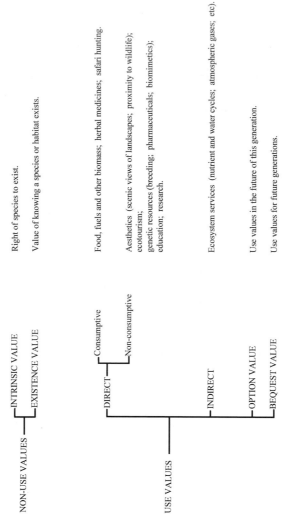

**Fig. 1.1.** The values of biodiversity, with examples.

Whilst some people believe biodiversity and conservation projects must pay their way, and others believe that non-human life forms must be put above economics, most conservationists take an intermediate position and have several motivations for their work. Indeed, no single argument is sufficient, and the relative strength of ethical and economic arguments will vary from case to case. The methods for evaluating the economic worth of species, landscapes and ecosystems will be considered in Section 9.1.

## 1.3.1  Ethics

Ethical arguments must date as far back as the earliest archaeological evidence of reverence for nature and sacred species. Recent philosophers such as E. Elliot have helped to formalise the field of environmental ethics. Many popular authors have contributed to the development of the ethic of conservation, as illustrated in Section 1.1.1. Amongst the first major philosophers of conservation – people who wrote extensively on themes and to whom particular schools of thought are often credited – were the North Americans Ralph Waldo Emerson, Aldo Leopold, Henry David Thoreau and John Muir.

One ethical position, developed by Leopold, suggests that we should maintain the integrity and complexity of systems for sustained use. Another suggests that we should strive for the greatest good for the most people for the longest time – a moral principle of equity and efficiency, which minimises waste. A third suggests that natural resources are an expression of God's Universe, and should be protected for aesthetic contemplation, healing, rest and relaxation.

Relatively idealistic conservationists support the proposal of an 'intrinsic right' of each species to exist, but philosophers are divided over its validity. Considering that ethics are a human construct, and in our absence biodiversity would continue to rise and fall on the planet, some argue that there is no defensible intrinsic right. The arguments for the rights of species may overlap with the ethics of animal welfare and suffering. Moreover, the intrinsic 'rights of species' have to be weighed against the very tangible needs and rights of existing people.

It is often argued that people are 'just another species', and we are part of a 'natural' process of extinction in which we need not intervene. The counter to this argument is that if we let natural processes take their course, the evidence is compelling that we are likely to end up in a world with more human suffering. If we behave like any other species, we will probably be controlled by mortality such as starvation, disease and pollution – just like any other species as its density increases. Evolution and ecology inform us that letting nature control our density and destiny is a very dangerous and unpleasant way to go! The evolutionary biologist and philosopher Richard Dawkins pointed out in *The Selfish Gene* in 1976 that religious objection to 'unnatural' family planning is likely to result in a natural method: 'It is called starvation'. Much human suffering might be avoided if we use our exceptional predictive capacities to conserve species and to reduce population growth – but we thereby set ourselves very far apart from nature.

The principle that future generations have a right to receive a world which has not been impoverished or degraded by the present generation is termed 'intergenerational equity'. Such a 'stewardship ethic' was promoted by President Roosevelt of the USA, and is reflected in the preamble of the Inter-American Conference on Conservation of Renewable Natural Resources, which stated in 1948: 'No generation can exclusively own the natural resources by which it lives. Successive generations are but trustees charged with maintaining unimpaired the inheritance of their successors. We hold the common wealth in trust for posterity, and to lessen or destroy it is to commit treason against the future'. The Environmental Strategy of the British Government (dated 1990) is based on the stewardship ethic: 'We have a moral duty to look after our planet and hand it on in good order to future generations', and in the Convention on Biological Diversity (Section 9.2.1) governments declare themselves determined to conserve and sustainably use biological diversity 'for the benefit of present and future generations'.

The loss of species, habitats and ecosystems with utilitarian value is thus seen by some as a failure of responsibility to protect the options of future generations. The counter argument to this is that since we do not know what future generations will need, we might be more ethically correct to concentrate on people of the current generation who have very clear and pressing needs – and if supplying their need involves reduction in biodiversity or pollution, so be it. Perhaps the future can look after itself? The uncertainty of the long-term benefits of conservation, when compared with the certain short-term benefits of, say, eating a fish or felling a tree, weaken the ethical arguments based on sustained utility, and this is part of the philosophical and economic debate about 'discounting' the future value (Section 9.1).

A further complication of the ethical argument is that many species (such as diseases, tigers and hippos) are harmful to people. Should the mosquitoes that carry malaria be conserved? Precaution would suggest so: it might be they are important in ecosystem processes, and their saliva might inspire anti-coagulants and painkillers. Should the last known smallpox viruses be destroyed in their laboratories – they might escape or be used by terrorists, but they might also have value in future medical advances. Whilst these few species are not likely to be lamented by many, Section 2.6 shows the ethics of conservation are deeply entwined with the ethics of health and development.

Ethical questions also arise in issues such as the 'shoot-to-kill' policy against poachers in Zimbabwe and elsewhere. If poachers are prepared to shoot park guards, then shooting back may be seen as a form of self-defence, but basically it is the few remaining individuals of species such as rhino and elephant that are being defended and valued above some human lives.

The *irreversibility* of biodiversity loss is central to the ethical arguments for conservation. Whilst matter can usually be converted and restored, given enough energy, it is not possible to re-create any but the simplest species once they are extinct. It is already theoretically possible to re-create a few very simple organisms (such as the smallpox virus) if the entire DNA sequence is known. But we will not be able to do this for the majority of species in the near future – not least because we have not even discovered the vast majority of them, let alone sequenced their DNA. It will never be possible to re-create what we never found. Moreover, the technical challenges of re-constructing more complex organisms may never be solved. There is much more to an organism than its genetic material. A human death is also irreversible, but it would happen in a few decades no matter what we do, whereas species would generally have lasted for the benefit of many future generations.

Irreversibility thus makes prevention of extinction a special case for philosophers, and might justify what many would otherwise regard as unethical management – such as the displacement of people from reserves, or prevention of hunting or logging. It may justify some reduction of human welfare or wealth in the short term, for the greater good of a greater number in the long term.

A precautionary approach has come to prominence in environmental ethics and policy in recent years, suggesting that conservation action should not be delayed until all scientific doubt is resolved (Section 10.2). However, precaution may seem excessive in the face of loss of jobs or other economic damage. There may be tensions between scientists (making decisions based on probability) and the public or politicians (who may make more subjective decisions). Yet in the context of complex ecosystems, the dynamics of which are not yet understood, it seems sensible not to perform substantial unplanned and irreversible experiments with the planet – such as exploring the consequences of extinction of species. Perhaps we should not let species become extinct if we are not sure we can do without them?

A suggested weakness of a precautionary approach is that it might be seen to prevent *any* new activity, since nothing is fully understood. However, the consequences of some changes, such as large-scale modifications of ecosystems, are less well known than the short-term and local changes we have often seen before, and it may be more appropriate to be more cautious when the risks are higher.

Another fairly common ethical position amongst conservationists and 'greens' is termed 'Deep Ecology'. This promotes a way of life which emphasises several factors: interconnectedness; social decentralisation; 'non-harmfulness' to other life and respect for the rights of other organisms; low consumption; and the need some people feel 'to be at one with the universe' – which is essentially a spiritual and aesthetic argument. Deep Ecology advocates a 'biocentric' position (rather than people's typically 'anthropocentric' position) in which non-human life, and even abiotic features such as mountains and rivers, are given moral rights and respected. The Deep Ecology movement has very little to do with the science of ecology – and indeed can be anti-scientific and sometimes counter-productive to conservation – but has important implications for policy. The writings of Wordsworth, J. Muir and A. Naess illustrate elements of Deep Ecology in their appreciation of nature, peacefulness, restraint and simplicity.

Whilst there is much philosophical debate about non-use values, many people with ethical concern for other species can also see uses for species, to which we now turn.

## 1.3.2   Aesthetics

One form of utilitarian argument which links ethics and economics is the aesthetic value of species and landscapes. Throughout the world and human history, people have found biodiversity beautiful and stimulating, and many believe that we should protect such beauty for this and for future generations. Common human behaviours illustrate the importance of enjoyment of animals and plants: pets are extremely popular in most cultures; the use of shells, feathers and skins in clothing, head-dresses and jewellery is very ancient and widespread; wildlife and landscapes are portrayed in art in many cultures, including pre-historic art; flowers are appreciated universally, and gardening is one of the most popular pastimes in several cultures. Humans might be able to survive in a world with very little biodiversity, but their quality of life might be very low.

Music, which provides a great aesthetic pleasure for many people, has often been inspired by nature and natural noises. The song of the nightingale is included in Beethoven's Pastoral Symphony, which includes movements titled 'The cheerful impressions excited on arrival in the country' and 'By the brook'. Similar inspiration is heard in 'The Lark ascending' by Vaughan Williams.

---

## Box 1.1
## Early statements of conservation ideals

We adore sacred groves and the very silence that reigns in them no less devoutly than the images that gleam in gold and ivory.

**Pliny the Elder, first century AD**

> There is a pleasure in the pathless woods,
> There is a rapture on the lonely shore,
> There is society, where none intrudes,
> By the deep sea, and music in its roar:
> I love not Man the less, but Nature more,
> From these our interviews, in which I steal
> From all I may be, or have been before,
> To mingle with the Universe, and feel
> What I can ne'er express, yet cannot all conceal.

**G. G. Byron, *Childe Harold*, 1812**

A scene in the English Lake District was nature ". . . putting on an aspect capable of satisfying the most intense cravings for the tranquil, the lovely, and the perfect, to which man, the noblest of her creatures, is subject."

**William Wordsworth, 1835**

Everybody needs beauty as well as bread, places to play in and pray in, where Nature may heal and cheer and give strength to body and soul alike.

**John Muir, 1912**

> What would the world be, once bereft
> Of wet and wilderness? Let them be left,
> O let them be left, wilderness and wet,
> Long live the weeds and the wilderness yet.

**G. M. Hopkins, 1881**

---

There is a great aesthetic value in the sense of 'wilderness', and great poets, writers and artists often make evocative references to wilderness. Box 1.1 gives examples of such writing. Many people seem at once attracted to, and in awe of, areas which *feel* empty of humans. Whilst those growing up in cities with little exposure to more natural habitats may be afraid of wilderness, on the whole it seems psychologically important to many people at some stages in their lives. The psychological value of landscapes and species has been recognised by the medical profession. In the developed countries there is firm evidence that stress can be reduced by contact with animals, whilst having a beautiful and tranquil view can be helpful to patients and the wider population alike.

The term 'biophilia' has been coined by E. O. Wilson to describe the apparently innate attraction and fascination which wildlife has for people.

An evolutionary reason for this psychological trait might be that our brains evolved to take an interest in other species – as prey, companions or danger. Alistair C. Hardy suggested that our obsession with going to coastlines and water may derive from a period of semi-aquatic existence in our evolutionary history, and an interest in savannah has also been suggested to reflect our evolutionary history; both these interests are evident in tourism and in the landscape design of country parks. I suggest that the widespread desire for wilderness might have developed from an evolutionary benefit in dispersing to less densely populated areas.

Wildlife gives people a sense of wonder, and Nigel J. Collar has argued that protecting it protects the freedom of species and the freedom of people to know they exist; Collar also argues that ethics are often a more enduring and honest reason for conservation than economics.

## 1.3.3  Economics

The utilitarian economic arguments for conservation are divided broadly into 'direct use value' and 'indirect use value' (Fig. 1.1). Direct use involves the harvesting of products of microbes, animals and plants. Indirect use includes the 'ecosystem services' that are provided by groups of species and habitats, such as promotion of rainfall, flood prevention, pollination, and the protection and aeration of soil. Methods for estimating the direct and indirect economic values are given in Section 9.1. The most substantial ecosystem service of all might be the stabilisation of certain features of the planetary environment as a consequence of abundant life: the concept of Gaia, as discussed in Section 1.4. Norman Myers was amongst the first and most inspiring scientists to discuss use values, and his books *The Sinking Ark* (1979) and *The Primary Source* (1984) did much to alert scientists and the public to the biodiversity crisis. E. S. Ayensu and colleagues have helped to strengthen the case for genetic resource conservation. The term 'genetic resources' is used to refer to any economically useful feature of biodiversity which is under genetic control.

Direct use also includes harvesting parts of living animals and plants (such as wool from llama), or products from the body. Species provide people with structural materials, such as thatch, threads, wood, and straw and dung for wattle and daub huts. Biodiversity provides many oils, pharmaceuticals, and medical benefits (Tables 1.3–1.5).

Most foods derive from living species, and most food comes from a very tiny range of domesticated plants and animals. Indeed, only 20 species provide 90% of our food energy, with wheat and rice providing 50%. Perhaps this is

Table 1.3 *Examples of the pharmaceutical uses of biodiversity*

| Organism | Illness, procedure or effect | Drug |
|---|---|---|
| Vampire bat | Clot dissolution for strokes | Desmoteplase (DSPA) |
| Jameson's mamba venom | Anticoagulant for strokes etc. | Dendroaspin |
| Cobra venom | Cancers: colorectal, etc. | Cobra Venom Factor |
| Korean pit viper venom | Cancers: melanoma, etc. | Salmosin |
| Puffer fish, toxic frogs | Painkiller in cancers, etc. | Tetrodotoxin |
| Cone shell (*Conus* spp.) venoms | Painkillers: non-addictive | Conotoxins, e.g. ACV1 |
| Medicinal leech** | Anticoagulant (strokes, microsurgery) | Hirudin |
| Green-bottle fly maggots | Wound healing (injury, ulcers) | 'Maggot therapy' |
| Honey bee (*Apis* species)** | Wound healing (antibiotic) | 'Honey therapy' |
| Sponge: *Cryptotheya crypta* | Cancers: blood, etc. | Cytarabine |
| Bread mould: *Penicillium* | Antibacterial antibiotic | Penicillin |
| Bacterium: *Bacillus subtilis* | Antibacterial antibiotic | Bacitracin |
| Soil bacterium (*Streptomyces*) | Antibacterial antibiotic | Streptomycin |
| Soil fungi | Immunosuppression for transplants | Cyclosporin, tacrolimus |
| Fungus: *Aspergillus terreus* | Colesterol reduction | Lovastatin |
| Cyanobacteria | Antiviral: HIV | Sulpholipids (lab trials) |
| Foxglove | Heart failure | Digitalis |
| Willow | Painkiller, etc. | Asprin |
| Opium poppy | Painkiller; coughs, diarrhoea | Morphine; codeine |
| St John's wort** | Depression | St John's wort |
| *Sceletium* species | Depression, addiction | Sceletium |
| Snakeroot** | Tranquilliser | Reserpine |
| Deadly nightshade | Pupil dilation, Parkinson's disease | Atropine |

(*cont.*)

Table 1.3 (*cont.*)

| Organism | Illness, procedure or effect | Drug |
|---|---|---|
| Corkwood | Sedation, sea-sickness, anaesthesia | Scopolamine |
| Black myrobalan** | Stress reduction | As part of Indian herbal mix |
| *Strychnos toxifera* | Muscle relaxant for surgery | Curare |
| *Cephaelis ipecacnanta* | Diarrhoea (amoebic) | Emethine |
| Jaborandi | Glaucoma | Pilocarpine |
| Ginger | Nausea | Ginger |
| *Hoodia*** | Obesity (appetite suppression) | In development |
| *Pterocarpus marsupium*** | Diabetes | In development |
| Cinchona | Malaria | Quinine |
| Moreton Bay chestnut | Viruses: HIV | Castanospermine |
| *Homolanthus acuminata*** | Viruses (yellow fever, HIV) | Prostatin |
| *Phyllanthus* species** | Hepatitis | In development |
| Siam weed** | Wound healing | Eupolin |
| Tumeric** | Wound healing | Tumeric |
| Garlic** | Antibacterial antibiotic | Allicin |
| Mexican yam | Arthritis, allergies; contraception | Cortisone; oestrogens |
| Cotton | Contraception (male) | Gossypol |
| Castor bean | Bone marrow transplant | Ricin |
| African bush willow | Cancers: lung, breast, prostate, etc. | Combretastatin |
| African sausage tree** | Cancers: skin | In development |
| Madagascar rosy periwinkle | Cancers: blood | Vinblastine/Vincristine |
| Pacific yew | Cancers: breast and ovarian | Taxol, taxotere |
| *Elentherococcus senticosus*** | Stamina, convalescence, anaemia | In development |
| *Clostridium botulinum* | Spina bifida; antispasmodic | Botox |

*Note:* ** denotes similar traditional use.

Table 1.4 *Examples of biodiversity used in medical/health products and studies*

| | |
|---|---|
| Marine plankton | Sunscreen: MAAs |
| Diatoms; Caribbean gorgon coral | Facial cream |
| Spider silk | Bandages, bone replacement |
| Shrimp shell | Wound dressing |
| Coral | Bone replacement |
| Manatee | Blood clotting studies |
| Cotton-topped marmoset | Lymphatic cancer studies |
| Rhesus monkey | Ozone links to asthma |
| Chimpanzee | HIV studies |
| Nine-banded armadillo | Leprosy studies |
| Nematode: *Caenorhabditis elegans* | Ageing studies |
| Sea slug. *Aplysia* | Memory studies |
| Horseshoe crab: *Limulus* | Light receptors/vision |

a risky situation? The capacity to feed the human population of the planet may depend on maintaining the green revolution. It will be necessary for crops to keep pace with environmental change – either through conventional breeding, or through the controversial methods of genetic engineering (Section 2.5). Change is likely in many factors: in climate (as under global warming); in levels of salt in the soil; in pests, diseases and weeds (as pesticide and herbicide resistance is selected for); and in demand.

There are many examples of agricultural improvements which have been possible through harnessing the natural variety of genetic resources of wild relatives of domesticated species (Table 1.6). A maize species called teosinte provided resistance to fungal diseases called rusts – and was found in a threatened forest in Mexico.

New organic farming methods may include the intermixing of plants. For example, silver leaf planted amongst maize in Kenya repels insects and suppresses weeds, while napier grass acts as a sacrificial crop to distract the corn borer pest. New and relatively benign pesticides and insecticides are likely to be developed from chemicals found amongst biodiversity, as with pyrethroids (which were based on a molecule discovered in chrysanthemums). Bacterial, viral and fungal pesticides and herbicides are being used in some countries and are being safety-tested in others.

The weakness of many of the utilitarian arguments for conservation is that 'high-technology fixes' may repair the damage, or provide substitutes – rendering genetic resources redundant. New drugs may be derived by using computer simulations. Models of molecules may permit the rational design

Table 1.5 *Examples of the non-medical utility of biodiversity*

| Organism | Use | Chemical or derivation |
|---|---|---|
| *Bacillus thuringiensis* | Insecticide | Bt toxin |
| African bugleweed | Insecticide | Ajugarin |
| Piquia | Biodegradable pesticide | Nuts |
| Neem | Insecticide/insect repellent | Azadirachtin in nuts |
| Neem | Fungicide | Secondary plant substance |
| Calabar bean | Methyl cabamate insecticides | Secondary plant substance |
| Lacepod, etc. | Fishing poison, insecticide | Rotenone |
| Rubber | Rubber | Sap |
| Chicle | Chewing gum | Sap |
| Guayule | Guayule (for tyres) | Sap |
| Jojoba | Machine oils | Seeds |
| Jojoba | Shampoo | Seeds |
| Microbe: *Thiobacillus ferrooxidans* | Metal leaching in mining | Enzymes |
| Hotspring microbe: *Thermus aquaticus* | DNA cloning (PCR) | Enzyme |
| Hotspring microbe: *Humicola languinosa* | Biological washing powder | High temp. lipase (enzyme) |
| Hotspring microbe: *Streptomyces* species | Dishwashing powder | High temp./alkalinity lipase |
| Crocus | Food colourant: saffron | Stigma pigments |
| Cochineal bug | Food colourant: carmine | Pigments |
| Lipstick tree | Makeup dyes | Pigments |
| *Bracon* spp. wasps | Detection of drugs, explosives | Antennae: trained behaviour |
| Whelk | Purple fabric dyes | Mucus |
| Lichen: *Parmelia omphalodes* | Brown tweed fabric dye | Whole organism |
| Lichen: *Ochrolechia tartarea* | Litmus paper dye | Whole organism |
| Algae: *Chlamydomonas reinhardtii* | Hydrogen fuel generation | Photosynthesis |
| Chrysanthemum | Pesticides | Secondary plant substance |
| Coconut, linseed | Plasticisers | Oils |

Table 1.5 (*cont.*)

| Organism | Use | Chemical or derivation |
|---|---|---|
| Buffalo gourd | Resins, paints, adhesives | Oils |
| Bladderpod | Plastics, hydraulic fluids | Oils |
| Crambe | Nylon 1313, surfactant, lubricant | Oils |
| Meadowfoam | Liquid wax, detergent | Oils |
| Spiders | Nanowires | Silk protein |
| Plants | Plastics, dynamite, fibres | Cell walls (e.g. cellulose) |

Table 1.6 *Crop improvements based on wild relatives*

| Crop | Disease resistance/ Improvement | Source of genetic resource |
|---|---|---|
| Rice | Rice grassy stunt virus | Uttar Pradesh, India: *Oryza nivara* |
| Rice | Yellow mottle virus | Africa |
| Rice | Hoja Blanca virus | South-East Asia: 'remaja' |
| Rice | Brown planthopper | South-East Asia: *Sativa officinalis* |
| Maize | Rust fungi | Mexico: 'teosinte' |
| Wheat | Yellow stripe rust, dwarf bunt | Turkey |
| Wheat | Increased production | Japan: dwarf race |
| Barley | Yellow dwarf virus | Ethiopia |
| Sorgum | Downy mildew | Ethiopia |
| Alfalfa | Stem nematodes | Iran |
| Vine rootstock | *Phylloxera* | America |
| Sugar cane | Yield doubled | Various |
| Sugar cane | Mosaic virus | Java |
| Potato | Blight *Phytopthora* | Andes |
| Potato | Nematode | Andes: *Solanum demissum* |
| Tomato | Fruit quality | Andes: *Lycopersicon chmielewskii* |
| Tomato | Fungus and insect resistance | Andes: *L. hirsutum* |
| Tomato | Virus resistance | Andes: *L. chilense* |
| Tomato | Nematode resistance | Andes: *L. peruvianum* |
| Tomato | Adverse environments | Andes: *L. cheesmanii* |

of drugs that block the active sites of enzymes, block or stimulate selected genes or neuroreceptors, or influence cell membranes. Vaccines (derived from the disease organisms themselves) may be more important in the treatment of AIDS or malaria than drugs gleaned by chance from plants. Nearly 100% of drugs in tribal societies derived from natural products, and over 55% of the top 150 prescription drugs in the USA still include such compounds – but in the future the importance of biodiversity for drugs, foods, oils or other products may continue to diminish.

Designer drugs and high-tech fixes may have fewer side-effects, and need a shorter period of safety-testing, than medicines from genetic resources. Pharmaceutical companies have rarely invested in biodiversity conservation because it is often easier, quicker and cheaper to modify existing drugs. The development period for new drugs is usually several years, and so income from 'bioprospecting' may take some time to feed back to local people; this has not encouraged conservation because future monetary values of products will be lower – the problem of 'discounting' (Section 9.1). Similarly, many ecosystem services such as hydrological stabilisation may be maintained or substituted with simpler systems such as plantations, rangelands, crops, or by physical and chemical ingenuity and engineering.

Hopes for some substitutes or fixes might prove overoptimistic, and if biodiversity is lost without trace we will have closed some options forever; again a precautionary approach suggests it is unwise to let this happen.

## 1.3.4 Scientific

Scientists interested in conservation may share some of the motivations outlined above, but may also be interested in the pure discovery that biodiversity permits – as the quote from Darwin in Section 1.1.1 illustrates. Studies of evolution, relevant to medicine but fascinating to many for their own sake, will be greatly impeded if a large fraction of the product of evolution is exterminated before it is discovered or documented.

Scientific and medical advances have been made following studies of the physiology of organisms and the interactions between them. Examples include: the discovery of drugs from the poisons used by organisms; unravelling the metabolic mechanisms of organisms; interpreting the behaviour of organisms (applied in the field of evolutionary psychology); and predicting the dynamics of fish and disease populations.

Evolution has produced may surprising and delightful solutions to engineering challenges – as illustrated in Table 1.7. Indeed, some engineers now

Table 1.7 *Examples of the values of biodiversity in design (biomimetics)*

| Organism | Feature mimicked | Product (* = suggested product) |
|---|---|---|
| Shark's skin denticles | Low-drag surface | Swimming costumes, boat surfaces |
| Arctic fish | Body fluids | Antifreeze* |
| Eels | Sinusoidal motion | Hydro-power generators*, robots |
| Bat | Sonar | Sonar for the blind |
| Bat | Wing | Sailboard wing |
| Whales | Skin | Antifouling paint* |
| Viper | Hollow fang | Hypodermic needle |
| Gecko | Foot | Sticky material |
| Vertebrates | Spinal column | Suspension bridges |
| Vertebrate bone | Bone | Eiffel Tower, helmets* |
| Wood-boring beetle | Insect mouthparts | Chainsaw blade |
| Crickets | Song from wings | Flat-plane loudspeaker* |
| Insects | Compound eyes/lenses | Solar panels* |
| Insects | Flight aerodynamics | Jet engines* |
| Hexapod insects | Walking gait | Robot leg movements |
| Animals | Muscle proteins | Robot muscles* |
| Polar bear, penguin | Hairs, down | Thermal insulators* |
| Lobster, scorpion | Senses/movements | Autonomous robots |
| Spider web | Spider | Bullet-proof vests* |
| Wood wasps | Ovipositor | Drilling* |
| Shipworm | Burrows | Tunnelling |
| Darkling beetle | Wing case surface | Fog-harvesting for water |
| Butterflies | Wing colours | Iridescent paint |
| Tenebrionid beetle | Body/wing attachment | Variable-strength attachments* |
| Hymenoptera | Wing/wing attachment | Novel zips* |
| Mussels (*Mytilus*) | Attachment to rocks | Water-resistant glue |
| Bristlestar (*Ophiocoma*) | Crystalline photoreceptors | Microlenses* |
| Tobacco Hornworm | Wing vortices | Micro Air Vehicles (MAVs)* |
| Trees | Wood structure: holes | Tough, light materials* |
| Lotus | Leaf surface | Self-cleaning lenses* and paint |
| Burdock | Sticky seeds | Velcro™ |
| Oyster (*Pinctada*) | Mother-of-pearl (= nacre) | Composite ceramics, combustion chamber |

simulate evolution itself, using natural selection between competing designs, in the development of structures such as bridges and aircraft. The development of designs from biological inspiration is called 'biomimetics'.

### 1.3.5  Cultural variation

Although science might suggest certain courses of action, conservation includes many areas where subjectivity and personal belief are very important in what we do. Since these vary between cultures, conservation organisations have attempted to find common ground amongst many of the larger faiths of the world, in an attempt to bring conservation into religious teaching.

Tribal peoples incorporate much which could be called conservation into their beliefs and teaching (Section 9.4.3). Examples include the protection of sacred forests, and lores relating to the harvesting of pregnant females. Close-seasons and forbidden methods may protect vulnerable individuals and habitats. In Madagascar, taboos termed 'fady' protect some species such as turtles and lemurs in some parts of their range – but Madagascar's varied cultural landscape also illustrates that such protection is somewhat accidental and arbitrary, and unless a fady is shared by all of the clans in a region it may be insufficient to protect a species. Unfortunately, fady, and similar systems elsewhere, may also dictate some species such as chameleons be killed. Moreover, cultural and religious traditions change and evolve rapidly, and may be abandoned.

Belief systems in the East, such as Hinduism and Buddhism, are frequently thought to be relatively pro-conservation, whilst those based on Christianity are more involved with 'dominion' over nature. Whilst the latter is now being interpreted as 'stewardship', the Biblical injunctions to go forth and multiply, and to exercise dominion over all the fowl and fish, are hardly helpful to conservation. Religions and beliefs which can be interpreted to promote human population growth, such as Catholicism, Islam and many African cults, may be relatively hard to reconcile with conservation. In Bhutan, a Buddhist population scorns those who hunt wildlife.

Despite such cultural variation, surveys asking people about their interest in conservation, and concern over extinction, have revealed some similarities between developing and developed countries (Table 9.1).

### 1.4  Gaia

In 1967, James E. Lovelock presented the idea of 'Gaia', which grew from his observation that the Earth exhibits stability of certain environmental states – despite the fact that some of these states are inherently unlikely. For example, the level of oxygen on Earth is very surprising in comparison to Mars and Venus. On those two planets, the atmosphere and rocks have achieved chemical equilibrium, and little oxygen survives free in the atmosphere. It is extraordinary that oxygen and methane both survive in free form in the Earth's atmosphere – the two would be expected to react. The diurnal temperature range on Earth is low compared with that on Mars, because clouds act as a blanket at night. The Earth's surface is surprisingly alkaline, and there is abundant free water.

Mars and Venus probably once had abundant water (some of which was delivered to these planets and to the Earth by comets). However, water can be lost through sunlight acting to break it down and release hydrogen (which escapes into space), and this 'photodissociation' has apparently removed a lot of water from Mars and Venus. On Earth, the abundant oxygen in the atmosphere slows down the loss of hydrogen, and thus helps the planet to retain water. Most of the oxygen is a product of photosynthesis in the oceans, and life in the oceans has also reduced the abundance of carbon dioxide in the atmosphere – which would otherwise have left the Earth with a much larger greenhouse effect. Lovelock argued that the highly anomalous physical and chemical condition of Earth compared with nearby planets was the result of the presence of abundant life, and that the biotic and abiotic components of the Earth are tightly coupled.

Discoveries in the past few decades lend weight to the idea of Gaia. For example, W. D. Hamilton and T. M. Lenton have suggested that most clouds may be the result of marine microbes manufacturing droplets – as tiny aeroplanes to disperse in. Indeed, microbes have recently been found to be active within clouds. Unfortunately, the oceans are being influenced in unpredictable ways by ozone depletion and fishing – and so the conservation of this ecosystem takes on a new dimension.

Gaia was once highly controversial amongst scientists, not because of the observations of stability, but because biologists did not agree with Lovelock's second postulation: that life has evolved to stabilise the planet for its own 'comfort' – that it is a super-organism with a 'homeostatic' mechanism. Lovelock's original 'Daisyworld' model of stability has an evolutionary fault (an inbuilt genetic bias), as pointed out by W. D. Hamilton. However, the idea of Gaia as 'global stability due to life' is now receiving attention because biologists have found ways in which evolutionary benefits to individual organisms may *incidentally* act to reduce changes at the global level.

Indeed, new mathematical models by P. A. Henderson and W. D. Hamilton suggest that Gaian stability may derive from the interactions of numerous species in ecosystems. Their 'Dam World' model has a stream flowing into a

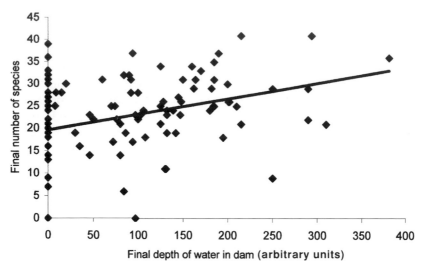

**Fig. 1.2.** The Dam World model of Gaian stability. For each run of the model, the species richness at the end of the run is plotted against the depth of water remaining in the dam. High final levels of water in the dam indicate a more stable system, and tend to be associated with higher numbers of species in the water. Greater species richness increases stability, through numerous density-dependent interactions. *Source:* P. A. Henderson & W. D. Hamilton (unpublished).

valley. In the water, some species secrete materials which tend to build a dam across the valley, and some species have behaviours which erode or burst it – so destabilising the level of water in the dam. A random set of imaginary species with a variety of diets, reproductive rates, etc., are introduced to the water. The depth of water in the valley tends to be higher at the end of the run of the model if more species are present at the time (Fig. 1.2), suggesting greater stability in rich systems. Some interactions between species (disease, competition and predation) become more intense as a species becomes more abundant. Such 'density-dependent' interactions tend to stabilise the system The relationships between the stability and functioning of ecosystems and their richness are unclear and controversial.

The mathematics of 'complexity theory' is relevant, because complex systems (with large numbers of species and interactions) may automatically be drawn towards stable states called 'attractors'. The new models suggest that loss of species and simplification of ecosystems may have unpredictable consequences, perhaps leading to unstoppable changes in the state of the planet. The level of oxygen on Earth may be a variable in a Dam World-type system, equivalent to the level of water in the dam.

If it proves that features such as the remarkably high and constant level of oxygen, the low level of the greenhouse gas carbon dioxide, the presence of abundant water and clouds, or the relatively stable temperature of our planet's surface are a consequence of a diversity of life, then maintenance of these services may require that we save as much of that biodiversity as possible.

Gaia suggests that a precautionary approach is important on large geographical scales, as well as at the level of loss of individual species. It highlights the inter-dependency of species. Ultimately, this may prove one of the most compelling reasons for conservation.

Whether the arguments in this chapter are sufficiently convincing to the public and politicians remains to be seen. If the reader remains in doubt, then the Further reading given at the end of this book will give more detail for the case. However, for the remainder of the book it will be assumed that at least some of the arguments carry some weight. So, given a need for conservation, how it can best be achieved? Firstly, we need to know the reasons for the decline in biodiversity and environmental quality – in order to plan measures to limit or redress the problems. The next chapter examines the threats which cause the conservation crisis.

# 2

# Threats to biodiversity

This chapter examines some of the main threats to biodiversity. No book can cover all of them. As we will see, extinctions and habitat alterations have been occurring for many thousands of years. We will examine the importance of human population growth, and our consumption of resources such as energy, food, water and land. We will also examine the problem of pollution, which occurs once the limited capacity of the environment to deal with waste is exceeded. We then turn to one of the oldest reasons for extinctions, introduced species, and relate this to the controversy over one of the potential new threats – genetically modified organisms (GMOs). Most species are threatened by several factors, some of which are not known. Threats may cause extinctions directly, or may cause 'secondary extinctions' of dependent specialist species.

One way to examine the threats is to look at the known causes of extinctions of species over the past 400 years (Fig. 2.1), and another is to look at the known threats to the species that are currently identified as officially threatened by the IUCN in their 'Red Lists' (Section 3.1.3 and Fig. 2.2). About 12% of vascular plant species, 25% of mammals, and 12% of birds, are listed as threatened. However, N. C. A. Pitman and P. M. Jørgansen have given more detailed consideration to the less well-studied tropical regions, and suggest that between a third and a half of the world's plant species are threatened.

## 2.1  Human population growth

Until the early 1990s, it was relatively taboo to talk about population growth as a 'problem' for humans. Yet in 1803, Thomas R. Malthus predicted that

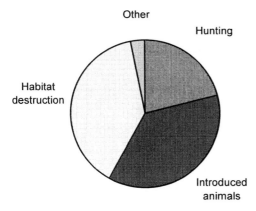

**Fig. 2.1.** Causes of animal extinctions since 1600, where known. This figure should be treated with caution: causes are known for only about 40% of extinctions in this period, and some causes are easier to identify than others. Extinctions may be caused by several factors.
*Source:* World Conservation Monitoring Centre. *Global Biodiversity: Status of the Earth's Living Resources.* (Chapman and Hall, London, 1992).

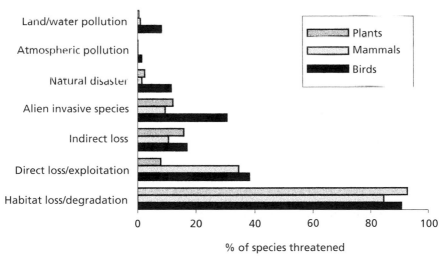

**Fig. 2.2.** Current threats to birds, mammals and plants. Indirect loss is through recreation, fires lit by vandals, etc. A species may be threatened by several factors.
*Source:* Modified from Hilton-Taylor, C. (Compiler). *2000 IUCN Red List of Threatened Species* (IUCN, Gland, Switzerland, 2000).

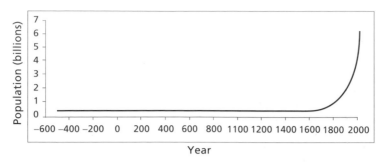

**Fig. 2.3.** Human population growth in the past 2500 years.
*Source:* McEvedy, C. & Jones, R. *Atlas of World Population History* (Penguin, Harmondsworth, 1978).

human populations would eventually undergo the same sorts of limitations on their growth as populations of other species do, and in particular he predicted large-scale famines. However, Malthus (and others more recently) underestimated the ability of technological improvements such as the 'Green Revolution' to increase our food supply, and so some authors believe the population problem has been exaggerated. Heated debates have raged over the true 'limits to growth' (see N. Myers and J. Simon, *Scarcity or Abundance?*, 1994). Fortunately, the World Conference on Population and Development, held in Cairo in 1994, demonstrated a change in opinion amongst politicians throughout the world – many of whom were under domestic pressure to help slow their national population growth.

Historically, human population growth has been exponential – as can be seen in Fig. 2.3. Indeed, the rate of increase in our numbers was for a while faster than exponential, which indicates an increase in human reproductive success through history! The global population growth rate hides local trends: in many countries, a 'demographic transition' has occurred, in which higher infant survival, the increasing cost of children, and better female literacy rates lead to a voluntary reduction in family size.

Biologists seeing exponential population growth in a population of lemmings or locusts, or in yeast cells in a Petri dish, would predict that such growth will naturally be halted by increased mortality. Natural populations are generally 'regulated' by 'density-dependent' factors – which are pressures that get stronger on a population as it grows, and weaker as it shrinks. Competition, disease and predation are the main factors. Sadly, disease is a major potential agent of regulation: for example, HIV, malaria, measles and tuberculosis are increasing. The human population presents a huge opportunity for diseases that can exploit our high population densities. Some of these may be familiar, whilst others may be 'emergent diseases', which we do not know how to tackle.

## Box 2.1
## Degradation of two islands

As Polynesian peoples expanded through the Pacific some 30 000–1000 years ago, they exterminated numerous endemic species from the islands. D. W. Steadman estimates that over 2000 species of birds were lost (*c.* 20% of the world total). At least 12 of the Pacific islands which were colonised had no human population by the time Europeans arrived in the sixteenth century. When Polynesians reached Easter Island about 1600 years ago, the natural vegetation was mainly forest, including endemic trees. As the population grew to some 7000 people over the next 1100 years, they completely deforested the island. Major colonies of several species of seabird were extirpated. Erosion, crop failure, warfare, and cannibalism followed. The population crashed, and the island still remains an irreversibly devastated grassland.

Similarly, people reached Henderson Island about 1200 years ago, and the population grew over the next 500 years. From analysis of their campsites and diet, G. M. Wragg has shown that they caused a cascade of extinctions amongst the birds (see Fig. 2.4). When the endemic pigeons were exterminated, people had to switch to eating seabirds. The human population then crashed, and vanished about 300 years ago – perhaps through lack of food. During Polynesian occupation, about half of the landbirds had been exterminated, much of the scrub on the island had been repeatedly burnt, and at least 40% of the land snail species had been lost (probably through habitat destruction and introduced mammals and ants). In addition to the snails and birds, which leave sub-fossil traces, many unique endemic species were doubtless lost without trace as people overexploited their environment.

The way human population growth rates change under the constraints of finite resources can be seen in two case studies on islands, which are presented in Box 2.1 and Fig. 2.4. There is evidence that excessive consumption of resources has happened in a number of human societies, leading to population declines and leaving a greatly impoverished natural environment. Within the Americas, parts of the populations of the Maya, the Inca, and the Pueblo Indians may have collapsed after overuse of resources rendered them sensitive to low crop yields in periods of adverse climate, whilst the Anastasi may have run out of wood. Human ingenuity and technology have permitted switching between resources, and extirpation or extinction of one resource species does not immediately lead to density-dependent feedback. Projections of the future human population growth rate and size are risky: changes in growth rates may be very rapid, as in Western Europe in the past century, and in Kenya and Bangladesh recently.

It is hard to quantify the proportion of an environmental impact, be it deforestation or pollution, that can be attributed to population growth.

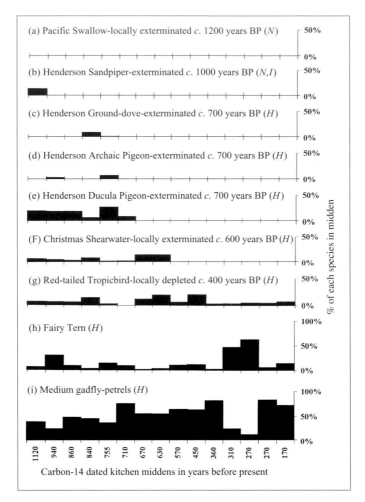

**Fig. 2.4.** The sequential loss of bird species on Henderson Island during the period of Polynesian occupation. The rate of exploitation of each species is deduced from the proportion of bones of each species in Polynesian kitchen middens. The probable, causes of decline are (in italics): N = interference with nesting; I = introduced rats; H = hunting.
*Source:* G. M. Wragg.

P. Harrison suggests the proportion of a problem due to population growth equals the proportional change in consumption (or pollution) divided by the proportional change in population. He suggests, for example, that population growth accounted for about 40% of the growth in greenhouse gas emissions from 1960 to 1988, 10% of the growth in CFCs from 1950 to 1985, and 80% of the deforestation between 1973 and 1988. Although this method can be criticised (because the growth in population and in threat may be coincidence) it provides a thought-provoking initial study.

However, we should never forget the compounding effect of high consumption and pollution 'per capita' (that is, per person). As we shall see, relatively small or low-density populations such as that of the USA or Australia can have disproportionate impacts on the environment when the average person in a society consumes relatively large amounts of resources such as energy, water or household space.

## 2.2   Human consumption patterns and habitat loss

Competition for food, water, land and shelter have been evident in local human populations for as long as we have records. In Ancient Greece, wars were fought over access to farmland. Competition for farmland or grazing has seen the rise of powerful warrior tribes such as the Mayans, Mongols and Maasai. Historians vary in the degree to which they would ascribe wars of conquest to competition, but it would be remarkable, biologically, if some were not driven by competition. The quest for 'living space' contributed to the Second World War. High-density populations, such as Britain's, can only survive by exploiting remote regions.

As noted above, there is debate over the capacity of our global population to feed itself. Some argue that much of the starvation on the planet – several million people per year – results from a problem in food distribution, rather than supply. Unfortunately, the obstacles to perfect, altruistic, distribution are evidently formidable. Food supply becomes an issue for conservation through hunting pressures and through competition for land between people and other organisms.

Globally, P. M. Vitousek has shown that humans now use some 40% of the energy captured by plants on land (the Net Primary Production, NPP); we also use some 10% of the production of the aquatic environments, a figure which would be hard to increase given the sparse production in the open ocean.

## 2.2.1   Hunting and harvesting

Direct exploitation including hunting threatens some 30–40% of the Red List birds and mammals, and about 10% of the Red List plants. Most human cultures eat large amounts of meat, if it is available. However, it is possible that the peak influence of hunting was several thousand years ago.

Hunting has been directly responsible for many extinctions over at least the past 50 000 years. There is still much controversy, but many scientists believe that human 'overkill' was the cause of most of the 'Pleistocene megafaunal extinction', in which many large (44 kg or more in weight) animals became extinct in the Pleistocene (Fig. 2.5). This view was proposed by P. S. Martin and R. G. Klein in 1984, and has been reviewed by J. M. Diamond. The view is supported by cuts and breaks in sub-fossil bones, associated weapons, the selective nature of the extinctions, and the timing of extinctions relative to other potential mechanisms. The main alternative argument, that climate change was responsible, can not explain the selective loss of large species, nor why the extinctions generally coincided with human colonisation of different parts of the globe rather than with global or local climate change. Moreover, many of these genera had existed for millions of years, and had survived through several ice ages. It would be remarkable if they then suddenly went extinct simply because of climatic changes which were typical of those they had already survived.

In some cases, however, hunting, introduced disease and climate may have interacted. In Australia, the Aboriginal use of fire (to drive game or in warfare) may have been important in the loss of its megafauna some 46 000 years ago. In Africa, fewer of the genera were lost in the Pleistocene – possibly because the species had time to evolve defences against human hunting over a long period of coexistence. Tables 2.1 and 2.2 illustrate the scale of the Pleistocene extinction.

Overkill of large animals can be seen most clearly in Madagascar and New Zealand. In the former, the giant flightless elephant birds were exterminated. Mathematical models assuming low rates of hunting, and archaeology, suggest that after the arrival of the Maori peoples in New Zealand about 1000 years ago the extirpation of the giant, flightless moas may have occurred within a mere 200 years! The process has been described as a 'blitzkrieg' against a fauna naïve to large predators. Only the earliest campsites of the first people have abundant moa bones – and it appears that by the fifteenth century over ten species had been eaten to extinction by a population of under 1000 people. Similarly, models by researchers including J. Alroy show that low levels of human hunting could easily have rapidly exterminated many large mammals in North America (Fig. 2.6), with consequential loss of large carnivores.

Overfishing has been occurring for thousands of years, causing major eco-system changes, but we have only recently begun to realise the impact of subsistence fishing in the pre-colonial era, because base-line information of population sizes has had to be deduced from archaeology and palaeoecology. J. B. C. Jackson and colleagues have reviewed the impact of fishing, and some

Table 2.1 *Examples of losses of large species in the Pleistocene extinction*

### North America
Mammoth (3 species); mastodon; sabre-tooth cats; bears; tapirs; peccaries; camels; ground sloths; glyptodonts; deer species; moose species; antelope species; cattle species; goat species; horse species; lion; cheetah; wolf species (e.g. dire wolf); giant condor; giant tortoises (3 *Geochelone* species); flightless duck; flamingo; condor, teratorn (giant scavenging bird); vultures; walking eagle.

### South America
Ground sloths; glyptodonts; rodents; sabre-toothed cats; wolves; peccaries; camels; deer; liptoterns; notoungulates; horses.

### Europe
Cave bear; straight-tusked elephant; spotted hyena; hippopotamus; giant deer (Irish elk); a rhino (*Dicerorhinus*); woolly rhino; woolly mammoth.

### Australia
Echidnas; marsupial carnivores (e.g. marsupial lion); wombats; diprotodonts; kangaroos; wallabies; giant horned tortoise (*Meiolania*); giant lizard (*Megalania*); large snake (*Wonambi*); giant flightless bird (*Genyornis*).

### Africa
African giant hertebeest; long-horned buffalo.

examples are given in Table 2.3. R. A. Myers and B. Worm report large marine predatory fish have declined about 90% in 50 years, and rarely reach their full size.

Hunting continues to cause extinctions. Almost a quarter of the 230 vertebrate species which we know to have become extinct in the past 400 years did so at least in part as a result of hunting pressure – although other factors such as habitat loss may have reduced their viability. Large mammals such as the aurochs and Caucasian bison in Europe, the Caribbean monk seal, the Atlantic race of the grey whale and Steller's sea cow were lost in recent centuries – the latter partly owing to pre-historic hunting. Other species currently endangered by human predation include most species of sea turtle, and many tortoises, primates, pigs and antelopes. Animals over 5 kg, such as tapir, are relatively scarce in the areas of Amazonian forest where there are subsistence hunters or tribal hunter-gatherers. The dugong of Queensland declined 97% between 1962 and 2001 – partly because of aboriginal hunting.

Even if hunting is stopped, it may be too late for some species. There is a chance some social species may not recover (Section 6.3.2). Many fish stocks are greatly depleted (Fig. 2.7), and some such as the bluefin tuna

(a)

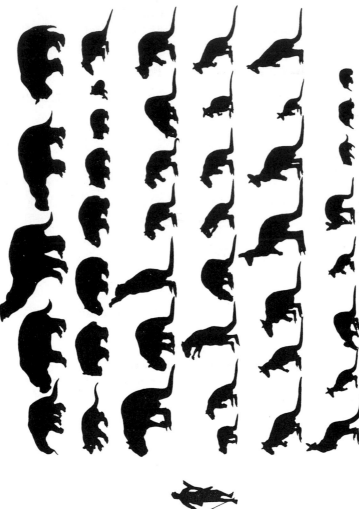

**Fig. 2.5.** Impressions of some extinct megafauna with a human for scale: (a) Australia; (b) North America.
*Sources:* (a) Figure from: Murray, P. In: Paul S. Martin & Richard G. Klein (Eds.), *Quaternary Extinctions: A Prehistoric Revolution*, pp. 600–628 (1984). Copyright 1984 The Arizona Board of Regents. Reprinted by permission of the University of Arizona Press. (b) Modified from: Stuart, A. J. *Biological Reviews* **66** (1991), 453–456. Reprinted with the permission of Cambridge University Press.

(b)

**Fig. 2.5.** (cont.)

Table 2.2 *Prehistoric extinctions*

(a) *The late Pleistocene megafaunal extinction, c. 100 000–10 000 years before present: known extinctions of mammals weighing over 44 kg, and approximate percentage of such genera lost*

| Region | Number of genera lost | Number genera known | Genera lost (%) |
|---|---|---|---|
| North America | 33 | 45 | 73 |
| South America | 46 | 58 | 80 |
| Africa (whole) | 7 | 49 | 14 |
| (sub-Saharan) | 2 | 44 | 5 |
| Europe | 7 | 24 | 30 |

(b) *Examples of faunal losses probably owing to human colonisation of islands*

| Islands | Species | Period (years BP) |
|---|---|---|
| Australia | 23 megafaunal genera (96% of known total) | 50 000–40 000 |
| Madagascar | Elephant birds; pygmy hippos; giant lemurs | 1500–500 |
| New Zealand | All species of moa; giant eagle | 1000–400 |
| Cyprus | Pygmy hippo; pygmy elephant | 10 500–6500? |
| Pacific | Possibly 2000 bird species | 30 000–1000 |
| Hawaii | Approximately 60 bird species | c. 2000–present |

BP = before present.
*Sources:* (a) Stuart, A. J. Mammalian extinctions in the Late Pleistocene of Northern Eurasia and North America. *Biological Reviews* **66** (1991), 453–562. (b) Various sources.

and Atlantic cod may become globally (or at least commercially) extinct owing to modern overkill. A single bluefin tuna may fetch over US $100 000 in Japan.

Hunting for fur, wool and skin products threatens species such as the Tibetan antelope, the crocodiles and the sable and the clouded leopard. Hunting for traditional medicinal ingredients such as bone, horn, gall bladder and penises threatens the tiger, saiga, all five species of rhino, and bear populations. Seahorses and sea cucumbers are being locally extirpated. Until recently, over 20 million seahorses were used in Chinese medicine each year. The enormous market in Asia is sufficient to drive almost any species with use

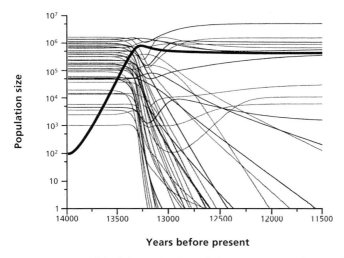

**Fig. 2.6.** A model of the extinction of Pleistocene megafauna of North America through hunting. The bold line shows the increase of the human population, and the fine lines show the fate of various species.
*Source:* Reprinted with permission from Alroy, J. A. *Science* **292** (2001), 1893–1896. Copyright 2001 American Association for the Advancement of Science.

as an aphrodisiac to extinction! Symbols of strength (such as bears and tigers) are also killed for traditional medicines believed to convey some features of the animal to the user. Many plants – such as ginkgo, *Adhatoda beddomei*, *Inula racemosa*, artichoke cactus and arnica – are overharvested for medicine, and a law was enacted as early as 1880 to protect plants in the Austrian Alps from herbalists.

Persecution of large predators has exterminated the thylacine of Australia, the Falklands wolf, and the wolf and lynx from Britain. Populations of coyote, wolverine, wolf, puma, and lynx have been fragmented throughout North America or Eurasia. Many populations of large carnivores and birds of prey, such as lions, wolves, dhole, kites, eagles, falcons and buzzards, have been extirpated. There is resistance from some farmers to the recovery of wolves in countries such as France and Norway, and from some gamekeepers to the recovery of birds of prey such as the red kite, hen harrier and golden eagle in Europe. In Africa, lions, cheetah and leopard bring prestige to warriors who kill them, whilst wild dogs and lions are persecuted to protect livestock. Seals and Cetacea are claimed to compete with fishermen and are used as scapegoats for declining marine fish catches, as in the Arctic and Mediterranean. Crocodilians are persecuted in Asia and Africa, dolphins in Venezuela, whilst otters, cormorants and heron are claimed to threaten freshwater fish stocks in Britain.

Table 2.3 *Examples of overfishing and associated changes (population sizes are estimates)*

| Species or feature | Region | Historical population or state (date) | Recent state |
|---|---|---|---|
| Steller's sea cow | Alaska | <5000 (c. 260 BP) | Extinct |
| Sea otter | Pacific | >100 000 (c. 260 BP) | 30 000 |
| Atlantic cod | Gulf of Maine | Mean body length 1.0 m (3550 BP) | Mean 0.3m |
| White abalone | California | 2000 per ha (30 BP) | c. 1 per ha |
| Green turtle | Caribbean | >33 million (>300 BP) | 1 million |
| Dugong | East Australia | 1 million (>100 BP) | 14 000 |
| Seagrass beds | Tampa Bay | c. 31 000 ha (c. 120 BP) | c. 11 000 ha |
| Staghorn coral | Caribbean | Dominated 63% of sites (125 000 BP) | Extirpated |
| Oysters | Tangier Sound | c. 45 km$^2$ (c. 125 BP) | Extirpated |
| Eutrophication | Baltic Sea | 3.2 gC m$^{-2}$ per year (c. 140 BP) | 70 gC m$^{-2}$ per year |
| Anoxia | Baltic Sea | 5% of sediment cores (100 BP) | 90% of cores |

*Note:* See Fig. 2.15 for linkage between overfishing and impacts. BP = years before present.
*Source:* Jackson *et al. Science* **293** (2001), 629–638.

There has been a recent upsurge in hunting as a serious threat to many species, as part of the growing trade in 'bushmeat' (wild game). Bushmeat is a traditional local food, but is also now being traded over great distances, and used by a greater total number of people – including urban populations in the same country or overseas. African bushmeat (including lion!) is available in London restaurants. Hunting methods such as snares, nets and guns have improved, whilst access to formerly difficult terrain has been made possible by logging tracks and improved roads. The bushmeat trade threatens primates such as the black mangabey, gorilla and pygmy chimpanzee, and some fruitbats. Hunting of species such as spider monkeys has knock-on effects when seed dispersal and other processes are disrupted. Numerous carnivores are being deprived of prey. An eventual consequence of uncontrolled bushmeat harvesting is 'empty forest syndrome' – where few mammals are present.

Harvesting of plants for horticulture has threatened a number of species. Orchids, succulents (including cacti), cycads and other popular house and

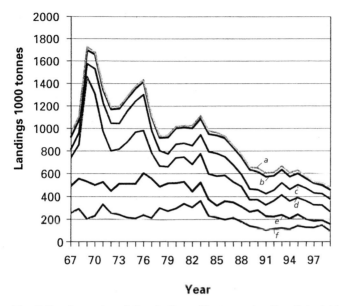

**Fig. 2.7.** Examples of the decline of bottom-dwelling fish yields in the North Sea (NS) region. Species: *a*, sole NS; *b*, plaice NS; *c*, saithe, NS and IIIa; *d*, haddock, NS and IIIa; *e*, whiting, NS and Eastern Channel; *f*, cod, NS, Skagerrak and Eastern Channel.
*Source: Fifth International Conference on the Protection of the North Sea 20–21 March 2002, Bergen, Norway. Progress Report* (Ministry of the Environment – Conference Secretariat, Norway).

garden plants have been widely overharvested. Species with populations threatened in this way include the lady's slipper and white nun orchids, saxifrages, irises, gentians and snowdrops in Europe, Greig's tulip in Asia, the saguaro cactus of North America, and the tree ferns of Madagascar (the stems are used as flower-pots). Horticulture has also led to destructive exploitation of peat, of limestone pavements for rockeries, and of lichens ('Spanish moss') in flower arrangements. The impact of harvesting kelp and other seaweeds for soil conditioners requires investigation.

Similarly, the pet trade threatens a number of species. Over 100 cage-bird species are threatened, including some 60 parrot species. The Bali starling is poached from reserves and captive breeding programmes. Tortoise species have been overharvested in Europe, Madagascar and Seychelles. Trade in insects (live and mounted) threatens species such as Queen Alexandra's birdwing butterfly and the Cape stag beetle.

Hunting is particularly threatening to large species, which have long lifetimes, small populations, and low reproductive rates; these are characteristics of '*K*-selected' species, and will be discussed in the context of sustainable harvesting in Section 7.2. Sadly, most of the really big and spectacular species present on Earth when humans first evolved are now extinct.

Hunting may threaten species indirectly through accidental capture, termed 'bycatch'. For example, sea turtles and dolphins may be drowned by fishing nets, whilst several albatross species are threatened by long-line fishing, which kills over 300 000 birds a year. The marine bycatch of some 40 million tonnes per year represents an enormous problem.

## 2.2.2  Land

Over 80% of the birds, mammals and plants in the Red List are threatened, at least in part, through habitat loss and degradation. Loss of tropical forest is the single greatest threat to terrestrial diversity (Section 3.4.2). Most societies require land for food production. Whilst the amount of land available per person declines as population soars, degradation of soils through erosion, salinification, nutrient exhaustion and pollution reduce the amount still further. Agricultural expansion in the past 10 000 years has been a major cause of extinction, and threatens some 70% of Red List birds. The relationship between the proportion of habitat lost, and the impact on biodiversity, is outlined in Sections 1.2.3 and 5.4.

There have been several attempts to estimate how many people the world can feed. The numbers depend on how much habitat we leave unfarmed, whether we can sustain agricultural inputs and associated energy consumption and pollution, and how much meat we eat. When animals are farmed to eat, there is a 90% wastage of energy through their metabolic processes. The total population that the planet could sustainably support may by now have been exceeded substantially – even if people converted all the wetlands and forest to agriculture.

Agriculture may have significance to conservation in a variety of ways, depending on the nature of exploitation. In Section 7.3 we will explore the derivation of 'semi-natural habitats' from traditional agriculture, and the conservation interest of such sites. Expansion of agriculture into wilderness is now mainly occurring in the developing world. In Western Europe and North America, the reverse is more often true; there, land is coming out of agricultural production owing to local surplus production under highly intensive (and arguably unsustainable) methods.

Norman Myers found that the agricultural expansion of poor peoples into new land is the primary cause of global tropical deforestation (Table 2.4 and

Table 2.4 *Causes of tropical deforestation, estimated in 1996 by N. Myers (total: 165 000 km² per year)*

| | |
|---|---|
| Slash-and-burn agriculture | 61% |
| Logging | 18% |
| Dams | 9% |
| Plantations | 6% |
| Cattle ranching | 6% |

Fig. 2.8), although ranching and logging are increasingly important. Such expansion is often accomplished by using 'slash-and-burn' methods – in which the slashing (cutting) helps to dry the forest vegetation and permit the burning. Massive deforestation of this type is occurring in Amazonia and Indonesia, creating plumes of smoke easily visible from space. Policies in many countries have encouraged expansion, sometimes accompanied by 'transmigration' (resettlement) as in Indonesia and Brazil. About half of the rainforest of the planet was lost between 1830 and 1984.

Agriculture may have impacts through its extent and its intensity. Expanding agriculture requires the conversion of large amounts of relatively pristine habitat. Intensive agriculture, using artificial fertilisers, may require less loss of natural habitat but requires inputs of energy and may lead to outputs of pollution from pesticides and herbicides (Section 2.3). Intensive agriculture may be in monocultures in large fields with few hedgerows or little cover at the margins. Whilst the popular 'green' lobby prefers extensive agriculture, there are other types of conservationists who prefer agriculture to be confined to more intensive use of a smaller expanse of land. The gains to biodiversity in promoting extensive systems (with hedgerows, mixed crops and low inputs) may be trivial, whilst the loss of wilderness is more irreversible. Hedgerows, given their transient and artificial character, are very unlikely to support globally rare species. In Europe and North America, some excess agricultural land is being 'set aside' for wildlife in blocks (Section 8.3.1), providing a higher quality of habitat than is possible within the fields themselves.

Recreational use of land, including climbing, sunbathing, off-road vehicles, rambling, dog-walking and photography may lead to disturbance, which is equivalent to reducing habitat area. Species on dunes, such as sea holly and sea bindweed in Europe, often suffer recreational damage. Wildfires are becoming increasingly frequent – possibly partly as a result of climate change (Section 2.3.3) and partly as a result of increased visitation and vandalism. Forest fires often rage in Australia, Russia, Indonesia, southern Europe and North America, whilst many grassland fires occur in Africa, and heathland fires are

(a)          Original extent            1950              1985

−15° S

−18° S

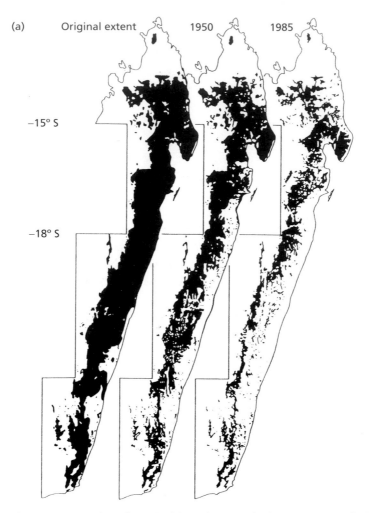

**Fig. 2.8.** Loss of rainforest in (a) Madagascar (only eastern part of island shown) and (b) Sumatra.
*Sources:* (a) Redrawn with permission from Green, G. M. & Sussman, R. W. *Science* **248** (1990), 212–215, copyright 1990 American Association for the Advancement of Science; (b) Collins, N. M., Sayer, J. A. & Whitmore, T. C. *The Conservation Atlas of Tropical Forests: Asia and the Pacific* (Macmillan Press Ltd., London, 1991). Copyright holder IUCN.

widespread in Europe. Dogs can cause more disturbance to wildlife than people or cars, since they resemble native predators.

In some regions, the loss of land to buildings ('urban sprawl') and roads threatens species. A trend to smaller households around the world is increasing the problem.

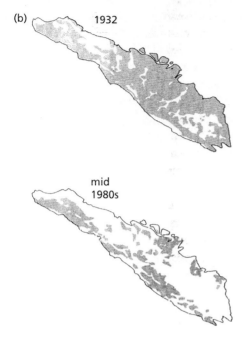

(b) 1932

mid 1980s

**Fig. 2.8.**  *(cont.)*

## 2.2.3 Water

Freshwater habitats are highly species-rich, and many are also very highly threatened. The demand for freshwater for drinking, bathing, washing, agriculture, livestock and industry is one of the most problematic issues in development. The world is already so short of freshwater that very serious political tensions – and even wars – are being related to it. Water supply can itself become a weapon. The internationally important marshlands of the Tigris and Euphrates rivers in Iraq have been largely destroyed since 1992 (Fig. 2.9), to suppress Marsh Arabs and because of dams in Turkey. Fresh water can be produced by desalinification of seawater, but this is expensive and would increase demand for energy.

Waterbodies around the world are drying out from overexploitation. People already use over a quarter of the global evapotranspiration from land, and over half the accessible run-off. The Aral Sea is now a ghost of its former self, with its water diverted to irrigation, and the Mesa Central of Mexico is threatened. The Florida Everglades have been suffering from profligate use of water – for example on golf courses, gardens, swimming-pools, showers and cars. The Volga has been reduced by dams almost to a series of lakes,

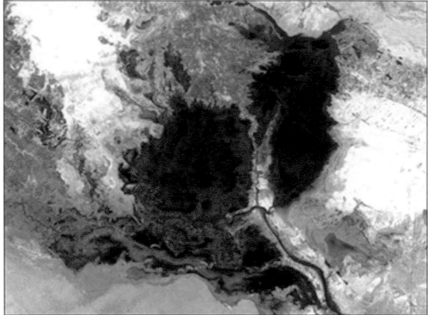

1973–1976

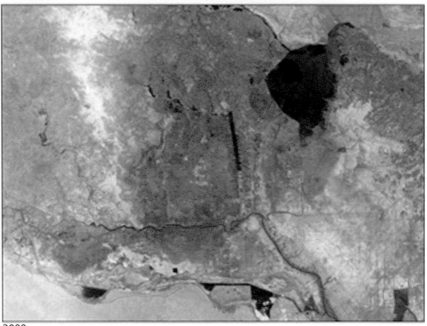

2000

**Fig. 2.9.** Drainage of marshland in Mesopotamia: remote sensing by Landsat shows most of the habitat was lost between 1970 and 2000. Most of the dark area is wetland.

*Source:* Image courtesy of Hasan Partow, UNEP.

with water taking 1.5 years to reach the Caspian Sea, when once it took 1.5 months.

The USA has serious water shortages in California and Florida, and has controversial intentions to import water from Canada on a massive scale. Spring habitats and species are particularly threatened. Overconsumption of water (for industry and irrigation) exterminated the Parras pupfish and stumptooth minnow from Mexico in about 1930, and threatens the Comanche Springs pupfish. In the Caribbean and Seychelles, water is diverted from coastal wetlands or a groundwater lens to supply locals and tourists. Southern Spain's water shortage threatens wetlands locally and elsewhere in Europe. The loss of wetland by drainage has been well documented for the Florida Everglades and the Somerset levels in Britain.

Rivers may now never reach the sea or their inland deltas. China's Yellow River is no longer perennial. Little water from the Colorado River now reaches its delta, and Colorado Delta clams are amongst the endangered species. In Britain, drought can lead to the drying up of streams such as the River Lavant in Kent, threatening populations of species including the brook lamprey. The Okavango Delta, a World Heritage Site in Botswana, is threatened by proposals to abstract water from its supply in Namibia and Angola, and other massive schemes are proposed in southern Africa.

Water levels are frequently controlled, and water courses diverted, straightened or built-up (canalised). There are massive proposed river diversion schemes in India and elsewhere. Water bodies are also used for transport and recreation: associated problems include bank erosion due to swell from boats, noise pollution from powerboats, and oil spills. Weirs, locks and dams are used to control water levels and flows, and in mining – a threat in southeast Madagascar; these obstacles have similar impacts to hydro-power (Section 2.2.6). Navigation weirs built on the River Severn in England in the nineteenth century extirpated shad and sea lamprey from the river, with the first weir, built in 1943, causing a very marked decline in migratory fish.

Wetland species are relatively highly threatened both globally and locally, although they are not a high proportion of known globally threatened species. The British Isles and New Zealand have probably lost some 80% of their wetlands in the past 1000 years – with the likely eventual loss of nearly 50% of the wetland specialists. Indeed, some 30% of the species of invertebrate that were locally extirpated from Britain in the past century were wetland specialists, whilst the same proportion of currently threatened British invertebrates inhabit wetlands. The United States has a rich freshwater fauna, of which, for example, some 70% of the freshwater mussels and 40% of the fish and amphibians are threatened. Freshwater animals are apparently one of the most threatened groups in the USA – and this is probably true of less well-surveyed regions.

## 2.2.4  Materials

Materials such as timber and minerals are vital to people, but there are many ways different products can be substituted, and so demand is hard to predict. Timber and tree products may have been exploited by the earliest humans – for example as bedding. Virtually all societies use wood for construction of shelters, boats, tools and weapons. The exploitation of wood is a form of hunting, although many species of plant can replace lost parts in a way many animals cannot – permitting exploitation of the same tree over many years. There is a great variety of growth forms and growth rates amongst woody plants, which makes species more or less susceptible to overharvesting (Chapter 7). The Juan Fernandez sandalwood was harvested to extinction.

Whole habitats, such as hardwood forests, may be overexploited, as with the deforestation of Philip Island and the general loss of large trees in Britain during numerous wars. Currently threatened habitats and species include the monkey-puzzle and alerce forests of Chile and Argentina, the dawn redwood forest of China, and afrormosia of Africa. Wood is also used in the carving of masks, musical instruments, bows and the like. Selective use of relatively slow-growing species may threaten them (Section 3.1.2), as with ebony, yew and rosewood. The brazilwood tree of Brazil is now very rare through 400 years of demand to make dyes and violin bows. The affluent use of hardwoods for furniture, veneers and disposable chopsticks has attracted much criticism.

'Selective logging' of lucrative species leaves the canopy relatively intact compared to clear felling. However, many species are sensitive to this type of disturbance, including some 370 species of birds (31% of all threatened birds). Dead-wood specialists amongst the birds and other taxa are often affected.

Large areas of forest have been cleared to make wood pulp, felling often being indiscriminate and wasting valuable timber species. It is easy and cheap to exploit forests with such unselective methods. In Indonesia, much forest has been pulped for paper, and the land then used for palm oil plantations. Tropical forest wood pulp is used in some plywoods and cardboard packaging, with Japanese operations and markets attracting much attention.

Mineral extraction procedures may be very damaging. Mining may produce pollution but also take land through spoil heaps. Open-cast mining can be very destructive – as in gold and bauxite (aluminium) mining in South American forests. Extraction methods may cause substantial pollution to freshwater systems, such as mercury contamination and siltation from gold mines in the Amazon. Settling ponds and transport links are often needed. Proposals for the mining of titanium in sands beneath relict coastal forests in Madagascar have provoked serious concern for endemic species and for species in nearby waterways. The extraction of precious stones, such as diamonds, may involve diversion of rivers. Mining for oil and gas, and its associated infrastructure such as pipelines (Section 2.7), may cause many problems. Oil and gas development involving helicopters can reduce this impact, as has been used by British Petroleum in South-East Asia, and at Camisea in Peru.

## 2.2.5  Grazing

Pastoral peoples are often at the centre of polarised debate. To some observers, the lifestyle is idyllic, benign and even natural; to others it leads to land degradation, deforestation and 'desertification'. Some of the benefits to conservation from grazing are discussed in Section 7.3. However, overgrazing has caused very extensive loss of habitat and biodiversity in many parts of the world. The species most often associated with overgrazing are goats (which can survive on very little freshwater), sheep, and cattle, but others such as camels can be important.

In the ancient Mediterranean there was much concern about overgrazing by goats. Goats can penetrate and destroy relict habitats that were otherwise protected by their inaccessibility or their unsuitability for crop production – for example forests on offshore islands such as the Radama group off Madagascar. On St Helena – an Atlantic island with 83% endemicity amongst its vascular plants – goats have been hugely destructive, contributing to the loss of 60 of these endemics. In southern Africa, erosion has increased as livestock numbers have increased, leading to massive gullying (Fig. 2.10). Concerns about overgrazing in eastern Africa were raised by Julian S. Huxley in 1931, who noted that it resulted from wealth being measured in head of cattle. In the Sahel, overgrazing is evident from comparison of repeated aerial surveys of livestock and erosion rates (Fig. 2.11). As human populations have increased, so erosion has increased in proportion.

It is often claimed, by those who credit tribal peoples with superior skills for managing the environment, that semi-arid systems such as savannah have a 'boom-and-bust' or 'non-equilibrium' ecology, in which unpredictable rainfall is more important than interactions between plants and animals. Some biologists believe that such systems have no 'carrying capacity' (limit to

**Fig. 2.10.**   An erosion gully in the Karoo, southern Africa, probably caused by overgrazing by livestock. Erosion is a major problem in many areas of the world. Further details of soil conservation problems are given by A. S. Goudie (2000). *Photograph:* Copyright James Keay-Bright.

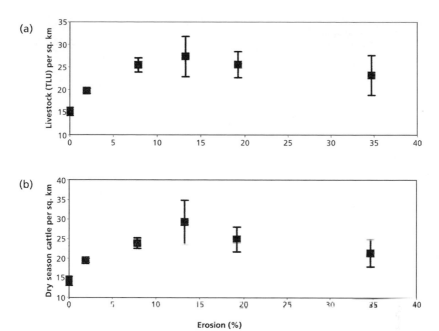

**Fig. 2.11.** The biomass (a) and density (b) of grazing livestock correlates significantly with erosion in Nigeria (means and standard error shown). Livestock density itself correlates with human population density. Data from 1980 to 1993. *Note:* TLU — Total Livestock Units, each equivalent to one camel.
*Source:* W. Wint & D. Bourn / Environmental Research Group Oxford (ERGO).

numbers due to competition) and cannot be overgrazed. However, recent research by A. W. Illius, and T. G. O'Connor has confirmed what ecologists such as M. J. Coe and A. R. E. Sinclair have observed over decades of study in the field: there is in fact a long-term equilibrium, and excessive populations of herbivores lead to density-dependent reductions in herbivore survival and reproduction in future seasons and years. A carrying capacity does exist, but it may be obscured by a time lag between a population increase in the wet season and decreased survival and reproduction in subsequent dry seasons. Illius and O'Connor deduced that the climatic variability of savannahs and arid areas makes them *especially* vulnerable to overgrazing.

The long-term population density of the savannah herbivores is determined by 'key resource areas', which they use in the dry season. These areas often have more permanently high soil moisture levels and plant productivity. If domestic animals are introduced to such an area, then this must inevitably be in competition with, and at the expense of, the wild species using the same food. The populations of wild herbivores, and the species which depend on

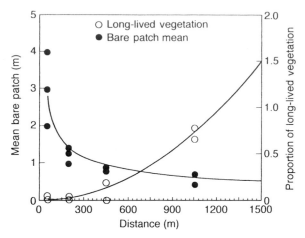

**Fig. 2.12.**  An impact of livestock grazing near wells in desert grassland in New Mexico. The size of bare patches of soil decreases with the square of the distance to wells, and the cover of perennial plants increases with the square of the distance. *Source:* Nash, M. S. *et al. Ecological Applications* **9** (1999), 814–823.

them, will often be suppressed by livestock – to believe otherwise would be similar to believing in perpetual motion.

Domestic livestock grazing is ecologically recent. Sheep and goats were introduced to Africa less than 10 000 years ago. Cattle were domesticated in Africa less than 10 000 years ago, reaching east Africa about 3000 years ago, whilst in Australia cattle have only been present since 1788, and in North America since 1521. The vegetation in many areas did not 'co-evolve' with these herbivores, and their trampling and dung may do more damage, per tonne of animal biomass supported, than native herbivores. Indeed, it was necessary to introduce dung beetles from Africa to help decompose cattle dung in Australia. Livestock may eat the vegetation in different ways to native herbivores – for example tugging it up rather than snipping off the grass. Overgrazing often causes loss of perennial plant species (Fig. 2.12).

Pastoralists such as the Maasai generally see the vegetation as 'theirs', with wildlife 'taking it', rather than the reverse. Pastoralists usually persecute species which they see as competing with livestock (such as the African wild ass, Tibetan gazelle and Asiatic ibex), or which 'degrade' rangeland (such as prairie-dogs, marmots and pika). Poisons used recently against voles in the Mongolian steppe killed demoiselle cranes and other wildlife. Wildlife may also be killed if it 'raids' forage crops, as with bears, wild boar, and blue sheep. The Hindu Kush–Himalayas region, and east Africa, support several wild ungulates threatened by a recent increase in livestock. Direct competition for forage is thought to threaten species such as wild Bactrian camel in Mongolia, wild ass in Africa and guanaco in Patagonia.

Grazing animals have indirect effects on wildlife. Pastoralists also persecute predators (Section 2.2.1). They also set fires at a far greater frequency than was natural (to clear scrub and to promote fresh growth for their herds) and so reduce the abundance of fire-sensitive trees. Burning of pasture changes the community composition of the grasslands, and fires may run out of control into adjacent habitats – damaging forest as in Mkomazi in Tanzania. Conversely, burning management, which is beneficial to some species, is discussed in Chapters 5 and 7. Burning to create new pasture ('the Hamburger Connection') accounted for most of the forest loss in Central America, and is an important cause of global forest decline.

Fire, and chains pulled behind tractors, have also been used to clear African scrub to reduce the abundance of tsetse flies, and so open areas for pastoralism. Diseases which livestock transmit to wildlife (such as rhinderpest and foot and mouth), or which wildlife transmit to livestock (such as tuberculosis, trypanosoniasis and foot and mouth) can lead to tensions between farmers and conservationists (Section 2.6). Use of artificial fertilizer to 'improve' pasture by increasing productivity leads to a decline in floristic richness (Section 7.3.2). Fences are used to reduce transmission of diseases between wildlife and livestock; this has killed wildlife directly, and impeded migration, as in the Kalahari.

Pens or corrals for livestock are often constructed using plants, and this can lead to local deforestation as with the 'boma' of the pastoralists in Africa. M. J. Coe and colleagues found it takes about 40 large bushes to make each boma for a family of 12 in South Turkana (Kenya), that bomas often last less than a year, and that this may have contributed significantly to deforestation over the past 200 years. Some of these bushes provided important foods such as fruit for other species, as well as being important in the structure of the habitat.

The carcasses of wild herbivores were part of the natural system, providing habitat for specialist species; however, livestock are generally removed and slaughtered. Livestock may require pesticidal dips and medicines, and these have ecological side-effects such as killing dung beetles and oxpeckers. Livestock also re-distribute nutrients.

Competition for water can be intense. In parts of the Turkana district of Kenya, S. D. Williams and A. P. W. Nelson found that threatened wildlife species such as Grevy's zebra may be excluded from water by thornbush fences. In the Marsabit District of Kenya, human activity near water has forced these zebra and other species to drink at night – exposing them to higher mortality from predators. Wild ass are threatened by exclusion from water in Africa.

Water holes created by or for pastoralists can lead to local declines in native herbivores, as witnessed in the lands of the Hadza hunter-gatherers in Tanzania, and elsewhere. Natural water holes may be drunk dry by livestock, and the areas around them degraded (see Fig. 2.12).

## 2.2.6  Energy

Energy is perhaps our most fundamental requirement after food and water, and it may be the most important of all in terms of conservation. Paul R. Ehrlich has suggested that the overall scale of the impact of the human population in an area can be estimated by multiplying the population size in the area by the energy usage per person in that area. Ehrlich estimates the total global consumption of energy in pre-agricultural times (some 10 000 years ago) was under $0.002 \times 10^{12}$ W; today it is about $13 \times 10^{12}$ W and it may reach ten times this figure under growth projected by the World Commission on Environment and Development.

If only we had a benign, cheap, abundant source of energy, we could solve many of the world's conservation problems. We could grow food in large quantities using artificial fertilisers or in microbial vats – without adding to the greenhouse effect. We could create and pump freshwater for irrigation – without the risk of salinification. We could prevent the deaths of thousands of infants per day – and so reduce birth rates. We could reduce the burning of fuelwood and dung, and the consequent spread of open, degraded land. The ecological impacts of various fuels are discussed below.

Fuelwood is the energy source used by most of the world's population, and is one of the most locally destructive sources of energy (Fig. 2.13). There is a global 'fuelwood crisis'. Charcoal burning is creating an expanding circle of deforestation around major cities such as Mexico City, and the biologically extraordinary Atlantic forests of Brazil have been largely lost to provide charcoal for industry. Charcoal production wastes 50% of the energy of the wood. In the Sahel, fuelwood is being stripped for domestic use far faster than it is replaced, and people may have to walk for several hours to collect it. The common practice of selective removal of dead or dying wood for fuel, whilst it might appear more benign than taking live wood, seriously threatens a large group of slow-growing species which feed specifically on dead wood (the 'saproxylic' species), as well as species which use dead wood for cover. Deforestation has numerous consequences for conservation (Sections 2.2 and 5.4). The generation of any type of 'biomass fuel', be it in fuelwood plantations, coppice, sugar-cane or water-hyacinths, will not occur without a local

**Fig. 2.13.** Fuelwood collection damages habitats, such as this mangrove in Haiti. *Photograph:* Copyright Mark Edwards/Still Pictures.

impact on wildlife – as will be shown for coppice in Section 7.3. Biogas fuel (methane generated from sewage and organic waste) is relatively ecologically benign.

Tidal power traps the water of an estuary behind a barrage at high tide, and lets it out slowly through turbines. This reduces the tidal range of the river and the expanse of highly fertile inter-tidal mudflats. Barrages therefore threaten invertebrates on the mudflats and the large populations of wading birds which eat them. In Britain, a proposed barrage across the River Severn threatens very serious damage to an area supporting huge populations of waterfowl – and indeed would be illegal under the Ramsar convention (Section 9.2). An alternative type of tidal power, using huge artificial islands with a series of reservoirs which fill as the tides rise, has been advocated for the Severn; it has not yet been evaluated for ecological impact such as mass mortality of fish in the turbines. Barrages also have major impacts on fish, similar to hydro-power.

Hydro-power (including 'mini-hydro' and 'micro-hydro') severely degrades river systems in many ways. Dams and weirs reduce flow rates and oxygenation, and are physical barriers to migrating fish such as shads, lampreys and sturgeon. Power turbines chop fish up, particularly long ones like eels and lamprey. Dams accumulate pollutants, and greenhouse gasses such as methane are released from rotting material in the water of new dams. The major dams on the Nile and the Amazon, and the new Three Gorges Dam on the Yangtze, illustrate environmental issues including the loss of important or beautiful terrestrial habitat. These problems are also true of small-scale dams, including the 'mini-hydro' schemes that many 'greens' favour. It is unclear, for example, what impact vast numbers of small hydro-power plants would have on the mountain ecology of China. The pumped-water storage system at Dinorwig, Wales, generates electricity when water that has been pumped into a high-altitude reservoir is released; the creation of the system extirpated an important population of a rare fish, the Arctic charr. To quote David Bellamy and B. Quayle, after the pivotal debate on the Franklin River Dam in Tasmania: 'No Dam' Good'!

Despite popular belief, nuclear power is highly acceptable from a conservation perspective. It requires relatively very small quantities of fuel (that is, it has a high 'energy density'). Damage results from strip-mining for uranium in Australia and South Africa. However, on a global scale this is much less extensive than open-cast mining for coal. Unlike fossil fuel, nuclear fuel produces *very* small quantities of waste, which is much more easily dealt with than carbon dioxide. Most species and individual organisms are far less sensitive to radiation than humans, since they have shorter lives, more offspring, and natural selection weeds out radiation-induced mutations in a way that is unacceptable in human populations. Measures which protect people from discharges of radioactive waste are more than sufficient for conservation. Catastrophic releases of radiation are far more damaging to people than wildlife. Indeed, the now-unpopulated region near Chernobyl has become a local haven for wildlife, whilst nuclear tests on Bikini Atoll have helped conserve outstandingly good undisturbed coral reef communities which are refuges from fishing. Cooling-water intakes for nuclear stations have caused significant mortality of fish in the English and Bristol Channels, and elsewhere.

Solar power and wind power have a low energy density, and thus require very extensive collecting surfaces. Solar power is relatively benign, but has damaged some desert habitats in North America. Solar power that reduces the need for fuelwood stoves might protect forests in the developing world – although fuelwood fires are often lit partly for warmth and for smoke to deter insects. Wind farm location and design must be considered very carefully, both onshore and offshore. In North America, wind farms kill migratory birds and legally protected species such as golden eagles (which may be attracted to the area by an increased food supply). According to one provisional estimate by M. Duchamp, based on extrapolation from studies at Navarra, wind turbines in Spain may kill approximately 150 000 birds each year (including some 10 000 raptors): clearly, more research is needed on their impacts.

There are also impacts from the turbines' foundations, cables, cable trenches, lighting and access roads, and disruption of bird migration. Undersea turbines exploiting water currents might have comparable effects on marine life. Wave power captured by bobbing devices in the open sea may also obstruct fishing, whilst wave-power devices on coastlines may be destructive to coastal wildlife.

Fossil fuel is one of the most destructive energy sources, and its use creates oxides of carbon, nitrogen and sulphur ($CO_2$, $NO_x$ and $SO_2$, respectively). These very important atmospheric pollutants are discussed in Section 2.3.3.

## 2.3 Pollution

The waste materials produced by individuals and society vary in their significance for conservation. Some (such as carbon dioxide) are relatively benign in low concentrations, others (such as arsenic) are acutely hazardous. Some (such as oil) act over short timescales, others (such as CFCs and radioactive isotopes) are persistent for hundreds of years. Some pollutants are dispersed through the atmosphere and affect both terrestrial and aquatic systems.

### 2.3.1 Terrestrial

Pollution in the terrestrial environment is often relatively conspicuous. Litter in the streets and the countryside, or contaminated land preventing agriculture or building, may have an aesthetic and health impact and may arouse public concern – in some cultures far more than others. The terrestrial environment does not disperse pollutants as readily as aquatic environments; this can be beneficial in localising impact and easing clean-up, or problematic in sustaining concentrated dosage of the pollutant.

Waste disposal is a major concern, as illustrated by the legendary 'Garbage Barge', which was sent from destination to destination along the east coast of the USA in an attempt to find somewhere to offload. Landfill sites are often used to bury waste in old pits and quarries, and this is a problem for conservation if these man-made pits have had centuries to acquire biological interest. For example, in Britain, old chalk pits are now refuges for rare chalk grassland species, whilst gravel pits may support notable wetland species such as great crested newts. Litter can threaten wildlife in a variety of ways. Birds may be strangled by the plastic rings used to bind drinks cans together. Rodents and reptiles may die trapped in glass bottles. Plastic bags have become a very conspicuous pollution problem in most countries, and may be damaging to ecotourism. Conversely, litter can provide structure and shelter in environments – in Britain, old tyres may have great crested newts beneath them, whilst bricks and corrugated sheeting lying on grassland can provide warm, dry cover for slow-worms and other reptiles. Similarly, flotsam on the strand-line of beaches can shelter rare coastal invertebrates.

Contaminated land has a variety of influences. In some areas, it protects species by deterring human use – as with contamination by radioactivity; however, few would argue that this excuses pollution. Contaminated land, although often problematic for people, is generally less of an issue for wildlife because many species are more tolerant of contaminants than are humans. For example, levels of lead on roadside verges (from petrol) have little impact on wildlife. Indeed, toxic waste from industry (such as spoil from lead-mining or alkaline and metal-rich waste from fuel-ash) may create 'extreme environments' which support rare specialist species such as orchids. Pollutants may attract species, as with oil spills in deserts (which resemble waterbodies and thus trap birds), or refuse dumps (which attract generalist predators). Oil spills on land are more common than in water, and may influence cold ecosystems such as the taiga and tundra for hundreds of years.

Light pollution is a problem for some species of vertebrate – attracting hatchling sea turtles towards beach-crest hotels, and birds to ships and lighthouses. On Réunion Island, 20–40% of fledgling Barau's petrels are attracted to lights. The effect of street lights on invertebrates such as moths and flies (which are attracted to them), and on birds and bats (whose diurnal rhythms are confused) is poorly known. Gloworms in Britain are adversely affected by domestic and other light.

## 2.3.2  Aquatic

Litter is an increasing problem in aquatic environments. Surveys of beaches on remote and uninhabited islands, such as Ducie, Aldabra and the Chagos islands, and the Antarctic coastline, reveal the great variety of litter now floating in the oceans (Fig. 2.14). Plastics are problematic in strangling and choking seabirds; 90% of albatross chicks on Midway island had plastic in the gullet. Some sea turtle species (particularly the leatherback) mistake plastic bags for their jellyfish food, and their guts become blocked. Discarded fishing lines and nets threaten turtles, cetaceans, seals, seabirds and waterbirds. Plastic particles less than 0.1 mm in diameter are changing the marine invertebrate communities of some coastlines.

**Fig. 2.14.** Litter on the shore of Laysan, an uninhabited Pacific island over 1000 km from the nearest heavily populated area.
*Photograph:* Copyright Milo Burcham.

One of the most recurrent and conspicuous conservation issues in the aquatic environment is the spillage of oil. Major incidents include the Atlantic Empress off Tobago in 1979 and the Exxon Valdez in Prince William Sound off Alaska in 1989. Ships may continue to release oil for many decades after sinking, as with the Royal Oak, which sank in the Scapa Flow in 1939, threatening an important seabird population. Oil may be released when ships flush their tanks – often illegally. Oil spills account for only 5% of the oil pollution reaching the sea, the rest being from run-off. Rivers influenced by oil spills include the St Laurence, Ohio and Gasconade of North America, and the Mangawhero of New Zealand.

In the marine environment, oil spills influence seabirds and mammals (such as the sea otter) directly through fouling their feathers (or fur) and through toxicity after ingestion of the oils during preening. Survivorship is low, even after cleaning the birds with detergent. Sea turtles, including hawksbills, are killed by ingestion of tar-balls they mistake for food. Oil in cold waters is removed less rapidly by natural processes (evaporation, ultraviolet light, and microbial activity) than oil spilled in tropical waters. In the Gulf War, for example, the damage to reefs and other habitats was relatively low – in contrast to the Exxon Valdez spill, which has continued to cause developmental anomalies in fish such as herring for over 10 years; the toxins responsible may include PAHs. Seabed communities had not recovered 10 years after the Amoco Cadiz spill in the English Channel in 1978.

Fertilisers and pesticides can be problematic where spray-drift or run-off may carry them into water courses. Pesticides and herbicides may be toxic to aquatic species. Fertilisers and sewage may lead to eutrophication of freshwater and marine environments such as the North Sea. Blooms of algae may develop; these are toxic in themselves or lead to de-oxygenation of stagnant water when they decay. Fish and amphibians in ponds may die owing to anoxia. Nutrient inputs from sewage may also be leading to algal growth on coral reefs, flipping the ecosystem into a new, less diverse, state. Eutrophication threatens Britain's rarest fish, the vendace, which is now confined to very clean lakes in the Lake District.

Seepage from waste tips, or spillages from industrial sources, can be acutely toxic. A spillage of millions of tonnes of mine waste into Spanish rivers and marshes in Europe in 1998 had acute toxic effects, and left lasting genetic changes in populations of white storks and other species of the Doñana National Park. Some compounds are extremely toxic to aquatic life, whilst having little known impact on people. Tributyl tin (TBT) is a compound used in some antifouling paints to stop marine organisms growing on ships; it has accumulated in European waters and caused local changes to ecosystems. In contrast, PCBs (derived from electrical insulation) are toxic to both people and wildlife; they are long-lived and 'bioaccumulate' in the food chain. Bioaccumulation is the accumulation of substances in species through eating other contaminated species; it is particularly problematic in top predators. PCBs have accumulated to harmful levels in mink in the Great Lakes of North America, English sole in Puget Sound and otters in parts of Europe and have unknown impact on species such as killer whales.

Derivatives of PCBs and some agrochemicals resemble thyroid hormones or oestrogen sex hormones: they are 'oestrogenic'. Oestrogens from contraceptive pills flow out of sewage treatment plants. These and other 'hormone disruptors' are leading to abnormal development in fish, amphibians and reptiles, including 'feminisation'. Such effects have been found in the Great Lakes

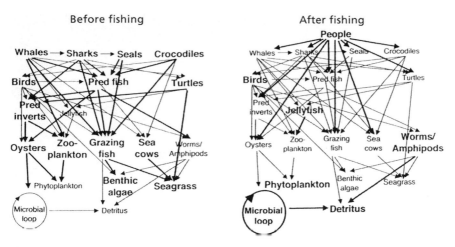

**Fig. 2.15.** Human fishing has resulted in increased microbial activity and sediment load in estuaries, owing to declines in filter-feeders such as oysters. **Bold** font shows abundance, Roman font shows rarity.
*Source:* Reprinted with permission from Jackson J. C. B. *et al. Science* **293** (2001), 629–638. Copyright 2001 American Association for the Advancement of Science.

of North America, in European estuaries such as the Thames, and in polar bears that have accumulated PCBs. Oestrogenics may be a part of the global 'amphibian decline syndrome'.

Siltation – the influx and deposition of suspended particles – is a major concern in many parts of the world. It can be exacerbated by overharvesting of shellfish (Fig. 2.15). As well as causing problems through nutrient enrichment, it has impacts through its physical properties. Many aquatic organisms filter-feed, and their feeding apparatus can become clogged; some species may be sessile and unable to evade smothering. The penetration of light through water is important to photosynthesis by phytoplankton, kelp, seagrass and corals. In Queensland, Australia, the creation of a road through the Wet Tropics World Heritage Area led to erosion onto important reefs, whilst silt damage to seagrass beds is one of the greatest threats to dugong in the Great Barrier Reef. In Madagascar, many of the rivers continuously run orange with silt, which then fans out of estuaries into the marine environment (Fig. 2.16); the impact of such plumes has never been assessed, because no base-line data on fish or invertebrates were collected when erosion began several hundred years ago. Siltation exterminated the harelip sucker – a fish which fed on the bottom of clear prairie streams in North America. In Britain, fine silt from clay pits damaged rivers and marine life in Cornwall.

**Fig. 2.16.**   A plume of silt from the delta of the Betsiboka River spreading into the
sea (left) off Madagascar. The silt is orange in colour in the original Space-Shuttle
photograph.
*Photograph:* Copyright: Corbis.

Heat energy can be a pollutant. 'Thermal pollution' from industrial or urban
water outflows is a problem in slow-moving freshwater. Warm water holds
less oxygen, and fish and other life may suffocate near outflows. Ironically,
however, in some areas such as the Severn Estuary in Britain, pollution has led
to large aggregations of birds, which feed where invertebrates are continuously
available in the warm outflows from power stations. The impact of such
aggregations on the natural system is unclear, and these sites may help species
which have declined elsewhere. Cold, de-oxygenated water released from dams

is a problem in some rivers. Light may be a pollutant in the deep sea, where oceanographic surveys can result in the permanent blinding of organisms such as shrimp near hydrothermal vents. Sound pollution is an increasingly serious problem in aquatic environments. There are many sources, frequencies and intensities of sound pollution, including ships' propellers, detonations for geological surveys, sonar, and other very high-intensity scanning. Sound can damage cetacean ears; it might interfere with whale song and sonar, and with other species of deep-sea organism that are sensitive to vibration.

Pollution is often unpredictable, and the consequences may only become evident after its accumulation through unforeseen pathways. For example, lead weights (used by anglers) accumulated in the gizzards of British mute swans, which mistook them for the grit they use to grind food. The resultant disfigurement and decline of swans (a bird protected by Royal decree) caused public outcry, and such weights have now been outlawed. Pollution is particularly likely to accumulate in relatively closed water bodies, such as the North American Great Lakes, the Mediterranean, and Lake Baikal.

## 2.3.3 Atmospheric

Atmospheric pollution is perhaps the biggest environmental problem humans have yet faced. The consequences of acid rain, ozone depletion or global warming, on health, buildings and agriculture, are potentially enormously costly. The impact on the biota, however, may be even more severe, long lasting, and ultimately may be one of the ways these pollutants most affect people.

Pesticides delivered from the air became one of the first issues for environmental campaigns – *Silent Spring*, written by Rachel Carlson in 1962, alerted many to the loss of birds in agricultural regions, and to potential health risks of spray drift. Organochloride pesticides such as DDT bioaccumulated in birds or prey, such as the sparrowhawk in Europe and peregrine falcons in Europe and North America, and thinned their eggshells, resulting in substantial population declines. Herbicides and pesticides now threaten species such as turtle doves in Britain, partly through reduction in availability of arable weed seeds.

Acid rain became one of the main environmental topics of the 1970s, after changes were observed by building conservationists, foresters and fisheries managers. After much debate and research, it was proved that waste gases containing sulphur and nitrogen, predominantly from the chimneys of major power stations, were causing severe pollution which flowed from Britain to Scandinavia, and from the USA to Canada. Whilst declining in developed countries, acid rain is increasingly a problem in developing countries.

Acid deposition has impacts on terrestrial systems through a variety of processes, which are similar for acids from both sulphur dioxide ($SO_2$) and various oxides of nitrogen ($NO_x$). These oxides may be deposited dry, or create sulphuric and nitric acids in mists, rain or snow. Acidification of the soil may lead to the mobilisation of metal ions and nutrients and their subsequent loss through leaching; this loss is more severe on soils lacking calcium carbonate. Contact with acid precipitation damages leaves. Nitrogen enrichment may occur. Although controversial, some believe that trees may suffer a combination of pathological features which taken together suggest that acid precipitation is the cause of injury or death. Some 50% of Europe's forest areas may have been affected. Maple forests in Ontario, Canada, have also suffered substantial acid damage. Unfortunately, some of the most pristine forests which have survived in Europe, such as Bialowieza National Park in Poland, now receive atmospheric pollution. 'Critical loads' of pollutants are being assessed and mapped. In 1995–1997, about 90% of British woodland exceeded the nitrogen deposition critical load, and 80% exceeded the acidity critical load.

Lichen assemblages can be influenced by a wide range of air pollutants, particularly gaseous $SO_2$ and $NO_x$; the latter acts through bark acidification and nutrient enrichment. In Europe, lichens sensitive to $SO_2$, such as *Ramalina farinacea* and numerous *Parmelia* species, have responded positively to reductions in emissions and are rapidly spreading or recolonising; furthermore, some species, such as *Parmeliopsis ambigua*, are extending their range owing to bark acidification, and many lichens, such as *Physcia* and *Xanthoria* species, are benefiting from nutrient inputs.

In aquatic systems, acidification may influence species directly or indirectly. Amphibian development is disrupted by low pH. Indirect effects include the accumulation of aluminium in fish; this may kill them by clogging their gills with mucous. Diatoms may also be affected indirectly, and thence the zooplankton which feed on them. Molluscs and crustacea, which use calcium carbonate in their shells, are stressed in acid waters, and sensitive groups include Ostracods, *Daphnia*, *Gammarus*, and crayfish. The loss of both the photosynthetic producers and the invertebrates has consequences up the food chain. In Ontario, Lumsden Lake lost all its eight fish species between 1950 and 1978, and, in 1980, 140 lakes in Ontario had no fish. In southern Norway, fish stocks have been halved since 1940, and many lakes still have no fish. In Britain, several fish species have been influenced, including the endemic race of the arctic charr. The dipper, an attractive bird which feeds on aquatic invertebrates, has also declined in the south of Britain.

Photochemical smogs in urban areas, including the constituents of acid rain, can generate ozone in the lower atmosphere, which is damaging to plants and animals. Meanwhile, ozone ($O_3$) is declining in the upper atmosphere.

Ozone depletion was first recorded in 1982, and occurred so massively and suddenly that scientists at first did not believe the data. Over the Antarctic, a 'hole' that was roughly the area of North America appeared in the layer of stratospheric ozone; in the spring, this hole is an almost complete absence of ozone. Ozone is a form of oxygen that absorbs certain wavelengths of sunlight – in particular ultraviolet light in the UVB wavelengths. These wavelengths do not normally reach the surface of the Earth in any quantity, and organisms have therefore not evolved defences against them. With a decrease in ozone of a few percent, the amount of UVB light at ground level increases by a few percent. This can lead to an increase of a few percent in skin cancers in humans.

The pollutants responsible for the ozone depletion were mainly chlorofluorocarbons (CFCs) – a range of almost entirely synthetic chemicals used as propellants in aerosols, as coolants and insulation in refrigerators, and as solvents. Another group of chemicals, the halons, contain bromine and are used in suppressing fires in confined areas. The largely inert character of these chemicals enables such applications, but the unfortunate consequence is that as pollutants they decay very slowly: CFC 12 has a half-life of over 110 years. Long survival in the atmosphere gives the chemicals time to move up into the stratosphere, where they are blown by the solar winds to the poles. At the winter of each pole, a 'polar vortex' appears, with winds circulating round the pole; these vortices insulate polar air from the heat of the tropics, whilst effectively creating very large reaction vessels in which ozone is depleted.

The mechanism for depletion of polar ozone depends on the cold atmospheric conditions in the Antarctic and Arctic winters. The surface of water droplets and ice crystals in cold polar stratospheric clouds catalyse the breakdown of CFCs and halons to release reactive free chloride and bromide ions (respectively). When the spring arrives in either pole, sunlight speeds up the breakdown of ozone to oxygen, and each ion can break down many ozone molecules. Thus the biggest depletions occur in the spring in each hemisphere. The depletion in the Arctic is less severe than in the Antarctic, because the vortex is weaker and its stratosphere warmer. In the summers, the vortices break up, and very low concentrations of ozone float away over areas such as Australia, South Africa and South America.

Increased ultraviolet light reaching the surface of the planet is not simply a health risk. Although most animals will not get skin cancers, they may develop cataracts (as in snow-blindness). There are suggestions that some mammals in South America are being influenced in this way. Marine algae are sensitive to increased ultraviolet radiation, and there is some evidence from satellite imagery that the phytoplankton of the southern ocean are being influenced. This could have very great implications for the ecology of the area, and important effects on fisheries. Worse, it might reduce the removal of carbon dioxide from the atmosphere by marine organisms. Ozone depletion could therefore be one of the largest conservation issues. The depletion will last at least 50 years, since although legal production of most of these pollutants stopped in 2000 (Section 9.2.1) many CFCs remain in the atmosphere. Indeed, because the increasing greenhouse effect leads to cooler stratospheres, the holes are still very severe. A new problem, depletion in mid-latitudes, is predicted as a result of increasing nitrous oxide pollution.

The greenhouse effect itself is potentially more damaging than any other pollution problem, and is arguably one of the greatest of all conservation problems. Various gases, particularly carbon dioxide, CFCs, and methane, are released by human activities and accumulate in the atmosphere. These gases, along with natural components of the atmosphere such as water vapour, are 'radiatively active' – that is, they can trap heat in the lower atmosphere. Solar energy which has been absorbed and then re-radiated from the planet's surface at a lower wavelength can be absorbed by these gases and re-radiated again – some towards the surface. This warms the lower atmosphere and cools the upper atmosphere.

The human amplification of the natural greenhouse effect will have a number of consequences, as discussed in the IPCC report *Climate Change 2001*. Basically, more energy is being trapped in the lower atmosphere, so the air, land and sea will warm. Global average temperature increased $0.6 \pm 0.2$ °C last century, and is predicted to rise by between 1.4 and 5.8 °C this century. The temperature rise will probably be greater towards the poles. More energy will be moved in the atmosphere and dissipated from the equator to the poles – and thus hurricanes are likely to increase in frequency. Sea-levels rose about 1–2 mm per year last century (through thermal expansion and melting of terrestrial ice caps), and are predicted to rise between 9 and 88 cm this century. The ocean currents may change very substantially as the vertical and latitudinal temperature gradients which drive them change. The 'El Niño' climate pattern may become frequent, rather than a 'freak' event. Global rainfall patterns will change, with wet areas generally getting wetter, and dry areas (including continental interiors) getting drier. Extreme events will become more common.

Positive feedbacks in the global warming process may explain the very rapid deglaciations after the ice ages. For example, darker surfaces are exposed when snow melts, absorbing more heat. There is a 'plankton multiplier' effect in which warmer sea-surface temperatures prevent nutrient mixing in the ocean, decreasing photosynthesis and thus leading to less carbon dioxide absorption in the oceans. Dying forests, stressed by drought, may burn more often, and there may be more major wildfires generally, as in Australia recently. Warming permafrost will release more methane, and increased biological activity in warmer soils will release carbon dioxide. As the ocean currents change, huge amounts of methane may be released from deposits of methane hydrates on the sea floor. Increased forest cover in cold latitudes may reduce the reflection of light back into space, particularly in winter when dark forest has replaced snow-covered grassland.

The biological and conservation impacts of climate change are likely to be very severe – indeed, perhaps the greatest cause of extinctions after deforestation. Most species on the planet have climatic preferences and tolerances. With rising temperature, climatic zones in different latitudes will be shifted, forcing the biogeographical zones (biomes) to move perhaps a few hundred kilometres towards the poles for each 1 °C rise in temperature. Similarly, the zones on mountains will move uphill – perhaps hundreds of metres per degree. In a 70–90 year interval, nine plant species in the Alps have moved 70–360 m in altitude. As habitats are forced up conical mountains, their area is reduced; however, the tops of mountains will always have more severe climates than near the bottoms, owing to higher windspeeds, and it is not clear how many species will have their climatic ranges pushed off the top of mountains. Heat-sensitive Antarctic marine species appear particularly vulnerable. Some examples of climate-related changes are reviewed by J. P. McCarty, and included in Table 4.2.

Although faster than any changes in the past 1000 years, these changes are probably within the dispersal abilities of many organisms, which have survived major climatic shifts before. However, in modern landscapes, which are generally fragmented by agriculture and urban development, it may now be impossible for the less-mobile species to keep within suitable climatic zones. Examples of species already apparently suffering from climate change include the ptarmigan in Britain (which needs a snow-covered landscape), capercaillie in Scotland (which need cold, dry climates), polar bears and penguins (which need ice cover), and the golden toad in Costa Rica (where altitudinal belts have shifted uphill, possibly exterminating this species). Communities may be disrupted where species have different dispersal abilities.

Reefs are very seriously and very imminently threatened by global warming. Sea-level rise and increased storm force are problems, but the greatest threat

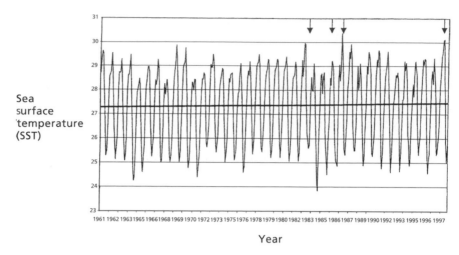

Sea surface temperature (SST)

Year

**Fig. 2.17.** Bleaching events have become more frequent in recent decades. Data from Mayotte, Western Indian Ocean, show bleaching (denoted by arrows) occurred above a threshold of 30 °C.
*Source:* Spencer, T. E. *et al. Marine Pollution Bulletin* **40** (2000), 569–586; copyright 2000 with permission from Elsevier Science.

is the rise in surface temperature in the seas. Reef corals grow near the upper limit of temperature they can endure, and if this is exceeded for several days, 'coral bleaching' occurs, in which the corals eject their symbiotic algae. Recent substantial bleaching has occurred in many regions. During the El Niño of 1998, over 15% of the world's reefs were killed, 87% of the inshore Great Barrier Reef was affected to some extent, whilst some 90% of the coral of the western Indian Ocean bleached. Historical records show that these bleaching events were infrequent through much of the past century, but are now occurring far more frequently (see Fig. 2.17). Indeed, examination of cores through corals have shown that in the reefs off Belize, the mass bleaching events since 1995 are unprecedented in at least the past 3000 years. Recovery is possible only if bleaching is not repeated frequently. Pollution can make bleaching more likely, and increased dissolved $CO_2$ may impede growth.

Mitigation efforts that have been proposed to reduce a build-up of $CO_2$ (such as adding iron to promote plankton in the oceans, some 'carbon offset forestry', and pumping the liquefied gas into the sea) are themselves a threat to some ecosystems.

The recently discovered 'Asian Brown Haze' is formed from a combination of chemicals and particles from a huge number of rural and urban sources (such as forest fires, fuelwood and traffic). This smog can extend over millions of square kilometres, and causes climatic disruption and toxic effects.

## 2.4   Introduced species

It has been suggested that up to 40% of extinctions in the past 400 years were the result of introduced species. Many of these have been on islands, and on the island continent of Australia, where the plants and animals have not evolved defences against the introduced species. However, there has been considerable invasion of continental areas, oceanic areas and freshwater systems by exotic species. Introduced diseases will be discussed in Section 2.6. The extinctions of most bird species since 1800 have been caused by introductions, with some 30% of currently threatened birds at risk from invasives. Introductions occur by accident or design. If the introduced species spread and breed beyond human control, they are termed 'feral species'. Tables 2.5(a), 2.5(b) and 2.6 illustrate the types of species that have been introduced, and the harm they have done. There may be a lag between introduction and rapid spread of a species: this lag was some 100 years for goats on Aldabra, and 20 years for cheatgrass in western North America.

Genetic pollution and hybridisation are further problems caused by introduced species. A super-weed, *Spartina anglica*, was created around British coasts by the hybridisation of the British *Spartina maritima* with the American *Spartina alterniflora*. The Leon Springs pupfish is extinct in the wild owing to hybridisation with introduced sheephead minnows. Release of Madacascar turtle doves (*Streptopelia pictrata pictrata*) in the Seychelles led to the 'genetic swamping' of the Seychelles subspecies (*S. pictrata rostrata*). The Ethiopian wolf is threatened by hybridisation with domestic dogs, and the African wild ass by hybridisation with domestic ass. The problems of 'introgression' of genes from one race or species into another are discussed further in Section 6.2.3.

## 2.4.1   Terrestrial: continents and islands

The reasons behind terrestrial introductions vary. Species such as mice and black rats have often escaped from ships where they were pests. Other species, such as the Polynesian rat, goats, pigs, rabbits and chickens, have probably been introduced as food. Some have been introduced for hunting (deer, red foxes, rabbits), or as beasts of burden (guanacos, camels, donkeys, horses).

Table 2.5(a) *Examples of threats from introduced species (terrestrial plant species)*

| Species or genus | Introduced to | Example of impact |
| --- | --- | --- |
| Gorse | New Zealand | Dominates vegetation |
| *Spartina* species | New Zealand, Australia | Dominates estuaries |
| Coco plum, cinnamon | Seychelles | Dominates vegetation |
| *Stachytarpheta jamaicensis* | Seychelles | Inhibits sooty tern nesting |
| Privet; guava | Mauritius | Threaten endemic trees, birds |
| Bramble, guava | Galapagos | Dominate vegetation |
| Spanish cedar | Galapagos | Replaces endemic *Scalesia* |
| Mexican thorn | Ascension Island | Obstructs nesting sea turtles |
| Rhododendron | Britain | Dominates vegetation |
| Bracken | Widespread | Dominates vegetation |
| Exotic grasses | North American prairies | Dominate vegetation |
| Musk thistle | North America | Degrades grassland |
| Saltcedar | North America | Replaces riparian communities |
| Cheatgrass | North America | Increased fire risk to steppes |
| Melaleuca tree | Florida Everglades | Dominates vegetation |
| Eucalyptus, acacia | South African fynbos | Dominate vegetation |
| *Opuntia* species | South Africa, Madagascar, Australia | Dominate vegetation |
| Lantana | Pan-tropical, e.g. South African veld | Habitat degradation: toxic |

Some feral species are pets which have escaped (e.g. Indian mynah birds in the Seychelles), or species kept on fur-farms (American mink in Europe and possum in New Zealand). Some were introduced to help colonial people feel at home – as with the house sparrow, which was moved from Britain to Australia and America.

On continental sites, species such as the rabbit, the fox and the cat have had tremendous impact. In Australia, cats and foxes have exterminated over 10 species of small marsupial mammal, whilst other marsupials, such as the burrowing bettong, are confined to islands and fenced reserves free of cats. It is estimated that there are over 10 million cats in Australia, killing over 10 billion native animals per year. In Britain, 9 million cats kill

Table 2.5(b) *Examples of threats from introduced species (terrestrial animal species)*

| Species or genus | Introduced to | Example of impact |
|---|---|---|
| Rabbits | Australia | Habitat destruction |
| Rabbits | Round Island (Mauritius) | Habitat destruction (boa, skink) |
| Rabbits | Robinson Crusoe Island | Habitat destruction |
| Deer | Britain; Mauritius | Forest degradation |
| Goats | Galapagos; Aldabra; Round Island | Habitat destruction (tortoises) |
| Red fox | Australia | Extinction of several marsupials |
| Cats | Australia | Extinction of several marsupials |
| Cats | Oceanic islands | Extirpate seabirds (Seychelles) |
| Cats | New Zealand | Extinction of Stevens Island wren |
| Cats | Seychelles | Near-extinction of magpie robin |
| Cats | Galapagos; Seychelles | Predate tortoises |
| Cats | Scotland | Hybridisation with wildcat |
| Dogs | Australia | Extinction of several marsupials |
| Dogs | Galapagos | Predate tortoises |
| Dogs | Macquarie Island (New Zealand) | Predate seals |
| Pigs | Galapagos | Predate tortoises |
| Pigs | Californian Channel Islands | Predate foxes and island jepsonia |
| Crab-eating macaque | Mauritius | Predate endangered birds |
| Polynesian rat | Pacific islands | Predate seabirds, e.g. Oeno atoll |
| Black rat | Aldabra | Extinction of Aldabra warbler? |
| Black rat | Seychelles; Galapagos | Predate tortoises |
| Brush-tailed possum | New Zealand | Extirpation of birds |

Table 2.5(b) (*cont.*)

| Species or genus | Introduced to | Example of impact |
|---|---|---|
| Hedgehog | British islands, e.g. South Uist | Predate dunlin, seabirds |
| Grey squirrel | Europe | Displacement of red squirrel, habitat degradation |
| Indian mynah | Oceanic islands, e.g. Seychelles | Predate endemic birds |
| Red-whiskered bulbul | Seychelles | Predate endemic birds |
| Canada goose | Europe | Overgrazes wetlands |
| Great kiskadee | Bermuda | Predate native birds |
| Mallard | Hawaii | Hybridisation with Hawaiian duck |
| Cane toad | Australia | Predate native species, toxic |
| Cane toad | Puerto Rica | Competition/predation native toad |
| Cuban tree frog | Florida | Predate native tree frogs |
| Brown anole | Florida | Replacing green anole |
| Brown tree snake | Guam | Extirpation of landbirds |
| c. 50 ant species | Hawaii | Extinction of endemic invertebrates |
| Red fire ant (*Solenopsis invicta*) | North America; Australia | Drive out native species |
| Ant (*Iridomyrex humilis*) | South Africa | Habitat destruction |
| Seychelles scale insect | Aldabra | Eats endemic plants |
| Gypsy moth | North America | Habitat degradation |
| Thistlehead feeding weevil | North America | Eats rare native thistles |
| Wasp (*Vespula*) species | New Zealand | Predate invertebrates, compete with birds for honeydew |

some 250 million vertebrates a year. It is possible that the Australian thylacine was hastened to extinction by competition with dogs (dingoes), which were introduced at least 3500 years ago by Aboriginal people. Introduced rabbits have changed landscapes dramatically – including Australia, Robinson Crusoe Island, Laysan (Hawaii) and Round Island (off Mauritius). Rabbits were introduced to Britain about 900 years ago, and were involved in creating

Table 2.6 *Examples of threats from introduced species (aquatic)*

| Species (and origin) | Introduced to | Example of impact or threatened species |
| --- | --- | --- |
| (a) *Freshwater* | | |
| Canadian pondweed (North America) | Europe | Dominates ponds |
| Lesser duckweed (Americas) | Britain | Smothering ponds |
| Water hyacinth (South America) | Africa | Smothering lakes |
| Water lettuce (widespread) | Seychelles; Australia | Smothering lakes |
| Nile perch (North Africa) | East Africa | Extinctions of fish in Lake Victoria |
| Tilapia (Africa) | Australia; Hawaii | Habitat degradation; predation |
| Trout – rainbow (east North America) | Colombian Andes | Extinction of Lake Tota fat fish |
| Trout – rainbow and brown (Europe) | New Zealand | Extinction of New Zealand grayling |
| Zander (continental Europe) | Britain | Decline in roach and other fish |
| Redbreast sunfish (North America) | Italy | Competes with/extirpates fish, e.g. bleak |
| Round goby (Asia) | North America | Competes with fish for food and nest sites |
| Chinese grass carp | Europe | Grazes waterplants |
| Sea lamprey (Atlantic) | North America | Parasitises fish in Great Lakes |
| American mink | Europe | Endanger European mink; Britain: extirpation of many water vole populations |
| Coypu (North America) | Britain | Habitat degradation, Norfolk Broads |
| Signal crayfish (America) | North America | Replaces European crayfish; bank erosion |
| Chinese mitten crab (East Asia) | Europe | Bank erosion; predates crayfish |

Table 2.6 (*cont.*)

| Species (and origin) | Introduced to | Example of impact or threatened species |
|---|---|---|
| Asiatic clam (South-East Asia) | North America | Competition with native species |
| Zebra mussel (Black and Caspian Seas) | North America | Hudson River and Great Lakes: competition with native mussels; herbivory of phytoplankton; ecosystem disruption |
| (b) *Marine* | | |
| Alga *Caulerpa taxifolia* (East Australia) | Mediterranean, North America, Australia | Smothers seabed: toxic |
| Meditteranean mussel | South African coast | Displaces native rocky shore species |
| Japanese oyster drill (Japan) | French coast | Predates whelk |
| European periwinkle | East North America | Denudation of intertidal rocks in Nova Scotia, extensive alteration to communities of rocky and soft substrates |
| Comb jelly *Mnemiopsis leidyi* (West Atlantic) | Black and Caspian Seas | Ecosystem change; eats plankton and fish larvae – ? starves Caspian seal |
| c. 20 molluscs including Asiatic clam | San Francisco Bay | Ecosystem change, e.g. proportions of plankton changed |

'semi-natural' habitats (Section 7.3). Grey Squirrels, introduced to Europe from North America, damage trees, predate birds, and have displaced a native species (Fig. 2.18).

Some of the most damaging introductions have been failed attempts at biological control, as with weasels and cats in New Zealand. Predatory snails (*Euglandina rosea*), intended to control the introduced African land snail, have exterminated several species of snail (e.g. *Partula* species) from Pacific islands.

**Red squirrels**

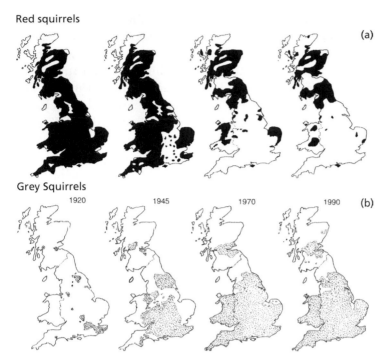

**Grey Squirrels**

**Fig. 2.18.** Red squirrels declined due to competition and disease as the grey squirrel spread in Britain.
*Source:* Yalden, D. *The History of British Mammals.* Reproduced with permission of T & A D. Poyser Ltd., London, and A. & C. Black Publishers Ltd., St. Neots (1999).

Mongooses in the Caribbean threaten endangered sea turtles and petrels. The pet trade is now amongst the most common routes – over 15% of Florida's reptiles and amphibians are exotics, many from the pet trade.

Feral plants may be crop plants, weeds, or garden ornamentals. They may come to dominate habitats, as with the species of *Opuntia* cactus in Australia, southern Africa and Madagascar. Introduced tree species threaten 900 plant species in the South African Cape. The natural rate of arrival of plants to Hawaii is estimated at one species per 100 000 years, whereas they are now being introduced at about four species per year; similarly, new plant species naturally arrived at the Galapagos about once per 10 000 years, whilst today they arrive at a rate of more than one per year. Over a quarter of Florida's plant species, and nearly a half of New Zealand's, are exotic. In San Francisco Bay, a new plant was established on average every 14 weeks between 1961 and 1995.

The introduction of invertebrate animals is happening increasingly often as global transportation increases. Recent examples include the New Zealand flatworm, which is damaging earthworm populations in Britain. Ants have probably exterminated many invertebrates including snails and spiders on Hawaii, and snails on Henderson island. Fire ants threaten many native species in the Galapagos, whilst Argentine ants, which do not bury seeds, are changing the ecology of the floristically rich fynbos of the South African Cape – threatening 1000 plant species. It is estimated that a few new species of invertebrate arrive in the Galapagos each year – in supplies and containers, and on tourists. About a tenth of Florida's arthropod species are thought to be exotic.

Introduced species may colonise disturbed areas even faster than natural areas, amplifying the existing damage, as do pigs in Hawaii. The main factors that promote feral species are a suitable climate and the number of introduction attempts, but in general it is difficult to predict if a species will establish itself.

## 2.4.2   Aquatic: freshwater

Freshwater aquatic systems have suffered greatly from introduced species. Such systems often resemble islands in having specialised species, isolated from the predators, competitors or disease in similar systems elsewhere. Aquatic species may have very high rates of reproduction: a zebra mussel may produce up to a million eggs per year. About a quarter of the freshwater fish in Britain and Florida are exotic. Since 1800, over 140 species of animals and plants have become established in the North American Great Lakes – over 40 of them since 1960. Some 50 species of fish have become established in the USA. Anglers and the pet trade are the main source of introductions. Roughly 200 species of exotic fish have been found in North American waters, with half of these from the aquarium trade and over 75 now breeding wild. Similarly, many exotic aquatic plants, such as the floating weeds invading Britain, several African lakes, and the Seychelles, derive from accidental releases of ornamental pondweeds.

Very many freshwater species have probably been lost without attracting public attention: the Lake Tota fat fish, of Lake Tota in Colombia, was probably exterminated by introduced rainbow trout. Over 200 species of cichlid fish in the African Rift Valley lakes were believed extinct following the introduction of Nile perch – although many have been re-discovered. Examples of invasions of freshwater systems, and their impacts, are given in Table 2.6(a).

## 2.4.3  Aquatic: marine

Introductions in the marine environment mainly comprise species transported in ships' ballast, and species transported for aquaculture. They also arrive on anchor chains and ships' hulls. Table 2.6(b) gives examples of the sources and impacts of such species. It is harder to measure the impacts of marine invasive species than on land or freshwater, and so less is known about them.

Links which people have created between marine systems have also presented problems. New species, including fish and crustacea, are spreading through the Suez Canal into the Mediterranean at the rate of about five a year, and establishing large populations with unknown impact. If a proposed sea-level, salt-water canal were created across Central America, it is feared many species of marine organism would invade through it.

## 2.5   Genetically Modified Organisms (GMOs)

In some countries there has been much public concern over genetically modified organisms (GMOs). Some of this concern borders on the hysterical, but some has a scientific basis. Several of the genetically modified organisms being considered are modified pathogens, such as bacteria or viruses, which are used as pesticides. It is important that the risks and benefits be evaluated as fully as possible, and that a precautionary approach is adopted. Otherwise, we risk making very serious mistakes   as in the early days of biological control. Fuller details of the controversies can be found under Further reading.

## 2.5.1  The ecological benefits

Any technology that permits more efficient use of existing agricultural land should help ease the pressure to expand agriculture into new wilderness areas – and so be a great asset to conservationists. Improved human health (for example through rice modified to provide vitamin A and iron) may lead to lower infant mortality, and thence lower human population growth. Genetic engineering might confer resistance to species threatened by disease, such as the American chestnut. Plants are being engineered to tolerate salt, which could help raise the productivity of land degraded by salinisation.

Reduced use of agrochemicals may be possible if plants are engineered to be resistant to herbicides or pests. A single dose may be needed to kill the weeds whilst killing few of the crop plants; this could lead to lower run-off. Microbial insecticides and herbicides might be more specific, and less persistent, than conventional agrochemicals.

## 2.5.2   The ecological risks

There is concern that genetically engineered species might themselves become a pest or weed. Furthermore, and more likely, genes may spread from engineered species into wild species, as occurs in the laboratory with sunflower and sugar beet. It is argued that such 'genetic pollution' might lead to insecticide-resistant weeds, pesticide-resistant insects, competitively superior plants, or plants that might spread into arid or salty areas. Any such species might alter natural systems.

Proponents of biotechnology argue that many engineered plants are dependent on, and unable to survive outside, intensive agriculture, and that gene-transfer in bioengineering is a tiny proportion of gene-transfer by natural microbial vectors. However, the deliberate linkage of traits may overcome evolutionary 'constraints on perfection' (see *The Extended Phenotype*, by R. Dawkins (1982)). The natural probability of such a combination of several important genes relating to productivity and resistance is low if they have evolved rarely and in different taxa. Genetic pollution is suspected in local varieties of maize in Mexico. This is disturbing because it is in one of the natural centres of diversity for maize (Section 3.1.1). There is also evidence of genes for herbicide resistance coming together ('stacking') in crops in Britain, highlighting the risk from 'super-weeds'.

Genetically engineered microbial insecticides may become a problem, particularly in countries where environmental safety standards are low. Laboratory 'safety-testing' prior to field-trials should examine a substantial number of species from a very wide range of taxa – rather than a few tens of species. The host range can change unpredictably after engineering. Similarly, pathogens modified to induce sterility in pest mammals such as rabbits might infect non-target species, and genes that modify the sex-ratio of animals such as fish might spread to non-target species.

## 2.6   Disease

Wildlife diseases – of both plants and animals – are increasingly of concern to conservationists. Diseases may have several hosts, including livestock, and may then cross over into wild animals. Hosts may also be people or domestic pets. Diseases have been implicated in the failure of some re-introduction efforts. Some examples of threats due to wildlife diseases are given in Table 2.7.

Rhinderpest provides a good example of the problems. This species is transmitted by contact, and thus requires high densities of hosts to survive. The disease, which originates in Asia, was brought into Africa with livestock. Although large wild herbivores naturally occur at too low a density for sustained rhinderpest epidemics, the proximity to high densities of livestock makes them vulnerable. Epidemiological predictions and past epidemics suggest a *cordon sanitaire* (comprising a belt of low livestock density over 60 km wide) is required to isolate herds from epidemics.

An emergent wildlife disease in amphibians, Chytridiomycosis, caused by the fungus *Batrachochytrium dendrobatidis,* may be the main cause of global amphibian decline, especially in cool waters. It can be spread by exotic species such as the cane toad, have reservoirs in common species, and so drive populations or species to extinction. Transport of amphibia, deliberately or accidentally, may have spread the disease globally.

Diseases spread by humans are a threat to primates, which are susceptible to many common human illnesses. There are concerns that ecotourism and local human populations could bring diseases, and endangered mountain gorillas in Rwanda may have acquired respiratory infections and nematode parasites from people. The risk of epidemics of diseases carried by pets increases as the density of people and thus pets increases, as with dogs in the east African savannah.

Some wildlife diseases threaten humans. The increasing proximity of people to relict populations of primates, together with increased use of bushmeat, could foster the advent of 'emergent diseases'. Such diseases could lead to calls for destruction of species and habitats. Malaria and dengue have been controlled through spraying and draining wetlands; malaria was eradicated in the Seychelles in the 1950s, using insecticides, and this might have exterminated unknown endemic wetland wildlife.

## 2.7   Infrastructure (including roads)

Roads are often seen as a sign of development and progress. Unfortunately, they are amongst the most destructive of human creations. Roads sever and fragment habitats directly, but worse, they can lead to the encroachment of slash-and-burn agriculture, hunting and other damaging activities into

Table 2.7 *Examples of wildlife diseases*

| (a) Animal disease | Origin/reservoir or vector | Past or present impact on |
|---|---|---|
| Tuberculosis | Humans | Meerkats in Botswana |
| Nematodes; measles | Humans | Mountain gorilla |
| Rhinderpest | Livestock | Game animals in southern Africa |
| Anthrax | Livestock | As above; plains bison |
| Foot-and-mouth | Livestock | European bison |
| Parvovirus | Domestic dogs | Wolves in North America |
| Canine distemper | Domestic dogs | Black-footed ferret; Catalina fox |
| Rabies | Domestic dog | Wild dog; Ethiopian wolf |
| Toxoplasma | Feral domestic cats | Australian mammals (e.g. bandicoot and kangaroo) |
| *Toxocara gondii* | Domestic and feral cats | Sea otters, North America |
| Brucellosis; tuberculosis | Plains bison | Wood bison |
| La Cross encephalitis | Asian tiger mosquito | Chipmunk and squirrel, North America |
| Parapox | Grey squirrel | Red squirrel, Europe |
| Avian malaria and pox | Asian birds | Range restriction of several endemic birds in Hawaii |
| Nematode: *Anguillicola* | Asian eel | European eel |
| Ranovirus | Amphibians and fish, USA | Frogs in Britain |
| Chytrid fungus | Amphibians | Amphibians (global) |
| Furunculosis | Farmed salmon and trout | Atlantic salmon in Europe, American salmonids |
| Virus? | Unknown | Vultures, especially *Gyps* species in and near India |
| Fluke: *Gyrodactylus* | Fish in farms | Salmon in Europe, e.g. Norway |
| Redmouth: *Yersinia* | Fathead minnow (America) | European fish declines |
| Fungus: *Aphanomyces* | American signal crayfish | European crayfish populations, e.g. *Austropotamobius pallipes*, Spain |

Table 2.7 (*cont.*)

| (b) Plant disease | Origin/reservoir | Past or present impact on |
|---|---|---|
| Dutch elm disease | North America | Most elms killed: Britain |
| Chestnut blight | Asia | Most American chestnut killed: East America |
| Takamaka wilt | ? | Many *Calophyllum* killed: Seychelles |
| Eelgrass wasting disease | ? native | Seagrass: Florida etc. |
| White pine blister rust | Asia | Several pine species: North America |
| *Phytopthora cinnamomi* | Europe | Many native plant species: Australasia |
| *Phytopthora ramorum* | ? | Oak, eastern North America |
| *Phytophtora lateralis* | ? Asia | Lawson cypress, Port-Orford cedars: North America |

previously inaccessible areas. The role of roads in precipitating habitat loss is illustrated by remote-sensing in Brazil (Fig. 2.19), and much of the Amazon forest will soon be under their influence. Logging roads have greatly increased hunting in areas such as the Congo. Some of the impacts of roads in developed countries have been reviewed by I. F. Spellerberg.

The impact of roads in interrupting movement of wildlife is illustrated in the Netherlands, where some highways act as almost complete barriers to amphibians through road-kill. A study of road-kill in the Organ Pipe Cactus National Monument, Arizona, found 22 dead snakes per kilometre, representing a threat to the Mexican rosy boa and other species. Over 32 000 vertebrates, from 100 species, were killed on a 3.6 km long stretch of road adjacent to Big Creek National Wildlife Area, Canada, in four years. Road-kill is the main cause of mortality of the protected badger in Britain; it threatens the Iberian lynx, several terrapins and tortoises in North America, and causes about a quarter of the mortality of the endangered wild dog in Africa. A road 20 km from Hwange National Park in Zimbabwe is the main cause of death amongst large carnivores using the reserve. Roads also present a different micro-climate, across which some organisms are reluctant to cross: in the Amazon, ant-following birds (Formicariidae) will rarely cross a road only 30–80 m wide. Roads, acting as fire-breaks, have changed the flora of some reserves in South Africa. Invasive species may be spread along roadsides. It has been estimated that roads have had an ecological impact on a fifth of the area of the USA.

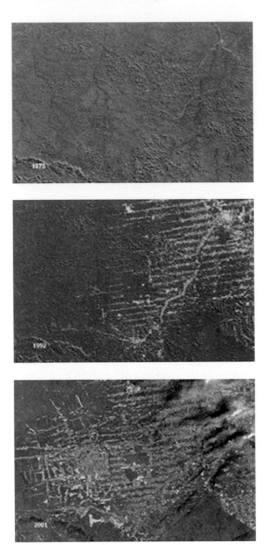

**Fig. 2.19.** Fragmentation of Amazonian forest in Rondonia, Brazil, after the development of roads. Clearings (pale areas) have spread along roads in a 'herringbone pattern'.
*Source:* NASA / Goddard Space Flight Center.

Pipelines and powerlines can have similar effects to roads and, indeed, roads often accompany pipelines. Pipelines may lead to damage during construction, and may impede movement of species. The pipelines in Alaska have been designed to reduce their impact as an obstacle to migrating caribou, but they still influence movement and mortality. Spillage from pipelines has

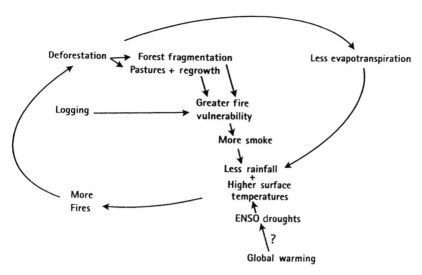

**Fig. 2.20.** Synergisms and positive feedbacks amongst threats can increase their magnitude and rate of impact unpredictably. The diagram shows some links between threats for the Amazon basin, all of which have been established except for that marked '?'.
*Source:* Laurance, W. F. & Williamson, G. B. *Conservation Biology* **15** (2001), 1529–1535.

caused damage in Russia (at Rostov), the Amazon forest and Kuwait. Thermal pollution from pipelines has been problematic in the Asian tundra. Canals may increase access, and serve as a barrier to movement. They may also act as huge pitfall traps for species, as in the 200 km long Eastern National Water Carrier of Namibia: dubbed the 'killer canal' it has been estimated to cause the death of 17 500 vertebrates a year. Collisions with powerlines kill California condors, whilst predation on forest birds' nests may be increased hundreds of metres from a powerline (Table 5.3).

Building of roads, pipelines, and railways has triggered numerous Environmental Impact Assessments. Such infrastructure may have to be relatively straight, and may expose much of the adjacent habitat to destruction: such 'edge effects' (Section 5.4.2) may extend hundreds of metres beyond the apparent width of the structure (Table 5.3). Whilst roads present a great problem in pristine habitats, in already highly fragmented landscapes such as the British Isles their potential impact can be over-stated. Roads, although unaesthetic, can contribute to conservation of rare species, as with the Aston Rowant National Nature Reserve in Oxfordshire, where the chalk cliffs created by a motorway cutting support rare plants. Similarly, active and disused railways and canals have become nature reserves in Britain – and may have relatively little direct human disturbance. Globally, infrastructure such as roads and pipelines threatens some 185 bird species.

Many of the threats in this chapter do not work in isolation, but interact and amplify their impacts 'synergistically'. This is illustrated in Fig. 2.20, which shows how synergisms and positive feedbacks may rapidly destroy much of the Amazon's rainforest and agriculture – and change the region permanently.

Having considered the threats to wildlife, we now turn to the ways we can select the best sites and the best species on which to spend funding to reduce these threats.

# 3

# Evaluation of priorities for species and habitats

Despite the high public interest in the environment in many parts of the world, conservationists are generally very short of funds. It is therefore essential to target the money that is available towards species or habitats where it will do the most good, and indeed to choose between an emphasis on species or on habitats. This may mean spending money in ways that might surprise people, for example on areas that are not the best of their type, or on species which are not the most highly endangered. Conservation requires money for research, for monitoring, for management, for education and for compensation. Many of the decisions in conservation relate to the availability and use of limited funds.

All decisions about priorities are subjective. The values attached to things, such as species or habitats, depend on the personal values of the people doing the evaluation. Just as beauty is in the eye of the beholder, different people with different motives for conservation (Chapter 1) will assign values in different ways. Faced with a diversity of values, there may be a diversity of aims in conservation. Choosing one aim may require a democratic decision, or expert opinion — and so debates and controversies are likely.

Before any evaluation it is therefore essential to define the aims. It is also necessary to decide the weightings which are to be given to the different reasons for conservation (such as rarity or diversity) in a particular case. Once the aims are explicit and clear, ecologists or other interested parties can often provide precise and objective rankings of priority species or habitats, using quantitative ecological methods (Chapter 4). They can also manage sites with a clear vision as to the desired result.

Whether to spend money conserving species or habitats is a fundamental issue in conservation. The two are separable because technology such as captive breeding has allowed conservation to protect some species outside their habitats (Section 6.5). Furthermore, protection of a species need not protect a specific habitat if the species is tolerant of habitat change – such as elephants, which are tolerant of deforestation. Legal protection is often afforded to species, rather than their habitats (Section 9.2). We shall see in Section 3.1.4 that conservationists may also separate species from habitat conservation by focusing on a limited subset of the biodiversity.

Historically, conservation often focused on species – for hunting or for their attractiveness. However, growth of interest in wilderness and national parks has emphasised landscape conservation. More recently, the emphasis has been on conservation of the habitats or whole ecosystems for the sake of the many species within them (biodiversity), rather than just for landscape appeal. There is also concern for 'ecosystem services' (Sections 1.3 and 9.1), which requires evaluation and planning on a larger scale.

Ultimately, both species and habitat conservation should be integrated. Both approaches have their strengths and weaknesses. It is sensible to adopt a flexible approach, and to emphasise one or the other according to circumstances.

In this chapter, we shall first review the methods used to choose between species, then examine the general methods to choose between habitats, and then finish with the choice of the most important habitat priorities in the world – the hotspots and Major Tropical Wilderness Areas, and the World Heritage Sites. In global conservation planning the reverse order would be sensible – starting with the most important first. However, it proves illuminating to see the problems of small-scale evaluation to help make a better job of large-scale action. Having considered the contents of sites, the ideal geometry of a set of reserves will be considered more fully in Chapter 5.

## 3.1   Choosing species to protect: species quality

Species may be considered to have high 'species quality' by conservationists (such as environmental consultants or managers) because they are in some sense a priority. There are too many species to list on any site, and we do not know the ecology of most of them. Conservationists therefore may focus efforts on species deemed to be important because they are, for example, highly threatened, specialised, charismatic, or useful – or have a combination of such features. Table 3.1 lists some of these features, and this chapter describes the

Table 3.1 *Some characteristics of 'high-quality species' useful in conservation evaluation*

| Characteristic | Reason |
|---|---|
| Endemics | Risk of global extinction |
| Low population size | Risk of global extinction |
| Low density | Risk of population extinction/need large areas |
| Increasing rarity | May be threatened |
| Low reproductive rate | Easily overexploited; slow recovery from disturbance |
| Slow maturation | Risk of mortality before reproduction |
| Longevity | Often have low reproductive rate and slow maturation |
| Large body size | Often have low reproductive rate and large ranges; often hunted |
| High natural mortality | Easily overexploited regardless of reproductive rate |
| Poor dispersal | Lower rescue of declining populations; poor recolonisation |
| Top carnivores | Often lost quickly from disturbed and managed ecosystems |
| Sensitivity | Easily disturbed, trampled etc. leading to low reproduction |
| High habitat specificity | Increasingly rare habitats (e.g. dead wood or large carrion) |
| Migratory species | Require networks of reserves/face several threats |
| Social species | Risk of Allee effect (Section 6.3.2) |
| Dominant species | Influence numerous other species and ecosystem services |
| Keystone species | Influence numerous other species and ecosystem services |
| 'Living fossils' | Evolutionary and genetic interest |
| High utility | Charismatic, attractive, or other high-use value |

importance of some of them, whilst Chapter 4 will describe how to quantify them.

## 3.1.1  Utility

As discussed in Chapter 1, species may provide foods, fabrics, medicines or structures, or be attractive to visitors. Such usefulness (or 'utility') of a species to people may be quantified using methods from the social sciences, such as

Table 3.2 *Some centres of origin for crop plants, and domestic animals*

| Centre of origin | Crop plants/animals |
| --- | --- |
| North America | Sunflower, cranberry; grape; tobacco; Jerusalem artichoke |
| Mexico/Central America | Maize (= corn); tomato; vanilla; common bean; sweet potato; hot peppers; cotton; cassava; papaya |
| South America: Andes | Peanut; potato; cotton; hot peppers |
| South America: Amazonia | Rubber; chocolate; pineapple; Brazil nut |
| Mediterranean | Cabbages; oat; mint; sugar beet |
| Near East | Wheat; rye; barley; pea; grape; goat; sheep; pig |
| North Africa | Marjoram; zebu cattle |
| Horn of Africa | Coffee; sorghum; wheat; pearl millet |
| Central Asia | Barley; carrot; garlic; onion; rhubarb; spinach; apple |
| Europe/Siberia | Gooseberry; cattle |
| South-East Asia (India, Indochina, Pacific Islands) | Sugar cane; citrus fruits; banana; yams; rice; mango; clove; cinnamon; aubergine; winged bean; chicken |
| East Asia/China | Rice; soybean; ginseng; ginger; foxtail millet; chive; buckwheat; radish; tea |

questionnaires, and the other tools of environmental economics (Section 9.1). Useful and valuable species may be very highly threatened, for example by over-hunting as in tuna, whales, rhino, or the Tibetan antelope. However, other species may be protected and the populations better managed because of their utility – for example, the commercially important fish species such as cod. Some species are bred commercially or domesticated, such as the crop plants, domestic animals, llama, Asian elephant, salmon and camels; whilst such species may not be at risk of global extinction, their genetic diversity may be diminishing.

There are regions which are particularly rich in genetic resources for crop species, and are therefore priority areas for conservation. The Russian geneticist N. I. Vavilov noted in the 1930s that there are regions on the planet supporting clusters of diversity of wild relatives of crop plants. These are often where the domesticated plant first evolved in the wild (Table 3.2). Such clusters are known as the Vavilov Centres. For example, maize ('corn') *Zea mays* has a centre of endemism for species in its genus *Zea*, which has already yielded important genes from the species *Zea diploperennis* (teosinte).

There are also centres of diversity for domestic animals. There are several endemic species of wild pig in South-East Asia, many of which are highly endangered (because they are good food). Several goat and sheep species are found in central Asia, and several of the cattle family (Bovidae) in South-East Asia. Such species may have the potential for improvement of domestic breeds – for example in modifying fat levels, hardiness, or drought and disease resistance.

## 3.1.2 Vulnerability and rarity

People like rare things: finding them tests and displays our skills. Rarity comes in at least seven different forms, each with different combinations of distribution and abundance. Species may naturally be few in total number, or be very sparsely dispersed, or be very local. Many naturally rare species are not threatened. Few species – other than humans and domestic species – have both wide geographical distributions and high densities. What matters to conservationists is whether a species is rare because of the action of people, and if it is getting rarer.

If a species is known to be vulnerable to *global* extinction, then it should be a prime candidate for conservation: if internationally rare and declining species are not protected, then their irreversible extinction may occur. Such species will of course be rare shortly before extinction, but many may not be rare initially. For example, the passenger pigeon of North America once occurred in populations of billions, and bluefin tuna were also once very abundant. Even blue whales once numbered some 200 000.

Rarity should therefore be assessed first on an international basis. However, there is a tendency for some conservationists to be 'parochial', meaning they favour species in their own region or country – and particularly the ones which are rare in their region. In this sense, the green mantra 'think globally, act locally' might be highly counter-productive to global conservation. For example, putting efforts into a species such as the adonis blue butterfly – which is rare in Britain but abundant in southern Europe, or to a species like the puffin which is rare in the south of North America but common in the north, may leave few resources for the species that are rare in the whole world.

An example of parochialism is given by a reserve near Oxford. The site was notable for one of the world's largest great crested newt populations. However, part of the habitat of the species was destroyed by grazing management aiming to introduce locally rare butterflies such as the chalkhill blue – a species that is very common in Europe and for which there were no previous records on the site.

Species may often be rare because they are on the edge of the climatic range they can tolerate. This is the case with many of the rare species in the British Isles or southern United States – and may have led to a great deal of effort focusing on these species whilst others became extinct. Populations at the edges of their ranges are sometimes interesting because these populations may be genetically unusual or distinctive, or because they are indicators of climate change, but they are less important to the survival of the species than those at the core of the species' range.

Another important factor in choosing species to protect is the 'life-history strategy' of the species – a term which describes the reproductive rate, dispersal ability and growth rate of the species. Species are spread along an ecological continuum of life-history strategies called the '$r$–$K$ continuum'. Species that are '$r$-selected' are in general relatively small, breed fast, disperse widely, grow fast – and die young. Conversely, '$K$-selected' species breed and mature slowly, disperse poorly and are long-lived. As will be seen in Chapter 7, $K$-selected species such as ebony tend to occur in 'late-successional' environments such as forests, whilst $r$-selected species such as dandelion occur in, and indeed require, habitats that are frequently disturbed or abiotically stressful. Within a taxon, a species may be relatively $K$-selected, and a species may be relatively $K$-selected in just some aspects of its life-history. For example, relatively large, long-lived invertebrates such as the robber crab, triton, queen conch, giant clams or birdwing butterflies are more $K$-selected than most invertebrate species – although they may produce many eggs. Similarly, some slow-growing trees, such as redwoods, produce many small seeds.

By their very nature, $K$-selected species are likely to be relatively rare to start with, and to be relatively vulnerable. Because of their low birth-rate and conspicuousness, they may be easily overhunted (Section 7.2). Because of their large size, they may be relatively useful – as food, or for material such as oil or wood. Because they use relatively stable habitats, such as primary forest, they may be sensitive to disturbance such as logging. Section 2.2 illustrates the selective loss of $K$-selected species.

Some $r$-selected species are also at risk. 'Metapopulations' of rapidly dispersing $r$-selected species may become too fragmented to survive (Section 6.1). Populations of $r$-selected species at the edge of their range may be highly vulnerable to year-by-year climatic changes, or to changes in habitat quality due to management (Section 7.3).

A general feature of vulnerable species is that they are habitat specialists, as opposed to generalists (which can use a wide range of alternative habitat types). Species that are very selective in the habitat they use are likely to become extinct when the habitat changes or is disturbed by people (although they must have been able to withstand the *natural* frequency of past habitat disturbance to have evolved at all). For example, a parasite specialised to live on a particular host may become extinct when the host is made extinct – as with the louse *Columbicola extincta* which was unique to the passenger pigeon. It is thought most species support at least one species of specialist parasite or endosymbiont. Species with specialist seed dispersal are relatively vulnerable, as in the fynbos, South Africa (Section 2.4.1). Species with specialist pollinators are also vulnerable, as illustrated by silversword species on Hawaii.

Species specialised to need two or more rather different habitats may be particularly vulnerable. For example, amphibians and dragonflies that have aquatic larvae and terrestrial adults may lose one or both habitats. The large blue butterfly in Europe needs short, hot grass with nests of the ant genus *Myrmica* in which it feeds as a caterpillar, whilst as an adult it needs longer grass with nectar-bearing flowers. Sea turtles need safe feeding grounds within range of safe nesting beaches.

## 3.1.3  The Red List and Red Data Books (RDBs)

The most threatened species in some of the better known groups of organisms have been monitored for some decades by the World Conservation Monitoring Centre (now the UNEP-WCMC, based in Cambridge, England). For the birds, the large mammals, the reptiles, the flowering plants, and a few of the invertebrates such as the swallowtail butterflies (Papilionidae), it is often possible to ascribe a degree of rarity or threat. Red Data Books (RDBs) have been published for such groups: these list the threatened species, and give details of ecology and threats to each. RDBs may include all the world's species in a taxon, or consider globally threatened species one region at a time, as with the birds of Africa. Every few years a global review of all known threatened species is published in the form of the 'Red List': this is published electronically by the IUCN and BirdLife International, and gives limited information about ecology and threats for each species.

Several categories are used by IUCN to describe the conservation priority of a species (Fig. 3.1) and these have been revised several times. Extinct species are included for illustrative purposes or in case they may have survived undetected – as did the takahe of New Zealand, the Vietnamese warty pig, or the Madeiran snail. The latest categories are in part based on the estimated probability of extinction over a given time interval. This has been accompanied by controversy over the 'spurious precision' involved in deciding the probabilities, given the limitations of predictive modelling (Section 6.3), and doubt as to

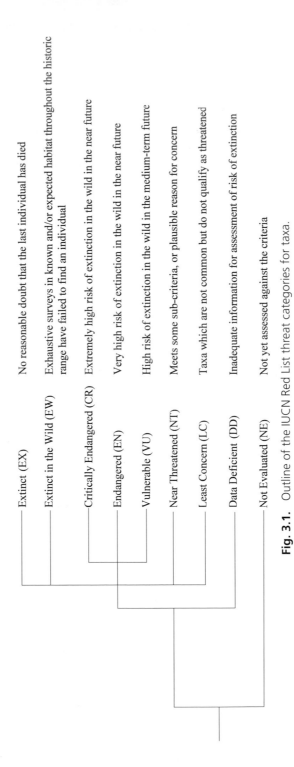

| Extinct (EX) | No reasonable doubt that the last individual has died |
| Extinct in the Wild (EW) | Exhaustive surveys in known and/or expected habitat throughout the historic range have failed to find an individual |
| Critically Endangered (CR) | Extremely high risk of extinction in the wild in the near future |
| Endangered (EN) | Very high risk of extinction in the wild in the near future |
| Vulnerable (VU) | High risk of extinction in the wild in the medium-term future |
| Near Threatened (NT) | Meets some sub-criteria, or plausible reason for concern |
| Least Concern (LC) | Taxa which are not common but do not qualify as threatened |
| Data Deficient (DD) | Inadequate information for assessment of risk of extinction |
| Not Evaluated (NE) | Not yet assessed against the criteria |

**Fig. 3.1.** Outline of the IUCN Red List threat categories for taxa.

whether any such evaluation can be objective. However, the new categories and their criteria are generally regarded as helpful in policy-making.

Some countries are producing their own RDBs, using different criteria. There are also national 'Red Lists': these include birds in Britain that have lost at least 50% of their range in 20 years, or species on the National Watch List in the USA that have a high score on a five-point index. In addition, there are some independent 'Red Books' and lists which have no official status, have not been reviewed by experts, and which might actually be counter-productive by being misleading or distracting. There is also a Blue List of species that have been removed from the Red List through successful conservation.

Species included in RDBs or Red Lists attract a lot of attention from conservationists – to ignore them would lead to global extinction or, in the case of a national RDB, local extirpation of the species.

## 3.1.4   Keystone, flagship and umbrella species

To preserve the integrity of a system it is essential to conserve species that are dominant through their high abundance or biomass. Some species may be food for a very large number of species – such as lugworms in mudflats, figs in rainforests, or krill in the Antarctic. The dominant plant types, be they tree species such as redwood or oak, or algae such as kelp, are central to their ecosystems. However, the really important species in ecosystem functioning may be much less conspicuous – such as plankton, or microbes involved in biogeochemical cycles.

Some species, termed 'keystone species', have an influence in their ecosystems far greater than would be guessed from their abundance or biomass. Their loss would lead to changes disproportionate to their biomass. They may be 'ecological engineers' – species whose activities modify the structure of the environment substantially. For example, the European and North American beavers strongly influence the local landscape. Gopher tortoises dig burrows in the forests of Californa, which are used by over 330 commensal species such as the gopher frog and the specialised beetle *Phylonthus gopheri*. American badgers create mounds supporting many prairie species. Elephants dig wells in savannah. Woodpeckers, burrowing into giant saguaro cacti, benefit other species such as elf owls, whilst red-cockaded woodpeckers make the only tree-holes in their old-growth forests, and these are used by over 22 other species.

Even if they are not keystone species, conspicuous and attractive species can be used as 'flagship species' to build public interest in an area or to raise funds for a habitat. Thus conservationists use the tiger in India to help protect the endangered swamp deer, whilst Fea's muntjac was protected in Thailand by an Operation Tiger reserve. The Aldabran giant tortoise and the Aldabra flightless rail helped to save all the wildlife of Aldabra – the former under the banner of 'a relict of the age of reptiles', and the latter under the banner of 'the last flightless bird in the western Indian Ocean'. The attractive avocet, emblem of Britain's Royal Society for the Protection of Birds, has provided aesthetic appeal which helps to raise funds for less popular species that share their rather unattractive mudflats. The giant panda, logo of the Wordwide Fund for Nature (WWF), has helped to protect threatened golden monkeys and bird species in reserves in China.

If an animal species has a particularly large home range then it can be argued that conservation of a viable population of such species will inevitably protect many other species which need smaller areas and which occur at higher densities. The borders of the Serengeti and adjacent reserves in east Africa were designed to include the migratory range of the wildebeest. Such species are termed 'umbrella species'. Bear and elk movements have helped define the borders of the Greater Yellowstone Area. Individual jaguar and tiger may range over 400 km$^2$, a pair of Philippines eagles may range over 100 km$^2$, and a pair of northern spotted owls use 800 ha of forest. Similarly, if a species has a particularly high sensitivity to 'edge effects' (Section 5.4.2), then protection of that species will require reserves with a 'core area' sufficient for many other less edge-sensitive species.

A species may fit into more than one of the categories: red-cockaded wood-peckers, or bears, are charismatic enough to be flagships whilst also being keystone and umbrella species. Reviews of the effectiveness of conservation programmes using keystone, umbrella or flagship species suggest they often fail. Conservation efforts for one species may conflict with those for another, as with the Everglades snail kite and the wood stork, which need different water levels. It could be argued that they are a distraction from more productive conservation methods, particularly the protection of habitats. However, in the absence of such efforts, the failures might have been even greater.

## 3.2   Choosing habitats to protect

Habitats are harder to define and characterise than species (Section 1.2). Priorities may be set based on a similar range of values to choosing species – from finance to aesthetics. As with choosing species, some habitats have higher quality than others. A range of attributes of habitats have been used to help decisions between the candidate sites for conservation. In this section

Table 3.3 *Examples of commonly used criteria for site evaluation, ranked by popularity*

Diversity (of habitats and/or species)
Area
Threat of human interference
Amenity value, education value, representativeness
Scientific value
Recorded history
Population size, typicalness
Ecological fragility, position in ecological/geographical unit, potential value, uniqueness
Archaeological interest, availability, importance for migratory wildfowl, management factors, replaceability, silvicultural gene bank, successional stage, wildlife reservoir potential

*Source:* After Usher, M. B. *Wildlife Conservation Evaluation*. (Chapman and Hall, 1986).

the attributes which have most general relevance are considered, whilst in Section 3.4 we examine the way the very highest priorities may be assigned.

There are many characteristics of sites that have been used to evaluate the conservation priority of habitats, as illustrated in Table 3.3. From an international perspective, the particularly common ones are naturalness, representativeness, and replaceability.

Britain was one of the first countries to evaluate its habitats systematically, in the government's Nature Conservation Review, which was undertaken to help designate National Nature Reserves and Sites of Special Scientific Interest (SSSIs). The attributes applicable to British terrestrial habitats were formalised by D. A. Ratcliffe in 1977, and similar ones are used in many countries. However, the attributes used in selecting sites for conservation vary somewhat from country to country and region to region, as will be seen in Section 3.2.1; this is very evident with one of the most popular, 'naturalness'. We will examine first the way a set of sites is chosen to give a broad and representative range of habitats within the region in question.

## 3.2.1   Representativeness and Gap Analysis

Representativeness is a property of a *set* of habitats or sites – rather than a single site. A site may be chosen to represent a particular type of habitat within a series which aims to protect the diversity of habitats (see Section 1.2). A site may be chosen because it is typical of that habitat, or because it is well preserved, or is large or otherwise important. Choosing the range of habitats to be represented involves minimising the gaps in representation.

In Britain there are more biological data with which to inform choice than are available for any other country, and Britain's site selection should thus be relatively rigorous and accurate. The first stage in prioritising habitats for Britain's Nature Conservation Review was to map the land area into distinctive habitat types ('formations'). This 'stratification' ensured that conservationists were at least aware of the range of potential habitats to save. An assessment has to be made as to the range of variation within the habitats, the degree of threat to them, the diversity of species within them, and other factors. This helps to inform the decision as to the number and extent of sites to be protected within each habitat type.

The importance of using more than one criterion with which to evaluate sites can be illustrated by examples from Britain. If, say, species richness per unit area were the only factor used in site choice, all the terrestrial reserves would be some type of woodland – probably coniferous. A further issue is that some habitats are only viable if large expanses are conserved (e.g. upland moor), whilst for others (e.g. calcareous fen) a small area can be viable and valuable. A pragmatic consideration overlying the choice is the cost of acquiring and managing the sites and habitats. This has contributed to the majority (some 50%) of the area of the protected area network in Britain being upland moorland – which, whilst important for some bird species, is generally of low national and international importance. Box 3.1 shows the details of the British Nature Conservation Review, which may be a useful model for areas where sufficient data are available.

In North America, the choice of National Parks reflects the history of the build-up of interest in wilderness, the recognition of its loss, and the identification of the most spectacular sites such as Yosemite, the geysers of Yellowstone, or the Grand Canyon. Naturalness was thus an important feature, but was secondary to spectacular aesthetic appeal. The selection of a wider range of smaller sites specifically to protect wildlife is undertaken primarily at a local government (State) level, based on features such as naturalness, outstanding populations of birds, migratory routes, and so on. The presence of species listed in the Endangered Species Act is very important in site selection at a local level. As in Britain, there is a bias towards upland sites and low-productivity land: 25% of the 400 000 km² of conservation area is on the least-productive soils, and 50% is on the highest elevations. Economically marginal upland also dominates in Sweden, Nepal, Australia, New Zealand

Box 3.1
## The British Nature Conservation Review

In order to identify the most valuable sites for conservation, a British government agency (the NCC) began a review of site quality in 1966, co-ordinated by D. A. Ratcliffe, and building on a series of representative sites chosen in 1947. Representativeness of the series was ensured by classifying sites into 'formations' – ecosystem types based primarily on established vegetation type – and then selecting at least one site in each formation. The following criteria were selected for sites: size, diversity, naturalness, rarity, fragility, typicalness, position in an ecological/geographical unit, recorded history, potential value and intrinsic appeal. The first five were the most important. Field survey lasted two years, including vascular plants, bryophytes, lichens, vertebrates and some invertebrate groups. Extra weight was given to sites of international importance, such as oceanic climate communities (ash, sphagnum), or supporting internationally important populations of birds (coastline, uplands; Britain supports over half the world population of some birds including puffins and Manx shearwaters). The SSSI network is envisioned to include about 5000 sites, and 10% of the land surface. Since publication of the results in Ratcliffe's *A nature conservation review* in 1977, many sites have been added or removed from the SSSI network – some because of damage. The Marine Nature Conservation Review has identified priority sites for a marine protected area network.

European and other international legislation (Section 9.2) has also provided guidelines for the selection of British sites, including Ramsar Sites. The Birds Directive has required the identification of sites of importance for rare and vulnerable birds, and for regular migrants: the Special Protection Areas, SPAs. These form part of the European Natura 2000 network. In Britain, over 240 SPAs cover some 1.5 million hectares. If a site is regularly used by more than 1% of the British population, or 1% of a migratory population, or 20 000 waterfowl, or 20 000 seabirds, then it automatically qualifies as an SPA. The SPA guidelines then select priority areas for species as follows: population size and density; species range (for geographical coverage); breeding success; history of occupancy; multi-species areas; naturalness; severe weather refuges.

and Canada. The largest reserve of the former USSR is the Taimyr of the Arctic – over 13 000 km$^2$.

The former USSR has a large total protected area. Here, selection of an extensive series of reserves was largely a scientific enterprise, with an emphasis on representativeness, uniqueness, rarity, genetic resources and landscape interest.

In an attempt to strengthen the representation of different habitats, on both a regional scale and globally, a technique called 'Gap Analysis' is being developed. Having decided on the list of habitats (or species) in a region,

---

**Box 3.2**
**Network Analysis and Gap Analysis**

Network analysis aims to identify sets of sites that complement each other, so that the network of sites includes representatives of all the desired taxa. In an early example on a global scale, R. I. Vane-Wright and colleagues chose endemic milkweed butterflies. The sites with the most endemic species are chosen first, then the one with the second, and the analysis is then repeated in a step-wise (iterative) process to add further sites until all the desired taxa are included; other species of milkweed butterfly were automatically included along with endemics, and a total of 31 sites were found which included the 158 known milkweed butterfly species. A similar exercise with swallowtail butterflies identified 51 sites (many congruent with the milkweed butterflies). A combined gap and richness hotspot analysis in Portugal identified a network of sites which would support all the country's bryophytes species. The procedure can also be used to obtain a representative sample of abiotic conditions in the network, or to test how outstanding a potential World Heritage Site is.

Gap Analysis is the identification of gaps in the protected areas network through the use of maps. In the USA, the Gap Analysis Program (GAP) began in 1988, mapping the ranges of indicator species on a national scale, predicting potential ranges from maps of suitable habitat, and comparing this with the existing protected areas network to help select future protected areas and increase representativeness. The aim is to represent all ecosystems and species-rich areas in areas managed for biodiversity, and so to reduce the number of species becoming threatened.

In evaluation of a protected areas network for the KwaZulu-Natal and the Cape regions of Africa, A. H. Maddock and colleagues used a geo-referenced database of abiotic and biotic information (including soils, contours, wetlands). GIS was used to set targets and rules (e.g. with regard to land claims). To identify gaps in datasets, biodiversity was broken down into elements: functional (demography, gene flow, population dynamics, etc.), structural (landscape pattern, etc.) and compositional (genes, species communities and landscapes). Whilst good data were available from reserves and near roads, there were deficiencies in areas of difficult terrain, and less popular taxa (e.g. invertebrates) were poorly mapped. The historical distributions of species were considered, and ordination identified vegetation types. Site selection considered endemicity, size, vegetation fragmentation, dispersion, transformation, provincial protection, overall protection, and irreplaceability. If possible, high priority sites with many endemics and a high level of threat were linked together.

---

this method seeks to identify gaps in representation of these habitats (or species) within the protected areas network (Box 3.2). Modern tools, such as Geographical Information Systems (GIS) and remote sensing (RS) have made the mapping, categorisation and Gap Analysis of large regions practicable. For example, a program called 'Worldmap' has been used to identify global map squares with high richness or endemism of plants; these are included in an idealised reserve network in sequence, starting with the richest square and continuing to add squares until all the species are represented in at least one reserve. A 'complimentarily algorithm' can be used for this iterative computation.

Sites chosen for their 'typicalness' of a region, such as lowland or prairie, are by definition relatively unspectacular but have value in ecological study – and may also be highly threatened.

## 3.2.2  Naturalness

Naturalness can be defined in a variety of ways, but the essence of naturalness is the degree of human influence. It should be remembered that people have been in some habitats, such as African coastlines and savannahs, for up to two million years. In other areas, such as the Amazon basin and Australia, there have been two main waves of human influence – firstly by the ancestors of Amerindians or Aborigines, and then, thousands of years later, by Europeans. Since climate change is so pervasive, no site on Earth, save perhaps ecosystems in the rocks kilometres below ground, is fully natural. 'Near-natural' sites have had little human impact, whilst the origins of more disturbed 'semi-natural' sites are discussed in Chapter 7.

There are a number of ways to identify and quantify naturalness, including the use of 'indicators' as described in Section 4.4.1. Often, some form of 'control' or 'reference' site is available by which the degree of recent human influence can be assessed.

One of the best arguments for maintaining some 'pristine' or 'fortress' nature reserves free of people (Chapter 5) is that they help us to recognise and understand natural systems. Such sites are sometimes said to provide 'biodiversity base-lines'. Thus the naturalness of a patch of coniferous forest in Scotland might be assessed in comparison with relict primary forest fragments in continental Eurasia. An area of 'primary' or 'old-growth' forest can serve as a base-line to identify the most similar of the logged forests in the region; similarly, an area of reef round an uninhabited island in the Chagos Islands of the Indian Ocean may illustrate the natural state of reefs, for comparison with others in the region such as in the Seychelles. An area of savannah that has no pastoral people (such as Mkomazi Game Reserve in Tanzania) can be used to examine the question of overgrazing. Pristine ecosystems in South America have shown us that our impression of the nitrogen cycle was fundamentally flawed because it had mainly been studied in polluted areas (where plants absorb more inorganic nitrogen than in natural conditions).

Some artificial habitats have acquired value for conservation, as with the Norfolk Broads wetlands in Britain, some brownfield sites (Section 8.6), and palm forest islands on abandoned pre-colombian sites in the Savannah of Bolivia which support the critically endangered blue-throated macaw.

In the tropical environments, and less densely populated regions, the choice of sites for protection may be influenced less by naturalness than in Europe – because there is generally more natural habitat remaining than in Europe, and so all the candidate sites may be fairly natural. Similarly, marine environments are often relatively natural, and discrimination between them requires other criteria. Generally, however, naturalness is a very high priority indeed for conservation, because natural habitats are very rare habitats, and becoming rarer. The loss of natural habitats is as irreversible as the extinction of species – which indeed is likely to accompany or cause their conversion to less natural states.

## 3.2.3  Diversity

Diversity (or 'biodiversity') can be measured in different ways, including species richness and habitat variety (Section 1.2). 'Diversity' is one of the most quoted and popular reasons for conserving or managing an area. However, the importance of diversity can be greatly overstated. Bringing in exotic species increases species richness. Disturbance, such as cutting a road or a mine or a gap for a farm in a forest often increases species richness *and* habitat diversity. For example, the richness of frogs and butterflies increase when the Amazonian forest is fragmented, as common generalist species move in. Similarly, selective logging in New South Wales (Australia) increases the richness of frogs in general at the expense of high-quality forest specialist frogs. Planting exotic conifers in the Flow Country in Scotland brought in woodland birds, and new habitats. However, none of these increases is compatible with naturalness or at all desirable for conservation. Species quality (Section 3.1) is often much more important than species or habitat diversity, although a diversity of high-quality species is generally desirable (Section 3.4).

To identify sites with a high diversity of habitats, it is important to consider the scale at which diversity is to be measured. Large sites will generally support more species, and more habitats, than small sites, as discussed in Sections 1.2 and 5.4, and so richness per unit area may be more informative than total richness. This will determine the resolution with which it is possible to map the habitats. For a very large region, tiny differences between habitats cannot be considered. It is simply hoped that within the large area there will be a lot of habitats, and a lot of species. For a small area, more subtle differences might be investigated. Diversity of aquatic habitats might include physical and chemical features such as dead wood, oxygenation, stream-flow, salinity, temperature, presence of a thermocline, nutrient status and other parameters. The techniques to identify and map habitats objectively, such as community ordination, are discussed in Section 4.2.1.

Diversity can be measured in political units as well as more natural geographical units. J. A. McNeely and colleagues suggest that some 12 'megadiverse countries' support up to 70% of the terrestrial species: these are Mexico, Colombia, Ecuador, Peru, Brazil, Zaire, Madagascar, China, India, Malaysia, Indonesia and Australia.

Richness should be compared between sites using the same groups of organisms (taxa), and sufficiently similar methods in all the sites to ensure that differences are not a result of the different methods used (Section 4.2). Richness will change through time, both within a year and between years. This turnover will be less for some groups, such as the plants or the breeding birds, than for the migrants or the flying insects.

Different taxa have different habitat requirements, so richness of one group may not coincide with richness in another group. The smaller the scale being considered, the less likely it is that a site will be rich in several taxa. Furthermore, different taxa respond differently to threats, so might show less overlap in disturbed regions. A. P. Dobson and colleagues found limited overlap in the sites for endangered species in the USA (Table 3.4), and J. R. Prendergast and colleagues showed that in the British Isles (which has detailed records) the richness of groups such as butterflies, dragonflies and birds and plants do not coincide (Fig. 3.2). The traditionally grazed and mown wet meadows in Britain, such as Port Meadow, Oxford, have high floristic richness and rarity, but much lower value for invertebrates due to the heavy trampling and simplified vegetation structure (Section 7.3).

Conversely, A. Balmford and colleagues found a high correlation between the richness (and uniqueness) of amphibians, snakes, birds and mammals in 1° map cells in Africa (Fig. 4.9). Similarly, A. Berg and colleagues found the best locations for nationally threatened species of forest specialist vascular plants, bryophytes, lichens, fungi, invertebrates and vertebrates were roughly the same in Swedish forests, and old forests proved particularly important for all these groups. The coincidence of diversity (richness) in different groups is termed 'congruence', and the degree of congruence is an important issue in site selection on a global scale (Section 3.4.1).

Another form of diversity, the ecological 'diversity index', measures the evenness (or 'equitability') of the relative abundances of species in a sample or

Table 3.4 *Congruence between sites for species listed in the Endangered Species list of the USA*

| Group | Percentage of species in other groups protected by protecting all endangered: | |
|---|---|---|
| | Birds | Plants |
| Birds | 100 | 94 |
| Plants | 38 | 100 |
| Mammals | 38 | 76 |
| Reptiles and amphibians | 35 | 74 |
| Fish | 13 | 55 |
| Molluscs | 2 | 39 |
| Arthropods | 12 | 54 |
| All others | 31 | 73 |
| Minimum percentage area of USA required to protect 100% of the species in the indicator group: | 2 | 10 |

*Source:* Adapted from Dobson, A. P., Rodriguez, J. P., Roberts, W. M. & Wilcove, D. S. Geographic distribution of Endangered Species in the United States. *Science* **275** (1997), 550–553.

site. This equitability can also be compared across sites visually by using 'rank abundance plots': these give more information and are generally far preferable to indices which can be misleading in conservation evaluation (Fig. 3.3). To be useful, the index must be calibrated against sites of known value, as has been done with flowering plants on 'calcareous' (chalk and limestone) grassland in Britain. There is no reason to believe such indices are desirable for many taxa: for example, predators should be rarer than prey in a site.

Phylogenetic diversity can be measured using evolutionary trees of groups of species (such as birds) in a site or a group of sites (Fig. 3.4). If the aim is to maximise genetic diversity in this way, then species which separated early in evolutionary time are chosen to complement each other. Species with long 'independent evolutionary history' will be separated by deep forks (nodes) in the phylogenetic tree, with long branches leading to each chosen species: choosing them results in 'branch length maximisation' for conservation. Species which would have high value in this way include living fossils such as the coelacanth, tuatara, Wollemi pine, dawn redwood, Cathay silver fir and ginkgo. However, it is not always the case that capturing such

**Fig. 3.2.** The sites in Britain which have the most species of various taxa are not congruent. The richest 5% of 10 km by 10 km map squares are shown for each taxon.
*Source:* Reprinted by permission from Nature: Prendergast, J. R. *et al. Nature* **365** (1993), 335–337; copyright (1993) Macmillan Publishers Ltd.

phylogenetic diversity will capture high numbers of genes, or useful genes. 'Worldmap' (Section 3.2.1) can be asked to give priority to high taxonomic distinctiveness.

Diversity, then, whilst popular in theory, is difficult to measure and can be *very* misleading. Sites that are diverse are not always important to conservation. Conversely, some sites with relatively low diversity of species or habitats, such as the Antarctic, mangrove forests, reedbeds or deserts, may be very important for other reasons such as naturalness, uniqueness, or for the ecosystem services they provide.

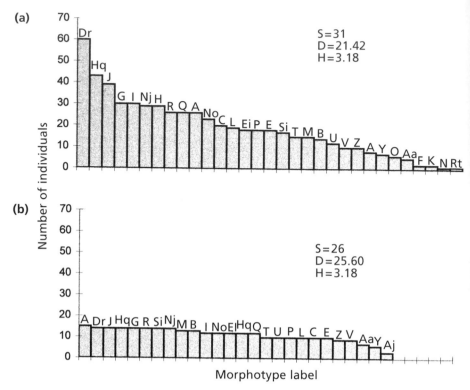

**Fig. 3.3.** Rank abundance plots and diversity indices for two sites. Species types are given by letters below the bars, and plotted in descending order of abundance. Diversity measures are: species richness, (S); Simpson's, (D); and Shannon–Wiener, (H). Note that low indices may occur on a site which has fewer of all species.

## 3.2.4   Replaceability and fragility

Replaceability of habitats includes a similar ethical dimension to extinction. If the loss of a habitat is irreversible, then, as with global extinction of a species, its loss becomes a matter of inter-generational equity (Section 1.3.1). Trivially, since all sites are unique, all are irreplaceable. However, some broad habitat types are evident, and we should attempt to save the rarer types as a matter of precaution. Fragile habitats are relatively easily damaged, and if they recover slowly they will also be less replaceable. Replaceability is an integration of attributes including typicalness, rarity, and fragility.

The early-successional habitats (such as a recent grassland or a secondary woodland) may be easier to replace than late successional habitats (such as semi-natural grassland or primary forest). Primary forest (old-growth forest)

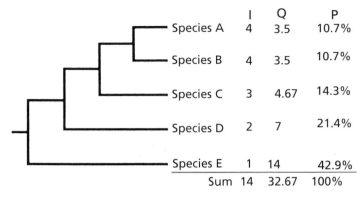

| | I | Q | P |
|---|---|---|---|
| Species A | 4 | 3.5 | 10.7% |
| Species B | 4 | 3.5 | 10.7% |
| Species C | 3 | 4.67 | 14.3% |
| Species D | 2 | 7 | 21.4% |
| Species E | 1 | 14 | 42.9% |
| Sum | 14 | 32.67 | 100% |

**Fig. 3.4.** Identification of evolutionarily distinctive species. Column P gives the percentage contribution of each species to the total diversity in this set of species. Column I gives the number of terminal groups to which each species belongs; column Q measures the information content in each branch as I/(sum of I); and P = 100 × Q/(sum of Q). The same method could be used for taxa other than species.
*Source:* Reprinted from Vane-Wright, R. I. *et al. Biological Conservation* **55** (1991), 235–254; copyright 1991 with permission from Elsevier Science.

cannot be replaced – by definition. Ancient woodland in Britain is, by definition, over 400 years old, and so would take at least 400 years to establish, whilst recent woodland could be replaced more rapidly if it were lost. Ancient woodland at a site has often existed there in some form back through time to the original 'wildwood', and C. W. D. Gibson's study of the history and species composition of different parts of Wytham Wood in Britain suggests that the characteristics of ancient woodland may take about 1000 years to develop – or replace.

However, some habitats which appear early-successional may actually have taken a very long time to establish. For example, the semi-natural limestone grasslands of Britain and montane grasslands of the Alps may have taken thousands of years to develop through a 'deflected succession' to a relatively stable 'plagioclimax', and would take as long again to recreate.

Early successional habitats, such as crumbling cliff-faces, mudflats, some wetlands, and some dunes, may be relatively robust to some types of disturbance. However, the ecology and history of a site has to be very well known to be sure that it can be replaced easily and rapidly. For example, titanium mining in sands of KwaZulu-Natal involved destruction of parts of an inherently dynamic and extensive littoral forest type, which could be quickly replaced with fast-spreading endemic trees. In contrast, similar mining proposals in south-east Madagascar threaten the last relics of a littoral forest type which appears more stable and less replaceable (in the absence of a tree species that has evolved for rapid colonisation and establishment). The methods for attempted replacement of habitats by restoration management are discussed in Chapter 8.

Fragile habitats include montane, polar and tundra habitats, upland bogs, and caves. These have relatively simple food-chains, and the productivity of terrestrial plants (if present) is very low, owing to the cold. Slow growth makes species vulnerable to many disturbances, including trampling, overgrazing, thermal pollution and fire. The vegetation in extremely cold environments is often a mat of lichens and mosses. A footprint in a Welsh *Sphagnum* bog may take 30 months to recover, whilst polar and montane plants may take many years to recover from a footprint and centuries to recover from a few seasons' visitor pressure; similarly vehicle tracks in the tundra last for many decades. Hot deserts may have similarly fragile communities.

## 3.2.5   Area, site geometry and other criteria

The area (size) of a reserve, and its shape may be very important criteria – if there is a choice in the matter! Usually, conservationists simply have to put up with what is available or can be afforded, and the boundaries of reserves are determined by pragmatic and logistical considerations such as existing habitat edges, land ownership, national boundaries, roads, rivers and so on. It may be desirable for the practicalities and effectiveness of management that an entire landscape feature be included in a reserve. There may be benefits to corridors, or, conversely, to isolation amongst sites (Section 5.4). Ideally, reserves should be large enough to support viable populations of the species which need the largest ranges, such as top predators (Section 3.1.4). Owing to species–area considerations (Section 5.4.1) there are diminishing returns as size increases. Indeed, some very small 'microreserves' of a few hectares can be important, as with conservation of rare plants in Valencia, Spain.

The ideal geometrical designs for reserves and groups of reserves, and the theories and evidence supporting them, are considered with the problems of fragmentation in Section 5.4. Generally, sites are more valuable if they are large, round and linked together by natural corridors – although there are many exceptions. The position of a site in a geographical unit may be important – the proximity of a site to a very high value or a very large site increases its value because the two sites may complement each other though dispersal of organisms between them. The National Wildlife Refuges assist bird migration along four major flyways in the USA.

The historical and archaeological records available for a site render it useful for scientific monitoring purposes. Very well studied sites, such as Tambopata and Manu in the Peruvian Amazon, the Serengeti and Mkomazi in Tanzania, Aldabra in the Indian Ocean, Barro Colorado island in the Panama Canal, and Wytham Wood in England, permit long-term trends to be detected, or the effects of historical management to be investigated. It is also worth considering the potential value of the site after any viable ecological restoration (Chapter 8).

Sites of geological interest, such as fossil beds, mineral deposits, or faulting, can help in the study of very long-term environmental and biological change. Geological SSSIs in Britain are designated to protect the integrity of sites or the presence of exposures – for example at Clevedon Shore in England; such sites are often also of biological importance.

## 3.3   Conservation indices

It would be very convenient if all of the important features of a site (including area, naturalness, rarity, etc.) could be boiled down into one figure, summarising the overall 'conservation value' of each site. This would greatly simplify the ranking of sites for their conservation priority – and have political appeal. Unfortunately, many attempts to create a general conservation index have failed.

To combine the scores for a site on the basis of a number of attributes, the attributes must be quantified and weighted in some way. But how is one to compare rarity with naturalness in the same units, so they can be added together? Another problem is that attributes are not independent: some may conflict, such as typicalness and rarity, whilst others such as rarity and naturalness may be correlated (non-independent). In an evaluation of wetlands in Sweden for their conservation value for birds, F. Gotmark and colleagues illustrated the problem of the subjectivity of weighting. A number of alternative indices were devised and tested against the consensus opinion of a team of expert ornithologists. The various indices gave different rankings, and only an index based on several measures of rarity came close to the team's subjective ranking.

An example of an apparently successful conservation index is that used for key coastal sites in the British Nature Conservation Review. A Comparative Biological Value (CBV) index was created by D. S. Ranwell. This included nine features of a site, such as area, diversity, education and research use, and physico-chemical distinctiveness. Each feature was rated on a scale of 1–3,

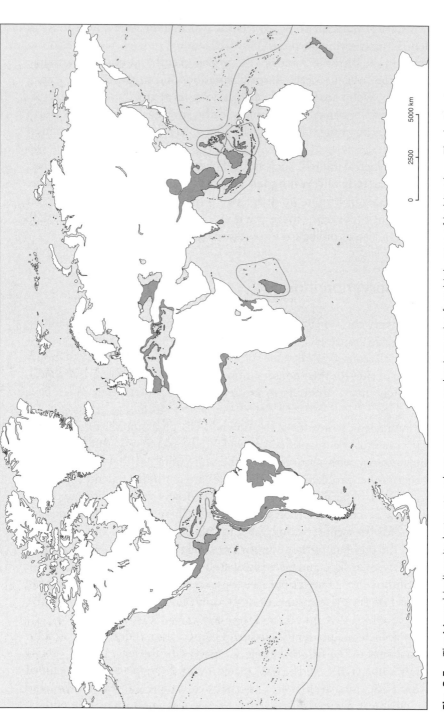

**Fig. 3.5.** The Myers biodiversity hotspots, where numerous endemic species face high rates of habitat loss. The hotspot expanse covers only part of the shaded areas.
*Source:* Redrawn from Myers, N. *et al.* Biodiversity hotspots for conservation priorities. *Nature* **403** (2000), 853–858.

and the features summed to give a score out of 27; each feature was therefore given equal 'weighting'.

An ideal evaluation might thus include the consensus opinion of a team of experts, including those expert in a range of taxonomic groups. A series of sites which have been ranked by experts can be used to calibrate indicators or indices, which can then be used as a short-cut on new sites (Section 4.4). Unfortunately time and money are often inadequate to complete an evaluation, and so evaluations often have to be revised as knowledge improves. In Britain, some sites of little interest to botanists, such as Richmond Park, have now been included in the SSSI series because of their value to invertebrates.

## 3.4    Hotspots for conservation

Is it possible to identify the most critically important sites in the world for conservation? In other words, where should we spend our limited money if we want to reduce the extinction rate fastest in the short-term? This question has been phrased and addressed by Norman Myers. Myers and colleagues have defined and identified the 'biodiversity hotspots' as those areas which have both high endemicity *and* a high level of threat (Fig. 3.5). Confusingly, some authors refer to 'hotspots' as areas of high richness, or high endemicity, without consideration of threat, and such usage should be specified.

To qualify as a terrestrial hotspot, an area must have 0.5% of the world's 300 000 vascular plant species *and* have lost at least 70% of its original expanse. This latter criterion is to focus attention on the areas where funding can do the most immediate good *to prevent extinction*. In the current total of 25 sites (just 1.4% of the land surface of the Earth) there are 44% of all endemic vascular plants, and 35% of the endemic vertebrates other than fish. Between a half and two thirds of threatened plants, and about 60% of threatened vertebrates, are endemics confined to the hotspots. More than two thirds of the world's most endangered mammals, and 80% of the most endangered birds, come from the hotspots, which have between them already lost 88% of their original habitat. The analysis is relatively insensitive to the cut-off levels chosen for endemicity and habitat loss. Fifteen hotspots have more than 2500 endemic plants, and ten have over 5000; choosing a threshold of 60% loss would bring in few other sites, whilst choosing a level of 90% would exclude eleven of them.

Similarly, to qualify as a 'marine hotspot', C. M. Roberts and colleagues decided that an area must be a marine centre of endemism with an average threat level of 1.67 on a three-point threat scale: these include about 50% of

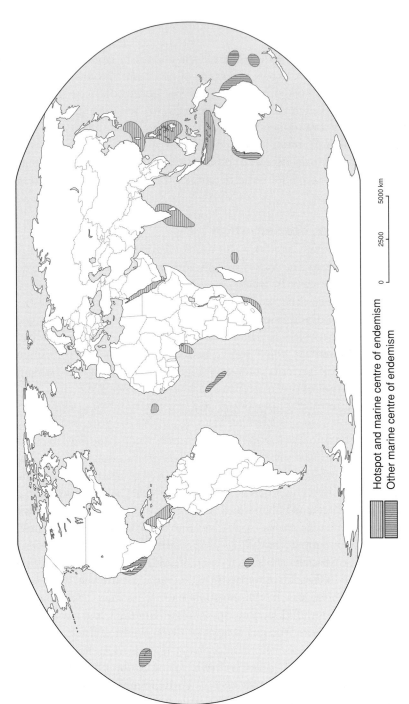

**Fig. 3.6.** Marine hotspots and other marine centres of endemism.
*Source*: Redrawn from Roberts, C. M. et al. *Science* **295** (2002), 1280–1284.

Hotspot and marine centre of endemism

Other marine centre of endemism

0          2500          5000 km

the restricted-range species in 16% of the area of reefs (0.012% of the oceanic area).

Eight of the ten marine biodiversity hotspots (and 14 out of the 18 marine centres of endemism), are adjacent to terrestrial hotspots (Fig. 3.6), suggesting an integrated approach to terrestrial and aquatic conservation in these areas would be extremely productive.

The designation of the Myers hotspots, and the priority they should receive for funding, have been the subject of intense debate. Many of the criticisms result from failure to read the original papers or to appreciate the aim of the hotspot analysis. Some of the criticisms of spending substantial funding on hotspots are: that there are sites with many endemics that are not included because there has not been so much loss of habitat (such as Papua New Guinea); that there is inadequate representation of the world's biomes; that they do not focus on species perceived to be useful; and that some taxa are not well represented in them. However, the hotspots were chosen by over 100 specialists in many disciplines, and as well as stimulating productive debate and focusing thoughts, they probably represent the nearest to a consensus on global priorities to date.

A similar global exercise in priority setting by consensus, using a large team of botanists, has identified nearly 250 Centres of Plant Diversity (CPDs); the criteria for these included richness, endemicity, habitat diversity, threat and richness of useful species.

## 3.4.1 Congruence

Congruence (the co-occurrence of areas of interest for different taxa) may occur between richness of species *overall* (Section 4.4), or between richness of endemic species. The issue of whether richness of *endemics* correlates well between taxa is particularly important. If the sites which had a high proportion of endemic species in one taxon also had high endemicity in most other taxa, then use of a well-known taxon such as the birds or the flowering plants would provide a short-cut to identifying the sites with the most endemics in other groups – such as mites, mosses or flies. The use of such indicators is discussed in the next section. The question of congruence is critical if we are to minimise extinction rates, but unfortunately it is very hard to answer. To demonstrate congruence, globally or for a region, there must be good maps of the distributions of endemic species, or of the number of endemics per unit area of the Earth's surface. Few such data are available. However, Fig. 3.7 shows that for tropical forests there is a global correlation between bird endemicity and mammal endemicity.

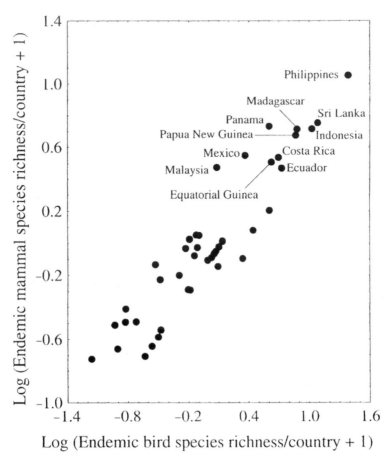

**Fig. 3.7.** Correlation between the richness of endemic mammal and bird species in countries with tropical forests (after correction for country area).
*Source:* Kerr, J. T. & Burkey, T. V. *Biodiversity and Conservation* **11** (2002), 695–704. With kind permission of the publisher, Kluwer Academic Publishers, and the authors.

To understand why we should expect congruence of endemics, it is important to understand the evolutionary processes creating endemic species. There are two main types of endemic species: those which have evolved in an area and have not spread far from that area, and those which used to have wider ranges but which now have only a relict population in one small area. The former may be called ancient endemics, and the latter relict endemics. Ancient endemics are likely to be found on isolated islands, lakes or mountains. Relict endemics are likely to be found on the edges of continents or in biomes where they have survived movements of habitat driven by climatic changes – as with the forests of the Ussuriland of far-East Asia. It is not always possible to tell the two types apart, and humans have complicated the situation. For example, the Stevens Island wren and was once thought to be endemic to a single island, but new archaeological evidence shows it occurred on the mainland of New Zealand and was probably exterminated there following the arrival of the Maoris. The Laysan duck occurred on several islands in Hawaii, where DNA evidence shows it was extirpated by Hawaiians. Endemism may also be considered from the perspective of political regions, or from the antiquity of their separation from other taxa, as discussed in the *Global Biodiversity Assessment* of 1995.

Endemicity requires sufficient isolation, and time, for new species to evolve: the more isolated and ancient the area, the more likely it is to have high endemicity. There is therefore likely to be high congruence on ancient oceanic islands, mountains, isolated lakes, and similar sites where genetic exchange with other populations is rare. Endemicity in the oceans occurs primarily on isolated sites (e.g. the Mascarene islands and Hawaii), and where cold currents isolate tropical communities (Fig. 3.6).

Most endemic species are in tropical sites – as are most species. This may relate to the 100 000 year cycle of glacial and interglacial periods over at least the past 2 million years (the 'Milankovitch cycles'), and similar wet/dry cycles in earlier times. These cyclical changes disrupt tropical sites less than temperate sites. For example, a glacier hundreds of metres deep forming over Scotland or Poland is more disruptive than woodland changing to savannah in the Amazon or Africa. Terrestrial species of temperate regions, which were able to move north or south as the ice advanced and retreated, were also able to move east and west. Consequently, terrestrial species in temperate regions generally have wide longditudinal (east–west) ranges, and are rarely endemic to small areas.

Mountain sites with demonstrably high congruence of endemicity across taxa include the Andes, the Himalayas, the Western Ghats, the Sichuan, the Cardamons, the Caucasus, Mt Kenya, Mt Nimba, Mt Cameroon, the Ethiopian Massif, the Eastern Arc mountains of Tanzania and the Mountains of the Moon in Rwanda and Uganda. Mountain lakes support several endemic birds and fish: in the Andes these include the Junin grebe, the recently extinct Colombian grebe and Lake Tota fat fish, Apolinar's marsh wren and the Bogota rail.

Sea-level rises and falls with the glacial cycles, flooding and exposing islands. Ancient, remote islands have marked endemicity. In Madagascar and New Zealand, floral endemicity is some 80%. Seven of the world's nine species of baobab occur only in Madagascar; 90% of Madagascar's reptiles are endemic, as are 99% of its amphibians. The granitic Seychelles (a fragment of an ancient continent) have 35% floristic endemicity. Remote tropical islands which are ancient volcanoes can also have high endemicity: the ancient 'high islands' in the Pacific support far more endemics than the recently flooded 'low islands'. The Hawaiian flora is 97% endemic. Similarly the Mascarene islands of the Indian Ocean have 73% floral endemicity. Isolated temperate islands can also show a high degree of endemicity: for example, Tristan da Cunha has 60% endemicity in its flowering plants. However, temperate sites do not support large numbers of species (because of the general 'latitudinal diversity gradient', in which richness declines away from the tropics).

Congruence requires more study in freshwater and marine habitats. Congruence is very likely in isolated freshwater habitats. The Amazon houses a very substantial amount of the world's freshwater, and has numerous tributaries. Endemicity of several taxa is high in the tributaries, and low in the main river. In the tributaries, many endemics are threatened by disturbance to watersheds. Other important mainland areas for freshwater endemicity include the African lakes (with hundreds of species of cichlid fish) and Lake Baikal (which has over 30 endemic species of fish, mainly in the suborder of Cottoids, and over 340 endemic amphipod species and subspecies). Freshwater species of many taxa reach high levels of endemicity on islands, as with fish in the Caribbean, Indonesia, Madagascar and New Guinea.

It has been presumed that endemicity within marine habitats might be low owing to dispersal of organisms in ocean currents, but the newly identified marine centres of endemicity dispel this view (Fig. 3.6). About one quarter of the world's fish species use coral reefs, which cover less than 2% of the Earth's surface area. Reefs are likely to be rich in numerous other taxa, such as molluscs. Within coral reefs, C. M. Roberts and colleagues found about 10% of corals, 25% of fish, 30% of snails and 55% of lobsters have 'restricted ranges' of less than $50\,000$ km$^2$, and there is high congruence of the top sites for endemicity in these taxa. A few fish with very narrow ranges are known on coral reefs, such as the splendid toadfish of Cozumel. Furthermore, work by P. Bouchet suggests high endemicity of certain microshell molluscs round New Caledonian islands and sea-mounts; endemicity of other weakly mobile taxa might be found to be high on similarly isolated topographic features including ocean trenches. Apart from reefs, kelp beds are considered highly important for many species which exploit kelp's great productivity and structural complexity, whilst seagrass beds support specialised turtles, fish and invertebrates. The Sargasso region has numerous distinctive species living in a gyre of floating seaweed. Deep ocean environments are largely unexplored, although hydrothermal vent communities and brine lakes may support distinctive organisms in many taxa.

## 3.4.2  Indicators of endemicity: the Endemic Bird Areas

Of all the features that an indicator group could usefully identify, one that can reveal the best sites for endemicity is particularly important for conservation, because endemic species become locally *and* globally extinct simultaneously. The birds, large mammals, and vascular plants are the best-recorded groups, and may help to indicate terrestrial sites with long periods of evolutionary isolation and high endemicity.

The birds are the best-recorded major taxon on Earth, and have been used as indicators of richness of endemic species in groups that are less well known. However, it should be remembered that birds are relatively good at dispersal. Taxa with poorer dispersal may therefore be endemic where the birds are not – as with the endemic plants on Mt Olympus, or the edelweiss of the Alps. Conversely, poor dispersal may preclude taxa reaching remote sites: other than bats, there are few endemic mammals on small islands. However, whilst they will not be present everywhere with endemic species, sites which have endemic birds will *always* have endemics in other groups.

It appears that amongst the birds it usually takes at least 10 000 years for endemic species to evolve. In Scotland, the Scottish crossbill is a distinctive race, but arguably not a full species. At most it has had 12 000 years to evolve in isolation since the ice ages. Correspondingly, in Scotland there are few endemics in any taxa. Similarly, in the atolls of the Chagos and Maldives archipelagos, which were last submerged about 5000 years ago, there are no endemic birds, although there are endemic subspecies of moth. In contrast, the raised atoll of Aldabra has been above sea-level for 80 000 years, and has at least 3 full species and 10 subspecies of endemic bird; Aldabra also has numerous endemics amongst many insect groups, and amongst the snails and plants.

Some taxa, including flowering plants, evolve endemicity faster than the birds: there are at least 15 flowering plant species endemic to the British Isles, such as the Lundy cabbage and Scottish primrose. The rate of evolution of a species unique to an area from its ancestral type will depend partly on its generation time and partly on its dispersal ability; endemicity will evolve relatively fast in species with short generations and poor dispersal. Some will evolve more slowly – such as trees or large mammals with long generations.

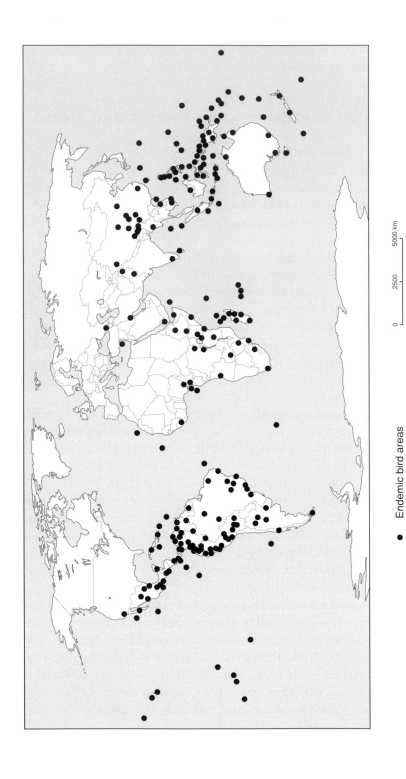

**Fig. 3.8.** Endemic Bird Areas (EBAs). Note that few sites occur in temperate regions, and many occur on islands or mountains. *Source:* Stattersfield A. J., Crosby, M. J., Long, A. J. & Wage, D. *Endemic Bird Areas of the World. Priorities for Biodiversity Conservation* (BirdLife International, Cambridge, 1998).

• Endemic bird areas

0     2500     5000 km

The distribution of terrestrial endemicity in the birds is illustrated by a map produced by BirdLife International. Firstly, 'Restricted Range Birds' (RRBs, defined as species with a global distribution of less than 50 000 km$^2$) were mapped. Sites with two or more such RRBs were then defined as 'Endemic Bird Areas' (EBAs). As can be seen from Fig. 3.8, the EBAs are clustered on islands and mountains in the tropics: 76% of the EBAs are in the tropics, and 50% of the RRBs occur on islands. The importance of ancient islands is indisputable: 75% of all animals which became extinct since 1600 were on islands, including 200 of the 217 extinct species and races of bird. Four fifths of the EBAs are in tropical forests, which support 70% of the threatened birds. Some 70% of EBAs overlap with Centres of Plant Diversity, whilst 60% of the CPDs overlap with EBAs. The roughly 220 EBAs add up to some 6.5 million km$^2$, which is only 2% of the land surface — yet they support 95% of the 2609 RRBs, and indeed 20% of all birds. This provides a very clear initial focus for conservation.

### 3.4.3  Important Bird Areas and threatened species

BirdLife International have identified areas that are important for birds other than just endemic species. Several criteria are used to assess importance, and it is anticipated that some 20 000 sites will be identified eventually.

Wetlands of international significance are protected under the Ramsar Convention (Section 9.2). Amongst the criteria which would quality an area as a Ramsar Site are that it regularly supports more than 1% of the international population of a waterbird, or more than 20 000 waterbirds.

A map has been created that shows the density of threatened bird species around the world (Fig. 3.9). This is the most detailed guide to the location of threatened species yet available for a major group of organisms. The areas that support the most threatened birds often support other threatened taxa. It should be remembered that threatened species are not always endemics, and maps of threatened species of different taxa may not show congruence. Figure 3.10 shows the locations of endangered birds and mammals. Mammals are more at risk from hunting than birds, and more endemic mammals occur in dry areas. The birds are not particularly good indicators of threats to desert or wetland species: only 10% of threatened birds occur in these habitats which support many other threatened taxa. However, J. R. Kerr and T. V. Burkey found that for countries with tropical forests, the proportion of threatened birds and mammals per country are correlated, with mammals being more

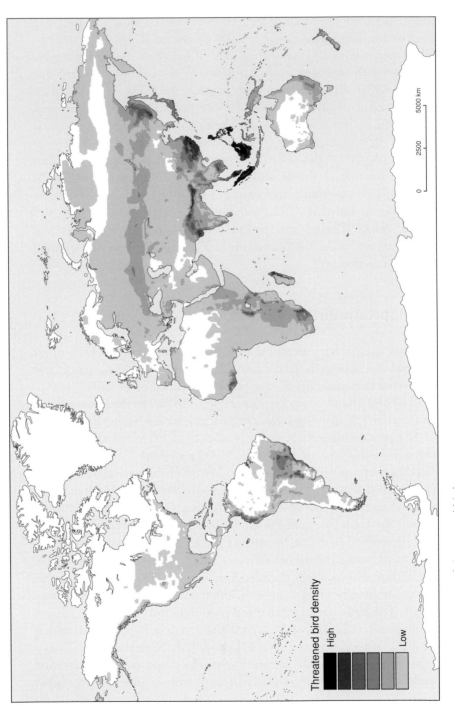

**Fig. 3.9.** Density map of threatened birds.
*Source:* Groombridge, B. & Jenkins, M. (Eds.) *World Atlas of Biodiversity: Earth's Living Resources in the 21st Century* (University of California Press, Berkeley, 2002). Copyright Bird Life International. Reproduced by kind permission of BirdLife International (2002).

Threatened bird density
High
Low

0    2500    5000 km

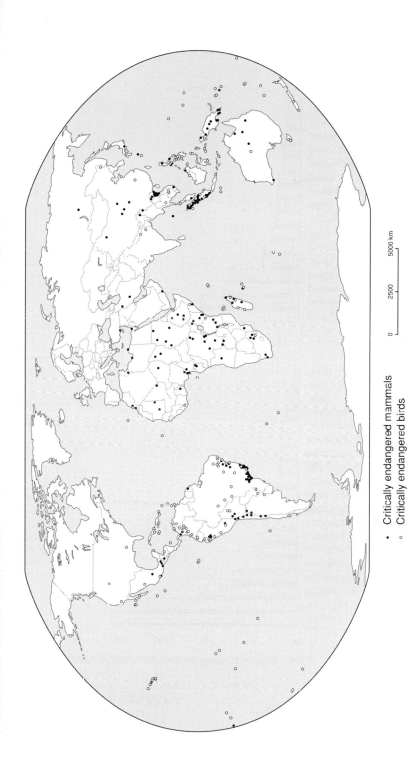

**Fig. 3.10.** Lack of congruence of critically endangered mammals and birds.
*Source:* Groombridge, B. & Jenkins, M. (Eds.) *World Atlas of Biodiversity. Earth's Living Resources in the 21st Century* (University of California Press, Berkeley, 2002). Redrawn with kind permission of UNEP-WCMC.

• Critically endangered mammals
○ Critically endangered birds

0    2500    5000 km

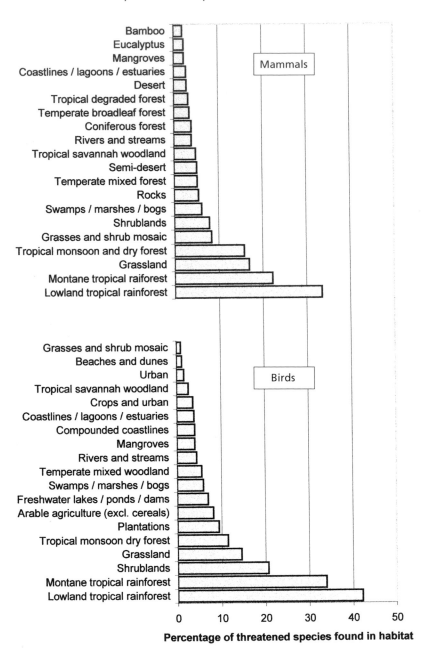

**Fig. 3.11.**  Threats to mammals and birds by habitat type.
*Source:* Hilton-Taylor, C. (compiler) *2000 IUCN Red List of Threatened Species* (IUCN, Gland, Switzerland & Cambridge, 2000).

highly threatened. Figure 3.11 shows the habitats which are important for birds, and for threatened mammals.

## 3.5 Major Tropical Wilderness Areas and ecoregions

The hotspots approach focuses attention on those areas which by definition have already been badly degraded. Such areas were never in themselves intended to be a complete list of the most important areas for conservation. They are intended to be complemented by other approaches, such as protection of 'Major Tropical Wilderness Areas' (MTWAs) (or 'good news areas'). Myers and colleagues have shown that a combined approach of hotspots and MTWAs could support 60% of all plant species in roughly 5% of the land surface. Much wilderness is in the temperate and polar biomes, but the tropical areas are a priority for protection of endemics.

As with hotspots, the terrestrial Major Tropical Wilderness Areas (MTWAs) were selected by a large team of specialists. They total some 6–7 million km$^2$, and include parts of the Amazon, Congo basin, and New Guinea regions. They retain at least 75% of their primary vegetation, and have fewer than five people per square kilometre. They also include many endemic species, such as the island of New Guinea with 15 000 endemic plants, the Guyana Shield, the lowlands of western Amazonia, and the Congolese forests (which support 30 000 endemic plants). What could be termed coral reef wilderness areas are evident from maps produced by C. M. Roberts and colleagues using a three-point scale of threat.

MTWAs will not be sufficient to include all the species absent from hotspots, nor all the threatened species. Numerous smaller, less rich, or more degraded sites, are also an integral part of the conservation programme.

Another complementary approach is to select representatives from all the Earth's 'ecoregions' for conservation. Ecoregions are rather vaguely defined large landscape areas containing one or more habitats considered by some researchers to be linked by features such as climate, proximity, geomorphology, soils, hydrology, ocean currents, potential vegetation or migratory species, which might be treated as a convenient unit for conservation. There have been attempts to categorise and prioritise ecoregions by degree of threat, in a similar way to the IUCN threat categories for species. However, the choice of boundaries for ecoregions, and the weightings which are applied to several features of interest within them, are highly subjective, and the scores for site quality do not indicate extinction risk as closely as do the hotspots. Consideration of ecoregions may help identify and protect a representative range of unique habitat types which are undergoing fragmentation. They may also help in landscape-scale management (Chapter 5), and help to define the aims of restoration in an area (Chapter 8).

## 3.6   World Heritage Sites

What are the very best, most spectacular, sites on Earth for conservation? It is impossible to answer this question objectively. However, there are people who believe that some of the natural wonders of the world are so interesting and special that they should be part of the 'global heritage'. In order to protect the very cream of the world's natural wonders, the United Nations Educational, Scientific and Cultural Organisation (UNESCO) helped develop the World Heritage Convention (Section 9.2.1).

The criteria for qualification as a World Heritage Site are very restrictive. There are three types of site (or 'Property'): Natural Properties are defined as 'natural sites or precisely delimited natural areas of outstanding universal value from the point of view of science, conservation or natural beauty'; a Cultural Property is intended for architectural conservation; and a Mixed Property includes elements of each – for example a landscape that has long human influence yet remains spectacular for its 'natural' features. Mixed Properties are 'works of man or the combined works of man and nature which are of outstanding universal value from the historical, aesthetic, ethnological or anthropological point of view'. Such sites may in fact be semi-natural habitat rather than natural, and need retention of the cultural management to remain intact (Section 7.3).

The List of World Heritage Sites now numbers over 140 Natural Properties and 25 Mixed Properties. It is anticipated that this list will not grow very much larger, to retain its elite character.

Following listing as a World Heritage Site, a plaque may be placed on the site by the sovereign nation recognising its international value to humanity (Fig. 3.12). The sites remain part of the sovereign nation, but there is strong international help (and pressure) to protect them. If UNESCO believe a site to be in need of urgent conservation operations, it may be placed on the List of World Heritage in Danger, and funds are available from UNESCO to help the sovereign country remedy the problems.

## 3.7   Conclusion and triage

As a conclusion to this chapter, there is no universal answer to the question of whether to prioritise the conservation of species or habitats. They are two

**Fig. 3.12.** Plaque on Aldabra World Heritage Property, which reads 'Aldabra, wonder of nature. Offered to Humanity by the People of the Republic of Seychelles'. *Photograph:* C. Hambler.

sides of the same coin, and both are important. The relative emphasis they require will depend on the case in question. Conservation of the integrity of a habitat may require the conservation of numerous individual species within it. There is no universally agreed list of global priorities for funding. Similarly, we shall see in Section 5.4 that there is no universally preferable geometrical design for reserves or systems of reserves.

Some, such as Norman Myers, would argue that the scarcity of funds for conservation forces us to consider the approach of 'triage'. This is the way casualties are assessed in war – doctors assess whether patients can be saved, and if so would the time taken on one patient with serious injuries be at the expense of saving a number of other patients? A patient may be given a low priority if he or she would be very hard to save. Perhaps some sites in the world are so badly damaged, and have such bleak prospects, that we should write them off? Should funding be sunk into the Philippines if the high rates of deforestation and high human population growth rate will negate most conservation efforts? Yet what appears to be a hopeless situation for one taxon may not be for others. Mauritius was once considered by many to have very poor prospects, but the situation on this small island has been turned around, and it is now a success story (Chapter 10). There is perhaps scope for a panel of experts to assess the prospects for some regions or species, and make tough decisions about funding. Such decisions need to be very transparent, to allow people who feel strongly (and have resources) to take up the effort if other conservation organisations pull out.

Decisions as to site selection and triage need to be taken with the best possible supporting information. None of the site attributes discussed above would be any use if it could not be measured reliably, so we now turn to the methodologies that can quantify features of ecological interest within sites.

# 4

# Monitoring and Environmental Impact Assessment

This chapter examines the methods for ecological survey that are required when evaluating sites for conservation. These methods are used for four main reasons: for base-line survey when choosing sites; for monitoring changes; for Environmental Impact Assessment (EIA) before developments; and for assessment of management methods – an evaluation before and after management will help detect and interpret changes due to that management. There are a number of basic principles and methods of ecological survey which must be understood in order to interpret survey results and reports. We will also examine the selection and use of indicator groups to give rapid assessment of sites, expanding concepts discussed in Sections 3.2 and 3.4.

The subject of this chapter is one of the most important to successful conservation, and is essential to those doing or interpreting field surveys. Similarly rigorous methods have been developed by social scientists, which can be used to obtain data on public opinion, local activities and local knowledge, as required in determining policy and management (Chapter 9). To avoid biases, questionnaires and interviews (including 'participatory rural appraisal') require careful design, piloting and distribution, and specialist texts should be consulted for such methods.

## 4.1 Aims and requirements

The aims of any survey must be very clearly defined, given the inevitable subjectivity of setting priorities. It must be absolutely clear from the start what will be considered a high-quality site. Just as there are too many species and sites to protect them all, there are too many species and habitats to survey or monitor them all, and selected samples must be made in the light of the changes which people aim to detect or predict. This is part of the wider problem of identification of conservation aims (Chapter 3).

Survey methods have to be considered in terms of ecological reliability and biases, cost, and practicality. The aims of the survey may be to record the richness of species, the density of species, or the relative abundance of species. This latter is related to equitability and the various 'diversity indices', as described in Section 3.2.3. Books on survey techniques and principles are given under Further reading, including books suitable for expedition survey.

Sampling will usually depend on the ability to identify species. Although short-cuts are sometimes used (Section 4.4.2), it is best to identify specimens to a species name if possible – so that the specialist requirements, rarity and quality of the species can be considered (Section 3.1). Sadly, the study of relationships between species – taxonomy – and training in how to identify specimens have both been greatly neglected in research and training. Courses in identification are available from museums and societies. The 'Traditional Ecological Knowledge' (TEK) of local people may be very helpful in identifying or finding animals from tracks and signs, or in identifying plants; it should be remembered that traditional cultures often group species together in different ways from scientists.

## 4.2   Sampling methods and analysis

Many principles of ecological survey apply to all groups of organisms. The techniques differ when counting whales or plankton or worms, but there are several general statistical requirements to consider in the design of any sampling project. Here we will examine a few critical features: replication; absolute versus relative sampling; standardisation of search effort; and standardisation of abiotic influences such as the weather. Unless such factors are considered, biases in the samples may render the results useless – or even counter-productive.

To compare different sites at different dates, the same methods should be used on each occasion. Similarly, a standardised methodology should be used to compare sites, so that genuine differences can be detected which are not due to changes in the sampling method.

The sampling methods should of course be as ethical as possible – minimising disturbance, stress or mortality to both the target organisms and to non-target species. Indeed, laws prevent some methods if damage to the habitat may occur, whilst ethical committees in scientific journals will bar the publication of results from unethical projects. For example, if pitfall traps sampling invertebrates in Britain were found to be collecting pygmy shrews or great crested newts, it would be illegal to continue. Disturbance to the habitat, either accidentally or through destructive sampling, is always undesirable – but it may sometimes be considered an acceptable cost to obtain essential data required for the wider survival and welfare of a species. Permits and licences may be required to sample species or sites, even as part of an impact assessment – for example if handling great crested newts or birds in Britain or many endangered species in the USA.

It is sometimes possible to record the *absence* of conspicuous species in a systematic survey – for example the absence of sea turtle tracks on beaches on particular days. Zeros in data sets can be very helpful in mapping and in detecting population trends, such as the recovery of nesting sea turtles on Aldabra, but the reliability of such data depends on very careful survey design.

## 4.2.1  Statistical methods

One of the commonest flaws in ecological surveys, be they for EIA or student projects, is that they are not designed with statistical analysis in mind. Statistics may be necessary when there is natural variation in the system in space or time, and we need to be convinced that the differences that have been observed are reliable.

Scientists need to know the risk that a difference which has been observed between sites or samples is the result of chance alone. If the result that has been obtained would only be expected once in 20 times by chance, this is accepted as 'significant at the 5% level'. If it is expected only once in 100 times, it is deemed 'significant at the 1% level'. 'Confidence Limits' or 'Standard Errors' can be calculated to illustrate the spread of the variation about the mean of the samples, and to find the chance that two means are different. Given that ecological systems are often very variable – for example the population size of a species or the richness of a square metre of grassland, such statements of the error estimates in a survey are very important if the conclusions are to be trusted.

To obtain error estimates for the mean, replicate samples are taken. The more replicate samples are used, the lower the Standard Error (SE). Statistical tests that may then be appropriate to test for difference between means include Paired t-tests and Analysis of Variance (ANOVA). These could tell the researcher that the average number of a particular species is higher in one area or another. Correlations and regressions are used to identify features which vary together, such as the abundances of two species. Multiple regressions are used to help identify which variables (e.g. temperature or predators) are the most important in predicting some feature – such as the abundance of a species. If a large number of statistical tests are used on the same data set, then there is a risk that some of the results are false. It is therefore often better to do a single test of many variables at once – so called 'multivariate analysis'.

Multivariate analysis may be used to help find the most important common features (variables) in a range of sites where the features have been recorded at the same time as the population size or species richness. For example, analysis can reveal the relative importance of wetness, logging intensity, or hunting pressure. To test which of the recorded abiotic or biotic variables are the most important in distinguishing the samples or habitats, PCA or DCA analyses are performed.

Multivariate analyses are also used in identifying, defining and comparing natural habitat types (Section 1.2.2). Important multivariate techniques for evaluation and monitoring include 'classification methods' (such as TWINSPAN) and 'ordination methods' (such as PCA or DCA). TWINSPAN presents a hierarchy of habitats showing the similarities between them, and the species that are the most important indicators which distinguish the different types of habitat. Such techniques were used for a 'National Vegetation Classification' (NVC), which mapped Britain's habitats into the types now used in ecological surveys. Examples of the use of multivariate analysis are shown in Figs. 4.1 and 4.2. These analyses can now be performed with various user-friendly computer programmes such as CAP; however, the assumptions of the analysis must be understood, and the interpretation of multivariate statistics may be difficult. Monte-Carlo tests can help to detect the significance of patterns in such analyses.

Unless the whole site is examined, a survey to record base-line data will need numerous replicate samples. If the site is to be re-surveyed at a future date, then consideration must be given to the way changes are to be detected. For the whole site, the total richness of a group such as plants or birds might be compared. If only part of the site is sampled in the base-line, detection of change will require a test for significant differences between the base-line and the subsequent samples. If general conclusions are to be made about the quality of a habitat, or the effects of a management, then the sampling must be adequately representative of those habitats and managements.

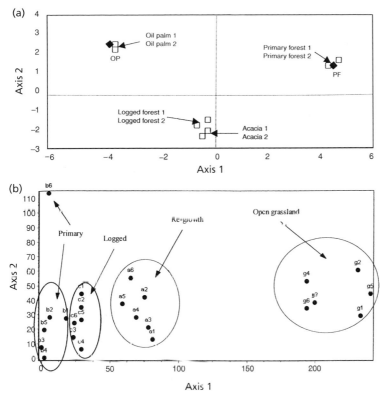

**Fig. 4.1.** Community analysis to test the impact of management. These are ordination diagrams in which the axes are scores calculated by the programme, and the points are individual samples with location labels. Axis 1 shows the strongest source of variation. (a) Beetle communities differ in the canopies of various forest types in Sabah, Malaysia. (b) Ant communities are sensitive to forest management in Kakamega Forest, Kenya: samples from four different management treatments cluster separately.
*Sources:* (a) Chung, A. Y. C. *et al. Bulletin of Entomological Research* **90** (2000), 475–496. (b) Espira, A. D. Phil. Thesis, University of Oxford (2001).

## 4.2.2 Replication, pseudoreplication and stratification

Many ecological studies have a fundamental flaw called 'pseudoreplication'. This is when there are only a few 'true' replicates of the habitat in question, but many samples within each one. The effects of location and management treatment are confounded. For example, to test if *in general* a grazed grassland has more species on average in a square metre than does

(a)

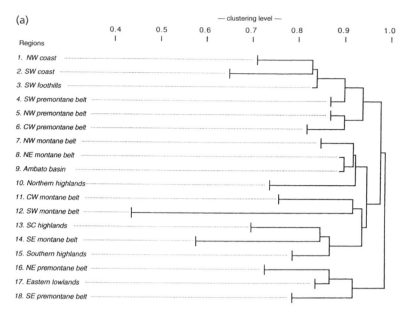

**Fig. 4.2.** Community analysis was used to map regions of plant endemicity in Ecuador. (a) A classification method repeatedly divides the communities into two groups based on restricted range species and altitude. The tips of the resulting dendrogram show regions which are similar. (b) The locations of the regions identified in the dendrogram. These correlate well with the local Endemic Bird Areas. *Source:* Borchsenius, F. *Biodiversity and Conservation* **6** (1997), 379–399.

an ungrazed one, it is not sufficient to sample very many times in just one grazed site, and in one ungrazed site. Instead of 50 samples in each of two sites, it would be better to have ten samples in each of five grazed sites, and ten in each of five ungrazed sites (Fig. 4.3). A mean level of richness can then be calculated for grazed sites, and compared statistically with the mean for ungrazed sites in that region. If only one grazed and one ungrazed site were examined, the differences found by intensive sampling within them may, arguably, simply reflect the fact that the grazed site happened to be wetter, or up a hill, or on different soils, or nearer to a town. Similarly, to see if logged forest is in general as good a habitat for lemurs as an unlogged primary forest, the population density in several logged and unlogged forests should be examined, rather than looking in great detail at many animals in just two sites.

Pseudoreplication may be difficult to avoid. For example, in surveys of forests prior to titanium mining in Madagascar, there was only one primary forest surviving in the area; in such cases, it is worth pseudoreplication in that forest, and true replication elsewhere – but more caution will be needed in

(b)

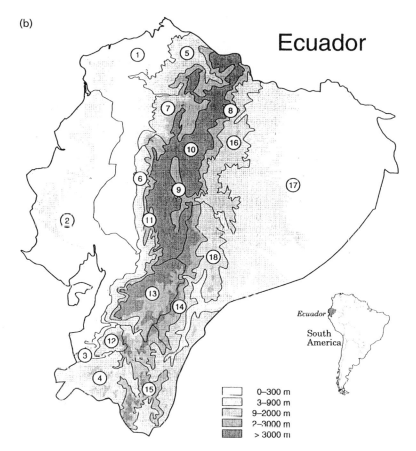

Fig. 4.2.   (cont.)

interpretation of the results and various alternative explanations would have to be tested. It is much harder to make generalisations from results of pseudo-replicated samples. Put simply, samples should ideally be as independent in space and time as is logistically possible, to increase the power to generalise to other sites.

   To survey sites each of which is known to include different habitats, or to survey a very large area, fully random placement of the samples may be unsatisfactory. Fully random sampling might, by chance, miss some habitat types. To avoid this problem, the sample may be 'stratified'. This means dividing the area into regions or types (strata), and ensuring that there is a sufficiently large number of samples in every type (Fig. 4.4). If samples are placed at random in each of the strata, it is called a 'stratified random design'. Sampling should aim to include as much of the conspicuous variation as possible – in which

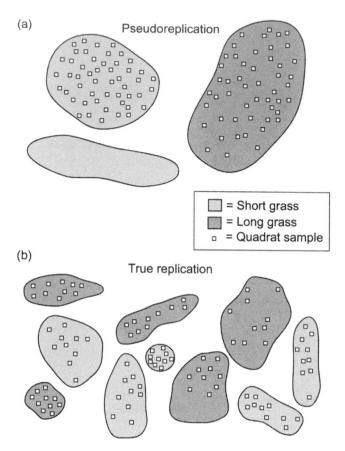

**Fig. 4.3.** Pseudoreplication places all the samples in a few examples of each habitat, whilst true replication spreads the samples across replicates of each habitat. Here the two habitats being compared (short and long grass) are the products of heavy or light grazing management treatments.

case differences that are found are more likely to result from, say, habitat age or management treatments, than from the chance placement of quadrats.

## 4.2.3   Relative and absolute sampling

Sampling can be done in two ways: 'relative sampling' and 'absolute sampling'. Relative sampling gives the count of organisms in one sample relative to another sample. For example, the number of species or individuals found in one site may be found to be double that in another. However, relative

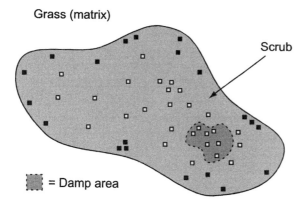

**Fig. 4.4.** A stratified random design to test for potential differences in a patch of scrub habitat. Within each potential habitat type, quadrat samples (indicated by small squares) are placed randomly. Quadrats near the edge which are hypothesised to differ from the core are recorded separately (quadrats marked in black), as are quadrats from the damp area. Pseudoreplication is unavoidable in this example, and the causes of any differences found between areas may therefore be hard to deduce.

sampling does not tell you the surface area (or the volume) of the habitat from which the samples were obtained. In contrast, absolute samples give a count of individuals per unit area (such as a square metre, a hectare, or a 100 km by 100 km grid square), or per unit volume (such as a cubic centimetre of seawater or a cubic metre of air).

If absolute samples are available for a series of sites or dates, it is possible to compare them with each other very directly – and to compare sites of different sizes by considering the different density of species or habitats within a site. Knowing the density of a species per unit area also allows the total population to be calculated for a site of known area.

Relative methods include moth-trapping, sweep-netting, counts of birds at a series of points, and simple counts along transects. For plants, point quadrats (described below) are a relative method. Absolute methods include quadrats, vacuum sampling, and knock-down sampling. These methods are discussed in more detail below, with the groups they are most often used for. There is some overlap in the methods for different taxa.

## 4.2.4  Sampling effort and species accumulation curves

In order to make comparisons between sites, by using either relative or absolute methods, it is important to know the effort put into sampling the sites.

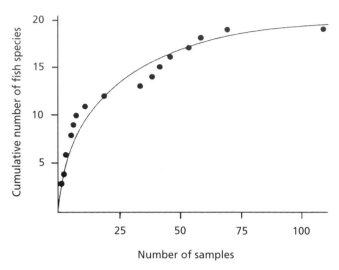

**Fig. 4.5.** A species accumulation curve for samples of the community of fish inhabiting leaf-litter in an Amazonian stream. An estimate of the asymptotic richness after 11 samples, using the Chao estimator, predicted 22 species – which is very close to the observed value.
*Source:* Henderson, P. A. & Walker, I. *Journal of Tropical Ecology* **2** (1986), 1–17, and Pisces Conservation Ltd.

The 'sampling effort' records variables which directly influence the number of organisms that can be sampled: these might include how much time was spent at each site, the number of traps used, the number of people sampling (and their level of skill), and the number of sweeps of a sweep-net. The species richness recorded at a site is very sensitive to the sampling effort and methods, and these must be known before interpreting the results of a particular survey. When attempting to measure species richness, it is seldom possible to record all the species resident in a site or which regularly use a site. However, if a large number of samples are taken then the total richness can be predicted. A 'species accumulation curve' can be plotted; this shows how the number of new species recorded declines as more and more samples are taken. This can be used to estimate the likely total number of species the sampling method would collect if it were used very many times in a site (Fig. 4.5). Various computer programmes are available which help predict the species richness.

For fair comparison between sites the seasons, the weather, and the time of day may need to be standardised, as well as the sampling method. For some groups this is easier or more important than others, as discussed below.

## 4.3 Methods for different groups

Sampling for plants is easier than for vertebrates, which themselves are easier to sample than invertebrates. Sampling for micro-organisms is in its infancy, and involves molecular probes. Several methods may be used simultaneously in a survey to broaden the number of taxa covered.

### 4.3.1 Plants

Plants are the least challenging organisms to survey, since they do not move – except for planktonic forms. The taxonomy and guides for identification of plants are relatively good, both for vascular plants and for cryptograms (mosses, liverworts, lichens, etc.). Plants do, however, present a number of challenges to sampling. Many are short-lived, such as annual plants, and can be seen for only part of the year. Others are very hard to identify unless in flower. Some can be identified only through tasting the bark, or by shooting flowers or fruit from the canopy with a catapult. Some species will be present in the seed bank, and not apparent for years. Others will colonise a site briefly, but die out. The list of plants in a site is not completely stable, but it is far more so than for animals.

There are several well-established methods for botanical sampling, but 'quadrats' are one of the commonest. They involve the marking out of a unit area of ground, which is often a square, although some are rectangles or circles. The area depends on the richness of species and the density of plants in the region. It is chosen to give a manageable count of species per quadrat. For tropical rainforests, plots of 1 ha, or 1 km$^2$ might be used for the woody plants – although epiphytes require other methods. For scrubland, plots 10 m by 10 m might be appropriate. For calcareous grassland in Britain or steppe in Russia – where there may be tens of species per square metre – a 1 m by 1 m quadrat would be suitable.

Quadrats are used to record the number of species per unit area. They can also be used to measure the percentage cover of a species, by subdividing the quadrat and recording the percentage of the divisions ('cells') in which a species is present. This can be used to measure the 'dominance' of species at a site, or the 'equitability' (how even the relative coverages of the species are, Section 3.2.3). Plant 'abundance' is measured only for those species where it is possible to identify what an individual plant is – particularly difficult if the species propagates through runners. 'Transects' are a popular technique,

Table 4.1 *Examples of types of plant architecture*

| | |
|---|---|
| Dead wood over 10 cm diameter | Leaf buds/scales |
| Dead wood over 2 cm diameter under 10 cm | Flowering scales |
| Dead wood under 2 cm diameter | Flower buds |
| Dead wood over 2 cm diameter under 10 cm | Open flowers |
| Dead wood under 2 cm diameter | Dead flowers |
| Bark on dead wood over 10 cm diameter | Ripening/ripe fruit |
| Bark on dead wood over 2 cm diameter under 10 cm | Old fruiting structures |
| Bark on dead wood under 2 cm diameter | Dead leaves |
| Bark on living wood over 10 cm diameter | Dead stems |
| Bark on living wood over 2 cm diameter under 10 cm | Mosses – epiphytes |
| Bark on living wood under 2 cm diameter | Mosses – on soil surface |
| Green stems | Liverworts – epiphytes |
| Leaves on monocotyledons | Liverworts – on soil surface |
| Leaf surface – upper (if distinguishable) | Fungal fruiting bodies – on vegetation |
| Leaf surface – lower (if distinguishable) | Fungal fruiting bodies – on soil surface |

*Source:* Southwood, T. R. E., Brown, V. K. & Reader, P. M. The relationships of plant and insect diversities in succession. *Biological Journal of the Linnean Society* **12** (1979), 327–348.

particularly where there is a gradient in vegetation (such as at the edges of habitats or between management regimes). They consist of a line, which is often straight but may simply be a path. The observer records along the line, up to a fixed width and a fixed length. The survey is usually done in sections; for example, a 100 m transect may be recorded in 10 m sections. There are special statistical methods to analyse such data, since there will be little independence of physical, chemical and biological conditions between adjacent sections.

The physical structure of the vegetation (termed its 'architecture') is very important to botanists, but also to vertebrates and invertebrates and epiphytic plants. Plant architecture can be recorded in a number of ways, and Table 4.1 lists some common types. The number of such types can be counted in quadrats or transects. Canopy cover can be recorded using quadrats or hemispherical photography. Size-classes of tree can be recorded by 'Diameter at Breast Height' (DBH). Dead plant material can be recorded using these techniques – as developed for the quantification of coarse woody debris by M. E. Harmon and colleagues and by K. J. Kirby. 'Point quadrats' are pins that are used to measure both diversity and vegetation structure. They may be very long poles, or a series of ten needles on a rack. The poles are marked with bands at height intervals, and, after placing the quadrat at random, the number of contacts with plant material at different heights is recorded, often with data on species and type of structure (e.g. stem, leaf, fruit).

Aquatic communities are sampled by a variety of techniques, depending where in the water column the sample is to be made. Nets and bottles can sample at chosen depths. Plankton are often sampled in bottles and then a smaller 'sub-sample' is taken from this onto microscope slides for counting. Other methods include taking mud-cores for dead diatoms from lake sediments (to study changes including acidification).

## 4.3.2  Vertebrates

Vertebrates present challenges in sampling for a variety of reasons. They may be highly mobile and they may migrate – if so, their density will vary through the year. They are generally sparsely distributed, although some species such as shoaling fish, bats and small mammals may be extremely abundant locally. Any aggregation or social behaviour may complicate the survey. The age of some vertebrates can be determined from their teeth or ear-bones. Some vertebrate populations can be surveyed by 'mark/recapture'. The proportion of marked animals caught in the second or subsequent samples may help in the calculation of the total population, provided the marked animals have mixed randomly amongst the unmarked ones between samples; for social or territorial animals, this will seldom be the case. Vertebrates may also be censused by the signs they leave – for example the tracks and nest-pits left by sea turtles on beaches, the latrines of badgers, or the dung of otters, deer or rhino.

Methods commonly used to give relative or absolute abundances for mammals, reptiles and amphibians include transects, point surveys, and quadrats. Detailed survey methods for birds are described by C. J. Bibby and colleagues, and many of these can be used for mammals. Birds, mammals, reptiles and adult amphibians are frequently recorded by sight or sound along transects. If the observer records the distance to the observed animal from the transect line, then a program called DISTANCE can calculate the absolute density of animals. An observer may also stop at points along a transect, and take a series of quadrat samples. Tape-recording of calls, and subsequent 'call-playback' are

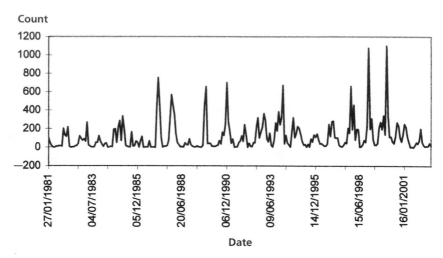

**Fig. 4.6.** Population changes of whiting in the Bristol Channel, England, based on samples from power-station water intakes.
*Source:* P. A. Henderson/Pisces Conservation Ltd.

frequently used to survey for the presence of birds, frogs and bats. Territory size can be used to estimate density and population: territorial encounters were used to estimate the average size of the territory of the Aldabra rail and then, knowing the extent of suitable habitat, an extrapolation was used to estimate its population.

For large mammals, such as elephants, which are dispersed over large ranges, stratified random sampling may be performed. The region to be censused is divided into habitats such as agriculture, open scrub or grassland. Within each of these strata, random transects are sampled by observers flying in a line at a known height, permitting calculation of the absolute density of large animals in open habitats. Relative methods which are used for small mammals include live-trapping, for example in Longworth and Sherman traps. Pitfall trapping may be used for small mammals or amphibians, with problems of bias as discussed for invertebrates below. Drift-fences may be used to lead small animals into buckets. Camera-traps can be used to search for, identify or count animals which trigger the shutter as they pass.

Freshwater fish may be sampled with netting, or electrofishing. Marine fish may be sampled by quadrats, transects, traps and nets. The large cooling water intakes of power-stations have provided data on population changes for many fish and other species in the Bristol Channel (Fig. 4.6). Counts per unit trapping effort are commonly used since true population censuses are so difficult; this has implications for sustainable management (Section 7.2).

## 4.3.3   Invertebrates

Invertebrates present many challenges in survey for conservation – being numerous, species-rich, small, highly seasonal and hard to identify. This is one of the reasons that they are relatively neglected in conservation, despite their great importance in ecosystems. In addition to problems of obtaining absolute counts of invertebrates, there are potential biases due to the activity and seasonality of the organisms. Since invertebrates usually have to be placed under a microscope to identify them with certainty, most methods require a sample to be killed. Conservationists must therefore balance destructive sampling against the benefits of better understanding and management of the community.

Absolute methods for invertebrates include a number of simple techniques that are easy to use, but also techniques that demand more specialised and expensive machinery. Searching quadrats by eye can be used for large invertebrates, such as some snails, and other slow-moving conspicuous species. The artefacts species make, such as webs, galls, and leaf-mines can also often be counted in the appropriate season and weather. Suction-sampling is used in grassland (Fig. 4.7), or on woodland floors, or in aquatic environments. In terrestrial environments, the 'D-vac' is an important machine; placing it twelve times in succession samples one metre square. It is good at collecting small invertebrates such as flies, wasps and some spiders, above the soil surface. Other suction samplers include the Univac, Vortis and Blowvac. These can be used for absolute samples in smaller areas of short grass: for example, after placing a quadrat with high sides, the contents are vacuumed into a net. Aquatic suction samplers have contributed to the evaluation of British marine sites.

Animals can be extracted from soil or litter by their response to warmth, water, light or heat. Soil-cores, bags of litter, or turves, can be gradually heated or floated to encourage animals to move and fall into preservative. Winkler bags, for example, are useful for extracting ants and other litter invertebrates.

The canopy of trees supports very large numbers of invertebrates that can be hard to find. For example, exotic conifer plantations in Britain were presumed to support few species or individuals compared with native broadleafs, because few animals are seen within them. However, this is a sampling bias due to the human eye! If the invertebrates in the canopy are extracted (as C. M. P. Ozanne has done), they prove to be far more abundant and rich than in native woodland, and so the value of conifers for conservation has been reassessed. To extract invertebrates (such as insects and spiders) from the canopy

**Fig. 4.7.** A vacuum sampler for invertebrates, in use on arable field margins at Wytham Farm, Oxford. The net is in the nozzle, and the petrol engine on the back of the operator.
*Photograph:* C. Hambler.

of forest or scrub, knockdown sampling can be used. This requires an operator trained in the use of pesticides. In low vegetation (up to about 20 m tall) a 'mist-blower' can be used. This delivers a strong flow of air carrying droplets of insecticide (and sometimes tracers to check the deposition of the mist). Mist-blowers can also be used on towers to sample biodiversity at different canopy heights. A. Y. C. Chung and V. K. Chey have done this to compare managed and unmanaged tropical high forest in Malaysia. Mist-blowers used by G. C. McGavin revealed high diversity in *Acacia* trees within African savannah (Fig. 4.8). For tall trees, a 'fogger' can be used to create a warm fog of fine insecticide droplets, which rise up into the canopy. These have been used extensively in tropical forests – most famously by Terry Erwin (see Section 1.2.1). The insecticides are short-lived pyrethroids, which do not spread far into other trees, particularly in mist-blowing. Absolute samples are collected when the invertebrates fall into funnels, usually of 1 m$^2$ area.

In freshwater habitats, 'kick-sampling' a standardised area of stream bed involves disturbing the stream-bed by kicking, and then collecting the material

**Fig. 4.8.** Insecticidal knock-down for canopy invertebrates, using a backpack mist-blower and 1 m² funnels. The habitat is savannah in Mkomazi Game Reserve, Tanzania. *Photograph:* Copyright: Royal Geographical Society, London.

in a net as it washes downstream. In marine and estuarine environments, plankton nets, bottom trawls, cores and other devices similar to those for aquatic plants can be used. Coral communities and architecture are sampled in similar ways to terrestrial vegetation.

Relative methods for trapping invertebrates include some very popular techniques that are sometimes used in surveys without an understanding of the sampling biases they create. This is particularly true of pitfall trapping. Pitfall trapping samples animals running on the floor of habitats. Unfortunately, the distance from which they have run is unclear, and this will depend on the activity of the animals – which itself is very sensitive to weather and season. In hot weather, or open exposed habitats, more animals and more species will be trapped. Furthermore, pitfall traps are more effective in those habitats in which animals apparently run more carelessly, such as short grass or bare soil, so biasing richness and abundances in catches towards these habitats. It is only when more individuals or species are found *despite* this bias that it can be interpreted. For example, if comparing long grassland with short grassland, there will be a bias against long grass, and finding more individuals in the traps in long grass would not be a sampling artefact. Similarly, there is probably a bias against dense, dark woodland. Baited pitfall traps are used to sample dung beetles, for example in tropical forests.

Moth-traps exploit the tendency of some moths (but not most of the 'microlepidopetra') to fly to light. An ultraviolet light is often used in association with a collecting surface or trap. Large 'mercury-vapour' traps sample over large areas, whilst small 'Heath traps' sample more locally. There are biases due to activity, and sites to be compared should be sampled in similar weather and seasons. Light will travel further in open habitats such as grasslands than in dense forest, creating bias. Sticky traps, such as coloured cards or sugar solutions on tree trunks, can be used to find certain species when their adults are feeding. Suction sampling from the atmosphere can be used to collect flying insects such as aphids. Flight interceptor traps such as the Malaise trap provide another way of capturing flying insects, which bump into a net and climb or fall into preservative in a collecting tube. A variety of such methods was used for an ecological inventory of savannah at Kora National Reserve, in Kenya.

Any method which attracts organisms risks recording many 'vagrants', or 'tourists' – species not resident in the site. For example, moths may be attracted to a trap from far outside the site under study: a moth-trap run by D. H. Sterling in a suburban English garden for 18 years recorded 970 species – nearly half the British total. When analysing the results, tourist species may have to be downweighted in the sample by analysing only the species for which several individuals have been collected.

## 4.4   Indicator groups and features

As noted in Chapter 3, conservationists often need to do economical and swift surveys of sites. However, it is very difficult to identify the majority of species from a site: most groups of organism are too poorly known, or too time-consuming to work on. Biologists therefore use certain easily studied groups of organism to identify features or changes in a site which may be relevant to many other organisms. Such 'indicator' species or taxa are used as a surrogate for some of the less well known groups, with which they are known – or more often assumed – to share features such as habitat requirements or diversity. Organisms sharing the same feeding specialism ('guild') might be used together even if they are taxonomically unrelated, as with 'saproxylic' (dead wood feeding) flies and beetles. In this section, we will examine the use of such indicators on a smaller scale than in Section 3.4, for the survey of small sets of similar sites or in the monitoring of a site.

It should always be remembered that the use of indicators is a short-cut which carries the high risk that important features are overlooked. Whenever possible, several indicator groups should be used for a fuller picture – each group may respond to different features of the environment. For example, ants, carabid beetles, tiger beetles, spiders and grasshoppers are responsive to many changes, and have been used as indicators in several studies; however, carabids sometimes give contrasting results to ants. The choice of the relevant indicator taxon or taxa will depend on the particular habitat and conservation aims; searches of the biological literature (using electronic databases such as Biological Abstracts) will show what is known of the responses of various species or groups to threats or changes within the region of study.

To be a good indicator species, the species must be easily sampled, identified, and be responsive to changes in habitat conditions. To be a good indicator group, members of the taxon of organisms (such as the dragonflies or the birds) must also be easily identified and sampled, abundant, and must vary in a useful way according to the features of the environment which are of interest. For example, if naturalness is important to the evaluation, then species sensitive to disturbance (such as trampling, hunting or pollution) are helpful. Any group whose richness or abundance has been shown to correlate with a feature of interest can be used as an indicator for that feature, but to be reliable this 'calibration' *must* be performed at many sites in the region and at many levels

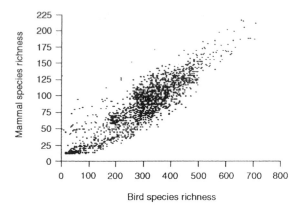

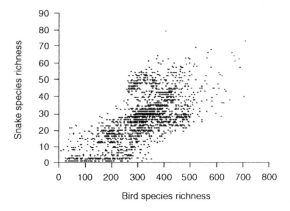

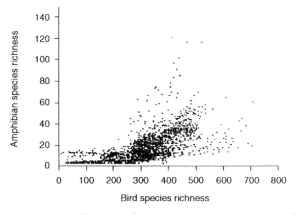

**Fig. 4.9.** Calibration of an indicator group. Birds correlate with other taxa in 1° map grid cells in sub-Saharan Africa.
*Source:* Balmford, A. In: Norris, K. & Pain, D. J. (Eds.) *Conserving Bird Biodiversity* (Cambridge University Press, Cambridge, 2002, pp. 74–104). Reprinted with the permission of Cambridge University Press.

of, for example, naturalness. Figure 4.9 illustrates how the calibration of an indicator group might be done.

The birds are amongst the most widely used of terrestrial indicator groups, particularly at coarse habitat scales. Owing to their great popularity, birds are exceptionally well known biologically. Amongst them, there are many specialist species – for example, those requiring open water, or mudflats, old trees, tall trees, particular fruit or insects. Birds have reached the most remote places on the planet, including the poles, mountain-tops and oceanic islands, and have often evolved specialisms in remote isolated habitats such as flightlessness or gigantism. Some are sensitive to pollution, or fishing. They may need extensive habitats – for example the Philippines eagle needs 20–50 km$^2$ of forest per pair, and the European goshawk may range over some 60 km$^2$. Rare birds have proved particularly fascinating, but even common species of bird receive attention – as observation of the recent decline of the house sparrow in Britain and North America testifies. The taxonomy of birds is relatively stable – there are few revisions of names. Most of the world's species have now been found – less than five new species are being described per year. Yet even for the birds, there is some under-recording of diversity: subtly different 'cryptic species' are still being found by splitting known species – as with four species of chiffchaff separated recently by their songs and DNA. There are now good field-guides to identification in most parts of the world, and atlases of distribution or even *changes* in distribution in some countries.

We shall examine the use of indicators to detect a number of attributes of a site. It is important to note that a site degraded from the perspective of one taxon may be more natural and important from the perspective of another. For example, Epping Forest in Britain has lost most of its lichen flora as a result of pollution, but has nonetheless retained a nationally important saproxylic fauna. Because features like naturalness, hunting and pollution are related, there is some overlap amongst the following sections.

## 4.4.1  Naturalness and continuity

Naturalness relates to the historical continuity of a habitat – the more continuous up to the present, the more natural. A potential measure of naturalness is to consider how much the site would change if human influence were removed. This may be easy to test experimentally in some habitats, such as grasslands, but very hard to test in forests or the ocean where turnover of species is very slow or the natural variability is not clear. Another measure is the magnitude, or frequency, of disturbance that is attributable to people in the area. For example, if a forest or grassland has been cut once by clear-felling it is more natural than one cut many times by coppicing (Section 7.3). A site with invasive exotic species is less natural than one without. A site which has had dynamite fishing is less natural than one which has had occasional hand-line fishing or lobster-potting. However, whilst it is possible to quantify the frequency or intensity of a particular type of disturbance, it is harder to compare sites influenced in different ways – for example, one which has been polluted compared to one which has been fished. Indicators of pollution are discussed in Section 4.4.3, and of hunting in Section 4.4.4.

Continuity is one component of naturalness (Section 3.2.2). It is helpful for conservationists to know as much detail as possible of the history of a site. This may be evident from archaeology. Pollen records, 'sub-fossil' beetles or sub-fossil bones may indicate what has lived on sites until recently. The record depends on suitable conditions for preservation: pollen occurs in acid, waterlogged sites, whereas snails and vertebrate bones survive better in alkaline sites. Human artefacts can give a clue to the history of a site – for example, evidence of habitation or agricultural use. Historical records, such as descriptions and maps, may also show major features such as forests or lakes. The presence of archaeological evidence such as buildings, palm nuts and utensils helped demonstrate that many forests in Central and South America, and West Africa, are secondary, and have grown up on old fields. Similarly, if 'ridge and furrow' structures are found beneath a wood in Britain they indicate that the trees have grown on a former mediaeval field.

Taken together, such evidence can identify sites with relatively little disturbance, or can reveal the nature of disturbances. Sites that are disturbed can then sometimes be compared with less-disturbed sites, to identify types of organism that have changed. In some cases, experimental manipulation may be possible to detect the sensitivities of different groups – as in the Biological Dynamics of Forest Fragments Project in the Amazon (Section 5.4).

Indicator species, chosen using what is known to be a relatively natural control site (Section 3.2.2), may help assess the naturalness of a habitat. A species or group of species that is vulnerable to disturbance can illustrate the lack of such disturbance in a site. The presence of sharks, fragile corals or precious shells might indicate naturalness on a reef, and the presence of pollution-sensitive dragonflies indicates naturalness of a stream.

Continuity of forest on a site can be evident from certain organisms that are easily lost when forest is cleared. Such species can be used as indicators of 'primary forest' (also known as 'old-growth forest'). Britain has been able to develop a system of 'ancient woodland indicators', because fairly good maps were available for woodland cover 400 years ago. Woods known to be 400 or more years old are termed 'ancient'. Many of these sites are also likely to have been wooded back to the time of the 'wildwood' (which pollen records suggest covered much of lowland Britain before the first human clearances some 8000 years ago). Comparison of woodland sites that are known to be at least 400 years old with more recent woodland sites identified those vascular plant species that are predominantly found in ancient woodland. The 100 that are most strongly associated with ancient woodland are termed ancient woodland indicators. These include primrose and wood anemone.

Ancient woodland plants also occur less commonly in other habitats (and in the wetter and cooler north of Britain they do not indicate woodland antiquity). They may occur occasionally in hedges, particularly old ones, and even, like the bluebell, in recent calcareous grassland. They may occur in recent woodland if it is adjacent to ancient sites. However, taken together, they are a useful tool for site survey. The presence of tens of such species at a site arouses interest, and may suggest that a site is ancient even if not recorded on the early maps. These plants may be more abundant in ancient sites because they are relatively sensitive to soil conditions: they indicate naturalness of the soil conditions and the lack of disturbance due to ploughing. They can survive limited grazing, and even canopy removal (as in clear-felling or coppicing), but not agriculture. They often have poor dispersal, with heavy seeds which can survive in a seed-bank for some years and then flower when gaps are created. They generally flower in the spring. Figure 4.10 illustrates the use of ancient woodland plants in surveys.

Amongst the vertebrates, specialists of old growth, or ancient forest, include the northern spotted owl in the Pacific north-west of America, the yellow-bellied glider in Queensland and the white-breasted guineafowl and black mangabey in Africa. However, it may be easier to use historical, archaeological or plant-structural evidence to identify primary forest in such regions.

The continuity of woodland can also be indicated by many specialist groups and species amongst the invertebrates, although these are less well studied. These indicators will often be relatively poor at dispersal, such as flightless moths and beetles. Ancient woodland species can also be specialist herbivores on ancient woodland plants. For example, the light orange underwing moth in Britain feeds on aspen. Moreover, it prefers tall trees on which to lay its eggs, so the presence of the moths indicates not only continuous availability of the food plant but also of a structural feature of the foodplant. Similarly, the termite *Syntermes chaquimyensis* declines in logged Amazonian forests.

Historical continuity of dead wood is required by many ancient woodland invertebrates. Dead wood supports a tremendous diversity of species,

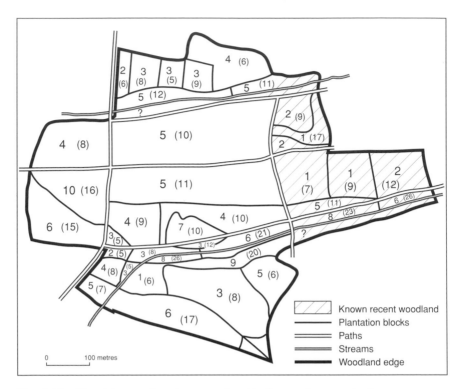

**Fig. 4.10.** The richness of ancient woodland indicator plant species in compartments of a mixed plantation woodland in southern England. The richness of all vascular plant species is given in brackets. Note some small compartments contain more indicators than large ones. Blocks of woodland along streams often have high richness, high indicator richness, and probably higher naturalness. Recent, drier blocks have very few indicators.

and is vital to the natural forest ecosystem. It has been described by Charles S. Elton as 'one of the two or three most important resources in a woodland ecosystem'. Yet it is often removed for fuelwood, for supposed forest hygiene or safety, or to 'tidy up' a woodland (Sections 2.2.6 and 7.3). The presence of saproxylic species, or of species which need mature timber, may indicate lack of disturbance even better than do the ancient woodland plants. Conversely, such species may survive despite major changes to the forest floor (such as grazing or ploughing), provided old trees remain. In Britain, ancient woodland invertebrates are found both in the few relatively natural (and possibly primary) woodlands in Devon and in Scotland, but are also particularly rich or abundant in sites with many trees which have been pollarded for centuries (such as wood-pastures and along riversides). A list is available for the best sites in Britain for the mature-timber specialist beetles: a score has been given to each species dependent on national rarity, and a total score for each site has been obtained by a variety of sampling methods including insecticidal knock-down; this score is an example of an 'Index of Ecological Continuity' (IEC). Similarly, some lichens, bryophytes and fungi have been found to be specialists of old-growth forests. These are often species that need dead wood, or are epiphytic, and have been used in Europe and North America to assess continuity.

Butterflies, a popular group often recorded by using standardised transects, can indicate land-use and climatic changes. Ant nests and termite mounds take a long time to establish, and so can indicate pressures such as ploughing or overgrazing. Abundant large ant nests help indicate ancient grassland in Britain, such as at Aston Rowant National Nature Reserve.

Indicators may be important when they are absent, rather than when they are present. If a species of organism occurs commonly in an area but not in a particular site, then it is possible that it is able to reach that site but cannot survive in the conditions within it. In eastern Africa, A. Espira has found that some ants, such as *Odotomachus assiniensis*, may indicate forest disturbance in that they occur commonly in disturbed and open habitats, but rarely in primary forest. The ants in general are responsive to habitat changes: for example, selective logging in Kenya, Malaysia and elsewhere has been found to influence richness, abundance and species composition. It is possible that sampling ants may help provide a guide to the more diverse and least disturbed areas to prioritise for conservation – at least in tropical forests. Dung beetles also respond to forest fragmentation, logging and edges.

In grassland, many plant species are sensitive to nutrient enrichment: species such as nettle flourish in phosphorous-enriched soil in western Europe, whilst thistles may indicate overgrazing in Europe. Some types of scrub (e.g. *Acacia senegal* ) indicate overgrazing in east African savannah.

## 4.4.2  Richness

It is never possible to get a full list of species from a site, and indeed the number of species changes continuously. Even a large team of people could never identify all the organisms such as microbes, seeds, springtails, nematodes or mites from a site. Indeed, very few of even the larger invertebrates such as insects can be identified in most parts of the world.

Biodiversity, in terms of species richness and genetic diversity, is largely a function of the number of invertebrate species at a site (although greater species diversity may occur amongst the micro-organisms). Even in well-studied regions, time often precludes identification of each specimen to the level of a described or undescribed species. In such cases, the richness of species can be estimated by using guesses as to which specimens look so alike that they are probably individuals of the same species. These are called 'morphospecies' or 'Recognisable Taxonomic Units' (RTUs). These can be used to compare sites where the identification criteria – and preferably those people identifying the organisms – are the same. Unfortunately, it is hard to add up morphospecies richness from separate studies because the overlap between species in the sites is not clear. Morphotyping underestimates the number of species in some taxa, owing to the microscopic subtleties of many differences between species, but overestimates it in others, owing to intraspecific variation. Morphospecies have been used to help identify high-priority sites amongst the tropical dry forests in Costa Rica. 'Parataxonomists' are researchers trained to distinguish morphospecies.

To identify sites with a high diversity of species, a convenient taxon is sometimes used as a presumed indicator of overall diversity. This taxon must itself exhibit a wide range of richness between sites, and this range must be correlated with the range of diversity of at least some other large taxa. If the indicator taxa are chosen to be sensitive to certain attributes of habitats, then they may show how the richness of other taxa with similar specialisms varies. Taxa respond in different ways to different habitat attributes, and so several indicator taxa, each sensitive to different attributes such as plant richness, plant architecture, and disturbance, should ideally be sampled simultaneously to test for consistency in the ranking of sites (for richness) that emerges. Popular groups that might serve as indicators of richness are those with a moderate number of species and that have also been well described by taxonomists. The birds, flowering plants, large mammals, dragonflies and swallowtail butterflies are amongst the best-known taxa that are often presumed to correlate with richness of several other terrestrial groups; unfortunately, very few studies have explicitly calibrated 'indicator' groups against richness of many other taxa in sites or samples. The richness of a number of taxa in 50 Ugandan forests was found not to be congruent, and Section 3.2.3 discusses this problem further.

Monitoring changes in calcareous grassland at Wytham in Britain, C. W. D. Gibson and colleagues found different groups of invertebrates have different sensitivities. Leaf-mining insects (which feed inside the plant leaf) were surveyed in 1 m$^2$ quadrats, and responded to the level and season of sheep-grazing. Leaf-hopping bugs (sampled by D-vac) are known to be similar. Spiders, by contrast (counted by their webs and by D-vac), responded far more strongly to changes in vegetation structure than to plant species composition, and should indicate the quality and richness of other taxa with similar structural and microclimatic requirements.

In temperate regions, butterflies have attracted attention as indicators of richness, being conspicuous and popular. However, this is highly problematic because there are relatively few species, they are highly seasonal, they represent predominantly herbivorous species, and they generally need a lot of sunshine. They are also large and bright, and indeed this very feature (which makes them popular) illustrates that they are atypical of invertebrates more generally. For example, butterflies will not be very sensitive to many very important variables such as the humidity, hydrology, or the amount of dead wood. T. H. Ricketts and colleagues found them poor indicators of moth diversity in Colorado. Butterfly diversity increases with some types of disturbance, such as making clearings in tropical forests.

As noted earlier, the ants are a potentially important indicator group. They are massively abundant and important in many ecosystems in the tropics (comprising up to half of the invertebrate abundance in some forest canopies). In some parts of the world, they have received a lot of attention from taxonomists; however, identifying the various species demands an understanding of the different specialised castes (which have such different shapes and sizes they might appear distinct species in a sample). They have been found to co-vary in richness with some other taxa, but can not be assumed to do so in most habitats.

The vascular plants are often used as indicators of site quality when other taxa are poorly known. It is often assumed that the richness of flowering plants will correlate with the richness of other species. However, despite many claims to the contrary, plants are *not* good indicators of overall biodiversity. Indeed, in some regions there may be an inverse relationship between the number of species of plant and the overall diversity – so high plant richness could sometimes indicate low site quality. Many conservationists erroneously talk of 'rich' or 'diverse' sites, when they should say 'rich in flowering plants', since the site may be low in richness of invertebrates per square metre (as with short calcareous grasslands or hay meadows) and thus not rich overall.

Flowering plants are unusual organisms in that, as 'autotrophs', they generally need high light levels for photosynthesis, whereas many invertebrates need shelter from the desiccating light. A moist microclimate may be far more important to invertebrates than to plants. Most animals are not specialist herbivores, so richness of plant species is less important to them than plant architecture or total plant biomass – as T. R. E. Southwood and colleagues showed for insects and R. H. MacArthur showed for forest birds. In terrestrial foodchains, approximately 70% of the energy goes into animals via the decomposers – which live off *dead* plant material – and decomposers are less sensitive to the type of plant than are the herbivores. Furthermore, plants are generally more species-rich in nutrient-poor soils (the 'Paradox of Enrichment', Section 7.3.1), whereas invertebrates and microbes may find more niches and nutrients where there is deep litter and abundant dead wood on the soil.

There are far more people competent to identify plants than invertebrates. However, many tropical plants are harder to sample, and there are relatively few botanists with tropical expertise. Similarly, there are few who can identify mosses, lichens and liverworts ('cryptograms') – these are important in many habitats, and many of the plants in polar regions may be cryptograms.

Ornithologists have data on the distributions, behaviour, and population changes of the vast majority of bird species. Identification of the sites with a high species richness of birds is a relatively easy sampling task. Sites that are notably rich in birds are usually rich in other groups – as with Tambopata in Peru or Bialoweiza forest in Poland – whilst few sites that are rich in birds are poor in all other taxa. A study in Poland found that woodpeckers are good indicators of the general richness of forest birds, and this sort of calibration needs to be performed elsewhere. The correlation of richness of birds with other taxa is illustrated in Figs. 4.9 and 5.7.

Richness in freshwater habitats and marine habitats is harder to measure than on land, owing to the subjectivity in the way people draw boundaries in these habitats and to problems in identification. Measuring richness of species in aquatic environments requires knowledge of invertebrates and fish. The invertebrates which are best-known are the Molluscs and the Crustacea. The fish are by far the richest and least well known vertebrate group, and many new species are being discovered each year. In identification of the richest coral reefs (Section 3.4), 3235 species of lobsters, corals, reef fish, and snails (cones, cowries and volutes) were used as indicators, with general but not full congruence across taxa.

## 4.4.3  Pollution

Pollution can be monitored by using species that are particularly sensitive to the pollutant, or species that bioaccumulate the pollutant (whether or not it harms them). Species that are sensitive to the pollutant may be affected for a number of reasons. They may be poisoned directly. For example, sulphur dioxide ($SO_2$) pollution (Section 2.3.3) kills certain lichens (such as *Lobaria* species) very quickly, and lichens have been recognised as indicators since the 1800s. In the aquatic environments, acidification can be detected through a decline in a number of groups that are known to be sensitive (Section 2.3.3).

Certain organisms may be good 'early-warning' indicators of pollution. For example fish, and fish-eating birds and mammals near urban centres, are particularly at risk of pollutants, and can be used to monitor contamination. Similarly, top-predators can be indicators of pesticides such as DDT (Section 2.3.3). Tissue samples can be used to detect pollution, as with swans in Britain suffering from lead poisoning. Toxins can be sequestered in the tissues of long-lived organisms, such as whales, or in corals, allowing the levels of pollution to be examined over recent history. For example, in the Chagos archipelago, corals and land crabs had virtually undetectable levels of petroleum compounds, sewage, metals and pesticides, indicating their pristine state in this regard; hermit crabs in Indonesia had pesticide levels 100–1000 times those in the Chagos.

Some scientists believe amphibians may be particularly sensitive to pollution, given their permeable skins and complex development. Amphibians are declining globally, for unknown reasons. Amphibian decline in upland Britain has been linked to acidification of breeding ponds.

Freshwater environments in developed countries are often well enough known to have water-quality indexes based on standardised biological assays (Box 4.1). Knowledge of which groups are the most sensitive to pollution (such as dragonflies and mayflies) allows a grade to be given for water quality.

Climate change related to pollution might be evident in the seasonality (phenology) of well-known species, such as birds in Britain (Section 4.6) Birds in the Arctic may be found to indicate sudden shifts of the community as expected from climate change. Remote sensing by satellites may be needed to monitor changes in marine phytoplankton in response to increased ultraviolet B (UVB) levels following stratospheric ozone depletion.

Increases in the abundance of some species can also be revealing. For example, acidification of tree bark in Europe has lead to an increase in the pollution-indicating alga *Pleurococcus viridis*. Nutrient enrichment due to acid rain is altering the balance of *Sphagnum* moss species in upland bogs in Britain.

## 4.4.4 Hunting and trampling

Species that are particularly prone to hunting, yet are relatively easily recorded, can be used as indicators of human influence and hence naturalness. Harvesting of some plants (as in selective logging) is a form of hunting.

---

**Box 4.1**
**The use of indicator groups in freshwater assessment**

Groups such as the mayflies (Ephemeroptera), stoneflies (Plecoptera), caddisflies (Trichoptera), flies (Diptera), beetles (Coleoptera) and dragonflies (Odonata) are found in freshwater almost throughout the world. Some of these are very sensitive to changes such as eutrophication and oxygen depletion – showing either population reduction or population booms. It is relatively easy to sample these groups from the bottom of the stream (e.g. by kick-sampling). Based on the abundances of the groups in sites of known pollution levels, indices have been drawn up for regions such as North America, or Britain, which can be used to compare watercourses in a watershed. The index provides a rough synthesis of the biological quality of the water in terms of pollution.

In North America, the Benthic index of Biological Integrity (the B-IBI) was developed by J. R. Karr and colleagues. The relative abundances of groups, such as filter feeders and predators, and the overall richness of the site, are combined in a formula to give an overall value which is calibrated against the most natural sites. A simpler alternative is the Ephemeroptera–Plecoptera–Trichoptera Index (the EPT), which is the total number of morphospecies of these taxa in the sample. These animals are very intolerant of pollution. However, this is only suitable in those regions of the world where they are naturally species-rich, and where good sites can be found for calibration. An Index of Biological Integrity for Fish has also been used successfully in parts of the Americas where there are many fish species. Similar indices are now being developed for terrestrial arthropods in North America.

---

Very often the top predators are removed relatively quickly when people are in close contact with wildlife (Chapter 2). Loss of top predators may lead to changes in those ecosystems that are subject to 'top-down' control of the abundance of competitive organisms. For example, removal of the predatory starfish *Piaster ochraceus* leads to the spread of mussels and thence a lower diversity of invertebrates and algae on reefs. Similarly, overharvesting of the triton mollusc and of large fish may encourage crown-of-thorns outbreaks on reefs. Such changes may be used to monitor the impact of removal of predators.

Sharks and other large predatory fish can serve as good indicators of the absence of fishing. For example, in the Chagos islands, a seven-fold decrease in sharks occurred when illegal shark-fin fishing increased. Similarly, on Aldabra, sharks and grouper declined during a lapse in wardening. In the case of relatively well-managed fisheries, as in New Zealand, the level of catch per unit fishing effort is recorded accurately and can be used to monitor certain changes in the system (Section 7.2).

Selectively or lightly logged forest can be detected from the stumps of certain hardwood trees such as mahogany, and, conversely, well-protected or primary forest may be indicated by the presence of species of high commercial value – as with the Ceylon ebony, which is virtually confined to reserves in Sri Lanka.

Any species with slow reproductive and growth rates, including many large predators but also species such as the elephants, ebonies and whales, may be useful as indicators. Certain corals grow slowly and are easily overharvested for ornaments (e.g. black corals). Brain coral colonies may live over 1000 years, but are easily destroyed for construction materials. The levels of damage due to trampling and to anchor-damage on coral reefs may be evident from broken corals. Permanent quadrats can be used on land to monitor trampling of plants. Trampling can also be detected by placing 'litter-bags' on the ground, into which spiders crawl. E. Duffey demonstrated that bags from more-trampled sites support fewer spiders.

## 4.5  Rapid Biodiversity Assessment (RBA)

In many cases of immediate threat to the environment, a shortage of time and money, and the lack of taxonomic expertise, preclude a detailed survey of more than a very few organisms. This is particularly true in developing countries in the tropics. In such cases, a small team comprising experts in certain indicator groups can be brought in to help assess the best sites, or the likely impacts of development, through quick and simple methods in a 'Rapid Biodiversity Assessment' (RBA). The team for an RBA almost always includes a botanist – but presently there are only a few in the world able to do such surveys, and many of these are specialised to have expert knowledge of a particular geographical region, such as the Neo-tropics. An ornithologist is often present – many of these can work widely in the world, owing to the manageable number of bird species, although familiarity with the calls of some species may again require specialisation within regions. Other groups that are often recorded in RBA include the primates and other large mammals, and the reptiles and amphibians. Habitat architecture such as dead wood may provide information on naturalness.

A survey of Wapoga River Area of Indonesia, as part of the Rapid Assessment Programme of threatened sites organised by Conservation International, found the area to be near pristine; the survey also found 94 species new to science (including aquatic insects, ants, fishes, frogs, lizards and plants).

RBA is increasingly being used in EIA (Section 4.7) for large or controversial developments. Given their necessarily superficial nature, the failure to detect features of interest often does *not* preclude their being present, but the discovery of features of interest in a rapid survey suggests more will be found in more-detailed survey, and this information may be sufficient to justify changes to development plans.

## 4.6   Long-term and large-scale monitoring

There is increasing interest in long-term changes in the environment. Some processes, such as climate change or pollution, may not have conspicuous immediate effects. Instead, it is necessary to examine data collected over many years to detect statistically significant trends which can be linked to conservation problems. Furthermore, it is recognised that conservation may require management of large areas, involving mapping and monitoring over whole ecosystems or even the whole planet. It may be necessary to monitor both at large spatial and temporal scales to detect changes such as deforestation. Standardisation of methods may prove difficult over long timeframes, because of changes in technology, and so new methods need to be calibrated carefully against old ones to stop 'drift' in methodology. New long-term programmes, such as the Environmental Change Network in Britain, have been designed to minimise methodological drift.

People may notice changes during their lifetime, but not realise how much the environment has changed over longer scales – for example the size that flocks of birds such as passenger pigeons reached, the numbers of sea turtles or seals on beaches, or the length that fish used to reach. This results in a 'shifting base-line', which underestimates the amount of environmental change over centuries or longer. Consistent long-term monitoring can reduce this bias in perception. Permanent quadrats, fixed-point photographic surveys, and filmed evidence can be particularly compelling.

The data required for long-term monitoring are particularly rare, whilst the huge datasets required for large-scale monitoring require specialist knowledge. Their great value is illustrated in detection of the influence of climate change, as in Table 4.2. Long-term data sets may reveal patterns that were not anticipated when the study was set up, such as ozone depletion or climate change. In the USA, the National Science Foundation established the Long Term Ecological Research Network (LTER) in 1980 to foster collaborative research and monitoring on long timescales and large spatial scales.

For research at large spatial scales, advances in techniques such as remote sensing and GIS are proving helpful. Satellite observations and aerial photography complement each other, the former now approaching the resolution of the latter. There is a compromise between the frequency at which a site

Table 4.2 *Examples of the value of long-term studies and historical observations*

| Species or region | Uses or discoveries (with date of first observations) |
| --- | --- |
| Serengeti: large herbivores | Long-term equilibrium through density dependence, despite climatic variability (1959) |
| Silver-studded blue, England | Development of metapopulation model, conservation genetics (1942) |
| Plants and ungulates, Swiss National Park | Density dependence and long-term equilibrium of chamois; alpine ecology (1918) |
| Baja Colorado, Panama | Decline in richness on isolation and reduction in area; vegetation richness (1923) |
| Lady Park Wood, England | Development of woodland without management (1944) |
| Monks Wood, England | Influence of various management treatments (1963) |
| Fixed vegetation quadrats, Wytham, England | Impact of deer in preventing regeneration of trees (1973) |
| Biological Dynamics of Forest Fragments Project, Brazil | Declines in richness and specialists: edge effects in forest fragments (1979) |
| Virgin Jungle Reserves, Malaysia | Natural dynamics of rainforests (1950) |
| Great tits, Wytham, England | Nesting shifted 12 days earlier over a 27 year period: influence of climate change (1947) |
| Edith's checkerspot butterfly, California | Range of species has moved 92 km in 100 years: influence of climate change (c. 1900) |
| Nineteen bird species, Fairfield Township, Wisconsin, USA | Migration date/first song of has advanced on average 4.4 days in 61 years (1936) |
| Flowering of 36 plant species, Wisconsin, USA | Advanced on average 8 days in 61 years: influence of climate change (1936) |
| Europe | Plant growing season extended c. 11 days in 34 years: influence of climate change (1959) |
| Alaskan Arctic | Increased shrub cover (1948) |
| Southern California Blight | Northern fish species decrease, southern species decline, in relation to climate (1974) |

Table 4.2 (*cont.*)

| Species or region | Uses or discoveries (with date of first observations) |
|---|---|
| Fish, Bristol Channel, England | Trophic interactions, community change, climate influences (1980) |
| Zooplankton and intertidal organisms, English Channel | Increase in warm-water species related to rising sea temperature (1920s) |
| Mute swan, Thames, England | Population dynamics, pollution (1823) |
| Moths and bugs, Rothamsted Insect Survey, Britain | Phenology and abundance in relation to climate and agriculture (1965) |
| Grassland, Park Grass Experiment, Rothamsted, England | Plant community changes in relation to nutrient inputs and levels, and rainfall (1856) |
| North American Breeding Bird Survey | Changes in breeding bird populations in America and Canada (1966) |
| Christmas Bird Count | Changes in winter bird populations in America and Canada (1900) |
| Common Bird Census | Changes in breeding bird populations in Britain; national red listing (1962) |

is recorded and the area which can be included in the image: in general, the finer the resolution required, the less often a satellite will record an area. The images may not be in natural colours, and indeed may be in wavelengths invisible to the human eye. Images may be processed mathematically (by 'Fourier Analysis') to discriminate and map habitats based on their seasonal changes. Table 4.3 gives some examples of the remote sensing tools currently available, and their applications.

A fundamental feature of satellite images is that they require expert 'ground-truthing' to help interpret them. Selected sites are chosen, visited and sampled to see how the colours in the image correspond to vegetation or other features on the ground: this is a form of calibration. Because ground-truthing is often difficult, it may be easier to detect changes in images than to know why they are occurring. To map habitats, each unit of the images (or 'pixel') may be 'classified' into vegetation types using the techniques in Section 4.2.1.

## 4.7   Environmental Impact Assessment (EIA)

Environmental Impact Assessment (EIA) includes many disciplines, such as health and pollution, but here we consider only the ecological component of an

Table 4.3 *Some remote sensing applications*

| Mapping | Example | Platform |
|---|---|---|
| Desertification and erosion | Sahel | Small plane |
| Human and livestock population growth | Sahel | Small plane |
| Habitat change | Pastoralism in East African savannah | Satellite |
| Forest fires | Indonesia; Amazonia | Satellite |
| Deforestation | Madagascar; Amazonia; Indonesia | Various |
| Clear-felling | Siberia | Satellite |
| Agricultural expansion near roads | Brazil | Aircraft |
| Loss of wilderness areas | Global | Satellite |
| Sea-mounts and troughs | Potential areas of marine endemicity | Satellite |
| Coral reefs and degradation | Global | Various |
| Ozone depletion | Antarctica and Arctic | Satellite |
| Sea-level | Global climate change | Satellite |
| Ice sheet extent | Global climate change | Satellite |
| Energy consumption at night | Global | Satellite |

EIA (or EcIA). An EIA is undertaken to assess the impact of a development, or to choose the least-damaging alternative from a range of development options. For example, would a particular dam or mine harm wildlife? Where should the hotel, or the road, or the new town be built?

The methodology for ecological EIAs is similar to Rapid Biodiversity Assessment (Section 4.5), but may include more or fewer taxa, depending on the habitat and impact. The sites that might be damaged are considered for their quality, using selected criteria from the list in Section 3.2, and methods described above. The EIA should aim to put the importance (quality) of the site in context – is it internationally or nationally important, or only locally valuable? Does it have very high-quality species (Section 3.1)? Understanding the context will require comparison of the quality of the site with sites of known quality in the region, and comparison of the quality of species on it with others in the region.

An EIA therefore involves a selective survey and inventory, followed by an assessment of whether the species and habitats are likely to be adversely impacted by the development – through, for example, loss of habitat, pollution, or disturbance. This will require knowledge of the biology of the species or habitats such as their sensitivity to pollution, and their 'Minimum Viable

Populations' (Section 6.3) or minimum habitat sizes (Section 5.4). Selected vulnerable species (such as great crested newts or rare succulents) may be sought intensively with appropriate methods. Indicator groups may be particularly important. The impact of the development or activity can then be predicted based on experience elsewhere – or if not a precautionary approach should be adopted. EIA will only be possible at the appropriate season(s) for surveys, unless there are already good biological records for a site.

Given the limitations of EIAs, and particularly the speed at which they usually have to be performed (often by expensive consultants), it would be far better to be pro-active than reactive. It is sensible to have mapped the important areas in a region long before any development is planned in detail, so that the most valuable sites are eliminated in the earliest stages of the process. Following an EIA, and approval of a development or activity, the site should ideally be monitored for decades – to be confident that the impacts have been detected or that any attempted mitigation has been successful (Sections 8.5 and 8.7).

The logic of an EIA can also be used to help choose and monitor management methods which, as we shall see in the next chapter, can make big changes in the landscape.

# 5

# Management of natural habitats

Management is a central feature of conservation, and an enormous subject. This chapter outlines the general features of management of natural systems, and gives some examples for major biomes of the world.

Management is required to maintain the features of interest of an area, which have been identified by the methods in Chapter 3. For strict nature reserves this is often a protection of naturalness against threats to the species and to the integrity of the habitats in the reserve. In highly natural sites, the threats often come from outside the site, but the more human influence there has been in a site the more management may be required within the site itself. Naturalness may be defined as the lack of human influence, or as how little the habitat would change if there were no people there (Sections 3.2.2 and 4.4.1). We should be careful not to 'overmanage' sites - and so do more harm than the threats we are trying to prevent. Overmanagement is a risk when we know little about the natural processes of a site. It is also a waste of effort.

The reason for 'detaching Man from Nature' through such definitions is that the human species, through consciousness and prediction, is alone in being able to manage the natural factors that would control its population (Section 1.3.1). Management of the biosphere will be essential to compensate for the power we have developed to overexploit it.

Management to maintain natural areas permits examination of how ecosystems work in our absence. In this way, we might learn how better to manage systems for both wildlife and people. Management will affect people in and near the reserve, requiring their integration into the management plan or compensation for loss of resources; such issues are discussed in Chapters 7 and 9.

**Fig. 5.1.** Overview of a management planning process.
*Source:* Adapted from Bangda, *Technical Manual for Preparation of a Provincial Coastal and Marine Management Strategy* (English version, Marine Evaluation and Planning Project (MREP) Report, Government of Indonesia, Jakarta, 1996).

As we saw in Chapter 3, few areas on the planet are completely natural. For example, human influence can be expected anywhere that is affected by climate. Even the ocean depths are not pristine: currents are changing owing to warming of the surface waters, and they may also be robbed of suitable organic detritus because of fishing in the surface waters. However, the magnitude of human influences may be relatively small in some areas, or small in relation to natural variations due to the physical environment. Perhaps under stones in the heart of Antarctica, or deep under the North Pole, or on the tops of mountains, there may be a few habitats where human influence is so tiny as to be effectively absent – although even in such sites ozone depletion may have some impact. No area on the planet is completely isolated from all others, and none can escape from influences on adjacent habitats. Terrestrial ecosystems exchange matter and energy with the freshwater systems, and with the oceans; indeed, the division of the Earth into these realms is somewhat subjective, but convenient. In theory, then, any site on the Earth might be threatened and require management.

---

## Box 5.1
## Management plans

Management plans vary, but ideally include some common features. An overview summarises the plan and the evaluation that led to protection. The plan states the management aims very clearly and explicitly. There are descriptions and maps of abiotic features (location, geology, hydrology, climate) and biotic features (ecosystem type, habitat types, species lists). Outstanding features (high-quality species and habitats) are identified and, if possible, mapped separately. A map divides the site into management compartments according to habitats and logistics. There is an analysis of general threats and a listing of potentially damaging activities in each compartment. Legal issues are considered for each compartment, including occupancy and access, safety, protected species, and exploitation rights. Management requirements and permissible uses for each compartment are identified. Data deficiencies for each compartment are identified, and the overall research and monitoring requirements are determined. Staffing requirements are determined. Contingency plans are made for emergencies such as pollution events. The plans are costed and expenditure monitored.

Tracing-paper overlays of different features, such as site history, plant communites, and individual management activities help to integrate the plan. Increasingly, Geographical Information Systems (GIS) and associated databases are used to map and monitor sites, with different layers for each feature and activity. Plans are reviewed on a regular basis appropriate to the region – for example every five years, or after a major change.

Ownership of reserves may be in private hands, and a management agreement is drawn up between government and landowner. Plans for each British SSSI identify a list of 'potentially damaging operations', which it is illegal to undertake on the site.

---

In this chapter we will first examine selected habitats, and then consider the problem of fragmentation. We then consider aquatic habitats. Since much management of natural habitats is essentially management of threats, the chapter expands on Chapter 2. The protection of specific species is examined in Chapter 6, whilst Chapter 8 illustrates how management may help to restore a degree of 'naturalness' to sites. Once the general aims of management are clear (Fig. 5.1), 'management plans' are drawn up to organise management on a site (Box 5.1).

Many habitats that at first sight appear natural are in fact 'semi-natural', meaning they are a product of a long period of human intervention in the system. The forms of management required for such habitats are discussed in Chapter 7. In the present chapter, disturbed (and possibly semi-natural) habitats such as many African and South American savannahs are considered since they are structurally similar to natural habitats, as is evident from the presence of specialist grassland species such as cheetah and guanaco. Some of the principles of fragmentation also apply to semi-natural habitats. It is important to note that management may be required in a site that is apparently natural, if it has become isolated during fragmentation. The isolation itself may create edge effects (Section 5.4.2), which render the fragment less natural. The isolation of reserves, and the frequently abrupt changes at their edges, are evident from Fig. 5.2.

It is also important to recognise that protection of a reserve may involve management of sites *remote from* the reserve itself. Management of problems related to climate change requires management on the scale of the entire planet, including manipulation of greenhouse gas production or storage, and legislation such as the Kyoto Protocol (Section 9.2). Reductions in vehicle emissions are a form of management. Similarly, the protection of polar regions from ozone depletion requires management (prevention) of CFC production. The management of exploitation and trade may require legal instruments such as CITES (Chapters 6 and 9) and includes enforcement at customs points in countries of origin and destination. The management of reefs may involve prevention of siltation through protection of distant watershed forests, which prevent erosion of soil into rivers. The management of natural areas involves many inter-linked issues, including social, political, economic, legal and ethical factors, in a world where human influence is increasing throughout.

This chapter examines the management of reserves that is required *once the primary aim of nature conservation has been established* for these areas, and considers the ideal management to protect biodiversity for the *long-term* benefit of human populations. Inevitably, this will lead to problems for many people in the short term, because their exploitation of the environment is curtailed. This should be ethically defensible if the need to protect biodiversity for the Earth's current and future population has been convincingly established (Chapter 1).

## 5.1 Continental biomes

### 5.1.1 Grasslands

Grasslands fascinate people. Many find the expansive landscape deeply satisfying. Archaeology, particularly the pollen record, suggests that a few thousand

(a)

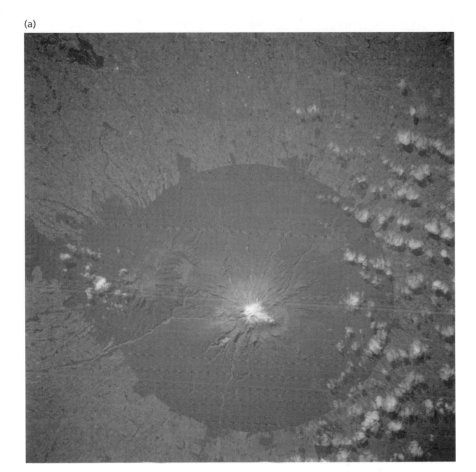

**Fig. 5.2.**   Some influences of fences. (a) A space-shuttle image shows how a fence has protected the national park on the top of Mt Egmont, New Zealand, from grazing and agriculture. (b) Elephant populations are high in the Mana Pools National Park, Zimbabwe, on the right of this boundary fence, causing loss of trees, growth of spiny scrub, and other degradation within the park. (c) Introduced goats were excluded from parts of Isla Santiago (Galapagos) in 1998, permitting recovery of native vegetation (left).
*Sources:* (a) Image courtesy of Earth Sciences & Image Analysis Laboratory, NASA, reference STS110-726-6. (b) Photograph: copyright D. H. M. Cumming (1996). (c) Photograph: copyright Marc Patry (2000).

(b)

(c)

**Fig. 5.2.** (*cont.*)

years ago grasslands naturally occurred in many parts of the planet. It is likely that over a quarter of the natural land vegetation was grassland. There are many areas (such as Madagascar and Britain) where their natural extent is debated. Grasslands are the natural climatic climax community where there is regular disturbance or stress which prevents scrub or tree cover developing. Low rainfall and fire may promote grasslands, as in Southern Africa, the Asian steppe, Australia, the American prairies, the Llanos and east Africa. Floods maintain some grassland. Low temperatures or high winds, as in the sub-Antarctic islands and on high mountains, may also preclude scrub or forest cover. Sporadic disturbance, or climate changes, may maintain 'shifting mosaics' of patches of grass and forest, in dynamic equilibrium, as with some savannahs. Grasslands were often grazed by native large herbivores, but the relative importance of grazing, fire and climate in the origin of grasslands are controversial and may vary with region.

The interaction between herbivores and climate is complex, and we may never fully understand it because most grasslands have now been so heavily influenced by people. Does climate create grassland, which herbivores exploit, or do herbivores create grassland, that then comes to have its own rainfall and fire regime? This uncertainty provides an argument for the conservation of some relatively natural grassland reserves as control sites for ecological examination of the effects of grazing or fire. Palaeobiology and dendrochronology may be useful in estimating the natural fire frequency.

Owing to frequent stresses, and their structural simplicity, grasslands are not highly diverse habitats, and support only 5% of all bird and mammal species and 6% of the threatened birds. Since grasslands have always been dynamic geographically, the species within them tend to have large geographical ranges and be able to tolerate some disturbed and modified habitats.

Grasslands have been extensively modified and degraded for a number of reasons. In particular, they are often on flat, fertile plains, which are easy to hunt, farm and build on. The Eurasian and North American grasslands supported herds of large herbivores, which moved north as the ice-cap retreated some 12 000 years ago, but a number of species of herbivore are now extinct (Section 2.2.1). Livestock, particularly sheep, may have replaced some native herbivores since pastoralism began over 10 000 years ago, but it is possible that forest has replaced grassland in some areas following the Pleistocene extinction. Large areas of prairie were maintained by fire by Native Americans, to favour bison. Owing to the extinction of large herbivores, it may be impossible to identify or retain the wholly natural disturbance regime, but the regime before European expansion might be taken as a target. Most, if not all, grassland in northern Europe is semi-natural (Chapter 7), and this may be true for Indian savannah.

Management of natural grasslands in general will require management of human encroachment, hunting, and fire. Natural shifts in the ranges of grasslands, and climate change, may be problematic in those areas that are densely occupied by people and livestock. Protection may be aided by highlighting flagship and umbrella species. These include various bustard species, saiga, steppe eagle, and demoiselle crane on the steppe, the plains-wanderer of Australia, the vicuna and bison in the Americas, and the charismatic megafauna of African savannahs.

The most extensive natural grasslands were probably the steppes of Eurasia, with associated herds of saiga antelope; however, only fragments of the steppe remain in an agricultural matrix, and management mainly involves protection against encroachment and poaching. The tallgrass prairies of North America have been almost eliminated, whilst the shortgrass prairies have been reduced to some 30% of their pre-European range. Most remnant prairies are as yet unprotected. Management of prairie includes removal of exotic species such as teasel and buckthorn by hand-pulling, cutting, ring-barking or herbicide, and burning on the 'natural' 1–5 year interval to kill exotic and woody species.

The African 'savannah' habitats are extensive grassland plains with varying degrees of scrub or tree cover, often in a shifting mosaic. These can be managed for ecotourism, owing to their beautiful landscapes and numerous, diverse and impressive large species. Ecotourism can be a disturbance to species such as cheetah, if unregulated, but can help reduce threats from poaching and livestock if the tourists require a 'wilderness experience'. Another form of tourism, game-hunting, is a controversial way to manage savannah species (Sections 1.1 and 6.4), and needs careful management not to deplete stocks, distort sex-ratios, cause suffering, or contribute to the evolution of features such as small tusks in elephants. Management of such hunting obviously requires zoning to separate it from other tourist uses, as with Mkomazi Game Reserve in Tanzania.

Hunting of the remaining large herbivores is a widespread threat to grassland systems, and must be regulated on reserves. The herds of tens of millions of North American bison were reduced to a few hundred animals in the 30 years following the completion of the railroad link to the Pacific in 1869. A few thousand now survive. Similarly, the saiga was reduced from millions to about 1000 by 1945. During the lifetime of the USSR, the saiga were relatively closely protected from hunting, and recovered to about two million, but have recently been hunted heavily again – particularly males. The huge herds of pampas deer reported by early explorers in Argentina have been almost exterminated by hunting and disease. Conversely, kangaroo populations may have increased as the Australian landscape was deforested. Management of the key species within savannahs may have to be quite intensive and severe, as with anti-poaching measures (Section 6.4.1). Maintaining elephant abundance is particularly important in the dynamics of the grassland–forest transition. Reductions in elephant density can lead to scrubbing-over and afforestation, whilst overgrazing by elephants or livestock can lead to the vegetation being dominated by unpalatable scrub (Fig. 5.2(b)).

Management of the density and composition of the herbivore communities will be required when native species have been depleted or extirpated, or when livestock grazing is permitted within the 'reserve'. I suggest (controversially) that domestic livestock *inevitably* have an impact on savannah (for the reasons given in Sections 2.2.5, 7.1 and 7.3), and must be carefully managed in the vicinity of reserves. Fencing may be required to exclude livestock, or a quota system used to limit livestock numbers (as in the Ngorongoro Crater in Tanzania). Fencing and other linear features may present problems on grassland where the key species are migratory (Section 2.7); the Kuki fence of the Central Kalahari Game Reserve killed numerous migrating wildebeest. Conversely, it is relatively easy to maintain fencing in grassland. Fencing may protect against diseases and poachers, help keep threatened wildlife in the reserve, or keep in wildlife which would cause disputes with neighbouring settlements (such as elephants in Tsavo, Kenya). Electric fencing has proved relatively effective in Tsavo and in southern Africa, including some private game sanctuaries.

Protection of grassland may include management of the fire risk from people in and around a protected area. There is controversy over the relative merits of management favouring frequent low-temperature fires versus infrequent hot fires. Whilst natural fires may occur rarely from lightning strikes, many fires are now set by local people to clear scrub, to encourage forage growth for livestock, to smoke out bees and for amusement. Firebreaks and pre-emptive burning may be required in some cases. Fire helped maintain Australian grasslands in pre-Aboriginal times, but since the arrival of people, fire intensity has increased, and grassland has expanded at the expense of forest. However, grazing by livestock such as sheep (to which the native flora has no defences) leads rapidly to degradation of Australian grassland, and fencing is required to protect it. The management of fire on relict North American prairies has also been the subject of much research. Management by fire is potentially highly destructive and on large sites is ideally left to nature, but if this proves insufficient to maintain the habitat (without sufficient herbivores) then it should usually be performed in rotation, as for semi-natural grasslands

(Section 7.3.3). Erosion and salinification have been problematic in grassland reserves in the steppe and Australia, and have been managed by planting trees as shelter-belts and to lower the water table.

## 5.1.2   Forests

Most of the world's forests have been modified far from their natural state, since most are in regions with a climate comfortable for people. Most forests have lost species in the megafaunal extinction (Section 2.2.1), have received introduced species, or have at some stage suffered cultivation, grazing, logging or clear-felling. The most natural continental forests are probably those of boreal Asia, such as the taiga of Russia. These expansive forests still have less extensive fragmentation than the forests of the Americas, Europe and Australia. The most natural of tropical forests are probably relict areas of mangrove, or are on islands with low human population density. In contrast, it is possible that most of the forest of the Amazon, Borneo and West Africa is secondary forest, which has grown up on sites cleared by thousands of years of rotational slash-and-burn cultivation. Certain palms, lianas, fruit or bamboo species, and charcoal deposits, can indicate past human clearance. In West Africa, archaeology reveals old field systems and habitation in areas once considered pristine primary forest, such as Okomo in Nigeria. The impact of the extinction of the megafauna of the Amazon is unknown.

Management of a natural forest for conservation should be highly protective and precautionary. The relict areas of the Earth's primary (old-growth) forest are irreplaceable and outstandingly important. Management may be needed to protect the extent of the forest, the structure of the forest, or the species composition – and these features will often interact. Hunting can be as serious a problem as direct habitat destruction – it will impoverish forests in the long term, and might prevent their recovery (Section 8.3). Hunting has left some isolated forests such as Bioko in Cameroon almost devoid of primates – the 'empty forest' syndrome. Poaching has nearly exterminated elephant in several west African reserves, even in World Heritage Sites such as the Tai forest in the Ivory Coast. Management of hunting can be very difficult in thick forest – as the problems of protection of mountain gorillas in the Parc des Volcanes illustrate: it is very labour intensive to seek wire snares, or people with guns, within forest reserves.

Fire management is a very controversial issue – particularly in Australia and North America. Management of 'semi-natural' forests with a long history of burning by tribal people, such as most *Eucalyptus* forests, is discussed in

Section 7.3. In North America, regular small fires had been considered essential to prevent the accumulation of combustible material which might lead to infrequent hot, extensive and destructive fires. However, such management of forests has been challenged, and a brave attempt has been made to let the natural fire regime recover in sites such as Yellowstone. So far, small fires created by lightning have prevented the conflagrations that were feared. Natural fires produce the small clearings that not only serve as firebreaks, but also support the assemblage of gap-demanding early successional species (Section 7.3.1). Subterranean peat fires in Indonesia may burn for years, occasionally igniting the forest, and can only be halted by cutting deep firebreaks. Fires started by vandals or recreation are increasingly common.

Management to protect forests from agricultural encroachment, grazing, logging, hunting and fire is essentially through enforcement, including patrols. This can provide some local employment, but will seldom be sufficient to offset the demand for food and land. Compensation will therefore be required (Section 9.1.2). Remote sensing, such as aerial and satellite monitoring, may be used to check for illegal fires, or gaps in forest canopies, but disturbance beneath the canopy might be missed without ground surveys.

Management that incorporates the activities of local people accepts the non-natural state of the reserve, but also accepts that this is often the least damaging option. The activities of ancient forest peoples, such as the Pygmies of west Africa, the longhouse dwellers of Malaysia, the many cultures of Papua New Guinea, and the Kyapo of Amazonia, may be relatively easily included into management plans. More recent colonists who dwell in and require forests include rubber-tappers and brazil-nut collectors – and these people, whilst linked to global trade and consumption, are less damaging than agriculturalists.

Management of the activities of 'indigenous' forest people raises issues of human rights and sovereignty, and stimulates calls for protection of their traditional homelands (Section 9.4). However, most populations are now non-traditional: they use tools such as chain-saws and metal axes, wire snares, fishing nets and guns, and they trade goods for money. Attempts to let local people manage 'their' forests have met with mixed success. In Korup, Cameroon, hunting of primates with guns has been excessive. In Paraguay, the transfer of rights to the Ache people led to deforestation for cash. Colombia has given limited land rights to indigenous people (including the Desana), extending over 180 000 km², which is about half the Colombian Amazon. This appears relatively successful; it may help that the Desana have tribal belief and incentive systems which limit their population growth in order to protect the 'energy' of the rainforest.

The simple act of isolation renders forests less natural in a variety of ways which may then necessitate remedial management. Deep edge effects might need to be managed (Section 5.4.2). Isolated patches of what was a very heterogenous landscape such as a rainforest may by chance be missing certain species, and if these are keystone species (Section 3.1.4) the remainder of the fragment may change. If the full richness of keystone fruit trees is not available at all seasons in a fragment of forest, fruit-eating primates, bats, and birds such as parrots and toucans, might be lost – causing further knock-on effects. The missing keystone species, such as fig species, may need to be planted into the reserve. It may thus be necessary to reduce naturalness in some ways to protect it in others.

Logging is always detrimental but may be managed in a variety of ways to reduce impact. Continuous-canopy forestry always leaves a canopy cover – protecting some species sensitive to microclimatic change. Selective logging is better than clear-felling. 'Low impact' or 'reduced impact' logging includes cutting lianas to prevent felled trees dragging down adjacent trees, and trees are then dragged carefully to sites for cutting and transport. For highly valuable species in fragile areas, balloons or helicopters may be used to lift the felled tree without the need for a road; forest roads threaten many species (Section 2.7) and compact the soil (which suppresses regrowth). Rotation lengths between cuts must be long enough to permit some recovery – at least 25 years for tropical forests – and the age-structure of the forest should be protected – particularly including the maintenance of dead timber. There are a variety of 'certification' standards for forest products which aim to demonstrate they have been obtained responsibly (Section 9.3).

Fully protected areas have proved important both as refuges and as baseline or control sites to compare with forest management options. For example, the Virgin Jungle Reserves (VJRs) of Malaysia have indicated which mammal species decline under selective logging and fragmentation.

## 5.1.3   Other terrestrial habitats

Polar regions may be highly natural, being so extremely inhospitable to humans. Antarctica has had less human habitation than the Arctic – where Eskimos have hunted seals and fish for thousands of years. The Antarctic has a larger land area and coastline than the Arctic, supporting very large numbers of breeding birds (such as penguins) and mammals (such as elephant seals). The birdlife of the Arctic is notably abundant, but there have been losses of common species such as the great auk. Polar environments will be affected by changes in their marine systems (Section 5.3), which provide much of the plant and animal productivity used by species breeding on land. Management of ozone depletion, and the greenhouse effect, will bring relatively large benefits to the polar ecosystems (Section 2.3.3).

Polar, tundra and montane habitats are relatively fragile (Section 3.2.4). Damage due to recreation has been monitored for years in sites including Tasmanian mountain reserves, Snowdonia in Wales, and the Olympic National Park in Washington State. In the Rocky Mountains National Park, species such as moss campion are very sensitive to visitor pressure, and asphalt or boardwalk paths are used to limit the impact of hill-walkers. Ski developments, hill-walking, mining, grazing and other disturbances need to be prevented or strictly limited

Deserts are often imagined to be natural, but many suffer intense disturbance. Deserts have low productivity (limited by water). Consequently, desert plants and animals grow slowly and are vulnerable to disturbance by vehicles, livestock, and collecting (Section 2.2). Lichens may be important in the food chain, as in the Skeleton Coast of Namibia, and are sensitive to dust and vehicles. Some vehicle tracks in deserts may last for hundreds of years. Many desert herbivores such as oryx have been overhunted and locally extirpated – they are very vulnerable in such open landscapes. Overgrazing is a common problem in the desert reserves of central Asia. In California, large numbers of livestock and roads have been removed, and mines closed, to protect desert tortoise and other species.

Many arid areas, such as the Namib and Kalahari, have had human influence since the early days of human evolution, and the hunter-gathering Bushmen of the Kalahari are possibly an example of a human community living within the limits of the system without causing recent extinctions. Whilst the Bushmen have declined, generally increasing human populations, technology such as off-road vehicles and guns, and modern use of oases encourage overexploitation. Livestock competes with desert herbivores for the low plant resources. Management of such impacts will involve enforcement and compensation schemes in and around most hot deserts of the world – no small task considering the scale involved and the low densities of desert species. Management of Asian desert reserves has included the planting of shelter-belts of trees to reduce erosion.

Scrub habitats are richer in species than grasslands, and are intermediate in stress regime and diversity between grassland and forest. Fire is very important to the floristically rich fynbos and Mediterranean scrubland habitats.

Hundreds of plant species in the fynbos need fire for germination, or need species of ants which are tolerant of fire to disperse the seeds (Section 2.4.1). Management of scrub involves determination and maintenance of the natural disturbance regime. Rotational management is often appropriate – using fire on large scales, or cutting on small scales. A public-relations exercise is also needed to overcome scrub's popular image as 'wasteland'.

Some of the earliest humans exploited coastlines, and by 2020, some 75% of the world's population may live within 60 km of the coast. Some coastal habitats may be inaccessible and highly natural, such as cliffs, or too unstable to develop for housing or agriculture. However, sheltered coastlines can be accessible by boats, and easily harvested. For example, few sea turtles and turtle nests survive uncollected in Madagascar, where the beaches are searched regularly using pirogues. In densely populated Britain, threats include gravel extraction from the internationally important shingle beach at Dungeness, and climbing and walking along cliffs which tramples plants and disturbs birds such as chough. Sand-dunes attract recreation, including vehicles, in many parts of the world – threatening many plants and sea turtle populations. Studies in the Parker River National Wildlife Refuge, USA, showed that even a little trampling reduced species diversity (Fig. 5.3), with sensitive species of the interdune community being replaced by species more typical of the foredune community. Management of dunes includes careful placement of developments such as hotels and beach facilities, constraining vehicle parking to small sites, boardwalks from car parks to the sea, patrols for beaches, and restraint in mineral extraction.

Cave systems are exceptionally interesting to conservationists because they may support unique, endemic 'cavernicolous' species. The older and more isolated the cave system, the more likely this is. Caves may support abundant bats and nesting swiftlets, such as those exploited for birds' nest soup in South-East Asia. Cave ecosystems are vulnerable to changes in hydrology, and to pollution. For example, the Bermuda Caves, Bermuda, support at least 25 endemic invertebrates, and are threatened by nutrients or pesticides running off from proposed development of golf-courses in the land above them. Cave faunas are also threatened by recreational caving and trampling. Management includes putting gates or grilles on cave entrances, policing of nest-collection, provision of alternative nesting sites (as in Malaysia) and monitoring and preventing changes in the watershed that might alter water volumes and quality.

Management of terrestrial habitats cannot be separated from management of aquatic habitats. This is particularly true of oceanic islands, which are strongly influenced by the state of the ocean from which many birds, turtles and mammals may arrive to nest.

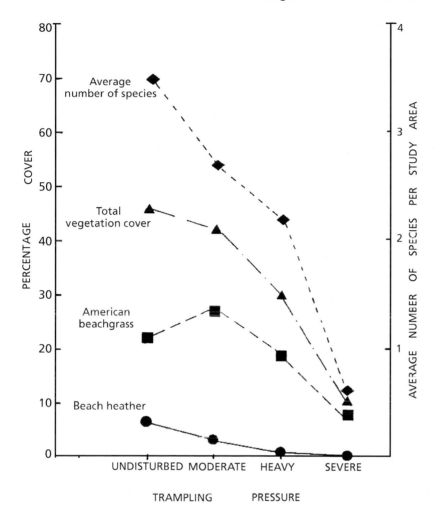

**Fig. 5.3.** The influence of trampling from recreation in the Parker River National Wildlife Refuge, Massachusetts. The total species richness of plants, and the percentage cover of interdune species (e.g. beach heather) declines relative to foredune species (e.g. American beachgrass).
*Source:* Redrawn from McDonnell, M. J. *Biological Conservation* **21** (1981), 289–301.

## 5.2   Management of oceanic islands

Oceanic islands present special problems – and great opportunities – for conservationists. In addition to the full range of threats present on continental sites, from hunting to agriculture and urbanisation, the ecosystems of islands have been particularly strongly influenced by introduced species (Section 2.4).

There is lively debate as to whether, or why, islands are more invasible than mainlands; however, their species appear often to be more vulnerable. Introduced species may become a larger proportion of the original flora and fauna than is possible on a mainland. The island forms may have no suitable defences against new herbivores or carnivores: large mammalian predators are often absent. Island species that are endemic have nowhere to retreat to if habitats are changed by people. The commonest problems on islands are hunting, loss of habitat, and introduced species. Hunting has been considered in Section 2.2.1, but may be particularly destructive for naïve species on islands, or species with smaller populations than usually occur on mainlands.

## 5.2.1 Loss of habitat

Loss of habitat has been a problem ever since human colonisation of islands. In the Pacific, all the forest of Easter Island was cleared by Polynesians in the period 900–1400. New Zealand lost about a third of its forest to Maori activities. Most of the scrub on Henderson Island in the Pacific was cleared or modified by fire in the period of Polynesian occupation (1200–200 years ago). The lowland forests of the granitic Seychelles were largely cleared for plantations of spice and coconut trees, and for hardwoods for ships and other construction. In Mauritius, deforestation cleared most of the lowlands, leaving forest mainly in the mountains of the Black River area. Grazing has devastated areas of Tristan da Cuna, the Galapagos and St Helena. Britain lost about 99% of its primary forest. On Madagascar, clearance of the forest has been very extensive (Fig. 2.8) and continues rapidly.

Wetlands are at risk on islands because they are often located on flat regions of the island (the coastal plateaux) and because competition for water is particularly severe on islands. Drainage of island wetlands has led to extirpation of populations of the Seychelles black paradise flycatcher on Mahé and Praslin. However, wetlands may support the best relict lowland forests remaining on islands, because the land may be hard to develop. Pollution can be intense on islands with dense populations using streams for washing and bathing. Management of islands to prevent loss of habitat requires sensitive zonation (Section 5.5), and sometimes restoration programmes including re-introductions (Chapter 8).

## 5.2.2 Introductions

Management of sites that are natural in being free of invasive species may include quarantine procedures to prevent them arriving. These procedures may be needed after an introduced species is removed: species may be accidentally or deliberately re-introduced, and this can be an act of ignorance, malice or vandalism. Management to remove introduced species is a form of restoration ecology (Section 8.2). Quarantine procedures may take a number of forms. Phytosanitary and animal quarantine controls (as part of the customs procedure) are primarily intended to prevent the introduction of diseases, but are increasingly seen as an important element in conservation.

Travellers and tourists may inadvertently (or deliberately) bring in viable plants and animals, and this can be a serious problem on sensitive island sites, which are intrinsically attractive to ecotourists. Ecotourism is also a relatively promising option on islands, such as the Seychelles and Madagascar, because of the beauty and uniqueness of the wildlife and the accessibility of marine life. Tourists need to check – or preferably change – their clothing prior to disembarking. This can be very important when tours move between mainland and islands, as with many cruises. Incoming agricultural produce and packaging should be thoroughly checked. However, this is very difficult: several species reach the Galapagos each year, and a gecko species was brought to Aldabra World Heritage Site with supplies.

The isolation of islands makes them both vulnerable and secure. Once cleared or protected from introduced species, the isolation and lack of human population on some islands may permit relatively simple, successful and highly satisfying management for conservation. Monitoring will often be required for existing or new exotic species. New problems can arise even when a species has apparently existed on an island with little impact to date (Section 2.4).

## 5.3  Management of aquatic habitats

Aquatic habitats have been neglected in selection and designation of reserves and in management. The low human population density in the marine environment has left some areas which are amongst the most natural areas on the planet, whilst the high population density around rivers, lakes, and coastlines make these amongst the most threatened systems.

## 5.3.1  Freshwater

Freshwater is such an important resource for people that freshwater systems have probably suffered more devastation than any other set of habitats. Management of freshwater systems is intimately linked to management of the watershed and floodplain. This is illustrated in the Amazon, where logging along the tributaries of the floodplain has probably led to the extinction of many endemic species specialised to use submerged dead wood. Indeed, P. A. Henderson has found that deforestation is a threat to far more Amazonian fish than is overfishing.

In Madagascar, deforestation of catchments has led to massive soil erosion and siltation of rivers, and unknown numbers of extinctions. The problem is compounded by a large human population using rivers for washing, waste and sewage disposal – a microcosm of other parts of the world. International aid may be required to provide better sanitation and reduce agricultural inputs near reserves. Management needs to control run-off, including protecting, planting and maintaining scrub or woodland 'riparian buffer strips' along waterbodies to help absorb nutrients and bind soil. Indeed, for many species, such as the water vole and otter in Britain, management of river banks is as important as management of the water quality. Speed restrictions on boats may be needed to protect banks from wash.

Industrial sources of pollution need to be inspected and settlement or chemical scrubbing may be required. Thermal pollution needs to be controlled by cooling-towers and weirs. Point sources of this type are easier to manage than diffuse sources. Sometimes the chemical 'fingerprint' of a pollution episode can be used to trace the source, as with oil spills.

Several globally endangered freshwater species occur in very limited waterbodies, such as springs and hotsprings a few tens of metres across. Management of the abstraction and quality of water in such systems is extremely important. In California, management for the desert pupfish includes creation of refuges from exotic species, maintenance of open water, annual monitoring, and removal of exotic salt cedar trees (which dry out the habitat). In Britain, the Environment Agency is responsible for managing the water table to prevent streams drying out, which may involve water conservation in dry years through hosepipe bans and manipulation of weirs.

Freshwater systems are important spawning areas for many fish which grow at sea. Management such as close-seasons on salmon nets across rivers, fish-ladders, and fish-lifts, are only partial solutions. Fish-ladders are less effective at helping migration than is often thought (Section 2.2.3).

Introduced species need to be controlled by quarantine. In Britain, informal guidelines suggest efforts such as cleaning pond-nets before surveys, to prevent the spread of lesser duckweed. Management of the signal crayfish in Britain includes intensive trapping on some rivers, including pheromone traps, and controls on the siting of crayfish farms. Low-frequency radio waves are being tested as a means of small-scale control of the zebra mussel in North America. Following the introduction of the ruff to the Great Lakes in ballast water, legislation has been suggested to require ships to flush ballast in mid-ocean, or treat it to kill potential invasives (Section 9.2.1). Ballast water can be purged of oxygen using nitrogen, or sterilised with ozone.

A good example of integrated management of river systems is provided by The Upper Colorado River Fish Recovery Programme, which protects several threatened endemics. It has removed hundreds of thousands of exotic fish and created obstacles to their movement. It has also purchased and created wetland habitat, and mimicked natural stream flow through timed release of water from dams. It also conducts research and education.

## 5.3.2  Brackish and intertidal

Estuaries and intertidal areas can be very important for biodiversity. The diversity of management problems is substantial, and threats from terrestrial, freshwater and marine sources may need to be prevented. The estuaries of the world are often highly productive areas, with numerous invertebrates exploiting the sediment and the structure of coastal vegetation such as mangrove. This in turn may foster large bird or fish communities. For example, the estuary of the River Severn in Britain has an exceptional tidal range, which exposes extensive rich mudflats at low tide, supporting over 100 000 waterfowl, including some internationally important populations. Parts of the deltas of major rivers such as the Niger and the Amazon may be relatively inaccessible, and support many birds, crocodilians and primates, as well as being spawning grounds for fish. Intertidal communities have often been threatened by overexploitation. Many mangrove forests are threatened by charcoal and timber cutting (Fig. 2.13), and by the creation of shrimp farms as in Mexico, Indonesia and Tanzania; recognising the problem, India has limited the expansion of aquaculture. In several British mudflats, lugworms are overharvested by fishermen for bait.

Pollution both from rivers and from marine sources threaten inter-tidal areas. Oil spills have been particularly notable, threatening species that feed near-shore or come ashore to rest or breed. Seabirds, sea otters and other marine mammals, as well as inter-tidal invertebrates, were severely disrupted by the Exxon Valdez spill (Section 2.3.2). Prevention of these disasters includes management of the behaviour of ships' crews and sensible shipping routes. Booms may be used to reduce the flow of oil onto the coast. Detergents and hot water used in clean-up have often proved counter-productive – killing, or slowing recovery of inter-tidal animals and plants. Sea-lochs may become highly polluted by aquaculture if the flushing of water through the loch is low.

A build up of pesticides, faeces or nutrients from fish-farms might be reduced by better placement and by increasing the diversity of fish species that are being farmed.

## 5.3.3  Marine

Conservation management of marine habitats presents great challenges associated with the scale and variety of the biomes and the relatively poor ecological knowledge of these systems. Few fully marine species are thought to have become extinct – although damage has probably been underestimated. Conservation of the marine realm involves activities in a great range of depths, distances from land, current regimes, substrates, and disturbance histories. In any event, the management of marine habitats and species involves consideration of very large geographical areas with ill-defined boundaries. Many marine areas are international property or 'open-access resources', and the 'tragedy of the commons' is therefore a very common issue in management and policy (Section 9.4.2).

Amongst the most important unresolved questions relating to conservation is the degree of endemicity and isolation of populations in the oceans (Sections 1.2.1 and 3.4.1). If endemicity is high in some parts of the ocean, such as in reefs around individual islands, then conservation will have to operate on a much finer scale, with numerous local management challenges.

Managers of marine systems may find it difficult to identify changes in, and threats to, the system. There are few long-term records of marine populations, and it should be a priority to start recording. Marine species such as cod or anchovy may be very difficult to census, and in general the base-line data required to inform management is very rare. It is therefore very important to retain some unmanaged areas or zones as controls, or 'biodiversity base-lines'.

As on land and freshwater, in general it is often the large, $K$-selected species such as sharks, groupers, rockfish, turtles, seals, manatees and whales that will require species-specific protective management. Catch-and-release big-game fishing, and whale watching, can provide motivation to conserve. There are also habitats and species fragile to trampling and to trade. Many marine species migrate great distances to feed and to reproduce, rendering them vulnerable to a variety of threats and difficult to manage. Eels, sturgeon, and salmon have suffered from problems in both freshwater and at sea, whilst seals, turtles and seabirds have suffered on land and at sea. Habitat management is required to protect the fuller diversity of these systems, with occasional focus on flagship, keystone or commercially important species.

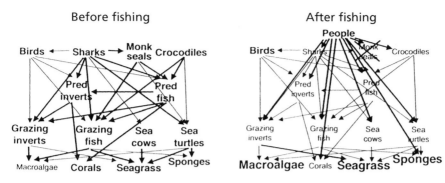

**Fig. 5.4.** Influences of long-term fishing on a complex marine food web. **Bold** font shows abundance, Roman font shows rarity. See also Fig. 2.15.
*Source:* Reprinted with permission from Jackson, J. C. B. *et al. Science* **293** (2001), 629–638. Copyright 2001 American Association for the Advancement of Science.

Habitats may change substantially after persecution of just a few species. The relatively complex inter-linkages of marine food-chains (Figs. 2.15 and 5.4) force management to be reactive to unpredictable changes, and management may need to be experimental ('adaptive'). The removal of predatory fish and triton molluscs has probably contributed to crown-of-thorns starfish epidemics on reefs. However, initial concern at the sudden unexpected increase in crown-of-thorns led to vigorous management to control them (a potential example of 'overmanagement'), including poisoning and removing the starfish. Harvesting of whales or krill may lead to substantial (and possibly irreversible) changes in the southern oceans. Loss of sea otters leads to changes in mollusc and echinoderm populations. Management of these dominant or keystone species (if they can be identified) should be particularly effective in protecting habitats. The impact of harvesting dominant marine seaweed species such as kelp and rockweed is poorly studied, but rotations of at least four years, and refuges, may be required to protect the structure and productivity of these species.

Strict Marine Protected Areas (MPAs) are required to protect threatened overfished species such as the barndoor skate of eastern North America, and the totoaba of the Sea of Cortez. The largest such reserve is the Great Barrier Reef Marine Park, totalling nearly 35 million hectares; the management of this reef is outlined in Section 5.5. When species aggregate, reserves on spawning grounds (as with the Downs Banks of the English Channel), and feeding grounds (as with the seagrass beds of Madagascar), may be particularly effective. MPAs in which fishing bans are enforced have been demonstrated to be effective both at maintaining high numbers of vulnerable species and at

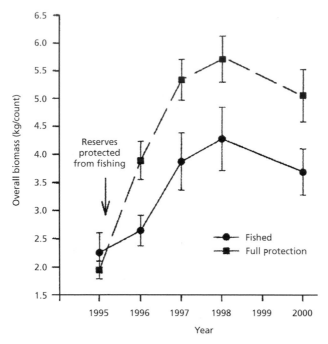

**Fig. 5.5.** Protection of areas of St Lucia (Caribbean) increases the biomass of commercially important fish, both in the marine protected areas and in unprotected (fished) areas adjacent to them.
*Source:* Reprinted with permission from Roberts, C. M. *et al. Science* **294** (2001), 1920–1923. Copyright 2001 American Association for the Advancement of Science.

providing 'spillover' of fish, which improves adjacent fisheries (Fig. 5.5). In St Lucia, after just five years of protection of 35% of the fishing area, yields in adjacent areas increased 46–90% (depending on the trap type). In Florida, 40 years of protection of an estuary adjacent to a space centre in Florida has resulted in large numbers of record sized fish being caught in adjacent waters. The UN World Summit on Sustainable Development in 2002 agreed to extend the global MPA system substantially to protect fish stocks.

Coral reefs have been more intensively studied than many marine systems, although they are still poorly understood. The threats to them and examples of management methods to address these problems are shown Table 5.1. Education and enforcement of policy are particularly important in these relatively accessible marine habitats.

Management of offshore waters includes quota systems and closed-seasons for attempted sustainability of fisheries stocks (Section 7.2). Flawed though these methods may be in preventing harm to other elements of the ecosystem, they probably help to protect or restore both naturalness, and yield, compared

Table 5.1 *Examples of management activities on coral reefs*

| Threat | Example of region | Management |
|---|---|---|
| *Pollution* | | |
| Sea temperature rise | Global | Curbs on greenhouse gases |
| Storm force rise | Global | Curbs on greenhouse gases |
| Eutrophication | Indonesia; East Africa; Hawaii | Treatment of sewage and control of run-off |
| Siltation – erosion | Madagascar; Caribbean; Fiji | Forest protection, reafforestation |
| Pesticides, etc. | Florida | Catchment water quality controls |
| Oil spills | Middle East; Panama | Contingency planning |
| *Destructive fishing* | | |
| Dynamite | South-East Asia | Legislation and enforcement; retraining |
| Cyanide, etc | South-East Asia | Legislation and enforcement; retraining |
| Muro-ami* | Philippines; Indonesia | Legislation and enforcement; retraining |
| Trawling | Deep water corals | Policy changes; protected areas and enforcement |
| *Overexploitation* | | |
| Sale of shells, etc. | Global | Trade restrictions: CITES; education; zonation |
| Seahorse trade | Philippines | Privatisation; community conservation; zonation |
| Spear-fishing | Global | Legislation and enforcement; zonation; education |
| Aquarium fish trade | Global | Legislation and enforcement (CITES); zonation |
| Herbivore decline | Caribbean | Zonation and protected areas |
| Sea cucumber | Global | Trade restrictions: CITES |
| Grouper and wrasse | South-East Asia; W. Pacific | Restrictions on live-fish trade for restaurants |
| Conch | Florida | Regulation of fisheries; zonation |
| *Coastal development* | | |
| Siltation – dredging | Japan; Seychelles; Singapore | Silt-screens during reclamation works |
| Mining of limestone | Jamaica; South Asia | Policy change: legislation and enforcement |
| Anchor damage | Global | Fixed anchor buoys; zonation |
| Trampling and diving | Middle East; Florida | Education of tourists; zonation |

* *Note:* Muro-ami involves a row of people pounding the coral with weighted bags, or poles, to drive fish into nets, and is extremely destructive.

with uncontrolled exploitation leading to commercial extinction of species. Driftnets (up to 60 km long), long-lines (up to 100 km long) and other highly destructive non-selective methods are becoming illegal in an increasing number of territorial waters. There is a global UN Moratorium on large-scale driftnetting, which is difficult to enforce. Management may include satellite or aerial monitoring of boats, and the use of impartial or international observers on boats.

Management is needed to reduce bycatch (Section 2.2.1). Shrimp nets, which are trawls with very fine mesh, are particularly problematic. There are technologies available to minimise the impact of long-lines, such as tubes to sink the lures before birds catch them, but these have not been widely adopted. The USA has begun to close shark, swordfish and tuna long-lining fisheries (including Hawaiian waters, the Desoto Canyon, and Grand Banks) at sensitive times for sea turtles, marine mammals and billfish. Ships are required to carry nets and clippers to help free turtles from long-lines. Devices can be fitted to nets to try to exclude or release species such as dolphins. Such methods are not always successful.

Management of the ocean floor is challenging owing to lack of information on the natural dynamics of these habitats. Ocean floors are being very seriously degraded by bottom-trawling, as with temperate reefs off Britain and New Zealand; corals over 4500 years old are being destroyed, and there may be few areas that are undisturbed. Similarly, mining for manganese nodules might damage extensive areas. Management requires provision of refuges – and this may fortuitously happen around wrecks, oil-platforms, offshore wind farms and other large rigid structures.

Pollution and introduced species should be reduced by legislation (Section 9.2), but little can be done to reverse them. Sonic pollution has been reduced by the US Navy halting some tests when sea turtles or marine mammals are spotted, although there is still concern about whale mortality from sonar. Management of oil-slicks at sea may involve the use of dispersants to prevent large slicks coming ashore, booms to contain the slick, fire, and seeding with microbes to degrade the oil. Quarantine is very difficult for expansive, inter-connected marine systems. Under its Marine Pests Program, Australia has implemented a National Ballast Water Management Regime, a National Marine Response System, and a GIS model of vessels likely to carry marine pests. Control of exotics, once established, is difficult and expensive (Section 8.2).

In the absence of detailed knowledge of marine systems, and in the light of knowledge of their importance to ecosystem services such as the oxygen supply or the carbon dioxide sink, minimising damage to marine systems should be a top priority in conservation policy and management.

## 5.4   Management of fragmented habitats

Habitat fragmentation is a major threat to biodiversity (Sections 1.2.3 and 2.2). Conservationists should aim to minimise the problems of fragmentation, through management at a landscape scale and within sites. The main management challenges of fragmented sites stem from three factors: their reduced area, changes at their edges termed 'edge effects', and increased isolation. We shall examine how these problems relate to the size, shape, linkage and relative positions of reserves – factors which can be termed 'reserve design' or 'reserve geometry'. There is a large body of science related to the issues of site geometry, much of which is also relevant to site management and selection (Section 3.2.5).

Sites that are to be conserved are usually isolated. They may be naturally isolated, as with oceanic islands, lakes, mountains, or caves. Increasingly, conservationists are able to preserve only tiny fragments of habitats as reserves, such as relict patches of forest, savannah, or chalk grassland. There may be several alternative fragments to select amongst. Certain questions arise frequently both in selection of sites and management to maintain and improve them. Should large sites be chosen over one or several small sites? Are certain shapes of reserve more viable? Are isolated sites more or less valuable and vulnerable? Are corridors between reserves desirable and functional?

To help answer these questions, conservationists have turned to theories of isolation within the discipline of biogeography. Biologists have long been attempting to find general principles that apply to isolated habitats, and are fascinated by comparisons between isolated fragments of habitats and isolated oceanic islands. It is tempting to view fragments of habitat as 'islands' in a 'sea' of modified habitat such as farmland. There are benefits and risks in making such comparisons, because fragmented habitats are intrinsically unnatural, even if they initially appear intact.

The main choices in the geometrical design of reserves are given in Fig. 5.6. Most of these designs were first presented in a classic paper by J. M. Diamond in 1975, and the 'better' designs were adopted somewhat uncritically by the World Conservation Strategy in 1980. We shall see that they are the right general aims – but they were originally chosen for the wrong reason! Table 5.2 summarises the pros and cons of these reserve designs.

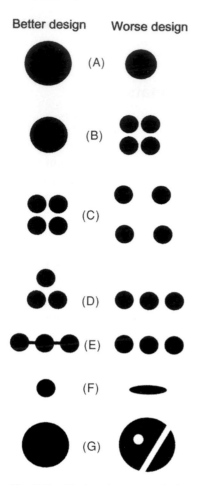

**Fig. 5.6.** Choices in reserve design. Designs (or options) on the left are, in general, preferable.
*Source:* (A) to (F) are based on Diamond, J. M. *Biological Conservation* **7** (1975), 119–146.

Three main models have been developed in relation to the ecology and conservation of patches of habitat: the Equilibrium Theory of Island Biogeography (ETIB), the Core Area Model, and the metapopulation model (Section 6.1). The models have been very influential in the development of conservation biology, yet remain controversial. We shall examine the relevance of these models to the choice of the best geometry for reserves, such area, shape and the importance of corridors.

Table 5.2 *Advantages and disadvantages of reserve design principles illustrated in Fig. 5.6*

| Design (and label as per Fig. 5.6) | | Advantages | Disadvantages |
|---|---|---|---|
| Large | (A) | lower edge effects<br>greater population viability<br>higher equilibrium richness? | cost of acquisition<br>cost of managing perimeter |
| Single large | (B) | lower edge effects<br>benefits core specialists<br><br>greater population viability | lower habitat diversity<br>lower total species richness<br>unsuitable for mutually exclusive species risk of catastrophe increased |
| Close together | (C, D) | greater population viability<br>higher equilibrium richness?<br>greater richness of specialists to a particular habitat | lower habitat diversity<br><br>lower total richness<br><br>lower endemicity<br><br><br>lower range of specialists? |
| Corridors present | (E) | greater population viability | greater risk of contagion (fire, disease) |
| Round | (F) | lower edge effects<br>increased dispersal within reserve | hard to acquire<br>lower immigration rates? |
| Solid | (G) | lower edge effects | hard to acquire<br>lower habitat diversity? |

*Note:* Advantages or disadvantages which may not be proven, or which may occur in some sites only, are indicated by '?'. The advantages and disadvantages refer to the left-hand option in Fig. 5.6.

## 5.4.1   Area: diversity and equilibria

The area (size) of a patch of habitat is one of its most important characteristics, apart from its state of naturalness. Indeed the two are inter-related, since, as we shall see in Section 5.4.2, small areas can seldom be natural given the intrusion of edge effects into small sites. Within any particular habitat type, there is a relatively simple relationship between the area of a patch of habitat and the number of species it is likely to contain. Studies of oceanic islands, and many other highly discrete habitats such as mountains, lakes and patches of grassland, show a remarkable and consistent pattern: if the area of an island is one tenth the area of another, it will support about half the number of species. The relationship between island area and species richness is called the 'species–area relationship'. For a given habitat, the number of species increases with area until no further species can be added from the total pool available in that type of habitat in the region. This leads to graph of area against richness as shown in Fig. 5.7(a). If the axes on this graph are plotted logarithmically, then the line becomes straight, as in Fig. 5.7(b).

The equation which describes these lines is $S = cA^z$, which can be transformed to $\log S = \log c + z \log A$. The term $c$ is the constant which defines the intercept with the $\log S$ axis. The term $z$ is more interesting, since it is the slope of the log–log plot of the graph, and thus shows how fast the number of species rises with area. The size of $z$ is generally between 0.20 and 0.35 on oceanic islands or isolated mainland habitats, and a figure of 0.25 is often used. For areas of habitat which are *not* isolated, $z$ is slightly lower (0.12–0.17), meaning that reserves which are still within a larger expanse of the same habitat will support more of the specialist species of that habitat than would isolated habitats, and the position of a reserve in a geographical unit is therefore important (Section 3.2.5).

Such a remarkable general pattern might have a fundamental biological cause. Two main hypotheses suggest why the species–area relationship occurs. One suggests that the bigger an island, the more habitat types it has on it: this begs the question as to why the rate of increase in habitat types with area should be so consistent. The other suggestion is the ETIB, which predicts that the number of species would increase with area even within a given habitat type. Unfortunately, the explanations have seldom been tested rigorously, since most islands have several habitats. Studies attempting to separate out the relative influence of habitat diversity, as opposed to equilibrium, on the species–area relationship suggest that in general habitat diversity is the more important factor. In an analysis of birds on islands round Britain, T. M. Reed found

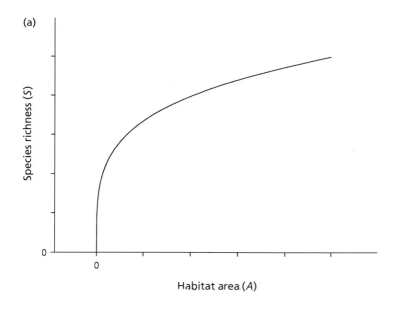

(a)

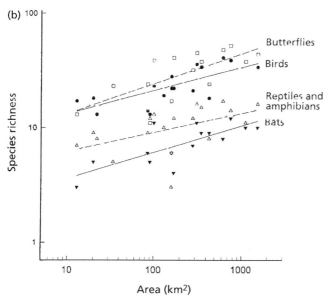

(b)

**Fig. 5.7.** (a) Species richness generally increases with area. (b) On a log/log scale, richness increases linearly with area, as for these four groups in the Lesser Antilles. Butterflies open squares and dashed line; birds, filled circles and solid line; reptiles and amphibians, open triangles and dashed line; bats filled triangles and solid line. *Source:* (b), Ricklefs, R. E. & Lovette, I. J. *Journal of Animal Ecology* **68** (1999), 1142–1160.

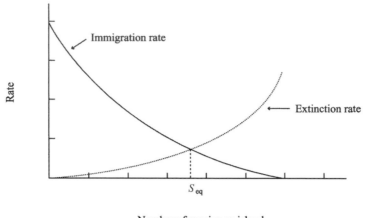

**Fig. 5.8.** Theoretical interplay between immigration and extinction on an island, tending towards equilibrium richness where the lines intersect at species richness $S$.

that most of the variation in richness could be explained simply by habitat diversity.

ETIB was proposed in 1967 by R. H. MacArthur and E. O. Wilson, who recognised it had several basic assumptions that might not be valid in many real-world situations. It is applicable only when dealing with islands of the same *homogeneous* habitat – or fragments of the same original habitat. The theory proposes that the number of species on an island increases with area in response to two factors: the immigration rate, and the extinction rate. Immigration is assumed to decrease with distance from a source of species (such as a mainland). Extinction is assumed to decrease as area increases. The interplay of these two processes can be seen in Fig. 5.8. As its name suggests, the theory predicts the species–area relationship once an equilibrium between immigration and extinction has had time to develop on each island, but it cannot predict how long this will take. Assuming sufficient time has elapsed for equilibrium to occur, remote and small islands will have the fewest species and large islands near mainlands will have the most.

How realistic are the assumptions of ETIB? It is not unreasonable to assume that, for most species, dispersal is limited by distance. Studies of recolonisation or colonisation of volcanic islands (such as the Krakatau group in Indonesia by R. H. Whittaker) show that species with nearby source populations generally arrive first. Birdwatchers get more exited about vagrants from afar than from nearby. Extinction rates are reasonably assumed to depend on area because small islands can support only small populations of a species, which may not be viable (Sections 6.2 and 6.3). An example of area-dependent extinctions comes from a very important project near Manaus, in Brazil (Fig. 5.9). Fragments to-be were surveyed for birds, primates, amphibia, butterflies and plants before they were isolated from other forest and surrounded by pasture: 'ecological relaxation' to a lower species number occurs faster in small fragments. Over about 10 years following isolation, around 50% of the abundant species of forest litter beetle were lost in fragments of 1 ha, whilst losses for 10 ha fragments were 30%, and for 100 ha fragments only about 15%. In general in these neotropical forests, a 1000-fold increase in fragment area translates to a 10-fold increase in the time it takes to lose half the species, and fragments under 1000 ha will lose many species within decades.

There is some evidence supporting the ETIB. Firstly, classic studies of invertebrates on islands off the Florida coast by D. Simberloff and E. O. Wilson showed that after species were removed by insecticide, the richness of several islands recovered to the original levels. As predicted, the new list of species on each island is different, although the total length of the list is roughly the same. Simberloff also showed that when these islands were reduced in size with saws, a decrease in invertebrate species richness occurred. Secondly, studies of archipelagos show that oceanic islands which are atypically rich in species are often recently isolated, whilst those which are poor in species have recently been disturbed. It might be predicted in these cases that richness of the recent isolates (such as the land-bridge islands off New Guinea) will lose species over thousands of years, whist disturbed islands (such as Krakatau after volcanic eruption) will gain species and equilibrate. These hypotheses will take far too long to test to be very helpful! A third line of evidence suggests that the variation in richnesses amongst islands that are in equilibrium will be relatively low, and the 'variance to mean ratio' of the number of species can be used to test for equilibria; in such a test J. Aho showed snails in a series of lakes in Finland are indeed in an equilibrium related to isolation and area.

ETIB does not allow for the evolution of endemic species on islands, which is generally on a longer timescale than conservation managers are considering. The assumption of habitat homogeneity means the theory should be applied only where all the islands or patches have very similar habitat (which is unusual in the real world).

Fortunately, whether ETIB or habitat diversity drive the relationship between area and richness is actually much less important to conservationists than the fact that richness usually decreases with area and during fragmentation (Figs. 5.10 and 5.11). Often 50% or more of the variance in log $S$ is explained by log $A$ (and for flies in wooded parks in Cincinnati it is some 90%). Nevertheless, there may be a lot of scatter in the graphs of richness versus area.

**Fig. 5.9.** The Biological Dynamics of Forest Fragments Project, Manaus, Brazil (formerly the Minimum Critical Size of Ecosystems Project). As rainforest fragmentation proceeds, these fragments are designed and studied. (a) Recently isolated 10 ha and 1 ha fragments. (b) A 10 ha fragment separated from continuous forest by a 100 m wide swath; this fragment has been isolated for a few years, and many of the large trees near its margin have died and been replaced by smaller pioneer trees.
*Source:* Photographs, copyright Richard O. Bierregaard; description, W. F. Laurance.

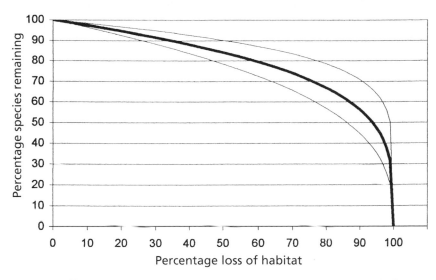

**Fig. 5.10.** The proportion of a habitat's species that can be supported declines with habitat area. The bold line shows the curve if $z = 0.25$, the upper line shows $z = 0.15$, and the lower line shows $z = 0.35$.

On the whole, choosing and maintaining a larger site is a relatively reliable way to protect more species without having to survey all of them. It is also clear that, for whatever reason, fragmentation leads eventually to extinctions (Section 1.2.3), and a further management implication is that to reduce such extinction, habitat area must be increased, through restoration management (Chapter 8).

As described in Section 3.1, conservationists are not always interested in protecting maximum species richness, but may be more interested in particular species and in species quality. Maintenance of species quality should require less management on large sites. High-quality species are more likely to be present in a large reserve, since larger sites will generally be less sensitive to edge effects, as discussed below. Studies by M. J. Usher and colleagues in the Vale of York in Britain show that, below 1.5 ha, woodlands have few woodland specialist plants, spiders moths or carabids, but above 5 ha such species start to appear. S. A. Hinsley and colleagues have shown that woodland birds in Britain have a high turnover even in woods of 30 ha, and that breeding probability and success increases with woodland size. Similarly, studies by N. R. Webb show that small heathland fragments do not support a specialist heathland invertebrate community.

Large reserves may be essential for large species, or migratory species. Desirable *natural* habitat diversity will also be greater in large sites. Furthermore, management may be simpler if the whole watershed is contained in

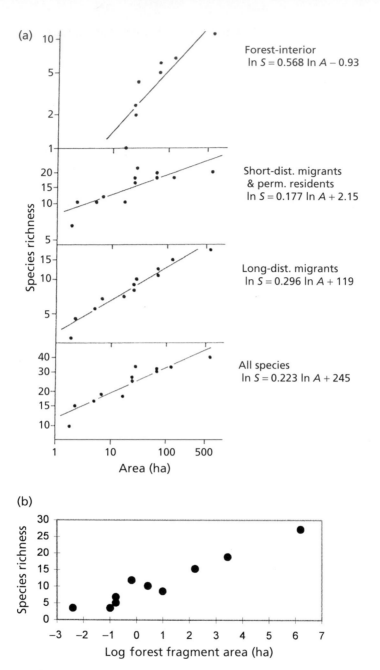

**Fig. 5.11.** Habitat fragmentation decreases richness. Note log scales on some axes. (a) Richness of all birds, and specialist groups of birds, declines with fragment area in Illinois. (b) Richness of forest understory birds declines with fragment area in the East Usambara Mountains, Tanzania.
*Sources:* (a) Blake, J. G. & Karr, J. R. *Biological Conservation* **30** (1984), 173–187; copyright 1984 with permission from Elsevier Science. (b) Newark, W. D. *Conservation Biology* **5** (1991), 67–78.

the reserve, and a manager can control the quality of the water flow to the system. However, large reserves are more expensive to purchase. The total cost of management may be higher. For example, the total length of the perimeter is longer – and this may cost more to fence and patrol. Patrolling large reserves is difficult. To prevent poaching of high-quality species like rhino, it may be easier to maintain small reserves with electric fencing (Section 6.4). Large reserves may attract unwanted attention. For example, Manu reserve in the Peruvian Amazon contains minerals, oil, timber, potential farmland, animals to eat, species important in trade, and so on. The political pressures to cut-off (de-gazette) parts of a large park and convert them to other uses might be higher than for a small site. The asymptote in the species–area curve means that if a park is large enough to support all the sensitive species of a region, it would be sensible to have other parks in other regions rather than an even bigger single park.

Within the biodiversity hotspots (Section 3.4), high rates of habitat loss are causing high rates of extinction of endemic species. T. M. Brooks and colleagues used the following equation to predict the eventual number of endemic species which will become extinct when an area of their habitat is reduced to a new size:

$$S_{original} - S_{new} = S_{original} - S_{original}(A_{new}/A_{original})^z,$$

where $z$ is approximately 0.25.

They found that the extent of habitat loss was a good predictor of the known number of extinct or threatened endemic species (based on independent measures), as with similar studies (Section 1.2.3).

## 5.4.2  Sub-division, shape, and edge effects

On the whole, few conservationists would prefer a single small park to one big park in a habitat. However, they may prefer several small parks to one big park of the same total area. The question of 'Single Large Or Several Small?' is known as the 'SLOSS' debate. The choice between a single large reserve or several small reserves is *not* (as sometimes assumed) related to equilibrium theory, but is closely related to the choice of reserve shape. These choices are linked by the problem of edge effects, in which damaging influences penetrate into a reserve. The choice has relevance to management or threats which might tend to fragment or diversify a reserve – for example, through the cutting of a clearing for a road, mine, pipeline or timber.

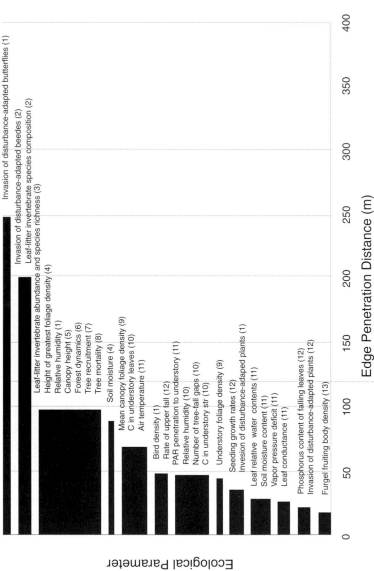

**Fig. 5.12.** Some edge effects and their detected penetration distance in the Amazon, from the project in Fig. 5.9.
*Source:* Laurance, W. F. Oryx **43** (2000), 39–45. Reprinted with the permission of Cambridge University Press.

The following labels appear on the chart:

- Invasion of disturbance-adapted butterflies (1)
- Invasion of disturbance-adapted beedes (2)
- Leaf-litter invertebrate species composition (2)
- Leaf-litter invertebrate abundance and species richness (3)
- Height of greatest foliage density (4)
- Relative humidity (1)
- Canopy height (5)
- Forest dynamics (6)
- Tree recruitment (7)
- Tree mortality (8)
- Soil moisture (4)
- Mean canopy foliage density (9)
- C in understory leaves (10)
- Air temperature (11)
- Bird density (1)
- Rate of upper fall (12)
- PAR penetration to understory (11)
- Relative humidity (10)
- Number of tree-fall gaps (10)
- C in understory str (10)
- Understory foliage density (9)
- Seeding growth rates (12)
- Invesion of disturbance-adaped plants (1)
- Leaf relative water contents (11)
- Soil moisture content (11)
- Vapor pressure deficit (11)
- Leaf conductance (11)
- Phosphorous content of failing leaves (12)
- Invasion of disturbance-adapted plants (12)
- Furgel fruiting body density (13)

Edge Penetration Distance (m)

Ecological Parameter

SLOSS is a very complex issue, and generalisations are risky. Species richness has usually been found to increase as the number of sites increases, both on islands and in fragments. This is most likely to be because more habitats are likely to be contained in several small sites, spread over different soils and climates. However, in some habitats, this relationship disappears at larger scales – for example, a study of the flora of sub-Arctic islands found that several small sites contained more species up to a total of 12 ha, above which most of the common species were present in either design. The extra species in several small sites may be desirable from the perspective of conservation of diversity, but when species quality is considered (Section 3.1), it appears that the opposite conclusion is generally true: single large sites are better. The reason is related to edge effects.

Edge effects are changes in the composition of communities at their boundaries. By definition, they do not occur in homogeneous habitats. The community of species in the 'core' of a large patch of habitat will differ from the community at the edge. This seems to be one of the most general principles in ecology. It was once thought that the edges of habitats were of particular importance to conservation – and desirable features in reserves. The places where habitats blend together, called 'ecotones', might support specialists of the ecotone. There may also be a suite of species which use – or need – both habitats (Section 3.2.3). Ecotones might thus be exceptionally rich areas. This is probably true for some *natural* edges, particularly if they are between relatively similar habitats such as grassland and forest, or very large (as with the interface of the Andes and Amazon). However, if an artificial edge is created by people, or if the natural patches are small, the resultant edge effects may reduce the number and quality of species present in the region as a whole.

Edges created by people generally have altered abiotic conditions. If a forest edge is created by clearing round a patch of forest, more sunlight reaches ground level. The humidity will decline. The temperature fluctuations through the day and the seasons will increase. Windspeeds will increase. Conversely, if a plantation is grown in an open landscape, the opposite changes may occur. Species evolved to live in the 'core' of a habitat may be threatened by the changes at the edge. Plants may dry out or be blown down – or conversely they may be shaded. Edge effects have now been found in any habitat that has been examined. The distance to which a particular effect penetrates, and the way the effect varies with distance is described by the 'edge function', and examples are given in Figs. 5.12 and 5.13, and in Tables 5.3 and 5.4.

The changes at the edge of a forest that has become surrounded by grassland or arable land during fragmentation are relatively well-known – and perhaps present an extreme case. Typically, the initial ('first-order') biological changes

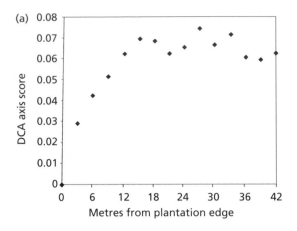

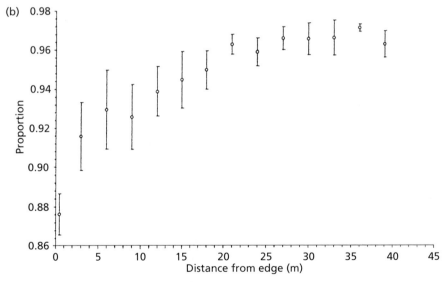

**Fig. 5.13.** Edge effects in the canopy of a Norway spruce plantation where it abuts grassland (England). (a) Community composition as measured by an ordination (DCA) score. (b) Proportion of small arthropods (under 2 mm in length).
*Sources:* Both with kind permission of the publisher, Kluwer Academic Publishers, and the authors: (a) Foggo, A. *et al. Plant Ecology* **153** (2001), 347–359. (b) Ozanne, C. M. P. *et al.* In: N. E. Stork, J. Adis & R. K. Didham (Eds.) *Canopy Arthropods* (Chapman & Hall, London, 1997, pp. 534–550).

Table 5.3 *Examples of recorded edge effects and edge functions*

| Habitat type and region | Edge type | Edge effect | Edge function (metres) |
|---|---|---|---|
| Rainforest: Manaus, Brazil | Fragment | See Fig. 5.12 | See Fig. 5.12 |
| Rainforest: Queensland, Australia | Fragment | Gap flora, exotics, lianas increase | 500 |
| | | Canopy cover decrease | 150 |
| | | Seeds from matrix increase | 80 |
| Moist forest: Rio Bravo, Belize | Minor road | Seed predation decrease | >100 |
| | | Egg predation increase | >30 |
| | | Density of forest increase | >30 |
| Conifer forest: Idaho, USA | Fragment | Soil temperature increase | >13 |
| Conifer forest: Sweden | Fragment | Egg predation increase | >30 |
| Conifer forest: Pacific NW, USA | Fragment | Humidity and wind increase | >240 |
| | | Sunlight increase | >30 |
| | | Growth of hemlock seedlings increase | 140 |
| | | Tree mortality increase | >120 |
| Conifer stand: England | Plantation | Light levels increase | >10 |
| | | Spider density decrease | >20 |
| | | Predator/prey ratio increase | >20 |
| | | Woodland spider density decrease | >5 |
| | | Arthropods <2 mm length decrease | 25 |
| Deciduous forest: Wisonsin, USA | Fragment | Nest predation/ parasitism increase* | >200 |
| Deciduous forest: Pennsylvania, USA | Fragment | Light increase | 35 |
| | | Humidity decrease | >50 |
| | | Temperature increase | >25 |
| | | Shrub cover increase | >30 |
| Deciduous forest: E Tennessee | Power-line: (80 m wide) | Forest-interior birds decline | >240 |
| | | Edge specialist birds increase | >120 |

*Note:* * See Table 5.4(a).

Table 5.4 *Edge effect on forest-interior birds in Wisconsin, USA*

**(a)** *Nesting success (despite predation and brood-parasitism)*

| Distance from edge (metres) | Nest success (% conspecifics fledged) |
|---|---|
| <100 | 18% |
| 100–200 | 58% |
| >200 | 70% |

**(b)** *Decline in a forest-interior species (American redstart)*

| Year of study | Presence in fragments of various sizes | | | |
|---|---|---|---|---|
| 1931 | Reported 'all woods', and 'common' | | | |
| 1957 | 4–9 ha | 10–20 ha | >20 ha | >100 ha |
|  | 7% | 16% | 39% | ? |
| 1980 | 0% | 0% | 0% | 75% |

*Note:* Forest specialist bird species include American redstart, wood thrush, yellow-throated vireo. Brood parasites include brown-headed cowbirds. Nest-predators include birds and mammals.
*Source:* Temple, S. A. & Cary, J. R. *Conservation Biology* **2** (1988), 340–347.

resulting directly from microclimatic changes include tree death and retreat of species needing dark conditions. 'Second-order' (indirect) effects may then follow as a consequence. Plants formerly found in forest gaps may be able to colonise the edge, and certain invertebrates and vertebrates may join them – for example butterflies which live on the flowers of the new plants. Birds may arrive which hunt in different ways to those of a forest core. Those birds that do not like to be near gaps retreat into the forest (and will often die under intensified competition). Large carnivores also retreat. Small omnivorous mammals replace them. 'Edge creep' describes the problem whereby edges move into a fragment as deeper and deeper layers are degraded by edge effects: a positive feedback may result, leading to rapid collapse of the interest of a small fragment.

Predation usually increases near edges, and in small fragments (Fig. 5.14). Human hunting is a very widespread edge effect with which managers often have to contend. People penetrate into reserves to hunt and obtain fuel, as in Mkomazi Game Reserve in Tanzania. Another edge effect is the risk of animals migrating or straying from a park into adjacent agricultural land and harming crops, livestock or people, leading to persecution. Moreover, animals may become exposed to risks such as road-traffic or disease – as with African wild dogs.

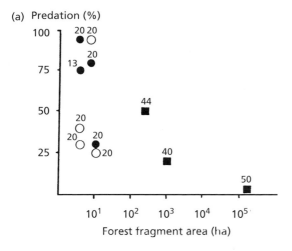

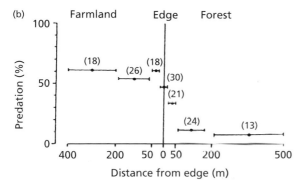

**Fig. 5.14.** An increase in predation is common near the edge of fragments. (a) Predation on dummy nests in the Maryland/Tennessee area of North America: large forest tracts (solid squares); rural fragments (open circles); suburban fragments (solid circles). (b) Predation on dummy nests in relation to a farmland–forest edge in south-central Sweden.
*Sources:* (a) Wilcove, D. S. *Ecology* **66** (1985), 1211–1214. (b) Andren, H. & Angelstam, P. *Ecology* **69** (1988), 544–547.

The edge may thus become a 'sink' for such species. This will be particularly problematic for large species, species with large territories, and species with large migratory or dispersal ranges. The selective loss of wide-ranging mammal species due to edge effects has been demonstrated by R. Woodroffe and J. F. Ginsberg, and probably also applies to birds such as raptors. Hunting at the edge influences lion social systems 80 km into Hwange National Park, Zimbabwe – leaving no part of its 14 900 km² area unaffected.

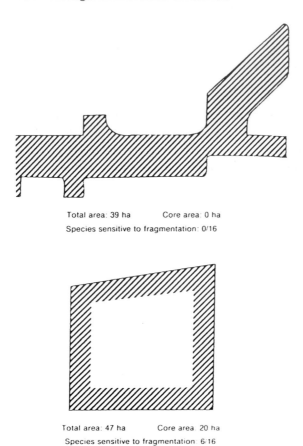

Total area: 39 ha          Core area: 0 ha
Species sensitive to fragmentation: 0/16

Total area: 47 ha          Core area: 20 ha
Species sensitive to fragmentation: 6/16

**Fig. 5.15.**   Application of the Core Area Model to two fragments of similar size in Wisconisn, USA, where the edge effect is taken to penetrate 100 m. The number of forest specialist birds sensitive to fragmentation in the region is 16: the top fragment supported none of these, and the bottom fragment supported 6.
*Source:* Temple, S. A. (1986). In: Verner, Jared, *et al.* (Eds.) *Wildlife 2000. Modelling Habitat Relationships of Terrestrial Vertebrates.* Copyright 1986. Reproduced by permission of The University of Wisconsin Press, Madison, Wisconsin, pp. 301–304.

The Core Area Model predicts the core available in any fragment shape or size, once the edge function is known. S. A. Temple found that this model is more successful at predicting the number of species of forest specialist birds in temperate forests in North America than is consideration of area alone (Fig. 5.15). Being widely threatened, forest specialists are high quality species. The amount of edge relative to core is lower in big sites and in rounder sites.

Management of fragmented habitats thus depends on knowledge of the most important edge effects, and the general limits to dispersal of species within the habitat. The monitoring of biotic conditions (such as humidity) and of particularly sensitive indicator species (core specialists and poor dispersers) might permit the identification of problems such as edge creep. Such indicator species have to be identified in comparative studies of large and small sites. Some form of management (such as growing plantations as buffers around the reserve, or extension of the reserve) might then mitigate the impact of edges. Similarly, the importance of dispersal might be tested through examination of highly isolated sites, or population genetics (Section 6.2.2).

Edge effects therefore fortuitously support four of the geometrical design principles in Fig. 5.6: large sites are preferable to small ones, single large sites to several small ones, and more circular shapes to more elongated, irregular or perforated shapes. Edge effects also have relevance to the value of corridors.

## 5.4.3 Corridors and isolation

Managers have long debated the value of strips of habitat, or 'corridors', which permit dispersal between reserves. The importance of dispersal to organisms is often overlooked. W. D. Hamilton, one of the greatest evolutionary biologists, considered dispersal the most important aspect of life after survival and reproduction. Corridors in theory have two advantages: they top-up populations which are too small to be viable on their own, by bringing in new individuals (Section 6.1). They may also increase the genetic diversity and thus the presumed viability of the populations that are linked (Sections 6.2 and 6.3): indeed, red squirrel genes have been shown to spread as fragmentation in Britain is reduced.

There is some evidence that corridors may help managers to maintain higher overall biodiversity – for example, from work by D. R. Perault and M. V. Lomolino on the mammals of the Olympic National Forest in Washington. Protection of community structure might be a cumulative result of benefits to many individual species, or benefit to a keystone species (Section 3.1.4). There are several examples of corridors working for individual species: chipmunks in an agricultural landscape in North America survived better when hedgerows increased the linkage of forest fragments, whilst red-backed voles use corridors between unlogged forests. Migrating toads, otters and badgers can use tunnels under roads in Britain. A review of the value of corridors by P. Beier and R. Noss found that several studies had shown benefits from corridors and none had proven they did harm; they conclude that a corridor should be assumed to be useful unless proven otherwise.

There are several theoretical reasons for why corridors may occasionally be counter-productive. The corridors may be insufficiently safe, with edge effects, and therefore act as population 'sinks'. Corridors might permit the spread of undesirable phenomena such as fire, diseases and exotic species. Regular boat journeys might be equivalent to a corridor, and present a risk in the Seychelles, where the endemic magpie robin and warbler have survived only because isolation prevented exotic predators reaching all the islands.

To have value, corridors should generally be wide enough to have a core area through which the species to be conserved can move without high mortality. Ideally, the corridor should be wide enough to permit breeding along its length. In KwaZulu-Natal, S. R. Pryke and M. J. Samways found grassland corridors amongst forests need to be over 250 m wide to be used as habitats by grassland specialist butterflies; butterflies move faster – if at all – through less hospitable narrow corridors, because they stop less often to feed, lay eggs or bask. The edge function can be a guide: to have a core along it, the corridor needs to be at least twice the width of the distance edge effects can penetrate. With edge functions of the order of kilometres in some tropical forests, very broad corridors may therefore be required. However, some species and habitats are less sensitive. On Dominica, P. G. H. Evans has found that a corridor only some 10 m wide (essentially a row of native trees) is sufficient to encourage native forest birds such as the brown trembler to move through the matrix (which is a banana and citrus plantation). Corridors may be enhanced by planting fruit trees, or digging water holes, as for elephants. Samways and colleagues have also found that the amount of disturbance in a corridor can be more important than width or location.

Corridors may need to be much wider than people realise: in Europe hedgerows on farms are often described as 'wildlife corridors', yet will not permit species which are strongly influenced by edges to move through them. For example, C. M. P. Ozanne and colleagues found that woodland specialist spiders are rare within 10 m of the edge of a forest – suggesting corridors at least 20 m wide may be required for such species. If there are species sensitive to the microclimatic differences which occur up to 50 m into some British forests, corridors would have to be over 100 m wide. Similarly, in dry forests in Costa Rica, forest birds such as the barred antshrike choose forest tracts, rather than hedgerows, for movement between fragments. The landscape may thus actually be far less connected than it appears. Highly edge-sensitive species might again be used by managers to provide a guide to minimum desirable corridor width.

'Landscape connectivity' describes the overall pattern of patches of habitat, including broad and narrow links between them. In British Columbia, S. W. Harrison found juvenile spruce grouse, a forest specialist, to have 31% mortality in more highly connected conifer forests, compared with 75% in forests with low connectivity.

In general, the use of corridors to increase connectivity in the landscape is a way of restoring naturalness, and is therefore desirable. Conversely, few would advocate linking sites that were not naturally linked. It seems that common-sense is required. If sites were once linked in a continuous patch, harm is unlikely if they are re-connected by managers (unless a new threat has arrived in the landscape, such as a disease, feral species, or increased fire-setting by farmers or vandals). Corridors are likely to remain a frequent source of debate amongst conservationists, some of whom believe there may often be cheaper management alternatives such as transfer of individuals (Chapters 6 and 8). Managers will need to monitor the effects and success of individual corridors, and if necessary choose to expand or sever them. Dispersal will be facilitated if a series of reserves are close together, even if there are no corridors. Sites that are closer together may share some of the benefits, and risks, of sites linked by corridors.

Landscape management which incorporates the biogeographical processes described above may lead to lower management costs overall, as fewer undesirable changes will occur spontaneously in the protected areas. Evolutionary processes involving dispersal or genetic gradients will also be better protected in a well-connected landscape.

## 5.4.4 Generalised or customised management?

General principles of reserve design and management are risky. For example, in the case of fragmented habitats, the importance of edges or the value of corridors varies between sites, habitats and species. The concept of 'variegation' develops the idea that species have different abilities to move through a landscape mosaic, which will 'filter' out the more specialised species; some habitat mosaics and edges are more selective filters than others. Some biologists such as D. Simberloff have argued that those designing and managing reserves should ideally work on a case-by-case, species-by-species basis. However, a shortage of time and money may preclude such an approach, and conservation biologists have sought sweeping generalities for reserve design.

A compromise is that generalisation on design and management should be as limited as possible, based only on local experimental evidence. Studies that might serve as local models include those on fragmentation of the Amazon by T. E. Lovejoy, W. F. Laurance and colleagues, on edge effects for North American forests by D. S. Wilcove, S. A. Temple and others, or on corridors in the Caribbean by P. G. H. Evans. Some mistakes will still be made – but probably fewer than with other universal management prescriptions or with numerous site-specific prescriptions that have been inadequately researched for lack of resources.

The management of individual sites may also be aided by detailed knowledge of the requirements of individual, high-profile species, for which substantial ecological research has been performed. There is a role for umbrella species (Section 3.1.4). Management of reserves for particularly sensitive, specialised species may protect the majority of high-quality species within them.

## 5.5   Zonation and Biosphere reserves

If a region cannot be protected throughout as wholly natural, yet it is of very high value, then a compromise may be found between use and protection. The compromise may involve 'sustainable' use throughout the site (Chapter 7), or may involve dividing the site into zones with different degrees of protection and use. Such zonation is a principle behind UNESCO's Man And the Biosphere Programme (MAB). In theory, the less heavily utilised zones provide benefits to the local people, such as watershed protection, and wider benefits such as protection of genetic diversity.

The MAB endorses 'Biosphere reserves', which form a World Network of over 400 sites with common standards. Their basic functions are conservation, development and logistic support of research, monitoring, and education. They have at least one core area that is relatively pristine and devoted to long-term protection. Core areas are adjacent to, or interspersed amongst, buffer zones of more intensive habitation or use, in which only activities compatible with protection of the core are permitted. There is an outer transition area in which sustainable resource use is encouraged (Fig. 5.16). Examples include the Pantanal of Brazil, Komodo in Indonesia, Sierra Nevada de Santa Marta in Colombia, Niagara Escarpment in Canada, Shennongjia in China, and the Caerlaverock coastal system in Britain.

Zonation has been a principle of conservation for many years. In the former USSR, the equivalent of Biosphere reserves have been designated since the 1920s, and were similar to the UNESCO pattern with an aim to protect landscape and genetic resources. Soviet Nature Reserves included a strict conservation area, which only scientists could visit, surrounded by a buffer zone,

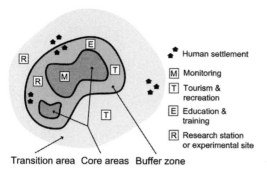

Transition area  Core areas  Buffer zone

**Fig. 5.16.** The general design principles of a UNESCO Biosphere reserve.
*Source:* Redrawn from the UNESCO Man and the Biosphere website.

which maintained existing economic activity provided it did not influence the reserve. The national parks of this region now have areas of habitation and public use, and a sanctuary area ('*zakaznik*') where tourism is excluded.

Zonation of reefs, such as the Great Barrier Reef, the Belize barrier reef, and reefs in Florida, involves evaluating the best areas for conservation and the local threats. Zones may permit or exclude specific activities such as fishing of various types, diving, and research – or exclude all intervention to provide control sites. The zonation system for two major reserves are illustrated in Fig 5.17. Zonation may be temporary. For example, parts of sites may be closed only during nesting seasons of birds or sea turtles. This leads us to the next chapter, where we consider the management designed around the needs of selected individual species.

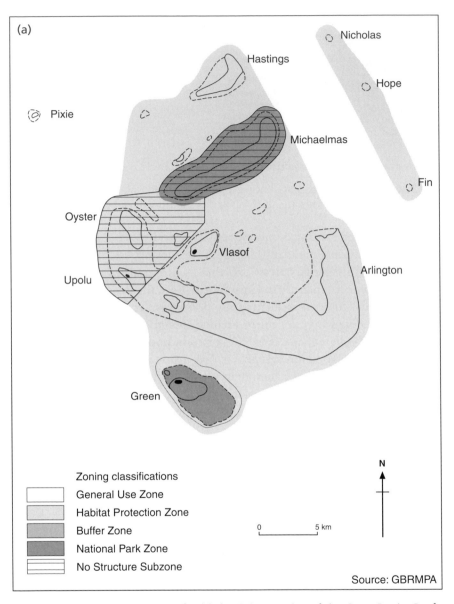

**Fig. 5.17.**  The zonation system for (a) the Cairns section of the Great Barrier Reef; (b) the Amazonian forest and freshwater reserve of Mamirauá.
*Sources:* Redrawn from (a) Kay, R. & Alder, A. *Coastal Planning and Management* (Routledge, New York, 1999). (b) Sociedade Civil Mamirauá. *Mamirauá – Plano de manejo* (Manaus, 1996).

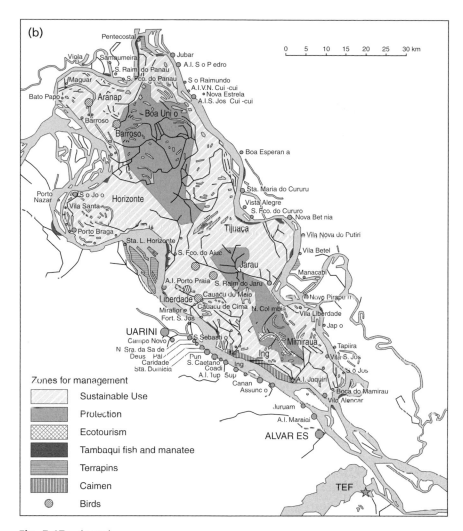

**Fig. 5.17.** *(cont.)*

# 6

# Management of species

Our limited resources preclude customised management for the majority of species. Indeed, most species and their requirements may never be known to science. However, the management of several individual species simultaneously may make a substantial contribution to management of habitats, and the management of keystone species may be a particularly important part of such management (Section 3.1.4). Conservation focused on species may be applied in the wild habitat of the organism ('*in situ* conservation'), or in captivity ('*ex situ* conservation'), or both. This chapter examines conservation of individual species, and of groups of related species which can be treated together because they have similar requirements, threats, or appeal.

Local populations are being extirpated much faster than entire species, and whilst this is generally less irreversible than the loss of species, it makes each species more vulnerable. Prioritisation of populations for conservation may use methods similar to the prioritisation of species and habitats (Chapter 3), considering factors such as population size, position in a geographical unit, genetic distinctiveness, and the risk of parochialism (Section 3.1.2). Genetic markers (e.g. DNA sequences) can be used to identify the linkage, taxonomic distinctiveness, and hence phylogenetic importance of populations.

One form of customised management is to identify the way the local populations of a species are connected together by dispersal, and how these populations are created or lost. Sometimes a species occurs in several populations, and the most important aim is to conserve the whole population, rather than any local population. Such situations may have relevance to the maintenance of species richness in naturally patchy habitats, or where the local populations have been created by habitat fragmentation (Section 5.4).

## 6.1   Metapopulations

A 'metapopulation' is a population of populations. If a species occurs in an area in several isolated patches of habitat, each of which might support a sub-population of the whole population, then it might be a metapopulation. The word is sometimes used rather loosely to describe any sub-divided population, and also in the context of captive breeding and translocation (where captive or isolated populations are considered part of a metapopulation). However, it is clearer to restrict the word to cases where the mathematical models discussed below may apply. These are essentially a form of equilibrium model, focused on the overall stability of a group of populations of a species. Conservationists may use metapopulation models to try to predict the survival of a species in a region.

The classic model of metapopulation dynamics was suggested by R. Levins in 1970. In a 'Levins-type' metapopulation, each patch of habitat is very similar in quality and area. Each patch may or may not be occupied by the species, which survives in an area because of an equilibrium between the chance extinction of sub-populations in patches, and the chance colonisation or re-colonisation of patches. Such a metapopulation can be recognised by the 'twinking' in and out of existence of sub-populations, whilst the whole population changes more slowly. It is similar to the ETIB in having an extinction–colonisation balance (Section 5.4.1), but considers only one or a very few species, not species richness.

Metapopulation dynamics are illustrated in Fig. 6.1. The critical feature is a high enough level of dispersal to replace local extinctions. Species that are likely to undergo such dynamics include 'pioneer species' exploiting naturally transient habitats (Section 7.3.1). A review by S. Harrison suggests most cases described as metapopulations are in fact better described as 'mainland–island populations' or 'source–sink populations' in which a relatively large source population survives continuously, occasionally topping up or replacing smaller populations that have become extinct. Some authors would argue this is another form of metapopulation with a different mathematical description. Table 6.1 shows some examples of species with particular population dynamics. The scale at which the landscape is viewed may influence whether a species is seen as having a metapopulation structure.

Small populations can serve as sinks because they lose individuals quickly through dispersal across a relatively large edge. Similarly, isolated populations

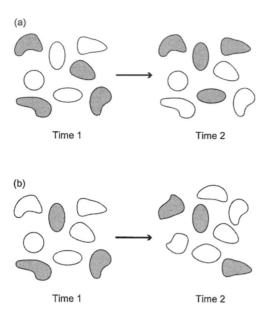

(a)

Time 1                    Time 2

(b)

Time 1                    Time 2

**Fig. 6.1.** Metapopulation dynamics. Individual patches of habitat temporarily support part of the metapopulation. Empty but suitable habitat patches are shown blank, occupied patches are shaded. Patches may be stationary (a), or move in a shifting mosaic (b).

suffer high extinction rates. C. D. Thomas has shown this effect with the silver-studded blue butterfly on patches of grassland in Britain, where suitable small or isolated patches were more often empty than predicted from their frequency.

A critical feature of metapopulations relevant to management is that removal of an *empty* patch is almost as detrimental to the species as removal of an occupied patch. Indeed, at any given time, more of the suitable habitat may be empty than occupied. Furthermore, a decreased dispersal rate (due to increased isolation of patches) may be very problematic. This has relevance to the debate on wildlife corridors between reserves (Section 5.4). Management of metapopulations includes protection of patches, and aiding dispersal (possibly through translocations, Section 8.1).

Since the model of the population dynamics of a species includes its dispersal ability and local extinction risk, a model developed for one species is only applicable to those few species which have very similar biology – if such species exist. For example, several of the butterflies of calcareous grassland in Britain might be served by minor adjustments to a single model template. To construct a metapopulation model, we need to know a great deal about the ecology of the species in question (its 'autecology'). This can take considerable

Table 6.1 *Some examples of population structure*

| Species | Observed structure of population | Type of population |
|---|---|---|
| Orb-spiders (Bahamas) | Few large populations, many small | Mainland–island |
| Bay checkerspot butterfly (USA) | One population of >500 000, nine of 10–400 | Mainland–island |
| Ragwort (Britain) | Continuous population over patchy habitat | Patchy |
| Boreal mammals (SW USA) | Relict population declining as climate warms | Non-equilibrium |
| Pool frog (Sweden) | Shifting mosaic in temporary ponds | Metapopulation |
| Furbish lousewort (USA) | Shifting mosaic on unstable riverbanks | Metapopulation |
| Silver-studded blue (Britain) | Shifting mosaic on early-successional grass | Metapopulation |
| Mosses (Scandinavia) | Shifting mosaic on decaying logs | Metapopulation |

*Source:* Compiled from Harrison, S. Metapopulations and conservation. In: Edwards P. J., May, R. M. & Webb, N. R. (Eds.) *Large Scale Ecology and Conservation* (Blackwell Scientific Publications, 1994).

amounts of fieldwork, and many years of measurement of the dispersal and extinction rates. The model needs to be continually refined in the light of new information. This form of very intensive care is only possible for very high-quality species.

Metapopulation models have been used successfully in reserve acquisition and management for butterflies in Britain, but conversely it has been argued that millions of dollars were wasted on the development of a related type of spatially structured model for the northern spotted owl in an attempt to predict the impacts of logging. In the latter case, a precautionary approach was adopted by a judge in the light of the uncertainties in the model. Metapopulation models are not accepted as realistic or safe by many biologists.

## 6.2   Conservation genetics

Genetics is a fast-moving subject which is important to conservationists in four main ways: to help maintain the genetic viability of small populations in the face of environmental changes; to help quantify how closely related individuals or populations are; to examine the phylogenetic relationship between species; and to help measure and maintain genetic resources. Conservation of genetic diversity depends on conservation genetics – for example, the knowledge that isolated populations on the edge of the range of the species, under local selection pressures, may be genetically distinctive and valuable.

## 6.2.1 Founder effects and bottlenecks

If a population is founded from a small number of individuals, this is equivalent to taking only a limited sample of the genetic variants (alleles) of the original population. In such circumstances, chance alone might mean that the sample includes alleles that are naturally rare in the main population, but now occur in a large fraction of the founder population. Whilst the new population expands, such alleles might remain at a frequency improbable in larger populations. A founder effect might be disadvantageous for a number of reasons: for example, the naturally common alleles might be beneficial to individuals under certain conditions. A possible example of a founder effect occurred with the Mauritian pink pigeon: several of the captive birds which had been bred in Mauritius from a few wild-caught birds had deformities of the feet or brain. Some disadvantageous alleles might even become 'fixed' – meaning they completely displace typical alleles. Conversely, founder effects in some alien species may permit rapid evolution and invasion.

'Bottlenecks' are periods when a population is small, and are more serious the narrower they are and the longer they persist. Alleles may be lost from a population by 'genetic drift' (chance changes in frequency of selectively neutral alleles), or by natural selection. Drift is faster in small populations, where it can become a more powerful force than selection in determining allele frequency. Experiments with some insects suggest a bottleneck of single generation may have little impact on the diversity of the alleles in a population (or may increase it), but the diversity drops rapidly as generations pass within the bottleneck. Bottlenecks may be more serious than they first appear, because only part of a population of size $N$ is reproductively active – the 'genetically effective population', $Ne$. This may be the result of biases in the sex ratio, age ratio, or incompatibilities in mating or pollination; some individuals may be relatively fecund and provide a greater fraction of the alleles to the next generation. A review by T. Crawford concluded that in many cases $Ne$ is only a tenth or less of $N$, and a figure of $Ne$ as approximately one fifth of $N$ has been widely adopted.

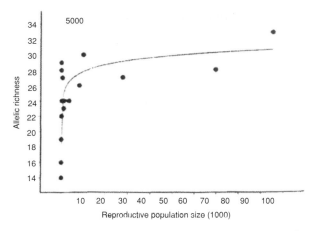

**Fig. 6.2.** Low genetic variation (allelic richness) in small populations of button wrinklewort (an endangered daisy of North America). Populations above 5000 individuals have high numbers of alleles.
*Source:* Young, A. G. *et al. Conservation Biology* **13** (1999), 256–265.

Theory suggests the rate of loss of alleles (genetic diversity) from a population by drift is approximately $1/(2Ne)$ per generation. Thus, if $Ne$ is 10, there will be a 40% loss in ten generations, whilst if $Ne$ is 100, the loss will be only 5% in ten generations. After a bottleneck, the expected proportion of the original heterozygosity which will remain is roughly $1 - 1/(2Ne)$. Genetic diversity can be measured by the average proportion of genes for which an individual has different alleles – the heterozygosity. The inbreeding coefficient, $F$, describes the reduction in heterozygosity due to inbreeding, and can be estimated from protein polymorphism (or pedigree records). The rate of change of $F$ due to drift is approximately $1/(2Ne)$ per generation.

The loss of variation in small populations is illustrated in Fig. 6.2. Without selection or mutation, most genetic variation would be lost in $2Ne$ generations. The rare alleles will generally be lost first. This could have significance if the rare alleles confer benefit such as resistance to disease. The loss of half a captive cheetah population in the USA to a viral disease which rarely kills domestic cats may illustrate the risks of low genetic diversity.

Populations expanding after a bottleneck may re-acquire genetic diversity through mutation, but this may take hundreds or thousands of generations. Studies of mitochondrial DNA sequences suggest that many species, including the polar bear, have been through natural bottlenecks. Some species are very tolerant of bottlenecks – indeed the 'pioneer species' (Section 7.3.1) specialise in survival in small populations. Species that have apparently survived bottlenecks in captivity include Przewalski's horse (once reduced to 13 individuals). However, experiments have shown that *Drosophila* populations which have been through bottlenecks cope less well with environmental change.

The isolation of a population will influence the flow of alleles into the population and the risk of genetic deterioration. It is widely believed that the arrival of only one immigrant per generation can significantly reduce random allele loss. However, the assumptions behind this suggestion may be unrealistic, and larger gene flows may be needed. Isolation has the consequence that, for self-pollinating plants and for some animals, there may be much greater genetic diversity between populations than within them.

If people change the environment they might change the selective advantage of some alleles, and eliminate some of them. If the environment were then allowed to return to normal, the population might not be able to respond fast enough. An example might be the extirpation of predators from an area, and a consequent reduction in anti-predator defences in the prey. The rate of change of the environment will be important in determining the outcome.

## 6.2.2 Inbreeding depression

'Inbreeding depression' is a decline in viability and/or fecundity of individuals resulting from mating between close relatives. Inbreeding is minimised in an 'idealised population', in which individuals mate randomly. However, populations may depart from this, giving a low $Ne$. When close relatives inter-breed, the parents share the same alleles for many genes, and these come together (become homozygous) in the offspring. Heterozygotes may have higher fitness than one or both homozygotes.

If deleterious recessive alleles become homozygous, pathological conditions result (Fig. 6.3). These are often witnessed in highly inbred pedigree domestic animals. Captive populations, such as those in zoos, are also good places to observe the problems of inbreeding. Wild populations are seldom sufficiently well known to witness inbreeding depression, although their $F$ can be measured. A range of problems which are thought to be the consequence of inbreeding are given in Table 6.2. The severity of inbreeding depression varies from species to species. Some are highly susceptible, whilst others (such as many invertebrates and plants) are highly tolerant. Inbreeding may affect one sex more than the other, and may skew the sex ratio creating further problems. A study of 38 species of mammals showed an average of 33% higher mortality in juveniles born to parent/sib or sib/sib matings. Problems of inbreeding may take thousands of years to show in a long-lived species of tree.

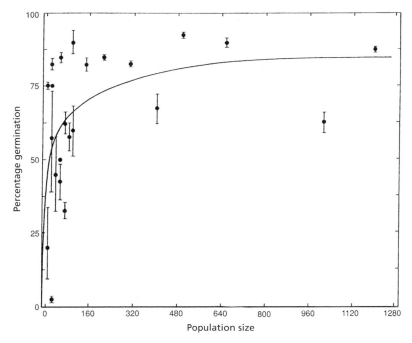

**Fig. 6.3.** Inbreeding depression lowers the germination success of the royal catchfly. *Source:* Menges, E. S. *Conservation Biology* **5** (1991), 158–164.

Homozygosity reduces the options for a varied immune system. A lack of variety in the offspring exposes them to a high risk of disease, climate change or other environmental unpredictability. Sexual reproduction evolved in part because it helps provide insurance against a variable and unpredictable environment: the genetically varied offspring sex produces are not all at the same risk.

## 6.2.3   Outbreeding depression

High heterozygosity can also be harmful to the viability of a population. Reduction in viability or fecundity due to mating with distant relatives is called 'outbreeding depression'. In extreme cases the problem of 'genetic assimilation' of novel alleles merges into the problems of 'introgression' after hybridisation with invasive species (Section 2.4 and Fig. 6.4). Breeding with individuals from remote populations risks diluting away locally advantageous alleles by an influx of novel alleles. The local alleles may be advantageous only infrequently, whilst incoming alleles may confer short-term benefits on individuals

Table 6.2 *Some examples of the consequences of inbreeding depression*

| (a) *Animals* | |
|---|---|
| Lion in Ngorongoro Crater | More sperm abnormalities; low sperm motility. |
| Cheetah (C) | Low sperm concentration; defective sperm; congenital abnormalities; high cub mortality. High vulnerability to infection. |
| Florida panther | Low sperm quality; small testes; vulnerable to microbial parasites. |
| Black-footed rock-wallaby | Female fecundity lower; sex-ratio skew; more fluctuating asymmetry (i.e. asymmetry on random side). |
| Okapi (C) | Higher juvenile mortality in parent/offspring or sib/sib mating; |
| Eland, Siberian tiger (C) | Decreased fertility and viability in zoos. |
| Takahe (C); common shrew (C, NT) | Survival of individuals released into wild problematic. |
| Great tits (NT) | Reduced nesting success; reduced hatching rate. |
| Desert topminnows | Slow growth; reduced fecundity; more fluctuating asymmetry; more developmental abnormalities; poor survival under stress; more parasites; weaker in competition. |
| Song sparrow (NT) | Reduced survival and female reproduction; low survival through storm. |
| Golden lion tamarin | Increased juvenile mortality. |
| (b) *Plants* | |
| Beraliya | Reduced seed set, germination, viability. |
| Torrey pine | Seeds trapped and germinate on plant; slow seed maturation. |
| Great blue lobelia (NT) | Reduced seed survival, decreased flower number. |

*Notes:* Results from captive populations marked (C); not threatened marked (NT). See Lacy, R. C. *Journal of Mammology* **78** (1997), 320–335, for more details.

('heterosis') and come to dominate the population. Locally adapted 'gene complexes' (combinations of alleles), if they exist, might be broken up.

Examples of outbreeding depression are relatively rare compared with inbreeding depression – perhaps partly because individuals may look very healthy. When ibex were reintroduced to Czechoslovakia, the initial population appeared successful, but further animals of different races were added

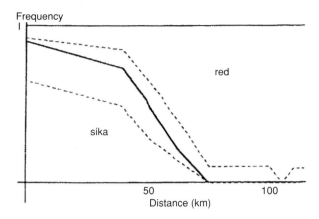

**Fig. 6.4.** Hybridisation between red deer and introduced sika deer in Argyll, Scotland, leading to genetic introgression. The shaded area between the dashed lines shows the proportion with alleles from both species: red deer alleles predominate above the solid line. Genes of sika ancestry have a higher frequency near the site of sika introduction.
*Source:* Goodman, S. J. *et al. Genetics* **152** (1999), 355–371. Copyright Genetics Society of America.

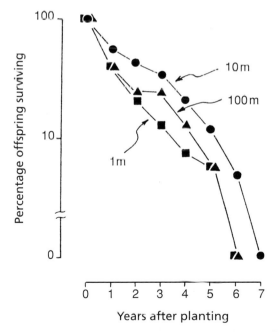

**Fig. 6.5.** Outbreeding depression in scarlet gilia. The survival of offspring is greatest when parents are from populations an intermediate distance apart (10 m) compared with 1 m or 100 m apart.
*Source:* Waser, N. M. & Price, M. V. *Evolution* **43** (1989), 1097–1109.

to hasten the recovery: the hybrids bred at the wrong season, and the population was extirpated. An experimental demonstration of outbreeding depression is given by the partridge pea, which is naturally inbred. The first generation after hybridisation between populations shows heterosis (hybrid vigour), but the third generation has reduced vigour (measured by germination, survivorship, biomass and fruit production). Experimental pollination of scarlet gilia showed outbreeding depression if the parents were 100 m apart (Fig. 6.5). Local adaptations were revealed when different stickleback populations were crossed in the laboratory. Outbreeding depression might occur if animals become displaced as 'refugees' from habitat destruction. Although there are few examples, outbreeding caries a risk to which a precautionary approach should be applied.

## 6.3   Population viability

How big does a population have to be to be 'viable' – meaning able to survive many generations without extinction? This depends on a number of features of the species, including its genetics, social structure and environment. R. Lande suggests that (other than after sudden bottlenecks) genetic threats often act over hundreds of generations, whilst small populations generally face more acute environmental or demographic threats.

### 6.3.1   Demographic stochasticity and catastrophes

The demography of a population means its size, sex ratio and age structure. If a population is reduced to very low levels (generally fewer than 100 individuals), then it becomes vulnerable to chance ('stochastic') changes in its demography. The population might become all one sex, or all too old to breed. A few species have been witnessed at populations so low that this has been a high risk. The black robin of New Zealand was reduced to three males and two females, but was saved by intensive management. Only two individuals of the palm *Ravenea moorei*, both female, could be found in its habitat on Grand Comore, and the future of this species is in doubt. Small populations face other problems. If they are all in one place, then there is the risk of catastrophe wiping all of them out: 'environmental stochasticity'. Endemic parrots in small patches of primary forest in Jamaica face such a threat from hurricanes.

## 6.3.2  The Allee effect

An 'Allee effect' is the rapid reduction in viability of a population when it falls below a threshold density. Below this threshold, recovery may be impossible. Some species are particularly vulnerable to reductions in population density. An Allee effect may have several causes. For example, some species live in only large populations, or come together in large populations to breed. One of the advantages of being in a large group was identified by W. D. Hamilton, who showed that individuals can hide amongst others of their species to avoid predators. If reproduction is synchronised, then there is the additional benefit that the predators may become 'saturated' (unable to take prey any faster). In such species, reproduction is often triggered by the sights and sounds of a large population. If numbers are reduced, reproduction will be reduced, and numbers will be lower in the next generation: this could lead to a positive feedback, or 'extinction vortex'. Many birds that nest in colonies or have co-operative breeding may be at risk of Allee effects.

It has been suggested that the passenger pigeon and the great auk succumbed when hunting took them below a threshold. Equivalent effects in plants might include the need for a large floral display to attract pollinators, or occasional 'mast years' of high seed production to saturate seed predators. It is possible that many social species (including primates and canids such as wild dogs), might suffer from Allee effects if living in groups helps in foraging, competition or defence. Some species may be reduced to such low density they may not be able to find each other to breed – a risk with species such as the North Atlantic right whale.

## 6.3.3  Population Viability Analysis (PVA)

The viability of species requires self-maintaining populations of healthy individuals. The true viability of populations will become evident only from long periods of observations – perhaps thousands of years. However, various theories and mathematical models are used to try to predict viability. In Population Viability Analysis (PVA), conservationists attempt to estimate the Minimum Viable Population (MVP). MVPs give a probability of survival of the population in successive generations. MVPs have often been based on genetic considerations. One consideration is how fast alleles will be lost from a population (Section 6.2). If a population begins to lose alleles through drift, then an extinction vortex may begin; for example, if the alleles permitting individual flowering plants to pollinate each other start to be lost, more self-pollination will result, with a consequent loss of heterozygosity and viability. Moreover, plants with self-incompatibility are at risk of extirpation in small populations if pollen cannot reach a compatible female plant, as suggested for the button wrinklewort.

The longer the population is to remain genetically viable, the larger it should be. The '50/500 rule' has been widely quoted: this suggested that populations should not fall below 50 in the short term, and should be kept over 500 for longer-term success. The derivation of the 'rule' was as follows: to prevent loss of heterozygosity through inbreeding, we use the empirical measurements which suggest that a rate of change of $F$ of 1% per generation is acceptable. So $1/2Ne = 0.01$, which gives $Ne = 50$. The mutation rate for a particular character was taken as roughly one in a thousand per generation. So, to offset drift with mutation, $1/2Ne = 0.001$, giving $Ne = 500$.

The numbers required are sensitive to the assumptions made about the genetics and environment of the species. The mutation rate used above is derived from cultivated species, whilst much lower rates may occur in some wild species, giving much higher $Ne$. R. Lande suggests that the rate of accumulation of relatively benign mutation may be much lower than the total mutation rate, suggesting a minimum $Ne$ of 5000. Mutation rates of one in a million apply to some genes, giving a minimum viable $Ne$ of 500 000. Since $Ne$ is generally much less than $N$, it appears that populations in the tens or hundreds of thousands are generally required in the long term to retain genetic variation. Inbreeding depression is hard to detect in the wild, and by the time it becomes conspicuous, the population may be genetically destined for extinction.

Various computer models are available for PVA (or Population and Habitat Viability Analysis, PVHA), based on explicit assumptions and empirical data. These include VORTEX and GAPPS (for general PVA), INMAT (for inbreeding effects), RAMAS/AGE (giving matrix-projections of population change). VORTEX includes environmental factors, and has been widely used by the Captive Breeding Specialist Group of the IUCN. Far too much faith can be placed in PVA models, since the relevant biological data are often limited: a study of the Capricorn silvereye showed that the PVA predictions based on five years of observations gave higher estimates of risk than those based on 27 years of data, and there is considerable variation in predicted viability (Fig. 6.6). Studies of the bird's-eye primrose have shown similar risks in extrapolation from limited data. However, models can help in clarifying quantitative targets and identifying gaps in knowledge. Despite the long timescales required to examine MVPs for large organisms, there are some relevant studies. J. Berger

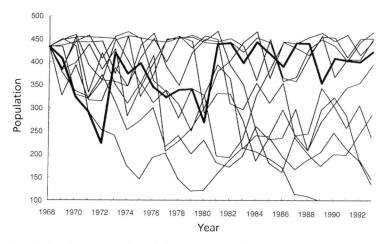

**Fig. 6.6.** The population of the Capricorn silvereye between 1968 and 1993 (thick line) compared with ten runs of a Population Viability Analysis model (VORTEX). Each run represents a replicate alternative path, showing variation due to chance.
*Source:* Brook, B. W. & Kikkawa, J. *Journal of Applied Ecology* **35** (1998), 491–503.

found bighorn sheep populations below 50 do not appear viable much beyond 50 years, whilst populations over 100 persisted for over 70 years.

## 6.4   *In situ* methods

A favoured few species receive close attention and monitoring from conservationists, and we now turn to some general methods used to help conserve selected species. Conservation of a species or taxon within its habitat requires both protection of the habitat (Chapters 5, 7 and 8) and protection of individuals.

## 6.4.1   Protection of individuals from specific threats

A range of threats to species and taxa has been illustrated in Chapter 2. The first problem in species conservation may be to identify the causal factors in the decline of the population, if possible through a 'key-factor analysis' (which identifies the most vulnerable stages in the life cycle). If and when the cause of decline is known, it should become apparent whether conservation in the natural habitat is practicable. If sufficient habitat remains, then it may be possible to control threats within it and maintain the species *in situ*.

The whales and dolphins (Cetacea) have been the focus of much conservation effort, and were amongst the first taxa to cause widespread public involvement in conservation. Populations of most of these species are now small fractions of the original numbers. Following public concern about the declines and animal welfare, many governments adopted a moratorium on the hunting of whales (Section 9.2.1). Controversially, hunting continues through so-called 'scientific whaling', and 'aboriginal' hunts. Some territorial waters have been declared whale sanctuaries by conservation-conscious countries and leaders, as in the Seychelles. Protection of the Cetacea is difficult owing to their large ranges and low densities, and the problems of handling individuals. Techniques such as satellite-tracking, DNA profiling, and ageing via ear bones have advanced our understanding of movement and reproductive rates. The long migrations around ocean basins, and the location of breeding grounds, have been clarified for some species; but even so, species such as the blue whale are very poorly known. Dolphins that live in rivers, such as the Indus and Yangtze, are highly endangered. Pollution, hunting, obstacles, water diversion and disturbance are hard to minimise on the large Asian rivers. Collisions between whales and boats are being reduced in some shipping lanes by looking for the sound-shadow whales produce when in front of rows of buoys containing microphones.

The large carnivores have attracted much sympathy and conservation effort, which is understandable given the popular appeal of cats and dogs, and the many threats. These species often live at low density, and have large home ranges, requiring substantial reserves. Furs of species such as snow leopards are still popular in many cultures; education programmes against their use may have little impact in rural areas of developing countries, and severe penalties may be the only option. Special 'guarding dogs' and fencing can be used to reduce the conflict between carnivores (such as cheetah) and livestock rearing.

'Operation Tiger' was one of the early projects of the WWF. The global tiger population declined 95% in the twentieth century, and under 7000 tigers survive in the wild. 'Tiger reserves' have been established in India and China. International trade in tiger products is restricted by legislation such as 'CITES' (Section 9.2.1). Camera-traps and footprints have proved valuable in monitoring individual tigers.

Wolves and foxes have attracted substantial conservation funding. These, and other canids, often respond quickly to conservation, and may increase rapidly once hunting is prevented. The great behavioural adaptability of canids helps in their acclimatisation and re-introduction (Section 8.1). Wild dog survival in Zimbabwe has been greatly increased by protective collars designed by G. S. A. Rasmussen after studies of behaviour and mortality

**Fig. 6.7.** African wild dog (painted hunting dog) fitted with a reflective studded collar to reduce road-kill and break snares. Without these collars, 87% of dogs die if caught in a snare, but if wearing them at least 92% survive snare events. *Photograph:* Copyright Peter Blinston/Painted Hunting Dog Research Zimbabwe.

(Fig. 6.7). Vaccination against rabies, canine distemper, or parvovirus has helped protect some populations (such as the Catalina Island fox). Attempts to reduce transmission include rabies vaccination of domestic dogs near reserves such as the Serengeti (to protect wild dogs) and Bale (to protect Ethiopian wolves).

Demand for rhino horn for medicine and for dagger-handles far outstrips its replacement rate, and the horn is worth more than its weight in gold. Figure 6.8 illustrates the decline in range of the black rhino, which in the late 1960s numbered some 70 000 and is now down to about 3000. The black rhino population of Kenya dropped from 30 000 in 1975 to 500 in 1990. Given the violence many poachers are prepared to use, anti-poaching measures have reached the level of 'shoot-to-kill' in some East African countries. It is difficult to patrol large areas for a few rhino and a few poachers, and in Cameroon individual black rhino have been protected by armed guards, which move with the animal. As a last resort, rhino have been de-horned (using saws) in some countries to render them less attractive to poachers – but at the risk of disrupted behaviour. Some fragmented wild rhino populations are now being managed genetically as if they were part of a zoo population; these include the 'managed breeding centre' at the Way Kambas National Park in Indonesia.

**Fig. 6.8.** Decline in the range of the black rhino: historical area (inside heavy black line); 1900 (hatched area); 1987 (black area).
*Source:* Ashley, M. V. *et al. Conservation Biology* **4** (1990), 71–77.

Rhino can be very difficult to survey, and camera-traps have helped monitor populations. Molecular fingerprinting of the horn may help track its origin.

Elephants have attracted considerable public interest and conservation efforts. It has only recently been discovered that the forest elephant of West Africa is a distinct species. Wild Asian elephants are threatened by habitat loss. All three species are threatened by demand for ivory, although some populations are thriving. The decline in elephants in East and southern Africa is illustrated in Fig. 6.9. Kenya banned big-game hunting in 1977, and thereby lost a source of revenue which could be directed against poachers; Kenya's elephant population declined severely, whilst that of Zimbabwe, and other well-protected areas in southern Africa, stabilised or increased in the same period. Some countries have conserved elephants so successfully that savannah is being degraded (Section 5.1.1; Fig 5.2(b)); there is little scope for migration outside reserves to alleviate the pressure on land. Countries with 'excess' elephants would like to resume trade in ivory, whilst others such as Kenya oppose this. Kenya made a very public statement of intent to stop

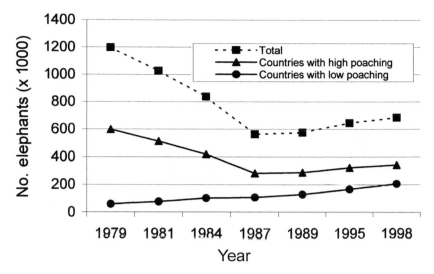

**Fig. 6.9.** Changes in the numbers of elephants in southern and East Africa in relation to a surge in poaching since the 1960s. Five countries having minimal controls on poaching (Angola, Malawi, Mozambique, Tanzania, Zambia) are contrasted with four having effective controls (Botswana, Namibia, South Africa, Zimbabwe).
*Source:* D. H. M. Cumming / IUCN African Elephant Database.

the ivory trade when it burnt a stockpile of 12 tonnes of tusks in 1989. Stable isotopes of chemical elements, which accumulate in different ratios in tusks from different areas, may help to separate legal and illegal trade in ivory. Big-game hunting is highly controversial on ethical grounds, even as part of a culling programme. Conservation of elephants has been improved with detailed knowledge of their social behaviour, migration routes and better population censuses – which have been facilitated by individual recognition of ear shape and the use of radio-collars. Contraceptive vaccines might provide an alternative to culling. Elephants in Kenya responded rapidly to the creation of a new reserve at Laikipia, illustrating their adaptability. Bee hives may help discourage elephants from crop-raiding in East Africa.

Many bird species and taxa have been the focus of conservation efforts. The charismatic birds of prey have been particularly favoured, and can often thrive once threats have been controlled. The northern spotted owl of the Pacific north-west of America was the focus of intensive study and controversy, eventually resulting in protection of its habitat from logging when its high habitat specificity became apparent. Substantial international public lobbying for this attractive bird proved very influential. CITES has been used to prosecute people trading in falcons. Similarly, many parrots and other popular cage birds command very high prices, and illegal trade needs to be stopped during the capture of birds and in smuggling. Migratory birds are particularly vulnerable to habitat loss, climate change and hunting. Specific legislation protects some migratory species (Section 9.2). Species that have communal nest sites may be very vulnerable to exotic species or hunting. Nest-predator control at seabird rookeries may include the deterrence of predators by using distasteful artificial eggs ('aversive conditioning').

Fish that migrate to spawn present great problems for conservationists: movement to the sea or to headwaters of rivers is increasingly difficult (Sections 2.2.3 and 5.3.1). High-quality species for which *in situ* conservation efforts are being made include several species of salmon and sturgeon. Strict management of harvests is required, and enforcement of quotas (such as that on caviar) has proved a problem. Populations ('stocks') are often boosted by fish raised in hatcheries. Genetic pollution from hatcheries, and fish-farms, presents an increasing problem, and may destroy local adaptation. Few (if any) genetically pure salmon survive; in the Oregon, controversy arose when a judge included hatchery-reared fish as part of the population of threatened coho salmon.

Many species of shark are declining under intense hunting pressure for the fins, and because of by-catch. Even very large, vulnerable species such as whale sharks and basking sharks are killed, despite the potential they offer for ecotourism. In the north-west Atlantic, populations of most species declined over 50% in the past 15 years, and hammerheads declined by 89%. Shark-nets (which protect bathing beaches in South Africa and Australia) kill species such as hammerheads. Certain species are receiving protection at least in some areas, such as the great white in South Africa. However, a ban on trade in many shark products is essential, although it will be very difficult to enforce and will need to be complimented by strict protective efforts in many countries. Trade in material from whale sharks and basking sharks is now regulated, and DNA technology can be used to identify the species of shark in a product. Many areas need protection from long-line fishing. Educational programmes are required to offset the negative image of sharks as dangerous pests, and to illustrate the grace, specialisms and value of many species.

Most turtle, terrapin and tortoise species (Chelonia) are declining very rapidly, and many populations have been extirpated. These species are vulnerable for a number of reasons. They may be slow moving, particularly when on land to breed. The freshwater species suffer from habitat loss, as in the Seychelles, and from overharvesting when they come ashore to breed, as in the Amazon. All sea turtles are endangered through overhunting and bycatch (Section 5.3.3). In the Seychelles, beaches which a few decades ago had thousands of green turtle nests each year are now almost empty as a result of hunting and egg-collecting. Sea turtles take decades to mature, and have imprinted fidelity to the area in which they hatched – delaying recovery on depleted beaches.

Protection of Chelonia includes bans on trade in pets or in products such as turtle soup or 'tortoiseshell' (from hawksbill carapace). Although many populations of sea turtle are legally protected, it is very difficult to patrol long stretches of beach, as in Madagascar. Hatching turtles orientate towards light, and so strict controls on developments are needed: these have caused conflict in the Mediterranean. Further conflict arises owing to the influence of beach parasols and sunbathing on sand temperature (which determines the sex of hatchlings). Fortunately, Chelonians appeal to many people, and ecotourism has been developed based on giant tortoises (as in the Seychelles), and on sea turtle nesting (as in Malaysia and Costa Rica). Satellite radio-transmitters and tagging have helped elucidate the large-scale movements and population dynamics of sea turtles. Individually numbered electronic tags ('PIT's) have been implanted subcutaneously into giant tortoises in Seychelles to reduce trade in pets and to monitor populations. Populations of sea turtles and tortoises are now recovering in the Seychelles whilst declining elsewhere in the region, confirming the threats have been identified and managed.

Succulent plants, including cacti, are often vulnerable because of very slow growth rates, which render them liable to overharvesting. Habitat destruction, including overgrazing, threatens many species. Trade in wild-dug plants has been reduced by CITES. Reserves have been set up specifically for some species, such as the saguaro cactus of North America. Transponders have been inserted into individuals of the Wright fishhook cactus in Nevada to track and catch 'cactus rustlers'.

There are various forms of intensive care in the wild. Silversword species in Hawaii require hand-pollination by people climbing down cliffs, because the moths that pollinated them appear to be very rare or extinct; captive populations have been used to augment the wild ones. Individual plants may need protection, such as the fencing and weeding round white forsythia in Korea. Translocation of individuals to new habitat is discussed in Chapter 8.

*In situ* conservation may include habitat enhancement – which may be a restoration effort or which may be a sacrifice of naturalness deemed acceptable given the rarity of the target species. For birds this often includes the use of nest-boxes, which has been important where the habitat has been degraded. For example, nest-boxes have been used for the ground hornbill, Seychelles black parrot and European barn owl, to compensate for a paucity of old, hollow trees (and barns). Nesting rafts have been provided for white pelicans on the

Volga Delta. Other enhancements include: artificial burrows; tunnels or ropes across roads; refuges; and supplementary feeding. Populations of giant panda are fed meat in cold periods, or when flowering of bamboo reduces their food supply – these measures compensate to some degree for the fragmentation of the habitat. Artificial habitat was created for the violet click beetle, a rare European species requiring hollow trees over 150 years old. The age structure of the woodland at its two remaining British sites was becoming short of suitable trees. To help the population through this period, substitute habitat was developed using compost bins containing a rotted-down mix of chicken droppings, sawdust, wood shavings, and dead rabbits; the bins take 5–10 years to prepare.

Adjustment of a management regime based on experience and experiment ('adaptive management') can be very revealing – as with the North Island kokako of New Zealand, where it was discovered that recovery was possible if rats and possums were reduced to very low levels at the start of the breeding season.

## 6.5  *Ex situ* methods

*Ex situ* methods are seldom sufficient in themselves as a conservation tool. There is a limit to the number of species which can be protected in this way, and there is often a limit to the amount of time that viable populations of species can be kept outside of their habitat. Almost any species could be preserved *ex situ* if enough money were devoted to it, but in practice it is usually high-quality species or races, such as relatives of crops, domestic animals and charismatic species which are protected in this way. The *ex situ* storage facilities for species and genotypes are often termed 'gene banks'. There is a bias to crop plants, and only 1% of the world's vascular plant species comprise around half of the germplasm being stored *ex situ*. Conservation of crop plants is co-ordinated by the Consultative Group on International Agricultural Research.

*Ex situ* methods have proved a very valuable complement to *in situ* methods, and a number of species would not have survived without the synergy between the two. Collection of species and races for *ex situ* conservation has now become a race against time, and a range of methods have been developed to collect pure strains, avoid hybridisation, and minimise impacts on wild populations. Some technologies used in *ex situ* conservation are illustrated in Table 6.3.

Apart from cost (which may be more or less than for *in situ* methods), there are other disadvantages to *ex situ* methods. Evolution with other species or in changing climates is halted, whilst the captive population is evolving to survive

Table 6.3 *Some technologies used for* ex situ *conservation*

| Method | Purpose | Example |
|---|---|---|
| Heat treatment | Breaking dormancy | Fynbos species |
| Smoke treatment | Breaking dormancy | *Audouinia capitata* |
| Storage of seeds in moist substrate | Breaking dormancy | Several species |
| Germination test | Checking survival *ex situ* | Cereals |
| Vitrification | Storage of seeds, etc. | *Eucalyptus graniticola* |
| Embryo axis cryopreservation | Storage of recalcitrant species | *Quercus* (oak) spp. |
| Cryopreservation of cell suspensions | As above | *Brunfelsia densifolia* |
| Mycorrhiza-assisted culture of orchids from seed | Reintroduction | Fen orchid |
| Cloning | Increasing population | |
| vegetative propagation | | *Isopogon fletcheri* |
| *in vitro* cloning from shoot tips of grafted plants | | Wyalkatchem foxglove |
| nutrient agar in a sterile jar air layering (stimulating roots from stem) | | *Begonia amphioxus* |
| nodal cuttings/internodal segments | | *Begonia* spp. |
| Somatic embryogenesis | As above | Bamboo cycad |
| *In vitro* fertilisation | As above | Yellow swainson pea |
| Asymbiotic culture of orchids from seed | As above | *Cymbidium rectum* |
| Embryo micropropagation | As above | *Restio abortivus* |
| Artificial insemination | As above | Tiger, giant panda |
| Embryo transfer within species | As above | Ocelot |
| Embryo transfer across species | As above | Guar into cow |
| Cross-fostering | As above | Black robin into Chatham Island tits |

in captivity. An aim of gene banks is to minimise this artificial selection on the *ex situ* population. *Ex situ* methods are vulnerable to changes in policy and funding, and to disasters; some have been lost in wars, as in Somalia. For some species, the collections are duplicated in a number of sites.

In a broad sense, *ex situ* conservation may also include captive rearing of species to take pressure off wild populations. 'Farming' of butterflies,

Table 6.4 *Examples of organisations involved in plant genetic diversity conservation*

| Organisation | Maintains |
| --- | --- |
| International Network for the Improvement of Banana and Plantain | About 600 species and cultivars |
| International Rice Research Institute | About 80 000 cultivars of rice |
| International Livestock Centre for Africa | About 7000 forage legumes |
| Conservatoire Nationale Botanique (France) | Seed bank and re-introductions |
| Rhenish Freilicht-museum, Kommerson (Germany) | Open air museum/rare plants |
| Western Regional Plant Introduction Station (USA) | Seed bank |
| National Seed Storage Laboratory (USA) | Large seed bank |
| Curepipe Botanic Gardens (Mauritius) | Endemic plants |
| Nordic Gene Bank (Sweden) | Seed bank |
| Millennium Seed Bank (Britain) | c. 10% of global flora and full British flora |
| Botanic gardens – all world | About 80 000 species |

aquarium fish, primates, succulents and medicinal plants can help meet demand. However, it is as yet technically difficult to farm many species (such as seahorses) on a large scale. Some farming methods which aim to augment wild populations may in fact be a drain on them: several of the hatcheries set up to rear hatchling sea turtles take eggs from the wild, and the survival of juveniles released to the sea from captivity may be low.

## 6.5.1   Seed banks

Seed banks have a very long history. All agricultural people store seeds from year to year. A variety of local species and races has been created and maintained in this way, including the many 'landraces' of crop plants grown by indigenous peoples. It is only in recent times that systematic efforts have been made to protect this diversity in specialised institutions. Some examples of seed banks for domestic and wild species are given in Table 6.4. These banks work well for certain types of plant, such as the grasses (cereals, millet, rice, maize, etc.), the brassicas (cabbages) and umbelifers (e.g. carrots). The bank stores seeds in cool dry conditions (typically −20 °C to 10 °C, with seeds dried to 5% moisture content). These conditions mimic or exaggerate the climate during the natural dormancy of the species. However, many species of plant, particularly from the humid tropics, do not have a natural dry-season dormancy which can be mimicked *ex situ*. They are very sensitive to reduced moisture content and are hard to store. Such seeds are termed 'recalcitrant'. These species, including many tropical and aquatic plants, can be maintained only by techniques described below.

## 6.5.2 Botanic gardens

Botanic gardens can help to protect many species, including those with recalcitrant seeds. Plants are grown in climates similar to the wild – either in the country of origin of the species, or in a country with a similar climate, or in greenhouses (as with the Eden Project in Britain). Some botanic gardens have satellite gardens protecting various habitats. Some species are cultivated in 'field gene banks', for example medicinal plants in an area of customised secondary forest at Trivandrum, India. About a third of the world's known flowering plants are held *ex situ*, and Botanic Gardens Conservation International helps co-ordinate the effort. Some 45% of the threatened palms of the world, 30% of threatened orchids and 85% of threatened cacti, are in botanic collections. Kew Gardens in Britain grows over 2000 threatened plant species. Some plant species are now extinct in the wild, including *Tulipa sprengeri* from Turkey. The palm *Hyophorbe amaricaulis* was reduced to a single specimen in the botanic garden in Mauritius. General problems with botanic gardens are that the total number of individuals which can be maintained is low, and hybridisation may occur – as with the mandrinette (*Hibiscus fragilis*) of Mauritius which hybridises with the garden plant *Hibiscus rosa-sinenis*.

## 6.5.3 Vegetative propagation and tissue culture

There are many methods to propagate (clone) plants vegetatively. Cuttings, bulbs, leaves, rhizomes or roots may be suitable. Rooting hormones and fungicides may be required. Grafting can be used for some species that do not root well. Cooke's kokio became extinct in the wild on Molokai (Hawaiian Islands), but is being cultivated on a rootstock of a related kokio species. The medium in which plants are cultured varies with the species, and may be sterile or non-sterile nutrient agar, or compost. The temperature of incubation is customised to each species. Species that do not propagate well are also termed 'recalcitrant'. Plants such as palms with a single apical meristem are problematic. A more recent and expensive technique is to clone plants by using *in vitro* tissue culture (IVC). Cells are taken from a tissue, generally the buds, and cultured in a pathogen-free environment. Populations of the lady's slipper orchid have been augmented (re-inforced) in Britain following such 'micropropagation' at Kew. Such cultures can increase populations rapidly, and are easily transported. Tissue can be collected directly from wild plants – '*in vitro* collection' (IVCN). Plants propagated vegetatively are genetically identical; they are therefore even more at risk of disease than inbred populations.

Plant tissues, including buds, meristems and some recalcitrant seeds, can be stored for many years frozen at low temperatures (e.g. $-160\,°C$), after drying to an optimum moisture content and protection with cryoprotectants. Such 'cryopreservation' is expensive, and practicable only for a limited number of species, such as the Wyalkatchem foxglove of Australia, which was reduced to three plants. The DNA of some species is now being isolated and stored for potential genetic engineering.

## 6.5.4  Zoos and cryopreservation

Animals have been maintained *ex situ* as pets or for curiosity for thousands of years. W. T. Hornaday, Director of the New York Zoological park, wrote in 1914: 'Today, the thing that stares me in the face every waking hour, like a grisly spectre with bloody fang and claw, is the extermination of species. To me that is a horrible thing'. Recently, some institutions have been dedicated specifically to conservation, beginning with Sir Peter Scott's Wildfowl and Wetland Trust in 1946 and with Gerald Durrell's Jersey Zoo in 1959.

Many of the world's zoos now help maintain threatened species. Early high-profile captive breeding programmes included the giant panda and the aye-aye. The World Zoo Organisation co-ordinates global programmes, and published the *World Zoo Conservation Strategy* in 1993. The institutions in the American Zoo and Aquarium Association (AZA) have had conservation as a principle aim since 1980: it has a programme which manages the mating and number of offspring of captive populations of threatened species, with co-operation between participating institutions and with *in situ* projects. There are similar associations and programmes in other regions. A database called the International Species Information System registers animals held in zoos and aquariums around the world. In the USA, Taxon Advisory Groups review,

Table 6.5 *Examples of captive breeding programmes leading to releases*

| Species | Site of release |
|---|---|
| Goitred gazelle; wild ass; Siberian crane | Former USSR |
| Houbara bustard | Saudi Arabia |
| Mauritius kestrel*; pink pigeon*; parakeet* | Mauritius |
| Black-footed ferret** | USA: Wyoming |
| Red wolf** | USA: Carolina |
| Puerto Rican crested toad | USA; Canada |
| Cheer pheasant; Swinhoe's pheasant | Pakistan; Taiwan |
| Przewalski's horse** | Mongolia |
| Pere David's deer** | China (semi-wild) |
| Aye-aye; jumping rat; ploughshare tortoise | Madagascar |
| Golden lion tamarin | Brazil |
| Arabian oryx** | Oman; Saudi Arabia; Israel; Jordan, etc. |
| European bison** | Poland (semi-wild) |
| Weta | New Zealand: Double Islands |
| California condor** | USA: California |
| Hawaiian goose (NeNe)* | USA: Hawaii |
| Bali starling (or mynah)* | Indonesia: Bali |
| Chinese alligator* | Yangtze Valley, China |
| Virgin Islands boa | Virgin Islands |
| Guam rail** | Guam; Rota (introduction) |
| Orthostoma cichlid** | Lake Victoria Basin |
| Toromiro** | Easter island |
| St Helena Redwood** | St Helena |
| *Dombeya mauritiana*** | Mauritius |

*Notes:* * = would probably be extinct without *ex situ* methods; ** = became extinct in the wild.

co-ordinate and produce Regional Collection Plans to help allocate available space for a taxon; Conservation Action Partnerships improve co-ordination between countries. 'Species Survival Plans' are used to manage a number of species held by the AZA.

Several species have been saved from extinction by *ex situ* methods (Table 6.5), and much has been learned from studies in zoos of the biology of threatened species. Experience from captive populations can be used in the wild, as with vaccination of mountain gorillas against measles. Maintaining species in captivity requires knowledge of their feeding and reproductive biology, and veterinary expertise. This knowledge may come partly from observations in the wild, and partly from comparisons with similar species. Zoos provide other valuable research opportunities: observing racoons at Calgary Zoo helped in the design of racoon-proof nest-boxes for the mountain bluebird of Canada.

Some species feed and breed readily in captivity. For example, some cats and dogs produce too many offspring for the world's zoos to maintain. Some 80% of carnivore species are kept in captivity, although only 40% of them breed regularly. The highly endangered Siberian tiger and Amur leopard have been bred in captivity, but only a few individuals of such large species can be maintained in any single collection. It is possible that some captive lions are derived relatively directly from the Barbary lion, which has been extinct in the wild since about 1920; the search is on for the animals with the closest similarity in DNA to that from skins of Barbary lions. Several waterfowl have been bred very successfully *ex situ*. One of the pioneering projects was the bolstering of the world population of the Hawaiian goose; about 50 individuals survived in 1947 (half of them in the wild), but by 1966 there were ten times this number, and by 1970 about 150 had been re-introduced to Mani island.

Foster parenting is commonly used for captive birds. A number of raptors have been bred using knowledge from falconry. The Mauritius kestrel was saved from extinction by Carl Jones, working in the Black River Aviaries in Mauritius and with Jersey Zoo; eggs were hatched in incubators, and young released into the nests of foster parents. Artificial eggs with devices to monitor temperature, movement and humidity can help customise artificial incubation, as with the white-naped crane. Many bird species will lay a second or further clutch if one is removed, and eggs can be obtained in this way for rearing under 'surrogate parents' from a common species. The risks of the animal imprinting on the surrogate parent species need to be considered. Imprinting is a risk in a number of species, and considerable efforts have been used to offset it. California condors were reduced to eight in the wild, and all of these were taken into captivity. Eggs were artificially incubated, and the young hand-reared. Glove-puppets resembling condor heads were used to present food to the young and so reduce imprinting on people. Birds were taught to avoid power-line poles through aversion training. Condors have now been released back into the wild, including some wild-caught birds as 'mentors' to transmit 'condor culture'; although poisoning from lead shot and other threats continue, there has been wild breeding after a 20 year gap. The captive breeding programme for condors costs about $1 million per year. Takahe in New Zealand have been reared in a similar way.

Some species or races do not breed well in captivity. The last individual of the Pinta Island race of Galapagos giant tortoises has not mated with females from similar races, and Aldabran giant tortoises do not breed well outside their range. In some species, particularly from temperate regions, reproduction may be triggered by photoperiod, or by specific climatic factors which are unknown or hard to imitate.

New reproductive technologies are being used where breeding is problematic. Eggs and sperm can be collected using methods developed for domestic species. In birds and mammals, artificial insemination is often possible. Hormones may be used to stimulate ovulation, as with the Puerto Rican crested toad and cheetah, or contraceptives used to control reproduction. Ovaries of endangered species can be transplanted to domestic species. In mammals, fertilisation can be performed '*in vitro*' (in test-tubes), and the embryos artificially implanted into a foster mother of the same or a related species. Some of these techniques have been used for high-profile species such as tigers. It is possible to monitor the reproductive state and levels of stress of individuals through samples of endocrine hormones in blood, faeces, or urine. It is now possible to sex birds using DNA from feathers. These techniques permit breeding and diversity in species which, owing to their size or social behaviour, would otherwise require very large enclosures – as with the white rhino.

Cryopreservation of ova, sperm or embryos involves freezing with liquid nitrogen. Techniques from domestic animal husbandry and human medicine have permitted 'frozen zoos' containing endangered species, such as that at the Zoological Society of San Diego. Cryopreservation permits maintenance of more individuals and genes than is possible with adult animals, but is too expensive to use for more than a small proportion of species. There is debate as to whether it will become possible to produce healthy clones of threatened species, and attempts have already been made with guar and Spanish goats. Only one sex can be cloned from an individual – in the case of the extinct Spanish goats, only females can be obtained from a tissue sample of the last individual.

The genetics of the captive stock needs to be monitored, with detailed pedigree (studbook) records whenever possible. Analysis of nuclear or mitochondrial DNA (including DNA fingerprinting), or protein polymorphisms, can help evaluate relatedness and genetic diversity in the populations. Gametes, embryos or animals can be moved around the world to reduce inbreeding.

Some animals have become extinct in the wild but survive in specialist programmes, such as the Leon Springs pupfish, which is conserved at Dexter National Fish Hatcheries (NFH), New Mexico. Various North American pupfish are kept at the NFHs. Similarly some *Partula* snails survive only in captivity, but unfortunately *P. targida* became extinct owing to a microsporidian parasite in captivity. Captive populations lose their endosymbionts under the artificial environment – a beautiful ciliate protozoan was glimpsed once from a wild-caught *Partula,* but has never been seen again. Captive populations of commercially valuable species face security problems: a substantial fraction of the captive population of Bali starlings in Indonesia has been stolen. Any *ex situ* store might be destroyed.

## 6.5.5   Private collections and feral populations

Private collectors have a mixed reputation amongst conservationists. Some have created demand for threatened species, whilst others have been generous in assisting *ex situ* programmes. Pere David's deer was taken from a private park in China to another in Woburn, England, where it survived exclusively in captivity for 800 years, before being re-introduced into semi-wild conditions in 1985. Other threatened species conserved in private ranches in North America and southern Africa include addax and rhinos.

Private collectors have fortuitously maintained populations of many fish species that may be extinct in the wild. Tens of species of cichlid fish of the African Rift lakes may survive only in aquariums. The succulent *Euphorbia mayurnathanii* survives only in cultivation. Several of the societies specialising in growing succulents now have a code of conduct to discourage trade in wild-dug plants, and maintain seed banks of families. Parrots are popular aviary birds, and the value of some species exceeds $10 000 per bird. They may be jealously guarded by collectors. When the Spix's macaw was reduced to a single male in the wild, several owners of captive birds co-operated in an attempt to release a mate; captive breeding of this species has now been successful, and releases of captive Illiger's macaws may help to plan re-introduction.

Collectors have been very important in the maintenance of the genetic diversity of domestic species, such as sheep, cattle, horses and pigs. 'Rare breeds' are often kept by enthusiasts, although there has been a loss of such diversity as costs rise. Rare Breeds International co-ordinates conservation of traditional races. Captive populations have to be protected against diseases such as foot-and-mouth.

Feral populations of species are generally undesirable (Section 2.4). Yet in a few cases, the feral population is thriving whilst the wild one declines. The introduced Reeves pheasant population in Europe is more secure than that in Asia, whilst Britain supports about a third of the world population of the threatened mandarin duck. Fortunately, in neither case do the feral species appear at present to be harming indigenous wildlife.

## 6.5.6   Release methods

The ultimate aim of captive breeding is usually to release individuals into the wild (Section 8.1). The release may be 'hard', in which the animals are placed directly into the wild, or 'soft', in which they are given some support on release, such as provision of food or shelter. They may be immediate, or delayed by release into a fenced area where they remain until acclimatised to the local environment. Some taxa, such as fish, can not easily be soft-released. To date, soft releases have apparently been no more successful than hard releases. Soft releases are more expensive. Species with highly developed social and cultural systems may be hard to release into fully wild conditions. They may not have the survival skills needed for foraging or escape from predators, and they may not be accepted by wild individuals. Primates that have been hand-reared in orphanages (including orang-utans, gorilla and chimpanzee) are generally released into semi-wild conditions, such as an isolated forest patch. Several species for which no secure or natural habitat remains have been released into semi-wild conditions in a managed park.

'Behavioural enrichment' of the zoo environment (by providing diverse enclosures) can be helpful preparation. Black-footed ferrets reared in artificial prairie-dog towns survived better on release than those reared in more artificial environments; juveniles fared better on release than adults, as did those given an opportunity to hunt whilst in captivity. A related species can be used to test release techniques: the Andean condor was used as a model for the California condor. Migratory species may be difficult to release, especially if there is cultural transmission of the migration route from generation to generation. In a few cases, reared animals have been shown the migration route by people flying ultralite planes, carrying a model to which the birds are imprinted. Sandhill cranes in North America were trained to fly 2000 km in this way!

## 6.5.7   Re-creation of extinct species

With a very few extinct animal species and races, there is some hope that selective breeding may help restore something resembling the original animal. Animals *visually* similar to the quagga of southern Africa have been produced from matings between the most quagga-like of other zebra. Hopes of re-creation of extinct species such as the mammoth and thylacine are regarded by experts in ancient DNA as fanciful. Despite apparently good preservation of flesh, the DNA of such animals is very highly fragmented, and it is probably impossible to link it together to create a genome. Similarly, cloning seems unlikely to work given the deterioration of the DNA and complete loss of natural cytoplasm. It is not inconceivable that one day it will be possible to splice bits of mammoth DNA into elephants, and create individuals with some mammoth-like traits, but these would be for curiosity rather than productive conservation.

# 7

# Sustainability, and the management of semi-natural habitats

This chapter examines the controversial issues of sustainable management of species and habitats. Species can be managed to maintain yield in the long term, but I suggest this may often be achieved at a risk to conservation. Similarly, habitats have been managed by traditional methods to achieve long-term use of many natural resources, but we will examine the validity of these methods as a model for conservation. Sustainability has been defined in a variety of ways. One of the early definitions of sustainable development comes from the World Commission on Sustainable Development, in *The Brundtland Report* of 1987: 'Sustainable development is development that meets the needs of the present without compromising the ability of future generations to meet their own needs'. Sustainability has been considered for many years by resource managers such as foresters and fisheries officers, who have attempted to harvest in ways which maintain long-term yields. A basic tenet of such managers is the concept of 'Maximum Sustainable Yield' ('MSY'), which we shall examine after considering how sustainability can be recognised.

## 7.1  Is sustainability an illusion?

With so many politicians and resource managers repeating the mantra of 'sustainable development' and 'sustainability', it would be easy to get the impression that the aim is realistic. But how can sustainability be detected and monitored? Are there proven examples of sustainability? And is sustainability in one sector only at the expense of another? In sum: is sustainability a comfortable illusion created by a lack of information?

Both the inter-connectedness of the species in ecosystems, and the basic laws of thermodynamics, suggest that humans cannot get something from the environment for nothing. If resources that were originally being exploited by other living organisms are taken from one part of the environment, then we are very likely to influence those other organisms. For example, if we can sustain a harvest of the Sun's energy, through solar panels or crops, might it be at the expense of other species which were using that sunlight?

If people manage a fishery to sustain a catch of one species of fish, then both that fish species and the people who eat them may appear to be in a stable equilibrium. But what of the alternative possible fates of the fish we eat? What might have eaten them, or their eggs, or their dead bodies? What might those fish have eaten – perhaps the algae growing on coral, or fish which eat fish which eat algae on coral? Might some species become more abundant when the target species is harvested, and other species less abundant? Might such non-target species suffer 'unsustainable' losses as a consequence of 'sustainable' use of a chosen species? Similarly, harvesting 'non-timber forest products' such as nuts will compete with wildlife and decrease tree replacement. Selective harvests may also alter the age and sex structure, and hence the evolution, of the harvested species.

Unfortunately, the interlinkages between species in any food chain are so complex that we have trouble discovering them, let alone understanding them. Work by R. M. May and colleagues in 1979 revealed the complexities of managing multi-species fisheries. We cannot easily predict the impact of harvesting a particular species on more than a few other species. We may have to rely on 'common sense' to guess what the impacts of harvesting might be.

This problem can be illustrated by considering the total marine environment. If people eventually stabilised their extraction of seafood, perhaps at 100 million tonnes per year, that might appear satisfactory and sustainable for us and for the fish. But this might mask changes going on elsewhere. What, for example, will happen to those species near the deep seabed that used to eat the larger remnants of dead fish? Or perhaps many deep sea 'detritivores' will become more common – as there are fewer fish to eat the plankton before it sinks to the depths? Extra nutrients would presumably influence other species of the depths. A similar issue has been debated with the harvesting of whales: might the species living in sulphur-rich whale carcasses on the sea floor have fewer places to live now whales are scarce? Even if the whale stocks stabilised, might such species become extinct? This controversy illustrates how little we know about the natural conditions of the deep sea. With so little base-line data, how can we detect and interpret changes to the communities of the sea floor – and convincingly demonstrate sustainability?

On land, some traditional agricultural, pastoral and forestry practices have been considered sustainable because they have apparently been continuously productive for hundreds or thousands of years. But what of the species that once used that land, and what of the species that would use the 'products' if people did not?

Sustainability may be an illusion fostered by a narrow focus in space and time. These issues will be explored in Section 7.3, where the generalities of traditional management are considered, along with the conservation interest of the practices themselves.

## 7.2   Maximum Sustainable Yields (MSYs)

Maximum Sustainable Yields are yields that give the greatest harvesting rate which the stock of organisms can maintain over the long term: birth and growth replace individuals (or the parts of them) which are harvested.

MSYs depend on the ideas of 'logistic growth' and 'density-dependent' competition. An organism at low population density in a safe environment full of food will reproduce at its maximum intrinsic rate; survival will be high, and exponential growth will occur. However, as density rises and resources decline, competition will reduce survival and reproductive rates, as individual organisms have fewer resources each. Eventually, in this simple model, the population may stabilise at a population level '$K$', which is set by the 'carrying capacity' of the local environment. (In the real world the population is more likely to crash, or undergo more complex dynamics.) A sigmoid growth curve will have been observed as illustrated in Fig. 7.1. This can be described by the 'logistic equation':

$$dN/dt = r N((K - N)/K).$$

In this equation, $N$ is the number of organisms (i.e. the population size), $dN/dt$ is the rate of growth of the population per unit time, $r$ is the intrinsic rate of increase (i.e. the maximum potential reproductive rate) and $K$ is the 'saturation density'. An alternative way of writing this equation is:

$$dN/dt = r N(1 - N/K).$$

To incorporate exploitation, the harvesting rate $H$ can be included:

$$dN/dt = r N((K - N)/K) - H.$$

The essence of this equation is that when there are very few individuals present, the rate of growth of the population is slow – because there are few individuals

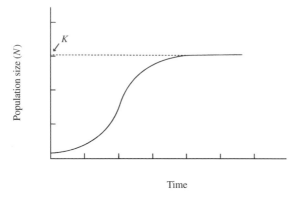

Fig. 7.1.  The sigmoid population growth curve described by the logistic equation. *K* is the population size at carrying capacity. Such growth is limited by intraspecific competition and would occur only in the absence of predation, disease, competing species, adverse weather, etc.

to breed. When the population is very high, population growth is again slow because each individual has too few resources to produce many young. In theory, then, the greatest growth rate, and so the greatest harvesting rate or yield, can be achieved in intermediate population densities. Maximum Sustainable Yields are achieved when $N$ is maintained at some point below $K$, and a harvest well below $r$ (Fig. 7.2), the actual values being dependent on the biology of each species. Harvesting rates higher than MSY will eventually drive the yield down, whilst lower rates are not the maximum which could be taken.

For harvest managers to use this model, $r$, $K$ and $N$ must be measured. Unfortunately, this is often *very* hard to do. It may be possible to find how many eggs a well-fed fish can lay in a year, or how many seeds a tree can produce – but it may be very hard to count the number of cod off Newfoundland or mature ebony in a forest. There is a risk of overharvesting, and once this happens the population will fall increasingly rapidly to extinction unless the harvest is reduced – the MSY is what mathematicians describe as an unstable equilibrium. A further problem is that $K$ is not constant, but changes with factors such as climate, currents and nutrient availability. It is important to harvest at a rate low enough to prevent overharvesting in the least-productive years. This is evident for sablefish stocks off Alaska, which have high variability with climate. In order to overcome this problem, managers may take a more cautious line: they may take a fixed, low proportion of the stock, again requiring knowledge of $N$. Large uncertainties and biases in population estimates make this and many other harvesting models unreliable.

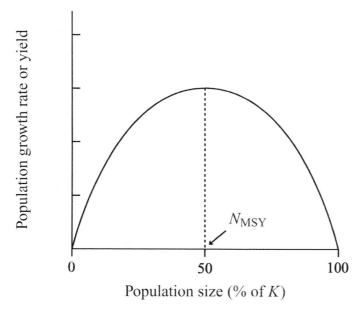

**Fig. 7.2.** The Maximum Sustainable Yield (MSY) occurs at population size $N = N_{MSY}$, when the population is a fraction of the number at carrying capacity (*K*). In some species, as in the graph, this would be at a population size 50% of *K*, but in some species such as whales it will be when the population is near to *K*.

In the absence of good population data – which is true for most fish and many terrestrial species – the safest way to harvest and conserve stocks is to monitor the hunting effort it takes to catch a certain amount of fish, or to find a mature hardwood tree. If the time and energy needed per unit of yield is increasing, the stock is being overharvested and the harvest is not sustainable (Fig. 7.3). The harvest should be reduced until catch per unit effort stabilises. For example, the number of tonnes of cod caught per season per net should be allowed to recover. Such experimental variation of the harvest is termed 'adaptive management'. Another indicator of overexploitation is a change in the age structure or sex structure of the population – for example the loss of older individuals.

By using a combination of ecology, policy and enforcement, it has indeed proved possible to sustain a harvest – as in the 'quota' system for fisheries in New Zealand (Section 9.4.2). The value of refuges to protect fish stocks is illustrated in Section 5.3.3. An example of successful protection of a fishery is the policy in New England of not harvesting large lobsters over about 1 kg, which are the key part of the breeding population: the largest lobsters live a long time and contribute a lot to recruitment.

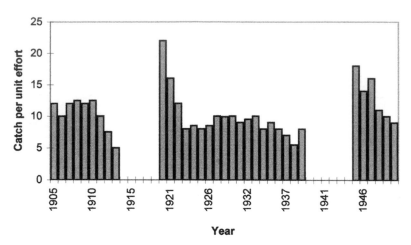

**Fig. 7.3.** Declines in catch per unit fishing effort indicate overexploitation of haddock in the North Sea. Population declines were reversed during the World Wars when fishing was reduced.
*Source:* P. A. Henderson/Pisces Conservation Ltd.

Because the potential yield of a particular species is proportional to nat-ural mortality, the yield at MSY is often said to be removing the 'surplus production' of the population, which would otherwise have been 'wasted'. However, this is a blinkered, anthropocentric and ecologically naïve view of sustainability.

The yield of a species in terms of number of individuals that can be har-vested per year is very sensitive to the reproductive rate, $r$. High reproductive rates are required to offset high natural mortality – and high inter-linkage with other species. Species with low reproductive rates such as whales, elephants and ebony can sustain only low rates of harvest, and are easily overexploited. Consequently, as noted in Section 3.1.2, such '$K$-selected' species are rel-atively highly threatened. Modelling by P. A. Stephens and colleagues has shown that social species are also more vulnerable to overharvesting, partly through Allee effects (Section 6.3.2), and this has relevance to safe harvesting levels.

'Proportional threshold harvesting' has been proposed by R. Lande as the safest approach for harvesting of species with highly erratic population sizes. A model of population viability is developed (Section 6.3) and a threshold de-cided below which chance environmental change might threaten the popula-tion; no exploitation is permitted when the population is below this threshold, whilst above it a harvesting rate is permitted in proportion to the population above the threshold. Regular and accurate population data are again required.

Overharvesting can lead to changes which are slow to reverse, or irreversible. Complex ecosystems may fall into new alternative states or attractors (Section 1.4), dominated by alternative species. The cod in Newfoundland had not recovered over 10 years after collapse and closure of the fishery. It has been hypothesised that overharvesting of cod leads to reduced predation by large cod on the predators of cod eggs or young; these predators might then become dominant, preventing most cod maturing. There may also be Allee effects in schooling species.

Despite the difficulties, harvesting of a target species, or several target species in a habitat, has in some cases demonstrably been sustained over long periods, leading to special issues in conservation to which we now turn.

## 7.3   Semi-natural habitats

When an area of land has been repeatedly exploited in a relatively constant manner for hundreds or thousands of years, in a way that determines the structure of the vegetation, the habitat that is created is described as 'semi-natural'. Such habitats differ substantially from natural habitats (Section 3.2.2). They also differ from 'near-natural' habitats, which are areas where human intervention has been more limited and temporary (such as a forest which has been felled once and has then regenerated). Semi-natural habitats are essentially nature's response to regular management of particular features of an area; people exploit and manipulate certain elements of the area deliberately, whilst other elements of the biodiversity are left to respond in their own way.

Semi-natural habitats are of very great interest in the context of sustainability. They illustrate how long-term, low-intensity exploitation of an area may lead to an equilibrium between inputs and outputs, whilst allowing the area to support desirable biodiversity. They also illustrate some of the compromises and choices that must be accepted in conservation management. Managers of semi-natural habitats need to be aware of many of the issues of management of natural areas described in Chapter 5, such as protection against encroachment and fragmentation. The special feature of management of semi-natural habitats is that the intrinsic processes which generate the habitat – the human exploitation regime and natural succession and recovery – must also be understood and managed.

Many of the ancient exploitative management techniques which have led to semi-natural habitats are described as 'traditional' – although it is subjective how long a management must have existed before it is perceived as traditional.

Management techniques may also have varied somewhat over the decades and centuries, leading to further debates over what 'traditition' is. Many agricultural practices (both for livestock and for crops), and much forest management, can lead to semi-natural habitats. Even traditional arable cropland can have value for conservation – as evident from the rising interest in conserving former arable weed species such as corn cockle, nigella and cornflower, which have become rare in intensive European farms. The distinction between natural, semi-natural and agricultural or forestry habitats is not clear-cut. For example, many Indian grasslands are degraded forests supporting grassland species – but not in ancient, distinctive communities.

Most land areas of the world have been populated and exploited by humans for many thousands of years. In general in such circumstances, the exploitation has proved unsustainable for some types of wildlife, whilst other species have found long-term opportunities in the habitats people create. With continuous exploitation of an area, the richness, distributions, and proportions of specialist species will change, and in some cases an equilibrium may be reached with a community of organisms emerging that is characteristic of the particular type of long-term exploitation.

Semi-natural habitats are very important to conservationists for several reasons. They give us insight into the potential for sustainable exploitation of communities. They provide ecological laboratories, where management (which can be treated as an experimental manipulation) has been running for hundreds or thousands of years – rather longer than any ecological experiment we can plan for today! They may support species which have now become rare in the general landscape. They may provide a mosaic of habitat types with associated specialist species. Finally, they are often aesthetically very appealing and historically fascinating, supporting attractive species in the relatively open landscapes which many people enjoy.

It is becoming clear that semi-natural habitats are much more widespread than was realised (Section 5.1). Many tropical forests have been repeatedly exploited in slash-and-burn rotations (as in much of the Amazon and West Africa), or burnt repeatedly to exploit game animals (as in Australia). Many temperate forests have been consistently 'coppiced' (Box 7.1 and Fig. 7.4), or grazed. Grasslands are often created by grazing livestock or by burning, be they 'chalk downlands' and alpine pastures in Europe, 'derived savannahs' in West Africa, 'prairies' in North America, or some 'paramo' grasslands in the Andes. Some forest patches within the grasslands of South America have been tended by peoples such as the Kayapo. There may also be aquatic semi-natural habitats, such as ancient fish-ponds or sea-shores, but aquatic systems are generally less well known than terrestrial ones – and are probably more often mistaken to be natural.

# Box 7.1

## Coppice management

Coppice management is the repeated cutting of certain tree species near to ground level, thereby forming a low, multi-stemmed stump or 'coppice stool'. The intended produce is numerous straight, narrow branches with a variety of uses such as fuel and fencing. A coppice woodland is often divided into sections, and the sections cut in rotation, creating a variety of heights of vegetation regrowth. Rotations are usually some 5–50 years. In some sites (called 'coppice with standards') certain tall tree species are left at low density and cut on a longer rotation to provide other produce. Coppice management has been practised in many parts of the world, including Africa, Europe and Asia – in some cases continuously for many centuries. There is a renewed interest in this management for renewable biomass fuel and for supposedly 'environmentally friendly' barbecue charcoal.

In Britain, coppice was often hazel, but hornbeam, and the exotic sweet-chestnut, were commonly coppiced in the south-east. The tall 'standards' were usually oak. There was often some deliberate encouragement of the hazel within such woodlands, but otherwise a semi-natural plagioclimax woodland developed. The short-term economic returns of this sustainable management protected such woodlands from conversion to agriculture. After industrialisation, and substitution of products, they have been fragmented, replanted with conifers, or left largely unmanaged to undergo succession ('neglected'). Most lowland woodland nature reserves in Britain are former coppice sites.

The long continuity of management, combined with particular types of structural diversity (including open areas and a variety of heights of taller regrowth), allowed numerous species to survive in or colonise coppice woodland. Such species may have been present in the gaps in natural woodland, or were present in other habitats but pre-adapted to exploit the microclimate of coppice. Many of these species are rare in the regions they now occur, and conservationists often attempt to re-instate management to foster them.

Coppice woodlands have lost species unable to tolerate the coppice cycle, particularly species of late-successional habitats needing dead wood, old trees, or moisture. Intensively coppiced woodlands such as Bradfield Wood in Suffolk are very rich in flowering plants, but notably poor for mosses and lichens. In Britain, some animals favour (but are not confined to) coppice woodlands, such as migrant warblers and various fritillary butterflies, whilst others such as woodpeckers and saproxylic flies and beetles cannot use them.

Since the full range of forest species cannot be conserved in a coppice system, conservationists must decide the aims of management on a site. The preferences of some taxa for different stages in the cycle have been established (Fig. 7.4). Decisions must be taken about the general suite of species which are to be maintained, and the successional states to be included. Following that, the frequency of cutting and the density of standard trees can be decided. Often, historical records can serve as a guide to management. If a British woodland has not been coppiced for over 50 years (as is often the case), it may no longer be viable to re-establish coppice-loving species, and conversion to high forest may need to be considered. In either case, restoration and re-introductions may be required (Chapter 8).

Studying coppice woodland helps give insight into the influences of forest managements in general, including clear-felling and selective logging.

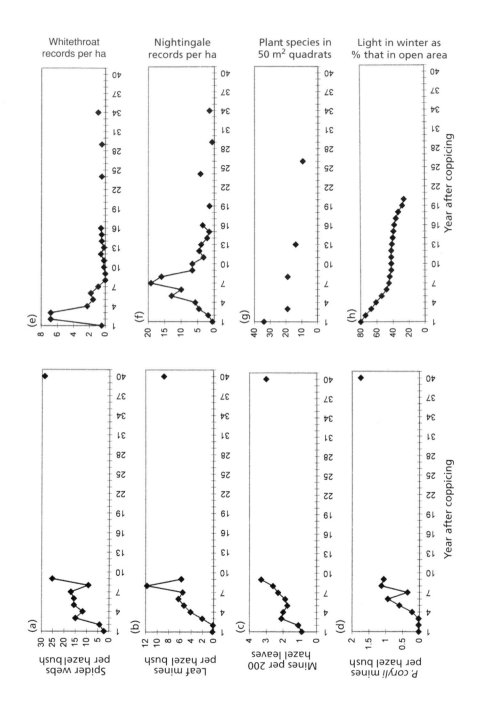

Semi-natural habitats may be structurally very similar to some of the original natural habitats of the region, and effectively extend the range of some habitats. Many inhabited and repeatedly managed habitats are widely treated as 'natural' – for example the Amazonian forest. Despite the great variety of semi-natural habitats in location and character, common themes emerge which have increasing relevance in the increasingly artificial modern global landscape.

Much of our knowledge of semi-natural habitats comes from studies in temperate regions, where the biology of the faunas and floras are relatively well known and the management history is relatively clear from historical and archaeological records. It may not be immediately obvious how management of, for example, chalk grassland or heathland in England is relevant to the sustainable exploitation of reefs, savannah or rainforests. However, it is likely that the relatively well understood managed systems will become valuable as models for long-term exploitation around the world.

In general, semi-natural habitats are maintained at an earlier stage of 'ecological succession' than is natural for the area. This has profound implications for the types of wildlife that can inhabit the area. In order to understand the derivation and maintenance of semi-natural habitats, it is necessary for us to examine briefly the basics of the process of succession. In particular, and unfortunately for ease of management, different types of organism respond in different ways to succession and management, meaning that no single management can be ideal for all of the species that might occur in a semi-natural habitat. When undertaking management activity, conservation practitioners should therefore think about whether and how they are modifying the

---

**Fig. 7.4.** Examples of the responses of different taxa to the coppice cycle in English hazel woods. The data from different sources are from different woods, but illustrate widespread patterns. (The data for leaf-mining moths, and spiders, are from the lowest 2 m of bushes – biasing against late year classes).
Sources: (a)–(d) Sterling, P. H. & Hambler, C. Coppicing for conservation: do hazel communities benefit? In: K. J. Kirby & F. J. Wright (Eds.) *Woodland Conservation and Research in the Clay Vale of Oxfordshire and Buckinghamshire* (NCC, Peterborough, UK, 1988).
(e) and (f) Fuller, R. J., Stuttard, P. & Ray, C. M. The distribution of breeding songbirds within mixed coppice woodland in Kent, England, in relation to vegetation age and structure. *Annales Zoologici Fennici* **26** (1989), 265–275.
(g) Ash, J. E. & Barckam, J. P. Change and variability in the field layer of a coppiced woodland in Norfolk, England. *Journal of Ecology* **64** (1976), 697–712.
(h) Salisbury, E. J. The effects of coppicing as illustrated by the woods of Hertfordshire. *Transactions of the Hertfordshire Natural History Society* **18** (1924), 1–21.

succession – and what the various consequences might be for different types of organism. In particular, a knowledge of succession will help to predict the types of organism that will benefit or suffer under a particular management regime, allowing informed decisions about which management to choose.

## 7.3.1 Patterns in succession

Succession is the process whereby areas devoid of life become colonised by a sequence of species. These species may remain in the area, or come and go as a variety of assemblages and habitats emerge and are replaced through time. There is usually some directionality and predictability in the process of succession. However, although we can often predict the type of vegetation structure that will emerge through time (e.g. forest or alpine grassland) it is harder to predict the composition of species within it. There is considerable debate as to whether successions reach a *relatively* stable end-point – a 'climax community' – or whether cycles or other changes will occur continuously. The architecture, microclimate and fauna of a climax community are often more stable than its plant species composition. From the perspective of conservation management, what matters most is that there are some changes common to the early stages of any succession. Succession is one of the most fundamental patterns in ecology – and in applied ecology for conservation. Marine successions are poorly known.

The various theoretical models of the mechanism of succession ('facilitation', 'inhibition' and 'tolerance') were clarified by J. H. Connell and R. O. Slatyer in 1977. Early in a terrestrial succession, species may build soil and render the area more suitable for (i.e. facilitate) other species. Later in succession, species (or teams of species) compete to hold their ground (inhibiting other species). H. S. Horn proposed 'transition matrix models', which have been used (with varying success) to predict future species compositions, or age class distributions. Horn was able to predict the forest types which follow disturbance in New Jersey. In these transition models, a measure is made of the frequency with which each species (or age class) replaces each of the others, and these frequencies are put into a mathematical matrix. Iterative multiplication of the matrix through itself again and again may lead to a stable predicted equilibrium community composition. If the transition frequencies change (are 'non-stationary') or depend on past history (are 'non-independent') then such models will fail, and indeed this seems to be a common problem.

Succession is generally initiated by disturbance, which creates an opportunity for species to colonise an area. Two main types of succession are recognised:

primary and secondary. If the disturbance creates colonisable ground which has not before supported life, the succession is termed primary. Examples are crumbling cliffs or emerging oceanic islands. If the succession occurs on an area where disturbance has created a gap in a habitat, it is a secondary succession. Such successions occur when a tree falls, is blown down, or is burnt; they also occur after tall grass is grazed to short grass, and when soil is exposed in various ways. Human activity may create opportunities for primary succession: mining, quarrying and building creates cliffs and islands. However, primary succession may take very many years, and most semi-natural habitats involve secondary successions.

Exploitation may repeatedly create gaps in natural habitats, which then undergo secondary succession. Some human activity (such as burning grassland or felling a tree) may be similar to natural disturbances, and relatively natural successional regeneration will begin afterwards with a range of species being ready and able to live in the disturbed area. For this reason, management of semi-natural habitats is often claimed to mimic natural gap-creating processes. When humans intervene repeatedly in a succession, and prevent dominance by natural communities, an equilibrium may nevertheless develop. This equilibrium state may have a distinctive community, with a limited turnover of species of animals and plants. Such a habitat is termed a 'plagioclimax', and succession has been 'deflected' by repeated intervention. The more ancient the exploitation or management regime, the more distinctive the plagioclimax community will be.

As succession proceeds there is a general accumulation of living and dead organic material, collectively known as 'biomass'. This continues either until a point is reached where no more biomass can be supported by the area, or until there is some disturbance to the area. In the absence of instabilities to the substrate, or of interruption, limits to the accumulation of biomass are generally climatic and biomechanical: there is a limit to the height and density of plants. In climatically stressed environments, such as at high latitudes and altitudes, the accumulation of above-ground biomass will be slower and lower. Even when biomass has ceased to accumulate above ground there may be accumulation in the area – through very slow peat and coal formation. As described in ecological textbooks such as that by C. Krebs, wetlands may go through a succession called a hydrosere to dryer land, but conversely some forests may eventually become wetlands.

Within the accumulating biomass, nutrients are sequestered – particularly carbon and nitrogen, but also other important elements such as phosphorous, potassium, sulphur, and trace elements. Many natural substrates are low in available nutrients – for example, porous calcareous rock, sand and cliffs. Some habitats lose nutrients readily, through leaching or erosion. In others, nutrients have not built up in the system, but will do so as colonisation and succession proceed. The specialised species of plant that exploit them are often able to fix nitrogen from the atmosphere. A little nitrogen is also fixed by lightning, and deposited in rainfall. Dust, surface water and animal faeces bring in nutrients. And weathering and erosion of rocks below and uphill of vegetation may provide some elements such as phosphorous. The relative importance of these factors in a region or site will depend on the bedrock, climate, aspect, area and surroundings of a site. For example, volcanic rock, or alluvial soil, is relatively nutrient-rich.

As vegetation is repeatedly removed from an area by an exploitative management such as coppicing, reed-cutting, or grazing, the nutrients within it are transported elsewhere in the produce. This results in 'nutrient stripping' from the habitat. Of these nutrients, nitrogen may be particularly relevant to diversity. Of the agents which remove vegetation, fire is the least selective, and results in the release and limited dispersal of nutrients through smoke. Heathlands and moorlands in Europe are traditionally managed by burning and grazing. Grazing an area with livestock traps nutrients in the animals as they grow, and when herds are moved elsewhere the nutrients within them are also moved. These nutrients may subsequently be concentrated in humans and their waste, particularly near settlements. In some cases, nutrients may be transferred to areas of land where livestock are folded temporarily. For example, in southern Britain, sheep traditionally grazed calcareous grasslands on hills by day, and were moved to low-lying areas at night. Since sheep dung is produced mainly at night, this transferred nutrients off the 'downlands' and onto arable land. Seasonal grazing of montane pasture in Europe and Japan has the same effect. Nutrients may become locked in sheep dung – particularly in arid areas.

The result of nutrient stripping is that the biomass an area can support is reduced, and the productivity (growth rate) of the vegetation is also diminished. The rainfall and rate of nutrient input will determine the rate at which material can be sustainably exploited, and thus also the rate at which a semi-natural site could be, or needs to be, managed. Nutrient stripping depletes the potential of an area for certain species, particularly those which require abundant resources for fast growth. Conversely nutrient stripping favours some species, particularly those adapted to some natural habitats which are low in nutrients.

Early in succession, when nutrients are very low, few plants can survive. As nutrients increase, more species can survive, and they begin to interact with each other through physical contact and competition. Whilst gaps occur between plants, or if gaps are regularly created in the plant cover, competition favours those species which can colonise them by rapid dispersal. When colonisable gaps no longer occur, competition increasingly favours species that can smother others. Eventually, accumulated nutrient levels may become sufficient for a few highly competitive, fast-growing, species to dominate; flowering plant richness will therefore begin to fall. This is important for conservationists who often witness the 'Paradox of Enrichment': the addition of nutrients to a semi-natural habitat (for example in agricultural 'improvement') leads to a decrease in the floristic diversity and interest. Plant species diversity is further enhanced in early-successional and semi-natural habitats by the gaps created by the activities of grazing animals.

Other important changes occur in succession. With increased biomass, there is increased water retention per unit area. This may be in the substrate – for example through roots impeding drainage. Water is also stored in biomass. Evaporation is reduced by the density of vegetation, which reduces desiccation by sunlight and by air currents, and a more humid microclimate will occur throughout the column of vegetation – particularly at ground level.

Whilst plants and animals follow similar patterns in the accumulation of biomass through succession, they follow different ones in terms of species richness. T. R. E. Southwood and colleagues demonstrated this in succession from grassland to woodland in Britain. Such differences have very important consequences for conservation management, as discussed in Section 7.3.3.

In contrast to plants, as the biomass and the total abundance of nutrients in a given area increase, animals and other non-photosynthetic taxa are presented with greater opportunity (or 'niche space'). As biomass increases, the height and structural complexity of the vegetation increases. There is more three-dimensional complexity in grassland than in a bed of lichen or moss. There is more again in a scrubland and, generally, most in a woodland. In late-successional habitats there are more opportunities for animals to shelter from abiotic pressures (such as desiccation, low temperatures and high windspeeds), or biotic pressures (such as predators). Consequently, a unit area of tall grass can generally support more invertebrate species and individuals than can the same area of short grass, and, as it is sometimes put, 'there are more ways of making a living on an oak tree than on a blade of grass'. A pioneer of ecology, Charles Elton, described this as 'the importance of cover'.

Contrary to many people's belief, most species of animals are detritivores, parasites or predators, rather than specialist herbivores (which can eat only a few types of plant). Therefore, animal diversity is potentially greater in later-successional habitats. Similarly, many fungi, cryptograms (such as mosses, liverworts and lichens) and ferns thrive in late-successional habitats: there is an increasing total surface area of substrate for epiphytic species, and the higher humidity which is often required by the fungi and cryptograms. It is also likely that microbial diversity will be high where there is high biomass, moisture and invertebrate species richness. The diversity and abundance of epiphytic flowering plants, including many bromeliads and orchids, increases with structural complexity and moisture availability. However, flowering plants in general are unusual amongst organisms in their high richness per unit area in certain early-successional, and plagioclimax, communities. Steppes of the former USSR may reach 80 plant species per square metre, and chalk downland in Britain over 50 species.

Removal of biomass during management renders semi-natural habitats structurally simplified when compared with natural habitats, at least on small scales. A late-successional habitat will have a greater range of age classes, from dead and senescent trees to seeds and seedlings. Semi-natural habitats generally lack large, old plants, although certain structural features may be long lived and more common than in the wider landscape. For example, 'pollarded' trees (where the main stems are cut off a few metres above ground), or ancient coppice stools, can survive hundreds of years if senescence is delayed by repeated cutting. In addition, the formerly large expanses of semi-natural habitats in the landscape contained a diversity of management types, intensities and habitat structures, allowing a range of species to exist in different areas. This landscape heterogeneity is one of the reasons it is impossible to cater for the full diversity of a semi-natural habitat type in a single nature reserve – the other reason being that small sites can support fewer species than whole regions (Section 7.3.3).

It is often argued that if management occurs in rotation, so that only part of a site is managed at one time, then the site as a whole will have a variety of structure and habitats greater than the same area left unmanaged throughout. This may appear to be the case on the scale humans view the environment, but other organisms might find greater habitat diversity if the whole site were a solid block of late-successional vegetation, in which there are structures and microclimates absent from early-successional vegetation – such as dead trees and high humidity. Considering species–area effects (Section 5.4.1), a large patch of late-successional habitat might sometimes support more species than an unnatural diversity of small, early-successional patches of the same total area. Such unresolved arguments about the impacts of rotations are important in the management of sites 'for diversity'. Examples of habitats formed by rotational management include coppice woodland (with its open, scrubby, and closed canopy patches), or savannah which is burned in patches.

Early-successional and semi-natural habitats will, then, support species with particular 'life-history' characteristics: species which can disperse well and produce many offspring will be able to find the recently disturbed areas, and such organisms often are small with short life-spans. They are relatively resistant to abiotic stresses in the gaps, but do poorly in the face of the biotic stress of competition. Such species are termed $r$-selected. Species with the opposite set of characteristics are termed $K$-selected, and predominate later in successions. As explained in Sections 3.1.2 and 7.2, $K$-selected species generally present the greatest challenges for conservationists.

   J. H. Connell's 'intermediate disturbance hypothesis' is sometimes invoked to justify management or exploitation. This hypothesis suggests that very high levels of disturbance lead to low species richness (owing to stress), as might very low levels of disturbance (which permit competitive exclusion of $r$-selected species). Richness may therefore peak at, and depend on, intermediate levels of disturbance. However, the hypothesis refers to the *natural* disturbance regime to which the region's wildlife is adapted, considers only species richness, not species quality (Section 3.1), and is applicable particularly to sessile plants and corals, not overall diversity. Over long timescales, it is the least disturbed habitats which acquire most species and inter-dependent co-evolved specialists (Section 3.4). It is an abuse of this hypothesis to use it to prescribe management of natural habitats unless the natural disturbance regime has been prevented, and it has questionable relevance to semi-natural habitats.

## 7.3.2   The origin and loss of semi-natural habitats

Semi-natural habitats were created, and are still being created, through long-term and regular exploitation management which removes nutrients roughly as fast as they arrive. Only a few species are exploited and managed directly and deliberately, such as hazel and oak in a coppiced British woodland, large herbivores in a calcareous grassland, or reeds in a reedbed. The repeated management may be designed to increase the food supply for large herbivores, such as for bison on the prairies of North America. Regular intervention through certain hunting techniques, as in fire-management to drive game by Aborigines in Australia, will also lead to a community more tolerant of the disturbance than was the natural one. Intervention will filter out species incapable of surviving the intensified disturbance regime.

   The microclimate of semi-natural habitats will generally be less humid than the natural habitat for the region, and will undergo greater fluctuations in temperature on daily and annual cycles. Windspeeds will also be increased. Such stresses limit the biodiversity an area can support to a subset of species from the original natural habitat which are relatively tolerant. However, they also present opportunities for some species of other natural habitats to extend their ranges. For example, C. J. Smith suggested many plant species of calcareous grassland in Britain naturally evolved and occurred on cliff faces and other areas with unstable soils, or in clearings made by natural herbivores. Species of African-derived savannahs evolved in natural grassland, desert and forest. Species in coppiced woodlands may have naturally been present only in woodland gaps, or in non-woodland habitats. Some warmth-loving ('thermophilous') species have been able to extend their ranges northwards in the artificially warm microclimates of European semi-natural habitats. Similarly, altitudinal shifts are possible: species may be able to live at higher or lower altitudes if the microclimate of a semi-natural habitat mimics that of their natural altitudinal range. Species of the paramo grasslands of the Andes may have moved downhill as forest was cleared and burnt, and some species of lowland semi-natural grassland and woodland in Europe may have been montane in origin.

Contrary to widespread belief, species very rarely completely depend on semi-natural habitats. They must have evolved, and usually survive, elsewhere. There has generally been insufficient time for the evolution of numerous distinct species in anthropogenic plagioclimaxes. Some behavioural adaptations (such as reduced mobility in butterflies) have been suggested, and some distinct races may perhaps have evolved recently only in semi-natural habitats (although none is yet known to have). However, semi-natural habitats are important to conservationists because they may now support the bulk of the populations of species in some areas. They may support 'relict populations' of species which have been made rare through destruction of the surrounding habitats – or through climate change; this has been suggested for thermophilous fritillary butterflies using coppiced woodland in Britain. In addition, the range extensions provide opportunities for scientists to study factors limiting distribution, and provide people with the opportunity to see, locally, interesting or attractive species which are more typical of other regions. Losses of semi-natural habitats, and local losses of their component species, therefore frequently provoke concern.

Semi-natural habitats are being lost or degraded through many of the processes which threaten unmanaged natural areas, such as development or pollution. For example, nitrogen input from acid rain and spray-drift threatens low-nutrient grasslands, heathlands and peatlands. Other site-specific or region-specific causes for loss include changes in climate or influential biotic factors. Britain's loss of calcareous grassland was partly the result of a decline in rabbits following the introduced disease myxomatosis. Ironically, rabbits were themselves introduced some 900 years ago, and became a major element in the landscape, creating very short, lightly trampled swards: arguably they had become a keystone species for some semi-natural British grassland communities.

However, a major reason for the decline of semi-natural habitats in the developed world is a technology-related change in land use, from extensive low-input low-output systems to intensive use of smaller areas of easily accessible land. The more intensively used areas, such as the 'improved pastures' in Britain, have regular input of artificial fertilisers to sustain high productivity, and can support high densities of livestock. In such environments, the species richness of the vegetation declines, and the invertebrate richness is constrained by the intensive grazing and trampling of the short swards. There may be changes in demand for agricultural and forest products. The extensive British downlands and heathlands were fragmented by agricultural intensification, including cereal production. Similarly, traditional European coppice products have been replaced by fossil fuel, concrete, and wire fencing. High-intensity plantations of exotic species have often replaced semi-natural woodlands. Species of reedbeds may be lost if wetlands are drained or succeed to drier land, when thatching is no longer economical. Agricultural weed species in western Europe have been lost to intensification, improved seed-sorting, and herbicides (although many are still weeds elsewhere in the world).

Traditional cultural practices are being lost in many areas of the world for a variety of reasons. Production intensity is being increased under population pressure, and traditional rotation lengths are declining (as in slash-and-burn agriculture). People are leaving rural areas, and the frequency and intensity of fires and grazing is changing. In the mountains of Japan, traditional grazing by war-horses created semi-natural, floristically rich pastures, and these are now being lost through a decline in grazing. In Britain, 95% of floristically rich grassland has been lost since 1969.

Many areas of semi-natural habitat are therefore being abandoned or 'neglected'. Succession is then released, and proceeds with eventual loss of the communities which require open plagioclimax conditions. Seeing the natural process of succession as an intrinsic threat is the interesting management paradox of those semi-natural habitats which have now become nature reserves or national parks.

With a loss and fragmentation of semi-natural habitats some species have become locally rare, particularly those requiring early-successional open habitats. Such species are often thermophilous species or specialist herbivores, such as the blue (Lycaenid) butterflies of the British grasslands and many arable weeds. The hairy spurge was extirpated from Britain partly through a decline in coppicing. The sea plantain on Peol Island, Germany, is highly dependent on cattle grazing of marshland. Birds such as ruff benefit from mowing to prevent the succession of the Matsalu watermeadows (in Estonia) to scrub. A decline or change in traditional aboriginal burning can threaten fire-dependent species in *Eucalyptus* forest, unable to cope with the conditions of the community that would develop in the area without human intervention in the succession.

### 7.3.3  Rotational management and refuges

It becomes apparent from the origin of semi-natural habitats, and the process of succession, that in order to maintain such habitats as nature reserves it is usually essential to manage them. Management may involve continuation or re-instatement of the traditional practices that created the habitats. Other options that need to be considered are: to cease active management on a site; to begin restoration management of a more natural habitat (Chapter 8); deliberate non-intervention or low-intervention management; or to manage only the exotic species on a site (Section 8.2). Furthermore, different species of animal and plant require different stages of the succession, such as short or tall grass, and there will be a choice of management options for different selections of these species.

Conservation management of semi-natural habitats is, therefore, a subjectively chosen activity – and is sometimes derided as 'gardening'. It assumes that the successional stages and communities that some people have created or prefer on the site are the most appropriate for conservation. However, each person will have a different appreciation of landscape and wildlife, and may in effect prefer different stages in the succession – or prefer groups of species which themselves need certain stages. The various people who will potentially benefit from the habitat (the stakeholders) should therefore be consulted before the successional stage or stages to be maintained are chosen.

The most important factor in management of semi-natural habitats is, therefore, to determine the aims. Moreover, even with management, semi-natural habitats will inevitably change – with the climate, and the natural population processes of species. Management may have to be monitored and modified regularly if the aim is to arrest change as completely as possible. Once the aims of habitat or species conservation at a site are clear, the appropriate management tool to interrupt succession or to promote a species can be chosen from a range tested on other sites.

Historically, the original intensity of management would often have been determined by economics, and conservationists will need to be aware of the financial implications of management of a semi-natural habitat on a nature reserve. When economic conditions no longer favour the traditional methods that created a semi-natural habitat, it may be costly to simulate them exactly. Less-costly alternatives may be attempted, such as substituting burning or cutting for grazing. In some nature reserves today, economic return from management, such as timber or livestock production, is expected – sometimes to help pay for conservation management. However, this risks compromising the nature-conservation aims: for example, on grassland, livestock may need supplementary feed in winter to maintain their healthy condition, and so their nutrient-stripping effect may be diminished. It may be difficult to find (or let the visitors see) a suitable skinny flock of sheep which will put on weight from grazing the reserve.

The aim of management of the semi-natural habitat in a region will usually be to preserve the full variety of species found in that region. Theoretically, this would be most easily and most effectively achieved by continuing the traditional management. However, this presents practical problems, since the original habitats were extensive, whilst the areas that are now available to be devoted to their conservation are small. Small habitats can support fewer species than extensive ones, and such species–area effects (Section 5.4) will limit the fraction of the assemblage of species typical of the semi-natural habitat which can use any small fragment of it. Nature reserves for semi-natural habitats must therefore usually have modest aims – and each site can aspire to only a particular subset of the assemblage present in the region. However, if a suite of nature reserves is created in an area to protect complementary fragments of a semi-natural habitat, then specialisation on each may be used to retain more of the original assemblage overall. Some may specialise in early stages of the succession (with short-rotation management), whilst others specialise in mid or late stages – but all within the limited range of successional stages encompassed in the original landscape.

In large sites, or in sets of sites, zoned or rotational management may be possible, as advocated by M. J. Morris and E. Duffey. Areas may be divided off, permanently or with temporary electric fencing. Only parts of the site are managed at a time – for example a fifth being grazed or burned every fifth year. The number of stages of the succession that can realistically be protected in such a site again depends on the species–area relationship: division of a reserve into too many small areas (each with a different stage) may mean that the total habitat available to some species is a small fraction of the reserve as a whole (Section 7.3.1). This fraction moves, and is subjected to edge effects from adjacent areas at different stages of the rotation (Section 5.4.2). The reserve could become mediocre for many species, but good for only a few.

Many species which specialise in a particular stage or stages of succession are threatened by interruption in the continuity of availability of those stages in space or time. When managing the entire site in one event (as in one of a suite of reserves) it is therefore essential to leave an area free from management – as a refuge for those species that are intolerant of the immediate effects of the management itself, but which require the conditions it creates. For example, many invertebrates, although requiring some short grazed grass, would be more sensitive to trampling and grazing than many vascular plants, and therefore require a temporary refuge from the grazing management. Although a site may not appear overgrazed to a botanist during management, it may be losing entomological value. Leaving corners, strips or islands of unmanaged habitats (which might move from year to year) may permit species of invertebrate to survive the grazing but then to expand from the refuge and re-colonise the managed areas. Similarly, fire-sensitive species within fire-maintained plagio-climaxes (such as some European heathlands or Australian *Eucalyptus* stands) may need to be protected by firebreaks.

A further advantage of rotations and refuges is that they may provide for species that demand two or more habitat types. For example, groups such as flies, beetles and butterflies have very different adult and larval stages, and may require floristically rich swards as larvae, rigid structures for overwintering, and abundant nectar sources as adults. The large blue butterfly in Britain uses both very short grass and taller flowers in close proximity.

Simulation of traditional management (such as substituting burning for cutting in reedbeds, changing the species of grazing herbivore, or favouring one tree species over another) will bring changes in the community, some of which may not be predictable; these must be examined experimentally. However, the simulated management may be easier to control – for example, cutting can be easier to perform than the management of sheep or rabbits. Arable weeds can be conserved by mimicking low-intensity methods – for example, annual ploughing without agrochemicals.

It must be remembered that semi-natural habitats, even more than many natural habitats, were dynamic. Traditions changed, climates changed, and wildlife assemblages changed with them. Despite this, as with the management of natural habitats, continuity of features of the habitat in space and time is important, both in the short term and the long term. It is possible through knowledge of succession and traditional cultures to conserve many of the species and communities of semi-natural habitats, and research can suggest optimal management prescriptions for such communities or for selected species within them.

Given the changes that have taken place in many semi-natural habitats after cessation of traditional managements, some form of Environmental Impact Assessment (Section 4.7) for the management options might help managers to decide whether to resume management, and the most appropriate prescription for a site. It is important to determine if the habitat is declining or increasing in conservation value as a result of loss of its semi-natural status.

With their high local appeal, it is likely that resources will be available for conservation of some semi-natural habitats that would not be available for conservation elsewhere. If funds and resources are not to be squandered on semi-natural habitats whilst natural ones are lost, it is important to ensure that the management aims are valid, realistic, and can be continued for the foreseeable future. Because the habitats are often recent, anthropogenic and early successional, the species in them are often relatively mobile, widespread and resilient to disturbance. It is also important to remember that, in general, semi-natural habitats can be restored and recreated much more easily than can natural ones. However, as recreation of limestone grassland at Wytham, England, shows (Section 8.3), it may still take hundreds of years to reach the desired state. The more ancient a semi-natural habitat, the less replaceable, and more valuable it is: it may support more specialist species and have more unusual soil conditions. Indeed, some semi-natural habitats may take longer to restore than some natural ones.

The fundamental subjectivity of management of semi-natural habitats must always be recognised. It is often valid to conserve such sites, but it is debatable how much effort should go into them. There are cases where clashes have occurred with other conservation activities. Management for semi-natural conditions and the species within them may be to the detriment of other habitats and species of greater rarity or quality (Section 3.1). The international context and rarity of species and habitats should be considered, as well as local, cultural values.

It can be argued that any management of habitats is an arrogant activity, particularly on nature reserves, and implies that we know enough about communities to improve on nature. However, there will probably always be great interest in maintaining traditional, semi-natural landscapes.

## 7.3.4  Sustainability and traditional management

Are semi-natural habitats good examples of sustainable management benefiting conservation? Such habitats generally illustrate a long-term, often unintentional, success in conservation of some species and ecological systems, but also show how that success can be fragile and occurs at the expense of other goals in conservation. It is indeed possible to use knowledge of semi-natural systems to maintain *low* yields for long periods, and this may be a compromise model for conservation in areas where the purist goal of conserving naturalness is impossible though the demands on the land.

Semi-natural habitats can supply a sustainable yield of material such as fuel, and sustain a fortuitous assemblage of species, but this is at the expense of some of the species that once used the natural habitat of the area. Some species, and particularly the specialists, may be confined to relict populations in the surviving fragments of the original habitat. In Britain, for example, no species need become globally or even nationally extinct if coppicing ceases, since species using semi-natural habitats have alternative habitats. The pearl-bordered and heath fritillary butterflies, for example, also occur in bracken and heathland habitats, respectively, and are common in Europe. In contrast, some 65% of the 150 threatened woodland invertebrate species in the British Red Data Book are at risk of national extirpation unless more high forest is restored. Restoration of semi-natural habitats to a more natural state might help protect these species, whilst continuing 'sustainable' management of habitats might lead to their extinction.

Initiating 'sustainable management' in a new area will have consequences similar to the initiation of coppicing or grazing in Europe thousands of years ago – and the changes will continue for thousands of years. The sustainability of management of a site should be judged in the light of its consequences to threatened species external to the site, as well as within it. Calls for traditional, sustainable management by indigenous people are frequently made without appreciating this is the lesser of two evils for biodiversity (Section 9.4.3). Any 'enhancement' of diversity, as is sometimes claimed for traditionally managed savannahs, or even the Amazon rainforest, will in reality often be an increase in richness of low-quality species at the expense of high-quality species (Sections 3.1 and 3.2.3). Genuine enhancement for biodiversity conservation would usually only come through restoration of as natural a system as possible.

The next chapter examines general methods for habitat restoration. These methods are relevant to conversion of semi-natural habitats to more natural ones, and also to 'restoring' semi-natural habitats from degraded or neglected states.

# 8

# Restoration, translocation and mitigation

The priorities in conservation should be to reduce extinction rates and to prevent further damage to 'high-quality' sites (Chapter 3). However, some sites which have already been damaged still retain valuable features and threatened species. There is increasing interest in attempting to rebuild such communities to a state more like the natural community. These efforts may prove to be particularly valuable when used to enlarge small fragments of habitat. Restoration has been defined by E. B. Welch and G. D. Cooke as 'any active attempt to return an ecosystem to an earlier condition following degradation resulting from any kind of disturbance'. This includes a return to desirable semi-natural conditions. Several management principles relevant to restoration can be found in Chapters 5 and 7, although those chapters focus more on protection of existing interest and on maintenance of the interest once it has been restored.

Restoration has a long history in conservation. For example, some reforestation of Trinidad and Tobago was undertaken in the eighteenth century, using exotic bamboo to protect soils from erosion. In the English Lake District in the early 1800s, the poet Wordsworth appealed for the release of lakeside back to nature, and advised the planting of native tree species to restore attractive forests. Aldo Leopold was amongst the first ecologists to attempt restoration. From 1934 he worked in an old pasture in Wisconsin, USA, aiming to create and study an imitation of the local tallgrass prairie. The University of Wisconsin's Arboretum in Maddison now supports a number of experimental restored habitats. Restoration ecology was promoted in America by the ecological devastation of the Dust Bowl and the deforestation of the Great Lakes area.

M. J. Morris recognised a difference in conservation methodology between 'maintenance management' and 'reclamation management'. The former aims to protect existing interest, whilst the latter aims to improve a site in some way by re-creating a habitat which is considered to have higher value. There is some overlap between the two – clearing exotic species from a habitat may help improve it, whilst re-introduction may prevent further damage to an ecosystem.

Restoration ecology provides insight about how natural ecosystems are assembled and function. An ability to restore an ecosystem (faster than nature can) shows we have some understanding of the system. Many disturbances that restoration seeks to remedy, such as mining and deforestation, can be used as large-scale or long-term ecological manipulation experiments – of the sort it would never be ethical to do deliberately! Working in Wisconsin, J. T. Curtis wrote in 1959 that 'The problems encountered in the attempts at artificial establishment of natural plant communities have demonstrated the complexities of community integration in a way that no other experience could provide'. Failures can be as revealing as successes. For example, the restoration at Wisconsin revealed much about the great importance of fire in prairie ecology, because the restoration failed before burning was tested. Soil formation has been studied in several restoration sites. Restoration of limestone grassland at Wytham, Oxford, has helped clarify the relevance of gaps, grazing and nutrients to grassland species richness. Restoration of lakes has improved our knowledge of nutrient dynamics. There are now several societies and journals focused on restoration ecology.

Restoration management aims to direct sites towards a more natural (or semi-natural) state, through techniques such as the removal of exotic species, the re-introduction of extinct species and the remediation of pollution of contaminated land or water. The Convention on Biological Diversity (Section 9.2) commits governments to attempt to restore species that have been extirpated in their territories – such as the beaver, lynx and wolf in many European countries; governments are also committed to stop the spread of invasive species and eradicate them if possible. Restoration may involve improvement of the quality of the matrix around relict habitats, through reduction in agricultural intensity, as in the 'wild farming' schemes in the USA and the Environmentally Sensitive Areas scheme in Europe. Wildlife corridors may be improved through large-scale restoration, as with tree-planting to help link the fragments of the Atlantic forests of Brazil.

There are several potential objectives of restoration, and in 1987 A. D. Bradshaw suggested these main targets: productivity; diversity; species composition; stabilisation of land surfaces; pollution control; visual improvement;

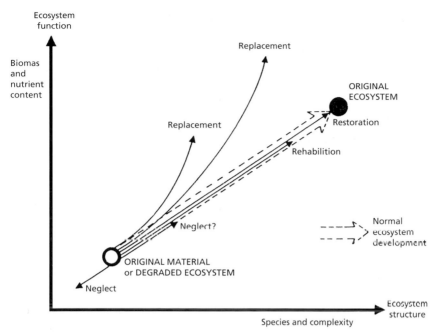

**Fig. 8.1.** True 'restoration' is achieved if the original ecosystem is produced. Partial success is called 'rehabilitation', and coverage by an alternative ecosystem is 'replacement'.
*Source:* Bradshaw, A. D. In: W. R. Jordan III (Ed.) *Restoration Ecology. A Synthetic Approach to Ecological Research* (Cambridge University Press, 1987, pp. 53–74). Reprinted with the permission of Cambridge University Press.

general amenity; and ecosystem function. It may be possible to restore certain facets of a system, such as the general structure of the habitat, but with a new species richness or composition. For example, the soil-binding and water-releasing characteristics of a forest may sometimes be restored by planting a grassland after deforestation. Indicators of successful restoration may include richness, species composition, vegetation structure (architecture), microbial profile, species quality, and ecosystem 'functioning' such as productivity, biomass, nutrient cycling and hydrology. Figure 8.1 illustrates different terms which may be applied to various outcomes of restoration.

Reaching the objectives may be theoretically or demonstrably possible, but impractical. The practical considerations that Bradshaw suggests are speed of attainment, cheapness, reliability in attainment, and stability of the product. He suggests the main benefit of restoration (over leaving a site to natural recovery through succession) is speed, although there will be cases where nature could never restore a species which has been regionally extirpated.

There is a further, modern impetus to the science and methodology of habitat restoration. If habitats can be re-created in their original location, then perhaps they can be re-created elsewhere? This has tempted developers and planners into attempts to move habitats and species which are in the way of a development. Restoration management and translocation management have both been embraced by developers aiming to offset the impact of a development by a form of compensatory payment-in-kind. Permission may be granted for development if policy makers and conservationists can be convinced that there will be a net gain for conservation – through the swapping of one habitat for another, the translocation of features of interest, and other methods often presumptuously described as 'mitigation' (Section 8.5).

There are many potential risks should we become overconfident that habitats can be replaced or exchanged. One of the most serious problems is long-term monitoring of the project – as yet there are few convincing examples of long-term success being achieved after restoration management. Until more research is done on success rates in different habitats, a precautionary approach should be adopted. Even without more research, we can already be confident that many forms of 'mitigation' *cannot* work. By definition, primary forests cannot be re-created.

There are three stages to restoration: recognising what is wrong with a system, taking appropriate corrective action, and demonstrating the system has returned to a desirable state. The desirable state may be similar to relatively natural sites in the region, and these are termed 'reference sites'. Reliable historical evidence is required to decide what we believe 'should' be on a site, in terms of species or habitats. We then need to know what species can realistically be replaced or removed. Managers need to consider whether it is theoretically possible to restore to a past state, because factors such as climate may have changed since that time. For example, whilst pollen shows that lime trees were common in the natural forests of southern Britain before deforestation, it is not clear if lime would thrive in the current climate. Moreover, many large mammals such as the wild boar, wolf and bear have been extirpated from Britain, and numerous mammal and tree species have been introduced, probably rendering restoration of anything like a natural forest impossible.

A general problem in restoration and re-introduction is that the site in question may be small and isolated from similar habitat, and so may suffer many of the problems of habitat fragmentation and population viability (Sections 5.4 and 6.3). The matrix which surrounds a restoration site may be damaging to the site, or contain property or forests of high commercial value.

There will be a species–area effect (limiting species richness), and edge effects (limiting specialist species). Edge effects have been observed in re-created prairies in North America. For example, shade round the edge of a restored prairie can lead to reduced vigour of grassland species, and so permit shrubs and trees to establish. Birds from forest (such as the indigo bunting and gray catbird) encroach into the prairie. The upland sandpiper, a prairie specialist bird, needs over 160 ha of habitat for a viable population unless the site is surrounded by open farmland. Small prairie fragments surrounded by corn suffer damage to sunflowers by corn rootworm beetles.

Isolated sites may suffer from a lack of colonists, slowing restoration, and so knowledge of the issues of re-introduction may be important to many forms of restoration. Bison and wolves cannot be re-introduced into small, recreated prairies. In many prairies and forests, the natural fire regime may be prohibited for safety reasons. We will examine obstacles to successful re-introduction, which then leads us into the controversies about translocation and mitigation.

## 8.1 Re-introduction

Re-introduction management has a relatively long history compared with other restoration methods. Capercaillie were extirpated from Scotland in the 1700s and re-introduced (from Sweden) in 1837. Large copper butterflies were extirpated in Britain in 1864, and first re-introduced in England in 1909. Arabian oryx were exterminated in the wild in the 1970s, but re-introduced to Oman in 1982.

There are various categories and definitions of management related to re-introduction.

- 'Re-introduction' is an attempt to establish a species in an area which was once part of its historical range.
- 'Re-establishment' is successful re-introduction.
- 'Conservation Introduction' is the attempt to establish a species, for the purpose of conservation, outside its recorded distribution but within an appropriate habitat and eco-geographical area.
- 'Translocation' is the deliberate and mediated movement of wild individuals or populations from one part of their range to another.
- 'Re-inforcement' is the addition of individuals to an existing population.

These definitions are expanded on the IUCN website. Confusingly, the term 'translocation' is often used more loosely as any movement of organisms or habitat from a development site, regardless of the suitability of the new site or the historical range (Sections 8.4 and 8.5). I shall refer to this as 'displacement', which might involve introduction, re-introduction or re-inforcement.

Re-inforcement is often an attempt to bolster populations and increase genetic diversity, or to improve the sex or age ratios of the population. Re-inforcement has been undertaken with crocodiles in China, rhinos in Africa, giant tortoises in Galapagos, otters and lady's slipper orchids in Britain, and kestrels and pink pigeons in Mauritius. Individuals are usually captive-bred (Section 6.5), or from a successful reserve (as with African elephant).

Re-introduction efforts will depend on suitable *ex situ* conservation methods (Section 6.5) during transport or captive breeding (if required). Ideally, the population that is to be used in re-introduction (the 'donor population') is genetically very close to the original population, to help increase the chances of it being suited to the local environmental conditions. However, if no such population exists, a closely similar race is chosen, as with the re-introductions of the large copper butterfly to Wicken Fen, England, and the large blue butterfly to south-west England. It quickly became apparent to conservationists that re-introductions were not always successful, despite the intensity of effort involved.

## 8.1.1   Obstacles and guidelines

Introductions are usually unacceptable. Conservation Introduction is risky since indigenous species may be harmed (Section 2.4). It is only acceptable in very special circumstances – where a species is likely to become extinct unless action is taken, and when the possible impact on the new site is judged by experts to be low enough to take the chance. For example, highly endangered flightless kakapo parrots were introduced to Little Barrier and Codfish Islands from the New Zealand mainland to create populations which were not at risk from exotic predators. This saved the species from extinction, with no apparent impact on the ecology of the host islands. Similarly, the Seychelles magpie robin – a critically endangered bird – may be introduced to selected coral atolls of low value, and the Guam rail was introduced to Rota Island. Unfortunately, it can be difficult to tell if a species naturally occurred in a region, but archaeological and 'sub-fossil' evidence may help.

Re-introductions raise complex issues. They carry a risk of damage to the new ecosystem, and a high chance of failure. There may be very good reasons why the species could not get to, or survive in, a site in the first place – unless it is poor at dispersal, as with the kakapo. Following a history of failures and

Table 8.1 *Selected guidelines for re-introductions, edited from those of IUCN*

- The original causes for extirpation *must* have been removed.
- Suitable habitat *must* be available for a viable population, ideally where the species occurred recently.
- A feasibility study should examine taxonomic, ecological and behavioural characteristics of the species.
- The fate of previous re-introductions of the same or similar species should be assessed.
- The release site should be within the former natural range, and be protected.
- The donor population must not be threatened by removing individuals.
- Re-introduced organisms must be genetically suitable, and screened for disease.
- Stock should, as far as possible, be prepared for the wild environment and local diseases.
- There should be consultation with all stakeholders, and minimal impact on local people.
- The released population should be monitored and managed.
- The welfare of animals should be paramount.
- Restocking is not recommended unless host populations are no longer viable.

*Note:* The full IUCN guidelines are at http://www.iucnsscrsg.org/pages/1/index.htm.

successes, the IUCN's SSC Re-Introduction Specialist Group have developed a series of guidelines on re-introductions. These are outlined in Table 8.1.

A review by B. Griffith and colleagues of 700 translocations found that success was more likely if the translocation was to the core of the former range of the species, and if the translocated individuals were wild-caught rather than captive-reared. The chances of successful establishment of a new population increase rapidly with the number of animals translocated, and then levels off at about 80–120 birds, or 20–40 mammals. Success is low if habitat quality is low. However, M. R. Oates and M. S. Warren found the success of butterfly re-introduction in Britain is apparently not related to the numbers released.

The most obvious requirement for re-introduction is that the population will not succumb to the same pressures that locally extirpated the species in the first place. Despite this, there have been many attempts to re-introduce without sufficient knowledge of such pressures. The reasons for the original extirpation should be studied in detail. Hunting, or an introduced species of predator or competitor, is often a relatively clear pressure. Unfortunately competition is often very difficult to detect: it took decades of research to prove that grey squirrels had competitively excluded red squirrels from parts of their range in Europe. It may also be very difficult to show that disease did not cause the extirpation – other species in the area might be reservoirs for diseases such as rabies. Changes in the landscape and habitat may have been only partially documented. For example, it was evident that drainage of the fens had reduced the range and abundance of the British race of the large copper butterfly; however, it was not clear exactly what the requirements for the species were, leading to a series of failed re-introduction attempts.

Detailed documentation of the decline of the species in question will help determine if the causal factors for decline might still operate. However, extirpation may have occurred tens or even thousands of years ago, and be poorly documented. Despite this, musk ox were successfully reintroduced from America to the Asian tundra 3000 years after hunting had exterminated them. It may not be until a re-introduction fails that the reasons for extirpation become clear – a risky experiment with rare species.

If the factors causing the original decline have now been removed, re-introduction may still prove futile – there may be new problems such as a reduction in the extent of the habitat, or a growing human population pressure in the area, or other changes in the landscape. It may be very difficult to re-introduce species which have become extinct in part as a result of habitat fragmentation. If the habitat is now too small to support a large population (Sections 5.4 and 6.3) this might have compounded a problem such as hunting or predation. For example, although the bear, lynx, wolf and beaver would no longer face major hunting threats in Britain, there may not be sufficient inter-connected land with a sufficiently low human population density to establish viable populations. The interchange of animals between wild populations and captive stock might help restore a few of these species in some areas.

It is often clear what caused the extirpation of many large mammals and birds in parts of Europe and America, and it is also fairly clear what the main obstacles are to their re-introduction (Table 8.2). The recovery of bears in America and wild boar in Europe now causes some concern where they are exploiting suburban or arable environments. Hunting may be a relatively clear pressure to identify, but a difficult problem to prevent. The persecution of the wolf in France is very deep-rooted, with much folk law about this 'evil' beast killing livestock and people. As the species re-colonises the Alps through natural dispersal (and possibly illegal re-introductions), the hunting lobby is pressing to exclude it and wolves are being illegally shot. Similarly, the apparently successful re-introduction of the wolf to Yellowstone Park in 1995

Table 8.2 *Reasons for extirpations of populations of some large species in the British Isles, with last record*

| Species | Last record | Likely reasons for extirpation | Re-introduction likely? |
|---|---|---|---|
| Bison | 27 650 BP? | Hunting for food; climate change | No: habitat area |
| Woolly rhino | 22 350 BP | Climate change; hunting | No: extinct |
| Woolly mammoth | 12 880 BP | Hunting for food; climate change | No: extinct |
| Arctic lemming | >10 000 BP | Climate change | No: climate |
| Arctic fox | 12 400 BP | Climate change; persecution? | No: climate |
| Saiga | 12 400 BP | Climate change; hunting for food? | No: climate |
| Wolverine | >8000 BP | Climate change; hunting? | No: habitat area |
| Wild horse | 9330 BP | Hunting for food; climate change | No: habitat area |
| Giant deer (Irish elk) | 9230 BP | Climate change; hunting for food? | No: extinct |
| Reindeer | 8300 BP | Hunting for food; climate change | Already successful |
| Elk (Moose) | 3400 BP? | Climate change; hunting for food | No: habitat area |
| Aurochs | 3250 BP? | Hunting for food | No: extinct |
| Lynx | 1700 BP (?AD 180) Persecution? | Habitat loss | Possible |
| Brown bear | 0–AD 1000 | Persecution | No: dangerous |
| Beaver | 1100s | Hunting for furs | In progress |
| Wild boar | 1295 | Hunting for food; persecution | Accidental success |
| Atlantic grey whale | 1610 | Hunting for food | No: extinct |
| Wolf (grey) | 1786 | Persecution | Possible: semi-wild |
| Pygmy cormorant? | c. 1500s | Climate change? habitat loss? | Unlikely |
| Eagle owl | c. 1930s | Habitat loss | No: habitat area |
| White stork | ?1416 (as resident) | Habitat loss; hunting? | No: habitat area |

(cont.)

Table 8.2 (*cont.*)

| Species | Last record | Likely reasons for extirpation | Re-introduction likely? |
|---|---|---|---|
| Capercaillie | c. 1790 | Hunting for food | Already successful |
| Great bustard | 1832 | Hunting for food; habitat loss | In progress |
| Great auk | 1840 | Hunting for food, feathers, eggs | No: extinct |
| White-tailed eagle | 1908 | Persecution | Already successful |

*Note:* England and Wales separated from continental Europe about 8600 years BP.
*Sources:* Various sources; most dates for mammals have been derived from Yalden, D. *The History of British Mammals* (T. & A. D. Poyser Ltd, London, 1999).

followed much heated public debate. Re-introduction of the beaver in Britain provoked concern at losses to forestry and property. These species illustrate, on a small scale, problems which will increasingly be faced world-wide as wilderness disappears.

Large fenced areas may be required to allay public concerns about livestock and safety, and substantial re-afforestation (of the sort the charity Trees for Life are undertaking in the Highlands of Scotland) might be a vital pre-cursor to re-introduction of large-mammals. Re-introduction forms part of what D. W. Macdonald sees as a potential 'radical future' for British mammals. Such changes in attitudes and landscape will require education, and compensatory payment for loss of land or livestock (Section 9.1). Public attitudes can change and permit re-introduction. Following persecution, the red kite became extinct in England in 1871. Now most of the public, farmers and gamekeepers have different views, and the red kite was re-introduced from continental Europe in 1989; it has bred and dispersed very successfully, increasing between 1974 and 1999 from 32 to 420 pairs in Britain. Some individuals have been poisoned by landowners, particularly in Scotland, but the public attitude is clearly sufficiently receptive. When white-tailed eagles were re-introduced to Britain from Norway in 1968, there was still a risk from egg-collectors (although this is both illegal and unfashionable) and persecution (which continues).

It may take some years to become confident that a re-introduction campaign has been successful, and that a viable population of the species has been established. For example, one re-introduction attempt for the large cop-per butterfly failed after several decades; only recently have laboratory studies demonstrated that waterlogging of the larvae in prolonged floods was prob-ably the major obstacle, leading to improved management prescriptions for future attempts. The importance of getting the most appropriate race of the species for the local conditions is illustrated by the re-introduction of the ibex (Section 6.2.3). In one of the most successful re-introductions, swift foxes have been released in Canada since 1983, and, by 2001, 99% of the population was wild born.

Contaminated land or water pollution can be an obstacle to restoration. Contamination by toxic or radioactive material may sometimes be reduced by removal of soil or by dredging of mud. Treating toxic soils is often termed 'rehabilitation'. Bioremediation involves the use of living organisms to destroy or sequester the undesirable chemicals. For example, reeds my be used to strip metals from freshwater. The plant or animal material must be harvested and disposed of on appropriate sites.

Parasites and parasitoids should also be re-introduced with their host; such species are often even rarer and more vulnerable than the host. A specific parasitoid of the swallowtail butterfly is a candidate to be re-introduced with its host to fenland sites in Britain.

## 8.2   Control of introduced species

Introduced species are a very common problem preventing re introduction – and are a common issue in restoration ecology generally. The terms 'intro-duced' and 'exotic' and 'alien' are used interchangeably. If an animal species escapes and breeds in the wild it is termed 'feral'. 'Invasive' implies an exotic species which is spreading fast. Introduced animals range from insects such as scale-insects and ants, through to large mammals such as camels and foxes (Section 2.4). Introduced plants include small annuals such as dandelions in South Georgia and trees such as cinnamon and albizia in Seychelles. Intro-duced species can be a substantial fraction of the fauna or flora – about 50% of the vascular plant species of New Zealand and Galapagos are exotic, and over 40% of the vascular plants in Seychelles – and they may cover substantial frac-tions of the land or freshwater surface. Management of exotic species to prepare for a re-introduction can be costly. There are some general questions and prin-ciples of management of exotics, which we will examine before considering particular cases. Key issues are whether to eradicate or control the introduced species, the risks to non-target species, and the welfare of the species.

Should introduced species be 'eradicated' (that is, entirely removed from the island) or 'controlled' at chosen numbers or densities? Since finding and removing the last few individuals of an introduced species may be very difficult and expensive, it might appear that control is the cheaper option. However, the timescale of management has to be considered. If the aim is to maintain a low population of the exotic species indefinitely, then eventually the costs of control will be greater than a one-off eradication. Failure to remove the last few individuals of an invasive species can result in recurrence of the problem. Exponential growth can very rapidly replace animals or plants that have been removed. For example, on Pinta Island in the Galapagos, three goats bred up to over 20 000 in 24 years. On Aldabra, the ability of goats to survive undetected and breed fast was repeatedly underestimated, and expensive repetition of an eradication programme was required.

Introduced species may be amongst the most intractable reasons preventing re-introduction. Numerous cichlid fish may have been extirpated from Lake Victoria by Nile perch, and may now exist only in captivity. The Nile perch is now a popular food in Lake Victoria, and eradication would be resisted by fishermen, even if it were technically possible (which it might never be). For large islands such as Madagascar and New Zealand, eradication of abundant species may be impossible. Even more impractical is the eradication of exotic species from whole continents, such as sparrows from North America, or rabbits from Australia. Specific diseases, if they exist, might eventually prove the only viable method. Intensive control of the species may be possible in some sensitive regions and periods. For example, part of an island may be cleared of feral predators in the bird breeding season by intensive poisoning. By controlling rats on Rarotonga in the breeding season, E. K. Saul saved the Rarotonga flycatcher from extinction.

Intensively managed parts of mainlands, termed 'mainland island' reserves, are now being created to protect and re-introduce species. An example of this is the control of predators in the breeding season of the yellow-eyed penguin, sooty shearwater and royal albatross, in Otago peninsula in New Zealand. Another mainland island reserve, the Northern Te Urewera of New Zealand, includes over 2500 ha of forest in which predators are eradicated, within a larger area in which possums are controlled. Wasps, magpies and other exotic species are controlled in various mainland islands in New Zealand. It is relatively easy to make mainland islands on peninsulas, which can be cleared with a 'rolling-front' of poisoned bait, or with a fenced, cleared zone and an outer zone where predators are controlled. Peninsulas are relatively easily fenced, and there are several projects in Australia to restore endangered mammals (including the burrowing bettong and western barred bandicoot) to the mainland from relict populations on islands.

Fenced enclosures have been used for re-introduced *Partula* snails in Polynesia, creating semi-wild populations protected from the predatory snail *Euglandina rosea*. Fencing can sometimes be used to divide areas into manageable units, as with the control of goats in Australia and Hawaii. Fences have been used to protect highly endangered marsupials in Australia from feral cats, foxes and dingoes. A 20 km long electrified fence protects 25 ha of Queensland for the bilbie. The Warrawong Earth Sanctuary was set up by J. Wamsley and demonstrated the benefits of feral-free reserves to species such as the woylie and numbat. A fence 4800 km long protects southeastern Australia from the dingo. Safe breeding refuges can be provided for species such as the water vole to escape exotics such as the American mink in Britain.

Eradication of aquatic species from extensive or well-connected water bodies is highly problematic; this is typically the case in marine systems. The spread of the toxic marine alga *Caulerpa taxifolia* might eventually be controlled in some areas by a specialised herbivorous sea slug such as *Elysia subornata*, although this is controversial; in California chlorinated water injected under tarpaulins has been used to poison the alga, whilst suction-dredging may be effective on soft substrates, and rock-salt can kill it in shallow waters.

A major consideration in the choice of method to remove introduced species is the risk to indigenous, 'non-target' species. There may also be a need to protect non-target individuals of the same species, such as domestic cats or goats owned by local people. This is a particular problem if biological control through disease ('microbiological control') is considered. Introduced invertebrates are often controlled biologically. If biological control is used, then it must be specific enough to preclude the control agent itself becoming invasive (Section 2.4). Highly specific predators and parasites have now been used with some success: these include the ladybird *Hyperapsis pantherina*, which protected the endemic gumwood of St Helena from ensign scale, and the alligator flea beetle, which cleared alligator weed from some North American wetlands. Diseases which trigger sterility (immunocontraceptives) are now being developed against rabbits and rats. Microbiological control is in its infancy as a science, and there are risks of repeating the problems encountered with other biological control organisms (Section 2.5).

Trapping methods, including snares, obviously carry substantial risk to non-target species of similar size and behaviour to the feral species. Poison baits may influence non-target species. They need to be delivered in a way that minimises such risk. Several poisons, such as Compound 1080 and 'second-generation anticoagulants' including Brodificoum, mainly influence mammals. Nonetheless, these should be dispersed in a way that reduces contact with native vertebrates. During several of the successful rat eradication projects on New Zealand's offshore islands, baits were dispersed in tubes to minimise such risks. Where there are no non-target species, but the terrain is difficult (such as mountains or thick scrub), baits can be dropped from special hoppers on helicopters – as against rats on Curieuse (Seychelles) and Kapiti Island (New Zealand). Poison bait was dropped on crazy ant colonies on Christmas Island, having first distracted robber crabs with alternative bait.

The welfare of the introduced species must be considered. Introduced vertebrates may suffer when poisoned or trapped (live or dead), and the control method should of course have the lowest risk of causing suffering. However, it should be noted that feral animals would suffer if left to reach a 'natural' population balance, for example through disease or starvation. There is often suffering amongst the individuals of the animals threatened by the introduced species – when eaten by cats, when starved, or if they catch diseases from them. Overall, the total amount of suffering in an area or species may be minimised by eradication. For some species, such as hedgehogs in Britain's Western Isles, live-trapping and lethal injection is possible. For larger species, the most specific and most humane method to eradicate or control introduced species is shooting, but this is relatively expensive. To get the last goats off an Island can cost thousands of pounds per goat. Shooting can be done on foot, but in rugged or remote terrain, helicopters are needed as shooting platforms.

In order to get the last few individuals, the 'Judas animal' technique can be used. When the introduced species is sociable, then the animals can be used to find others of the species more efficiently than can people. A radio-collar is fitted to the Judas animal, which is then released. It finds other individuals, which are shot. This is repeated until all of the animals have been betrayed by the Judas animal. When the Judas animal can find no others, or can only find other Judas animals, these too are shot. This technique has been used successfully against goats on San Clemente Island (California), and against feral pig colonies in Australia and New Zealand. On Aldabra, Seychelles, difficult terrain precluded Judas goats finding all other goats in the timescale of the eradication attempt.

Introduced land plants can be controlled by hand in small areas. On Aldabra, cutting of sisal has limited its spread for decades. Cutting of rhododendron ('rhodie-bashing') is a common management in several British nature reserves. Herbicides (including some dropped from helicopter) have been used against several species such as mysore thorn on Raoul Island (New Zealand). Backpack sprayers (applying Krenite) have been used successfully against birch on British heathland. If herbicides are used against plants, they might kill native plants, and initial survey work should examine this risk. The risk to native plants can be reduced by a herbicide gel developed in New Zealand, which is applied directly to the exotic plants. Tree stumps may also be hand-painted with herbicide to prevent regrowth. Introduced aquatic plants such as water hyacinth are sometimes harvested by machine. Livestock on Ascension Island has been fenced-in to reduce the spread of Mexican thorn bush.

The various introduced species may require different considerations and techniques on different islands, depending on terrain and the combination of native and other introduced species present. There may be interactions between introduced species to consider. For example, following eradication of exotic goats on Round Island (off Mauritius), it was found that they had been controlling a pan-rropical weed (*Tylophora taevigata*), and control of this plant may require introduction of tortoises. Rats have increased on several islands, such as Pitcairn, after removal of cats. In western Australia, a policy of controlling foxes was found to be counter-productive because foxes suppress cat populations – which are more damaging to marsupials. There may often be a logical sequence to removing introduced species. Pigs need to be removed before goats, or else regrowth of vegetation will make finding pigs harder. Feral species should be eradicated before re-introduction of species which might tolerate the feral species but be susceptible to the eradication methods.

Examples of successful and unsuccessful management of introduced species are given in Table 8.3. Once exotics have been controlled, monitoring and quarantine may be needed if there is a risk of population increase or re-invasion.

## 8.3   Restoration management

Restoration of species into habitats by re-introduction may depend on an initial management of the site to a state more suitable for the re-introduced species. Re-introduction of many species may be undertaken simultaneously – as with seeding plants into a prairie, wetland or limestone grassland. Often, some vegetation must be re-established before animals or other plants can be re-introduced or can colonise naturally. And even before the vegetation is established, the abiotic features such as soil quality and hydrology must be checked or made suitable. Restoration may begin on a damaged site which retains relicts or elements of the original habitat. This may be termed habitat enhancement. Alternatively, the restoration may be on a site lacking most or

Table 8.3 *Examples of control or eradication of exotic species*

| Species | Location | Aim | Protected |
|---|---|---|---|
| (a) Successful | | | |
| Goats | Pinta Island (Galapagos) | E | Ecosystem; endemic species |
| Goats, rabbits | Round Island (Mauritius) | E | Endemic plants and reptiles |
| Pigs | Santiago | E | Ecosystem; endemic species |
| Cats | Fregate Island (Seychelles) | E | Seychelles magpie robin |
| Polynesian rats | Oeno and Ducie (Pitcairn Islands) | E | Seabird nest sites |
| Brown rats | Langara Island (Canada) | E | Seabirds, e.g. ancient murrelet |
| Opuntia | Australia | C | Scrubland |
| Alligator weed | North America | C | Freshwater systems |
| Crazy ant | Christmas Island | C | Red land crab; ecosystem |
| (b) Initially unsuccessful projects | | | Reason for failure |
| Goats | Aldabra (Seychelles) | E | Terrain: helicopters required |
| Goats | Pinta Island (Galapagos) | E | Judas goats required |
| Polynesian rats | Pitcairn Island (Pacific) | E | Terrain: refuges from bait |

*Notes:* E = eradication; C = control at greatly reduced abundance.

all features of the original habitat, in which case it may be termed habitat creation. Some of the principles of restoration apply to both terrestrial and aquatic systems.

Restoration may involve the introduction or removal of selected species for a particular role. Some of these may be exotics, acting as 'ecological analogues' in mimicking an extinct species. For example, in some reserves in Costa Rica, D. H. Janzen and P. S. Martin have encouraged the use of horses and cattle to mimic the extinct megafauna as agents of seed dispersal; plants such as jicaro and guanacaste have benefited from livestock in parks. Similarly, Aldabran giant tortoises are used as ecological analogues for extinct tortoises on Ile aux Aigrettes, Mauritius. Exotic species may be used to build soil structure, strip toxins from soil, and restore soil nutrient levels. On old mine spoil in the eastern USA, the black locust has been used to fix nitrogen, and poplar used to pump cations to the soil surface. These species are later displaced by native species. 'Biomanipulation' of lakes may involve the introduction of exotic species; however, these are relatively extreme measures which should be used with great care.

Some types of improvement of the agricultural landscape for wildlife may not involve true restoration of native habitat, but nevertheless provide more pleasant scenery and help some valuable species. Many of the agri-environment schemes aim to create interesting grassland (although true restoration would aim for woodland). Unfortunately, few of these schemes have been monitored closely enough to demonstrate benefits to wildlife. However, studies by J. W. Dover and the Game Conservancy Trust have shown local benefits to butter-flies of reduced insecticide and herbicide use at field margins ('conservation headlands'); insectivorous birds are also known to benefit.

Restoration of some characteristics of the original ecosystem is now possible in most terrestrial environments. However, this certainly does not mean that the new sites are as valuable for conservation as the original – particularly in the quality of the species they support (Section 3.1). In order to improve or protect species quality, translocation of species or habitats has been attempted – with variable success.

## 8.3.1   Terrestrial systems

In the extreme case of 'derelict' land, soils are often entirely absent or skeletal. This may occur after erosion. To build soil structure, or increase soil nutrients (if desirable), or permit the growth of specialist plants, it is often necessary to promote the early re-establishment of the microbiological community, for example through inoculation of the soil with mycorrhizal fungi. Topsoil that has been stored may be deficient in mycorrhizal spores. Plants that are capable of supporting mycorrhizae may have to be introduced to a site early on, and many late successional plants require established mycorrhizae. To restore forest and reverse salinification at Nambling, western Australia, ramial chipped wood mulch (RCM) was added to promote *Basidiomycetes* mycorrhyzae.

Restoration management often involves manipulating a succession, which may be a primary succession if the topsoil has been lost, or a secondary succession on less degraded sites. There are principles in common with the management of semi-natural habitats (Section 7.3). Restoration will often be cheaper, but slower, if natural successional processes such as soil-building or

Table 8.4 *Some basic considerations in restoration of derelict land*

| Category | Problem | Immediate treatment | Long-term treatment |
|---|---|---|---|
| Physical structure | Too compact | Rip or scarify | Vegetation |
| | Too open | Compact or cover with fine material | Vegetation |
| Stability | Unstable | Stabiliser/mulch | Regrade; vegetation |
| Moisture | Too wet | Drain | Drain |
| | Too dry | Organic mulch | Vegetation |
| Nutrition | | | |
| Macronutrients | Nitrogen | Fertiliser | Legume |
| | Others | Fertiliser and lime | Fertiliser and lime |
| Micronutrients | | Fertiliser | |
| Toxicity | | | |
| pH | Too high | Pyritic waste or organic mater | Weathering |
| | Too low | Lime or leaching | Lime or weathering |
| Heavy metals | Too high | Organic mulch or metal tolerant plants | Inert covering or tolerant plants |
| Salinity | Too high | Weathering or irrigation | Tolerant plants |
| Animals and plants | Absent or slow colonisation | Reintroductions | Monitoring and management |

*Source:* Adapted from Bradshaw, A. D. The reclamation of derelict land and the ecology of ecosystems. In: Jordan III, W. R., Gilpin, M. E. and Aber, J. D. *Restoration Ecology* (Cambridge University Press, 1987, pp. 53–74).

colonisation are exploited. Restoration through succession often takes a similar timescale to primary succession on bare rock in the region, for example several decades for a forest to appear, but centuries or millennia for many specialist species to establish. The process will take much longer on extreme soils with high toxicity such as on waste from mines or industry.

The general underlying problems of restoring derelict land were identified by Bradshaw in 1983 and are summarised in Table 8.4. These are applicable to any soil in the world. Bradshaw suggests these reflect 'the very simple needs of plants for: (1) a medium into which they are physically able to root, (2) an adequate water supply, (3) an adequate nutrient supply, and (4) lack of toxicity'.

It is critically important that the hydrology of the site is rendered suitable by management. The water table may need to be raised before wetland plants and animals can establish. However, except in the case of areas damaged by dams or irrigation, creation of drier habitat would seldom be defensible, given the relative rarity and value of wetland.

The physical character of the soil is very important to establishment. Soil may need to be created, or improved for planting, through ripping the subsoil and substrate, and a seedbed of fine soil prepared on top. Organic matter or earthworms may be introduced to maintain the physical quality of the soil.

The soil nutrient content must be examined and, if necessary, managed to permit the desired plant species to establish. Soil nutrient levels are fundamental to the ecology of habitats. 'Semi-natural' habitats have low nutrient status, whilst various natural habitats may have either low or high status – but usually relatively high levels of nutrient (per unit area) within the vegetation. To restore semi-natural habitats, nutrients must often be removed, whilst to restore natural habitats, they must often be added. Nitrogen appears a particularly important nutrient in restoration. Nutrients will gradually accumulate in an area through natural inputs, and succession will tend towards restoration of a more natural habitat (Section 7.3). Topsoil rich in nutrients may be used to accelerate restoration. Fertiliser including nitrogen, phosphorous and potassium may be added to skeletal soils in quarries to help establish grassland. Fertiliser may also be added in forest restoration.

To restore semi-natural habitats, the reverse of this natural process is usually required. Succession must be arrested or reversed. Many semi-natural sites have been 'degraded' by natural succession after grazing declined, or have been converted to cropland, or were subject to agricultural improvement, all of which increase soil nutrient levels. It may be possible to reduce the nutrient levels by 'nutrient stripping'. Nutrient stripping may be achieved by cropping of any plant material, such as through cutting and removal of cuttings, or by grazing with livestock which are gaining in weight. A more rapid method, of value on arable land which is relatively disturbed and rich in nutrients, is to plant an agricultural crop which is demanding of nutrients. When this crop is harvested, the nutrients are removed from the land. At the wet grassland of De Veenkampen in Holland, topsoil was removed to strip nutrients.

The use and effect of nutrient stripping is illustrated by the experimental attempted restoration of limestone grassland at Upper Seeds, Wytham Woods,

(a)

**Fig. 8.2.** Changes in the floristic richness in Upper Seeds limestone grassland (Wytham, Oxford, England), under different restoration management treatments since agriculture ended in 1980. (a) The experimental grazing treatments, with some treatments replicated in blocks. (b) The frequency of late-successional specialist species in two ancient grasslands (upper two lines) compared with the slow rise in experimental treatments (lower lines). A = short-period autumn grazing; AA = long-period autumn grazing; C = ungrazed control; S = short-period spring grazing; BO and SH = local ancient grasslands of moderate richness; SA = long-period spring and autumn grazing. (c) Enlargement of the lower section of (b), showing only restoration treatments.
*Source:* (a) BBC; (b) and (c) C. W. D. Gibson of Bioscan UK Ltd.

England, by C. W. D. Gibson. This is an area with a well-recorded flora and history of land use. As with many agriculturally marginal areas on calcareous rocks in southern Britain, Upper Seeds was a semi-natural limestone grassland which had a brief history of use for cereal production this century – it was used for cereal production between 1960 and 1981. A cereal crop was grown without fertiliser in the first year of restoration; it was not harvested, and then self-seeded. In the second year, the soil nutrient level was now so low that the self-seeded cereal grew very poorly, and the land was therefore ready for conversion to grassland. Sheep were used to strip nutrients in the vegetation, through grazing. Seeds and animals colonised from the adjacent areas and grew from the seed bank. Three grazing regimes have been tested for their ability to direct the succession towards a limestone grassland community.

The changes in floristic richness at Upper Seeds under different experimental management treatments are illustrated in Fig. 8.2. The grasslands are very slowly accumulating high-quality species typical of traditional limestone grassland. Results suggest that a sophisticated grazing management

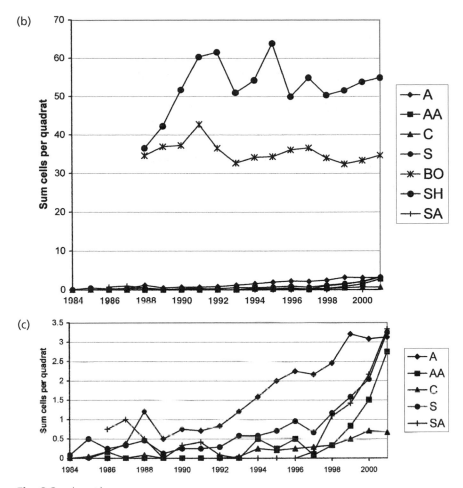

**Fig. 8.2.**  (cont.)

regime may be required over many decades to direct the succession on such sites towards a floristically rich grassland. At Upper Seeds, the proximity of floristically rich limestone grassland rendered re-introduction redundant for many species. However, it is possible that the soil is now suitable for some species that may not yet have colonised because they have weaker dispersal. Re-introductions might be considered to overcome this problem on similar sites (although not on an experimental site where natural dispersal can be investigated).

When habitats are being created from highly disturbed land, intensive preparation and management may be needed to speed up the process. This will be particularly true when seed banks have been lost, and expansive agriculture limits natural dispersal. There is often an interest in encouraging wildlife onto 'surplus' arable land, as with the 'set-aside' and other agri-environment schemes in Europe and America. In an experiment by D. W. Macdonald and colleagues at Wytham Farm, field-margins were set-aside to create grassland (Fig. 4.7). Nutrient status was a possible problem and there was a risk of nutrient-demanding weed species (such as nettles and thistles) flourishing in this ex-arable land. Several management treatments were therefore tested to find a way to maximise attractive diversity and beneficial arthropods such as spiders and carabid beetles, whilst minimising the risk of weeds. The results suggested that seeding with a wildflower mix hastens the development of an attractive and beneficial margin. The introduction or re-introduction of seeds in this way hastened the development of architecturally complex, flower-rich, margins, supporting butterflies and predators. Similarly, seeding hastened wetland creation in Wisconsin. In the prairie restoration project at the Fermilab site (Illinois, USA), restoration has three phases of re-introductions: a prairie mix of seeds is used to cover the ground and suppress weeds. Several years later, seeds of forbs and grasses are sown, and as these establish, more sensitive prairie species such as downy gentian are planted as seedlings.

The use of wildflower seed mixes to restore habitats is controversial. When restoring habitats in or near nature reserves, it is important that the seeds are from native species, and preferably local races – to reduce damage to existing populations through outbreeding depression and introgression (Sections 2.4 and 6.2.3). In the past, professional seed-collectors, and special seed-harvesting machines have been used to gather seeds, sometimes at remote sites. It is better to obtain seeds of local provenance. For restoration of the prairies, seeds are collected by seed-harvesting machines or by hand from as local a source as possible. In the restoration of Somerford Mead, Oxford, A. W. McDonald collected seeds from hay meadow reserves only 2 km away, using a mechanical sampler. These seeds were applied to a fine seed bed on a site which had been nutrient stripped with a barley crop; 19 of 22 characteristic plant species were established in the sward within 3 years.

Similarly, when woodlands are re-created, local seeds or saplings should be used. In Britain, it is not uncommon to find that well-meaning conservation volunteers have planted numerous exotic tree species, or races, onto nature reserves. This can be problematic when mapping the distribution of native species. The importance of obtaining seeds of local provenance is illustrated by restoration of mineral sand mines in Australia: the seaward and landward populations of several scrub and tree species of the dunes differ, and grow poorly in the other's habitat. Environmental education (Section 9.3) will often be important in restoration to help explain the management aims and the changes anticipated in the landscape.

Experimental work on a series of sites can help identify the limiting factors in restoration – such as immigration, nutrients, or area. Translocation of a species can illustrate whether it had failed to establish through dispersal or unsuitable site characteristics. This would be more ethical with plants than animals, and with common or captive-bred species. For example, translocation of plants to alkaline reclamation sites in north-west England showed the spread of yellow rattle and yellow-wort had been limited by dispersal, whilst cowslip was limited by nutrients. Lack of animals can prevent animal-dispersed plants from colonising secondary tropical forest, and such plants may need to be re-introduced.

In addition to adding species, some competitive plants may have to be removed prior to restoration. In prairie restoration, the ground may first be sterilised by a short-lived herbicide to clear agricultural weeds. Weeding (an expensive option) may subsequently be required to aid the colonisation by desirable species. Manipulation of the fire regime (which kills many perennial species) has proved very important in prairie management, and this would probably be true for restoration of many savannah habitats. Pollinator species may need to be protected or promoted – as with the hawkmoths which pollinate the eastern prairie fringed orchid.

An artificial age structure, and particularly a lack of dead wood, are common features of secondary and managed forests. To restore more natural forest, trees may be wounded (for example by ring-barking) to hasten their death and decay, as in Moccas Park in Britain. Former coppiced woodland in Britain may be restored to high-forest by 'singling' – the promotion of a single main stem from the coppiced tree. Grazing by deer or livestock may need to be prevented.

## 8.3.2 Aquatic systems

Restoration of freshwater habitats has often been fairly successful, perhaps because of the naturally dynamic nature of many wetlands. Indeed, many of the best wetlands in Britain (such as the Norfolk Broads) are in former peat cuttings or quarries that have become colonised by wetland species. Reedbeds can be created by cutting and levelling the substrate, although it has often proved difficult to re-create the homogenous surface of the original mud. Freshwater and marine sites may require preparation of the abiotic substrate. Methods include dredging or blasting, or increasing the variety of flow conditions by

(a)

**Fig. 8.3.** Restoration of the River Brede floodplain. (a) Part of the restored area.
(b) Examples of restoration activity.
*Source:* (a) County of South Jutland, Denmark, J. W. Luftfoto. (b) Benstead, P. *et al.*
*European Wet Grassland: Guidelines for Management and Restoration* (RSPB, Sandy,
1999).

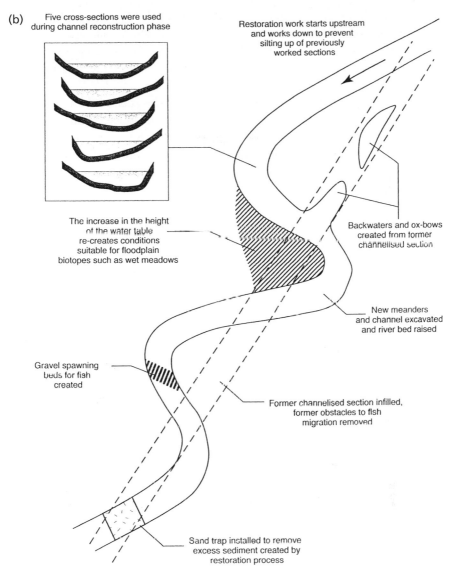

(b)

Five cross-sections were used during channel reconstruction phase

Restoration work starts upstream and works down to prevent silting up of previously worked sections

The increase in the height of the water table re-creates conditions suitable for floodplain biotopes such as wet meadows

Backwaters and ox-bows created from former channelised section

New meanders and channel excavated and river bed raised

Gravel spawning beds for fish created

Former channelised section infilled, former obstacles to fish migration removed

Sand trap installed to remove excess sediment created by restoration process

**Fig. 8.3.** (cont.)

adding boulders or gravel. Bank slopes may be made less steep by cutting or dumping. Gravel may be dumped in ridges to create spawning beds for fish, as for salmonids in several restored Danish streams. Gravel in spawning grounds may be flushed clean of silt. Meanders may be restored by cutting and blocking channels. Dead wood can be placed in rivers and streams. Dead salmon have been dumped in North American salmon streams to provide nutrients for juveniles, mimicing natural post-spawning death of adults. Reduction in pollution levels in French rivers, such as the Loire, has been followed by natural re-colonisation by species such as shad. Over 25 km of the floodplain of the River Brede in Denmark has been restored by various engineering methods (Fig. 8.3).

Restoration may also include removal of obstacles such as dams, and provision of better fish-ladders or lifts. Four mini-hydro-power dams are being removed from the Sandy River Valley in Oregon, USA, to restore fish runs. Controlled flooding may be used to mimic seasonal floods, as in the Grand Canyon of the Colorado River. Connectivity is being restored in the Florida Everglades.

Lakes are increasingly being restored under laws relating to water quality. In the USA, the Environment Protection Agency's Clean Lakes Programme accelerated restoration after 1980, leading to several informative successes and failures. Eutrophication, following pollution by nutrients, is the commonest problem in lakes. Diversion or purification of the rivers supplying the lake water may be required. Eutrophication may be reduced by flushing or dredging of nutrient-rich sediments, as in Lake Trumen in Sweden and Moses Lake, Washington, USA. Macrophytes may be harvested to strip nutrients. A chemical is sometimes added to precipitate the nutrients (such as phosphorous) and bind them in the sediment. Often, care must be taken not to stir nutrients from the lake bed, but in some cases stirring of the water column can help remove nutrients from the lake. Acidification can be remedied by application of powdered lime to the lake or watershed, as in many Scandinavian lakes. Fish of local origin often need to be re-introduced as part of freshwater restoration.

Restoration of marine environments is in its infancy – we know less of the natural diversity and dynamics of these systems. Mangrove habitats have been planted amidst reclaimed land in Seychelles. Several salt marshes are being restored through policies of 'managed retreat' of agriculture and housing. Managed retreat has been widely adopted in Britain, where rising sea-level may be too expensive to fight, and this is an opportunity to reverse the extensive drainage and loss of these important habitats. New coral and cold-water reefs have been founded on structurally complex substrates, including scuppered ships, old typewriters and car bodies. Limestone boulders have been used to repair major gaps in reefs. Concrete 'Reef Balls' of various sizes have been designed to encourage colonisation by temperate or tropical species. These are placed where the substrate has been damaged by fishing gear, ships grounding, or other processes. Regeneration of several reefs has been aided using electrolysis to help deposit calcium carbonate ('biorock') onto a metal frame. The proximity of a 'source reef' may be important to re-colonisation (Section 6.1).

Many juvenile fish and other organisms have a preference for their natal reef, and this may slow restoration unless re-introduction is used. Broken fragments of corals have been fixed onto artificial substrates to hasten regrowth. Restoration of reefs is likely to take decades to centuries, given the slow growth-rate of corals. A living 'model' coral reef in a tank at the Smithsonian Institution has helped in the understanding of reef dynamics and inter-linkages. The importance of understanding natural dynamics before attempting restoration is illustrated by the early efforts to restore reefs through managing crown-of-thorns outbreaks (Section 5.3.3).

## 8.4   Translocation of habitats

Habitat translocation takes introduction or re-introduction to extremes. Habitats are sometimes moved from one site to another, generally to permit lucrative development (Section 8.1), but sometimes to hasten restoration. The habitat is often moved in pieces, such as soil, turves of grass, or whole trees. Plants such as orchids may be moved individually. The site which receives the habitat is generally chosen because the habitat was once also found there, but there have been cases where it was not, and these are technically 'introductions' and unacceptable under IUCN guidelines (Section 8.1).

For habitat translocation to succeed, the conditions at the new location (the 'receptor site') need to be closely similar to the original 'donor site' in terms of climate, geology, hydrology and soil characteristics. Unless this is true, the new habitat is most unlikely to resemble the old one and will lose and gain species according to their tolerance of the new substrate and the new management conditions.

Grassland and heathland have been translocated at a number of sites in Britain. Initial results of such translocations suggest that some species may survive or benefit, whilst others such as ants, and species of spider which exploit ant nests, are not able to withstand the mechanical disturbance in translocation; recovery (if it occurs) may take well over a decade. Similarly, after 50 years of the prairie restoration project in Wisconsin, ants had spread very little from relict patches of natural prairie into the restored prairie. Translocation of heathland was attempted during a development which was about to destroy a colony of the silver-studded blue in Suffolk, England, despite their dependence on ant colonies. Heathland was skimmed into turves a few centimetres deep, but the butterflies did not establish in the new site.

A likely general problem of translocation is that the soil structure is altered, particularly through compaction and inversion, leading to reduced plant rooting depth and disturbance to macro-invertebrates and their nests.

In an apparently successful translocation, turves were taken from a floodplain meadow of the Morava River (an important site in Slovakia) and used to help restore a nearby meadow. The transplanted turves retained their flora, whilst the gaps in the donor site were rapidly filled. Translocation of recent grassland or other early-successional habitats seems less likely to fail than translocation of scrubland or woodland. The woodland soil is likely to be deeper, and in the case of natural sites less often disturbed, than a grassland. There have been few attempts to move woodlands, but, in the exceptional case of the Channel Tunnel between England and France, resources were available. Biggins Wood SSSI was moved by transporting topsoil and tree seedlings from the location where the British terminal was to be built to a nearby location; whilst this has been described by some as total destruction, it will take years to evaluate what, if anything, has been relocated successfully.

In an attempted translocation of ancient neutral grassland at Brock's Farm, Devon, England, turves 50 cm deep were moved very carefully following best practice; initial impressions were of success, but after five years the translocated flora showed increasingly rapid deterioration (divergence from control sites), illustrating the need for detailed long-term monitoring of habitat translocations, and the very high risk of failure.

## 8.5   Mitigation

Restoration of habitats is often attractive to developers, since they believe it may weaken the case for protection of a site if it can be shown that the features of interest can be translocated, re-created, created or restored somewhere else less inconvenient to the developer. This has encouraged a series of 'swaps', which are similar to 'planning-gain' in development. A deal is made between developers, conservationists and enforcement agencies in which some habitat is lost, in exchange for some mitigation measures elsewhere. D. W. Macdonald has suggested there are two main types of swap: 'like-for-like' (in which the same habitats are involved), or 'like-for-unlike' (in which a habitat of a different sort is protected as supposed compensation for a development).

Mitigation may be considered only within the site in question, or alternatively the net global impacts may be considered. In European environmental assessments, the term 'mitigation' is becoming increasingly restricted to *on-site* management which genuinely *does* reduce local impact, whilst 'compensation' includes other efforts. In other contexts, 'mitigation' may include any overall reduction of impact on the planet, habitat type or species.

Mitigation has been formalised in the USA through a mechanism called Habitat Conservation Plans (HCP). Developers benefit from the fact that the Endangered Species Act (Section 9.2.2) may permit a certain amount of 'take' of the habitat of a protected species – which was intended to prevent the Act blocking an excessively large number of developments. If exceptional circumstances exist, it may be deemed appropriate to protect a comparable region of habitat elsewhere. This is not always satisfactory, since the habitat may not be identical. Taking a precautionary approach – to allow for uncertainties in the ecology – it is therefore typical for the habitat to be protected to be several times the area that is to be destroyed. The ratio of mitigation area to area to be sacrificed is termed the 'mitigation ratio', and in wetlands of the USA these range from 1:1 If the existing site is degraded, to over 10:1 if mature wetland is to be lost. The Wetland Mitigation Banking system of the USA allows developers to trade in permits to destroy wetlands, provided there is 'no net loss' of habitat – which is rarely the case (Box 8.1).

In Britain, there have been similarly controversial 'translocations' of species or habitats, some involving 'Section 106 Agreements' under the Town and Country Planning Act. Such displacements, as I shall call them, may take several forms. Movement to a previously unoccupied site is an introduction and therefore usually unacceptable under IUCN guidelines (Section 8.1). The same may be true of translocation to newly created habitat. In translocation to restored habitat in the historical range (re-introduction) there is again uncertainty as to whether the new site will be suitable for the species (Section 8.1). In translocation to apparently suitable but empty existing habitat, the guidelines for introductions and re-introductions also apply: there may be important reasons why the species is not already there, other than limited powers of dispersal.

Some displacements move organisms to newly created habitat in the region, such as new ponds – blurring the distinction between introduction and re-introduction, particularly for species whose habitat shifted naturally and the term 'range' is more vague (Sections 5.1.1 and 6.1). For example, over 24 700 great crested newts were moved from one of the largest colonies in Europe, at Orton Brick Pits, England, before the site was largely destroyed; the success of the newts in the new habitat designed for them nearby remains uncertain.

Translocation off-site, and other risky 'compensation', is usually illegal for species listed under the Berne Convention (Section 9.2.2), such as great crested newts. Weakness in the British environmental laws, or their enforcement, often permits such development, and has led to several translocation attempts.

---

## Box 8.1
## Wetland Mitigation Banking

In the USA, a programme of wetland mitigation has been developed since 1980 which is often seen as a model. The Clean Water Act of 1972 has been interpreted to stipulate that a developer who wishes to damage a wetland must obtain a permit from The US Army Corps of Engineers. There should be 'no net loss' of wetland (which currently covers 42 million hectares). It has been assumed that an artificial wetland can replace a natural one. Mitigation ratios of up to 10:1 were established according to the quality of the site to be lost and the quality of sites to be used in mitigation. A Wetland Mitigation Bank was set up, enabling developers to buy credits in restoration. Some of the mitigation schemes have run into millions of dollars, and the expectation has been that damage will be compensated within 5–10 years.

However, studies by scientists such as S. C. Brown, and a report by the National Research Council (NRC) in 2001, have shown that replacement wetlands are poor substitutes for natural ones. A review has shown that, between 1993 and 2001, 17 000 ha had been created for 9500 ha lost, but the restored sites often are little more than ornamental ponds. Some mitigation projects are never begun or completed. The natural flooding regime (critical for marshland dynamics) is very seldom re-created, but instead dykes and overflows regulate the level. Base-line surveys of site quality are seldom performed, and changes in ecosystem processes are rarely documented. Exotic species and cattail may dominate the vegetation, and the vegetation structure may be unsuitable for nesting species such as the clapper rail. A study in San Diego by J. B. Zedler and J. C. Callaway suggested it might take 40 years for some ecosystem processes to reach natural levels in wetlands.

Inadequate monitoring of mitigation projects, and inadequate attention to habitat quality, have permitted loss of sites. The NRC now recommends that wetlands which are hard to re-create such as fens and bogs should not be developed, and the whole watershed should be considered to get maximum benefit. A study in Oxfordshire and Cambridgeshire, England, showed that public interest in wetlands has risen considerably, with a generally favourable attitude to their restoration. It is possible that wetland and other mitigation schemes do not meet the requirements of laws, public opinion or wildlife.

---

Translocation of individuals to ease development may be undesirable on both conservation and welfare grounds. If the receptor habitat is unsuitable, the individuals will die of starvation, predation or stress. Yet if the receptor habitat is suitable and occupied, it should be assumed to be already saturated with the species, and adding more individuals will probably cause death through density-dependent factors (Sections 1.4 and 7.2). For example, studies of translocated hedgehogs in Britain found that translocated animals suffered over 40% mortality in the first month, owing to increased competition and predation, whilst the recipient population suffered 20% mortality in that month, and the total population at the recipient site quickly declined to pre-translocation numbers. Perhaps the same fate happens to rattlesnakes in the United States when they are rounded up and moved to protect people, and to other 'nuisance' species, which are translocated into apparently suitable habitat as a matter of public convenience, conscience or safety. There is also a risk that translocated animals may carry disease or genetically pollute the recipient population. Scottish Natural Heritage (the government organisation responsible for conservation in Scotland) noted the undesirability of translocating hedgehogs when eradicating them on the Western Isles.

Although reviews show that most displacements are unsuccessful, their ecological consequences are largely unknown. Displacements to ease development are risky but may often appear the lesser of two evils, and may occur as a result of inadequate legal protection. I suggest that for legal purposes, particularly for protected species, such a 'translocation' should usually be treated as killing the individuals – with the burden of proof in a case being on developers to show it will not do so.

An example of swapping 'like-for-unlike' would be to swap an environmental 'bad', such as pollution, for an environmental 'good', such as habitat protection. For example, carbon offset forestry has been suggested (and heavily criticised) as a way of compensating for the damage done due to carbon dioxide release and the greenhouse effect. Relatively direct mitigation includes protection of existing forests which would otherwise have been burned, to compensate for the release from power stations or cars. This 'deforestation foregone' approach invites the abuse of polluters claiming that forests would have been burnt, even when they would not. Another way to compensate would be for polluters to pay towards protection of those sites that will be most affected by their actions – such as coastal sites, montane forests and reefs in the case of the greenhouse effect.

One way to mediate such swaps would be to use a panel of experts (in various subjects) to help assess the 'exchange rate' of goods and bads for various habitats, and to assign priorities for conservation (Chapter 3). Polluters and developers could pay into an 'environmental fund', in proportion to the damage they are doing, and that fund could then be used to pay for compensatory action (Section 9.1.2).

Whilst generally questionable, 'mitigation' in some cases leads to genuine conservation gains, particularly when developers can provide funds on a scale rarely available to conservation agencies and groups.

## 8.6   Urban wildlife

The wildlife of urban and suburban areas gives considerable pleasure to many people. With half of the world's population now living in cities, the interest in the urban environment is disproportionate to the amount of biodiversity which these highly artificial environments can support. Restoration and mitigation management may be required to make the best of the opportunities such areas present, or to minimise their impact.

Some urban wildlife sites are of national or even international importance. Rainham Marshes, beside the Thames in east London, are important for waterfowl, water voles, and raptors. They provide an important wildlife, wilderness and cultural resource for many people, and have been described in novels such as *David Copperfield*. With its accessible location, the site has been threatened with numerous developments. However, a major ecological restoration programme is now being advanced in Rainham Marshes, led by the Royal Society for the Protection of Birds, who have bought much of the land. Some sites become urban wildlife areas through the growth of cities: the Mai Po marshes of Hong Kong are internationally important, yet close to rapid urban expansion.

Urban environments are generally highly unnatural. However, they may support a high richness of species, many of them exotic, in a diversity of habitats such as gardens, parks, riversides and waste-ground. Many of the familiar species of gardens have popular appeal, even if, as with the grey squirrel in Britain, they are a threat to native species.

Conservation in urban areas may have two main themes: one is the protection of genuinely important species and habitats, and the other is maintenance and enhancement of wildlife for amenity. The two may overlap if the high-quality species (Section 3.1) are also attractive. An example is provided by peregrine falcons in cities such as New York. The artificial cliffs that tall buildings create are used by the falcon for nesting, and with a plentiful urban pigeon population for food this charismatic raptor has been able to expand its range. The Karori Reservoir Native Wildlife Sanctuary in Wellington City, New Zealand, is a regenerating hardwood forest fenced off against exotic predators; this site has high public support and is funded by a trust.

'Brownfield' sites are derelict areas that were once developed for housing, industry or other use. There is increasing pressure to build new houses on such land in Europe and America, in order to reduce 'urban sprawl' (meaning building on 'greenfield' agricultural or more natural sites). Whilst this is generally a good idea, some brownfield sites are surprisingly rich in wildlife. Derelict land in London supports black redstart – a bird typical of cliffs which is rare in Britain. If derelict sites have been unmanaged for several decades, they may support grassland, scrub, or even woodland communities. Whilst these areas are usually fairly small, and seldom have notable large animals, they may have rare species of invertebrate and plant. C. W. D. Gibson has demonstrated the importance of many brownfield sites in Britain for British Red Data Book species. Many of these species are rare in Britain because they need hot, dry habitats, and such thermophilous species find suitable structure and microclimate in derelict inner-city land. Although all of these species are more common in warmer continental Europe, the sites which support them should perhaps present similar interest to conservationists and the public as do the semi-natural habitats with warm microclimates (Section 7.3).

The Trap Grounds in Oxford, England, is a derelict urban site, including tipped and contaminated land. Yet it supports at least ten national 'Biodiversity Action Plan priority species' (Section 9.4.1) including water vole and turtle dove, and other regional priority species. This site, like many other urban sites, is under intense pressure for housing development. Urban wetlands, including the banks of rivers and canals, may support some nationally or locally notable species: for example, the London Wetland Centre supports water voles and bittern.

Because of the large numbers of local people, many of whom like to be involved in conservation, and their accessibility, urban sites present great opportunities for restoration and for environmental education. Urban wildlife groups often help to encourage species onto such sites. Such activity should be carefully controlled, particularly on more notable sites. However, there is often greater flexibility than on a more natural reserve to introduce or retain species to enhance appeal — for example by providing nectar for attractive butterflies, or fruit for birds. The special circumstances which excuse this should be made clear in educational and display material. Such sites may be seen as large wildlife gardens.

Whilst urban sites are rarely important in conserving globally threatened species, their importance in exposing people to biodiversity should not be overlooked. As urban and suburban environments sprawl outwards, these habitats may come to be the main − or only − places where many people encounter wildlife. It is futile to attempt to restore them to very high-quality habitats, but also a mistake to scorn them.

## 8.7  Measuring success and cost-effectiveness

Success of restoration, translocation and mitigation should be judged by criteria stated *at the beginning* of the project. The desired community of plants and animals or desired ecological processes should be identified. The character of the site to be translocated or developed should be recorded by a base-line survey of appropriate indicator groups (Section 4.3). Success should also be considered against control or 'reference' sites: ideally, several control sites should be left without the restoration management, in order to see how much of an improvement (in terms of completeness and speed) the management makes compared to natural re-colonisation. This will also help to find how cost-effective restoration is. Each element and alternative sequence of restoration could ideally be tested if sufficient replicate sites were available.

Typical prairie plants were used by J. T. Curtis to monitor restoration at Maddison, and ancient grassland plants indicated change in translocated habitat at Brocks Farm (Section 8.4). The distribution and architecture of the plants is as important as the diversity. For example, restored prairies may have many of the species of a natural prairie, but in clumps, rather than as small plants spread evenly in the grassland. This was also true in the restoration of watermeadows discussed above. Keystone species, such as ants and termites in grassland or woodpeckers in forests, might be used as indicators of success. Similarly, the presence and abundance of high-quality species (Chapter 3, and Fig. 8.2) could be compared in restored and natural control sites, and targets set for their populations. Ancient woodland indicators – both plant and invertebrate – should provide a sensitive guide to the success of woodland translocation.

The designation of a restored site in Britain as a Site of Special Scientific Interest (SSSI), as with the limestone grassland at Upper Seeds, indicates national recognition of some success in a restoration project.

To judge the success of a translocation of a species it is important to demonstrate the persistence of the new population of the species though many generations or decades. For success in translocation or re-creation of a habitat, community analysis techniques such as DCA and TWINSPAN (Section 4.2.1) can help determine if the new habitat fits and persists within the variation of the old or natural habitat in the region. Long-term monitoring of the success of displacement ('translocation') has been a major failing: the fate of many populations is not known, even for protected species (such as displaced great crested newts or badgers in Britain, or gopher tortoises in the USA). Radio-tracking has been used to monitor translocated animals.

Control sites may help to separate natural trends (due to climate or other changes) from trends due to inadequate management. Success should be measured by real data, rather than predictions based on presumed 'trajectories' in the community. Experience in wetland construction and mitigation in

San Diego Bay suggests that trajectories are unreliable in naturally dynamic systems.

Successful restoration of water quality may be claimed when the output water quality is of the original natural quality. This may be problematic unless good records are available of the pre-disturbance state of the system (as they are with the Hubbard Brook project in America).

A database should be developed of global and national efforts at restoration management, which would allow analysis and comparison of sites and methods. This could provide results which may not be available from single projects (such as the minimum viable size or scale of restoration for a habitat or species), and would help identify other features which lead to success.

Restoration projects are often expensive. The proposed restoration of the Little Pedder lake in Tasmania was encouraged as 'symbolic' by IUCN, but in 1995 it was estimated this could cost up to 2.5 billion Australian dollars. The Florida Everglades restoration budget is 8 million US dollars. Such costs have to be considered against alternatives, such as preservation of existing habitats – no matter how attractive the restoration might appear. The maximum potential quality of the restored habitat should be evaluated (as in Chapter 3) against other conservation priorities. However, the lessons learned from the restoration and monitoring may have higher value than the restored habitat itself. Furthermore, the appeal and positive feel of restoration means that funding may be available through developers and corporate sponsors that would not be available for other purposes.

# 9

# Environmental economics, law and education

In this chapter we will examine briefly some of the economic issues in conservation. We will also consider the legal framework of conservation, and broader conservation policy. Since these topics change fast, and there are many differences between countries, specialist texts should be consulted for the latest situation. Conservation policy needs to be developed in the light of public opinion, which can indicate the social benefits of the policy. The results of some relevant opinion surveys are given in Table 9.1 and Fig. 9.1; these might overestimate the strength of opinion since it costs the respondent nothing to profess interest in conservation, but nevertheless the level of consistency across countries is interesting.

## 9.1 Economics

There are many circumstances when it is helpful to put a financial value on wildlife – for example to compare the costs and benefits of development and conservation options. Some people feel that valuation is an impossible task, because of the uncertainties in the numbers of species or their uses and because some values are hard to compare in the same units (they are economic 'incommensurables'). Others (especially economists) feel this is a problem that economics can cope with. Some believe the very attempt to give wildlife an economic value is immoral, and that we should consider the intrinsic right of species to exist (Chapter 1). As the ethical arguments demonstrate, economics should be only one consideration amongst many in defining policy.

Table 9.1 *Selected examples of surveys testing public interest in conservation*

| (a) General Country | Group | Opinion/reasons for conservation |
|---|---|---|
| **Surveys in 1970s** | | |
| Africa | General public | 75% want more done to conserve wildlife/species |
| Western Europe | General public | 89% as above |
| India | General public | 46% as above |
| USA | General public | 87% as above |
| Japan | General public | 85% as above |
| Latin America | General public | 94% as above |
| **Surveys in 1980s** | | |
| Tanzania | School children | 53% utilitarian 37% ethical |
| Rwanda | Farmers near parks | 49% did not think park should be converted to agriculture |
| Brazil | Landowners | 74% would protect wildlife on their property |
| USA | General public | 42% of people liked wolves |
| **Surveys in 1990s** | | |
| Norway | General public | 76% say pristine nature must be saved even if not useful |
| Norway | General public | 83% agreed all ecosystems have a right to exist |
| Sweden | General public | 78% consider intrinsic value important |
| Netherlands | General public | 92% agree the intrinsic value of nature is important |
| USA | Students | 80% agree intrinsic value of nature is important |
| USA | General public | ≫50% agree intrinsic value of nature is important |
| USA | General public | 87% say maintaining biodiversity is important to them |
| USA | General public | 71% want to leave the Earth in good shape for future generations |
| Britain | General pubic | 82% are concerned about loss of plants and animals |
| Senegal, Ireland, USA | Students | 61% of favourite places are part of natural environment |
| Global (60 countries) | Adult population | 2/3 say their government has done too little to protect the environment |

*(cont.)*

Table 9.1 (*cont.*)

| (b) Netherlands (1990s) | | | |
|---|---|---|---|
| 'What are the reasons why nature is important?' | | 'The value of nature is found in . . . ' | |
| Health | 65% | Intrinsic value | 59% |
| Future generations | 40% | Future generations | 39% |
| Intrinsic value | 38% | Usefulness for humans | 35% |
| Beauty | 32% | Responsibility for evolution | 24% |
| Enjoying plants and animals | 30% | It being God's creation | 14% |
| Memory of the origin of life | 30% | Nothing | 2% |
| Relaxation | 28% | | |
| Agriculture | 14% | | |
| Science | 7% | | |
| Recreation | 5% | | |
| Nature study | 1% | | |

*Sources:* Section (a) various. Section (b): Van Den Born, R. J. G, Lenders, R. H. J, de Groot, W. T. & Huijsman, E. The new biophilia: an exploration of visions of nature in Western countries. *Environmental Conservation* **28** (2001), 65–75.

The value of natural resources to the economy is frequently overlooked, yet as the economist Partha Dasgupta says: 'Whether it is consumption or production, or whether it is exchange, the commodities and services that are involved can be traced to constituents provided by Nature.'

## 9.1.1  Valuing wildlife

Wildlife (biodiversity) can be valued in several different ways, which were illustrated in Fig. 1.1. A major distinction is between 'use values' and 'non-use values' (including intrinsic values, Section 1.3). Use values are those which derive from exploiting a species, habitat or ecosystem in some way, whilst non-use values are ethical. The meanings of these values are given in Table 9.2; different authors may use some of these terms in slightly different ways.

How can we quantify the use value? In the 1970s, D. R. Helliwell examined individual species such as oak trees and combined values based on abundance, consciousness and material value into an index or 'shadow price'.

(a)

(b)

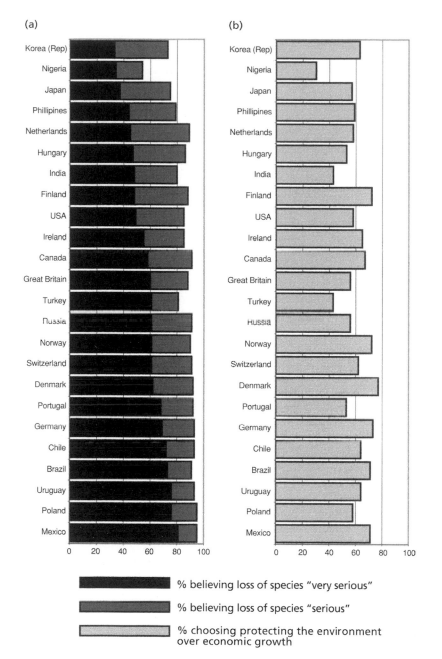

% believing loss of species "very serious"

% believing loss of species "serious"

% choosing protecting the environment over economic growth

**Fig. 9.1.** Public attitudes to the environment in 24 countries, in 1992.
(a) Percentage of people who believe the loss of species is 'very serious' or 'serious'.
(b) Percentage who choose protecting the environment over economic growth.
*Source:* Dunlap, R. E. *et al. The Health of the Planet Survey* (The George H. Gallup International Institute, Princeton, 1993).

Table 9.2 *Examples of values of wildlife, with some estimates*

| Type of value | Example | Estimate (and date) billion $US per year | Typical valuation methods |
|---|---|---|---|
| **Use values** | | | |
| Direct | Foods | 1386 (1997) | Direct |
| | Traditional medicines | 20–40 (2001) | Direct |
| | Pharmaceuticals | 75–150 (2001) | Direct |
| | Raw materials including fuelwood | 721 (1997) | Direct |
| Indirect | Prevention of erosion | 576 (1997) | Experimental; Hedonic prices |
| | Nutrient cycle/decomposition | 17 075 (1997) | Experimental; Hedonic prices |
| | Rainfall generation | ? | Hedonic prices |
| | Cloud formation | ? | Hedonic prices |
| | Atmospheric gas composition | 1341 (1997) | Experimental; Hedonic prices |
| | Green sponge and flood reduction | 2807 (1997) | Experimental; Hedonic prices; flood damage |
| | Pollination | 117 (1997) | Experimental or Direct (specific crops) |
| | Ecotourism and recreation | 815 (1997) | Direct; Experimental |
| | Biological control | 417 (1997) | Experimental; Hedonic prices |
| | Aesthetic, spiritual, scientific, etc. | 3015 (1997) | Experimental; Hedonic prices |
| Option | Future direct and indirect use values | | Opportunity cost |
| Non-use | Intrinsic/existence value | | Willingness to pay |

*Notes:*
Methods for measuring non-market values:
   Direct: e.g. Travel Cost Method; market prices.
   Experimental: elicit preferences by constructing a market or hypothetical settings (contingent valuation, such as Willingness to Pay).
   Hedonic: valuation by comparison, e.g. with other commodities or through house prices.
Existence value is the value of knowing something exists.
Opportunity cost is the value of all alternative uses which are forsaken.
*Source:* 1997 valuations from Costanza, R. *et al. Nature* **387** (1997), 253–260 using largely Experimental methods.

More recently, D. Pearce, D. Helm, P. S. Dasgupta and others have clarified the methods of environmental economics.

Market research and other social science surveys may be helpful to find the uses to which a species is put, including the market price of products it provides. For example, pet hyacinth macaws may be selling for over $10 000 each. Tiger bone may fetch a known price per gram, and ebony a known price per cubic metre. Game hunters may be prepared to pay $15 000 to shoot a lion. The value of species may be highly speculative: a species which has a potential for development of a medicine may attract attention just as a new mineral deposit might. Over half of the top 150 prescription drugs in the USA are linked to discoveries in wild organisms, with an annual value in the USA of about $80 billion. Globally, the value of pharmaceuticals derived from genetic resources was estimated at up to $150 billion per year in 1997, and the value of crop improvements from wild genotypes at over $1 billion per year. The San Bushmen are to receive royalty payments for anti-obesity drugs in development from *Hoodia* succulents used in traditional medicine as appetite-suppressors, and Samoa will get revenue from Prostatin, a drug derived from a plant which their healers used against yellow fever virus (Table 1.3).

However, for the vast majority of species there is no known use at present – and there probably will never be one. Such species may contribute to the use value of ecosystems, but the inter-linkage between most species and their influence on ecosystem processes and stability cannot be disentangled (Section 1.4), so the contribution of each species to the value of the system may never be measurable. Some 'ecosystem services' are listed in Section 1.3 and Table 9.2. Conventional economics often does not include these services – taking them as free. One first attempt to estimate their global use value was made by R. Costanza and colleagues (Table 9.3): in 1997 they calculated the total of ecosystem services and resources as over $33 trillion dollars ($33 \times 10^{12}$), which is double the global Gross Domestic Product.

Conventional economics have failed the environment by passing on the costs of destructive activities to other places and future generations. Such 'externalities' include the global costs of pollution. One ethical way to internalise these costs is the principle that 'the polluter pays'. For example, the costs of an oil spill, including restoring the wildlife, should fall on the polluter. On a larger scale, the costs of greenhouse gases should fall on the users, transferring the value of local and global damage into the price of fuel.

One method of valuing wildlife is to ask people in social surveys how much they are prepared to sacrifice to save a species, or habitat, or to pay for the knowledge that a species exists. Such estimation by 'willingness to pay' often

Table 9.3 *Initial estimates of minimum values of some ecosystem services and genetic resources (1994 prices, US$)*

| Service or resource | Value (US$) |
| --- | --- |
| Gas regulation | 1 341 000 000 |
| Climate regulation | 684 000 000 |
| Disturbance regulation | 1 779 000 000 |
| Water regulation | 1 115 000 000 |
| Water supply | 1 692 000 000 |
| Erosion control | 576 000 000 |
| Soil formation | 53 000 000 |
| Nutrient cycling | 17 075 000 000 |
| Waste treatment | 2 277 000 000 |
| Pollination | 117 000 000 |
| Biological control | 417 000 000 |
| Habitat/refugia (e.g. fish nurseries) | 124 000 000 |
| Food production (e.g. fish, game, crops, fruit) | 1 386 000 000 |
| Raw materials (e.g. timber, fuel, fodder) | 721 000 000 |
| Genetic resources (e.g. medicines, horticulture) | 79 000 000 |
| Recreation | 815 000 000 |
| Cultural (e.g. spiritual, aesthetic, educational) | 3 015 000 000 |
| Total | 33 268 000 000 |
| Range (depending on assumptions): | 16 000 000 000 to over 54 000 000 000 |

*Source:* Costanza, R. *et al.* The value of the world's ecosystem services and natural capital. *Nature* **387** (1997), 253–260.

overvalues the resource because it costs nothing at the time the question is asked. However, looking at how far somebody has actually travelled ('travel cost' methodology) to see a wildlife spectacle can be helpful; for example, each year people spend a total of over a billion dollars on tourism to see whales.

Three problems are commonly encountered in economic evaluations of wildlife (and in economics in general). Substitution of the product may occur, which means that a cheaper alternative is discovered which competes with the wildlife resource and reduces its value. For example, the value of whale oil crashed when petroleum oils were introduced. Price collapse may also occur if supply increases relative to demand. For example, in 1989, C. M. Peters and colleagues valued non-timber forest products in a Peruvian rainforest as over $6000 per hectare, six times the value from logging, yet if many people elsewhere started to gather and sell these fruits, nuts, gums and other products their value might drop – as has happened with farmed butterflies. Inflation also reduces how much wildlife a given amount of money will buy you in the future.

Such problems contribute to the value of goods being less clear, and lower, the further into the future one looks. Economic 'discounting' formalises this reduction. Discounting rates of 5% to over 20% may be used by governments and investors. Species which grow and breed slowly accumulate value slowly, and C. W. Clark pointed out in 1973 that if the rate of growth in the resource is less than the discount rate, it makes economic sense for private investors to harvest all the stock immediately ('liquidate' it) – and invest the profit. It makes good economic sense to harvest whales and ebony to extinction, considering only the values of flesh and wood. Unpredictability of future resources compared with clear present needs is a widespread pressure for short-term exploitation, rather than management for long-term rewards.

A further problem of economic evaluation is that if money is allowed to be paramount when proposing a conservation project, then it is hypocritical to continue to defend the project if it becomes uneconomical. For example, it might become more economical to chop down a forest and substitute its ecosystem services value (as a green-sponge or in soil-binding) with a plantation or grassland with similar effect. Economic arguments are probably more perishable than ethical arguments.

An unusual feature of human resource use, compared with other species, is that as resources get rarer we may value them more highly – even if they are non-essential. This status accorded to rare objects is probably a reflection of the 'handicap theory' (the ability to bear a cost is an honest signal of mate quality) and helps drive species to extinction – as with macaws. It also makes conservation more expensive and difficult.

## 9.1.2 The costs of conservation

In 1970, Peter Scott wrote: 'And it is going to cost a lot to defend the biosphere, to defend our spaceship earth – probably as much as it costs us to defend our frontiers and our national sovereignties. In the end, of course, the money will have to come from governments and international aid programmes . . .'. His words are valid today. Despite popular belief, limits to the productivity of populations mean wildlife can seldom 'pay its way'.

Conservation *in situ* commonly involves costs of land purchase or rent. Management (such as fencing, patrolling, control of exotic species, or grazing) and research (for evaluation and monitoring) may involve costs of

Table 9.4 *Estimated annual budget for conservation (1996 prices, US$)*

| Operation | Cost per year (to nearest billion) |
|---|---|
| Management of existing reserves – present expenditure | 6 billion |
| Management of existing reserves – extra required | 2 billion |
| Compensation of opportunity costs of local people | 5 billion |
| Acquisition of new reserves (includes survey and purchase) | 11 billion |
| Management of new reserves (includes administration) | 3 billion |
| Total required for terrestrial protected areas | 28 billion |
| Total required for conservation in matrix and seas | 290 billion |
| Total *cost* of comprehensive global conservation | 300 billion |
| Total *available* from abolishing perverse subsidies | 950–1450 billion |
| Total *value* of ecosystem services | 3000 billion |

*Source:* Derived from James, A. N., Gaston, K. J. and Balmford, A. Balancing the Earth's accounts. *Nature* **401** (1999), 323–324.

employment, equipment and materials. Total costs for conserving terrestrial protected areas have been estimated at about $28 billion per year, and for conservation of the matrix at about $290 billion per year (Table 9.4). In 2002, A. Balmford and colleagues estimated the annual cost of an effective marine protected areas network would be about $23 billion plus $6 billion in start-up costs.

Compensation payments are frequently required for local people and other stakeholders, who are prevented from exploiting land or species, and this may become much truer in the future as population and land prices rise. Conservation entails 'opportunity costs', which include the values of resources such as farmland, timber or meat that have to be forsaken. Examples of compensation schemes are given in Table 9.5. Compensation payments may not be socially acceptable, often being seen as paternalistic. They may also be abused. Land owners may claim they are going to drain land for farming, and demand payment if they are prevented because it is to be a reserve. Farmers may claim a sheep was killed by a wolf or lynx, rather than a dog. Trust, and policing, will be required to prevent such exploitation of legal loopholes. Conservation may entail many other costs: biodiversity may be dangerous to people and crops – as with elephants and tigers. Species and ecosystems may harbour diseases such as malaria, HIV and ebola.

Direct payment for conservation is likely to become more frequent in the future, under various names including conservation concessions, investment,

Table 9.5 *Examples of compensation costs in conservation*

| Nature of loss | Conservation value | Region | Nature of compensation |
|---|---|---|---|
| Livestock killed | Wolves, lynx | Europe | Reimbursement |
| Livestock killed | Tiger | India; China | Reimbursement |
| Livestock forage | Wild ass | Ladakh (India) | Reimbursement |
| Livestock killed | Large predators | Ladakh; Mongolia | Reimbursement |
| Fuelwood | Forest wildlife | Lake Malawi | Plantation forestry |
| Crop damage; risk | Elephant | Indonesia; China | Reimbursement |
| Grazing land | Savannah ecosystem | Tanzania | Outreach programme |
| Fishing losses; risk | Alligator | China | Reimbursement |
| Fishing losses | Stock protection | USA | Reimbursement |
| Bushmeat hunting | Game species | Botswana | Retraining |
| Land use | Wildlife on SSSIs | Britain | Reimbursement |
| Reindeer killed | Wolverine dens | Sweden | Payment per den |
| Agricultural | Farmland diversity in ESA* | Britain | Subsidies |
| Hunting / products | Wildlife | New Zealand | Land purchase/ swaps |

*Note:* * ESA = Environmentally Sensitive Area

and stewardship schemes. Examples include the 'Payments for Environmental Services Program' in Costa Rica, paying a lease to local people in Kenya for wildlife corridors, and paying farmers to promote desirable landscapes and species in the North York Moors, England. The advantages of such performance-related payments over payments to community-based schemes (see Section 9.4.3) have been reviewed by P. J. Ferraro and A. Kiss, and include simplicity and cost-effectiveness.

## 9.1.3 Funding for conservation

Where will the money come from for conservation? Ethically, surely protection of the global heritage must be shared by all governments and every person? Biodiversity has been described by some economists as a 'public good'.

International funding for conservation includes the Global Environmental Facility (GEF). This fund was set up during the Earth Summit in Rio in 1992, and is run by the World Bank. At Rio, governments recognised the need to conserve biodiversity – and that the bulk of known biodiversity is in poor developing countries. The richer countries can subsidise conservation elsewhere by paying into the GEF, which is a multi-billion dollar fund to protect the environment and promote sustainable development. Unfortunately, many governments have been slow to exploit this resource, which could, for example, compensate farmers for not expanding into wildlife habitat, subsidise improved farming methods, and pay for stewardship of resources. Other international support can come from development aid and from intergovernmental organisations, such as UNESCO's World Heritage Fund, which supports preparation, training, education, equipment, and emergency assistance for the World Heritage Sites.

Governments fund their official conservation agencies from general tax income. They may also raise special funds through environmental taxes, as on leaded fuel, plastic bags, water or tourism. The British government runs the Darwin Initiative for the Survival of Species, funding conservation work around the world. National research councils and institutions fund selected conservation science. National lotteries have provided millions of pounds.

Norman Myers pointed out in 1998 that many government subsidies to lobby groups are doubly foolish in that they use taxpayers' money for an uneconomic product which then damages the environment *and* the economy. Such 'perverse subsidies' have supported the German coal industry, European agriculture and fishing, and deforestation in the USA and Ivory Coast. A global total of about 1.5 trillion dollars per year in perverse subsidies is 2.5 times the amount that governments at Rio in 1992 estimated was required for sustainable development – and then claimed was unavailable. The total cost required for protected areas on land and sea is only about 2–5% of the total spent on perverse subsidies, and the total required for comprehensive conservation (including the matrix) is only 20%.

Similarly, A. Balmford and colleagues have calculated that conversion (destruction) of natural areas is highly uneconomic because of lost ecosystem services, and a protected areas network would thus easily pay for itself if all values were included: not converting wild areas would save some $250 billion per year.

'Debt-for-Nature' schemes involve organisations or governments entering into agreement with a country to pay off some of the national debt in exchange for conservation. In 1987, Conservation International cancelled $650 000 of debt in Bolivia to support the Beni Biosphere Reserve; habitats in Poland and the Philippines have been protected in this way. The Tropical Forest Conservation Act of 1998 enables the USA to forgive debt it is owed, in exchange for conservation. More controversially, forests may protected as carbon stores to gain carbon credits to sell under the Kyoto Protocol: such 'deforestation foregone' and other 'carbon offset forestry' such as re-forestation might raise billions of dollars (although it can offset only a few percent of global carbon emissions).

Non-governmental organisations (NGOs) such as the World Wide Fund for Nature (WWF), BirdLife International, and Conservation International raise money from members and donors, or advise others on the direction of funds to selected projects. The WWF has spent over half a billion dollars since 1961, and Conservation International will govern the direction of hundreds of millions of dollars towards the Myers biodiversity hotspots. Various organisations support conservation expeditions, including the Royal Geographical Society in Britain, and the National Geographic Society in the USA.

Well-managed ecotourism is a growth industry, and provides a major source of income for countries such as Kenya, the Seychelles, Ecuador and Costa Rica. Although unpredictable, this source of income may be more secure than agriculture – where prices of crops can crash rapidly and permanently. It is important to reduce the 'leakage' of benefits out of the local economy and country. Unfortunately, many reserves receive very few tourists. 'Green-hunting' (using tranquilliser darts), may replace some safari hunting as a way to combine trophy hunting and research, as with tag-and-release big-game fishing.

Groups of shareholders have been formed to conserve some areas – as with some Australian mainland islands and with private purchases of areas of Amazonia or the Scottish Flow Country to block destructive agriculture or forestry. Interested individuals may contribute to specific causes, such as condors or Florida panthers. There are many dedicated charities and trust funds. For example, the Diane Fossey Gorilla Fund helps with 'outreach programs' which provide training, employment and micro-capital support to communities around national parks in Rwanda and elsewhere. Sponsorship schemes include adoption of animals in zoos or the wild; for example, Minesota Zoo sponsored Ujung Kulon National Park in Indonesia – buying equipment such as boats and radios. Private funds have protected Aride Island in Seychelles, and private reserves are spreading widely.

Business is increasingly involved in conservation and biodiversity. Motivations include concerned managers, improved public relations, shareholder satisfaction, networking and savings ('win-win' scenarios). Some businesses see biodiversity conservation as a good investment, as with some pharmaceutical companies in Costa Rica. Some consumers will pay premium prices for products they see as environmentally sound. Unfortunately, some businesses boast of their environmental sensitivity whilst in reality being extremely destructive, and the environmental record of any company should be closely scrutinised. I suggest an 'Environmental Pool' of money should be created, into which businesses make contributions. Businesses could be rewarded with a 'Green Star' rating for their products and the proportion of their profit they contribute to the Pool, which would help consumers identify the most genuinely conscientious businesses. The Pool could help priority conservation products selected by experts and the public.

Reduced affluence could help substantially; for example, the annual pocket money of children under 17 in Western Europe and the USA is some $60 billion – double what is needed to fund terrestrial protected areas. Moreover, global defence spending is 16 times the roughly $50 billion per year required for an effective global protected areas network.

## 9.2 Law

### 9.2.1 International laws

International laws may be binding, in which case they are incorporated into national laws. Alternatively, they may effectively be commitments, in which case there are no supporting laws; however, 'non-compliance' with the Treaty or Protocol brings assistance to help the country in breach of the law to meet its commitments – and eventually shame or rebuff from the international community. Most international environmental laws ('legal instruments') are not enforceable by penalties such as fines or sanctions. They generally commit states to 'due diligence' rather than liability, and to reduce impacts rather than prevent problems. Some of the 1000 or so international laws relevant to conservation are listed in Table 9.6.

One of the most far-reaching conservation laws is the Convention on Biological Diversity (CBD). Formulated at the Earth Summit in 1992, it has three main objectives: the conservation of biological diversity, the sustainable use of its components, and the fair and equitable sharing of benefits arising out of the utilisation of genetic resources. The contracting parties (states) are 'Conscious of the intrinsic value of biological diversity and of the ecological, genetic, social, economic, scientific, educational, cultural recreational and aesthetic values of biological diversity and its components'. They 'Affirm that the conservation of biological diversity is a common concern of humankind', and are 'Determined to conserve and sustainably use biological diversity for the

Table 9.6 *Examples of conservation laws and agreements (abbreviated names)*

| Law or Agreement | Aim or target of conservation |
| --- | --- |
| (a) International | |
| Stockholm Declaration: Principle 21 | Reduction of transboundary impacts |
| Convention on Biological Diversity (CBD) | Biodiversity; intellectual property rights |
| World Heritage Convention | Globally outstanding sites |
| Ramsar Convention | Important wetlands and reefs |
| UN Convention on the Law of the Sea | Reduced pollution and impact |
| Convention on Migratory Species (Bonn Convention) | Migratory species |
| UN moratorium on large driftnets | Discourages use of driftnets on high seas |
| MARPOL | Ocean pollution |
| Rio Forest Principles | Forests |
| Kyoto Protocol | Atmospheric composition |
| Montreal Protocol | Ozone layer |
| IWC Moratorium on commercial whaling | Most whales; creates whale sanctuaries |
| Agreement on the Conservation of Albatrosses and Petrels (ACAP) | Protection of albatrosses and petrels from fishing |
| (b) Regional or national | |
| Antarctic Treaty | Wildlife; prevention of pollution |
| Convention on Antarctic Marine Living Resources | Wildlife preservation |
| Convention for the Conservation of Southern Bluefin Tuna | Sustainable fishery |
| Habitats Directive (EU) | Selected habitats |
| Wild Birds Directive (EU) | All wild birds in Europe |
| Berne Convention (Europe) | Selected species and their habitats |
| Wildlife & Countryside Act (UK) | Selected species and habitats |
| Endangered Species Act (USA) | Selected species and their habitats |
| Great Ape Conservation Act (USA) | Support for great ape conservation overseas |
| National Ballast Water Management Regime (Australia) and equivalents in USA, New Zealand, Chile, Israel, etc. | Reduced import of exotic marine species |
| Great Barrier Reef Marine Park Act (Australia) | Great Barrier Reef |

(cont.)

Table 9.6 (*cont.*)

| Law or Agreement | Aim or target of conservation |
|---|---|
| Law for the Conservation of Endangered Species of Wild Flora and Fauna (Japan) | Japanese wildlife; CITES listed species |
| Federal Law on Specially Protected Natural Ranges (Russian Federation) | Habitats and natural complexes |
| Conservation of Living Resources and their Ecosystems Act (Indonesia) | General; education as part of management |
| Patent laws | Intellectual property rights |
| Water quality laws | Drinking water, wildlife |

benefit of present and future generations'. States have sovereign rights over their biological diversity. They note that 'the fundamental requirement for the conservation of biological diversity is the *in situ* conservation of ecosystems and natural habitats and the maintenance and recovery of viable populations of species in their natural surroundings'. They will take an holistic, ecosystem-orientated approach, using scientific adaptive management. These are very powerful words, and if implemented really could change the prospects of conservation. Unfortunately, not all nations have ratified or enforced the Convention.

The Convention on International Trade in Endangered Species (CITES) is another powerful tool in conservation. Over 150 countries have signed this agreement. It lists species in three Appendices. Species in Appendix I cannot be traded (intact or in products from body parts). Species in Appendix II are traded with an export license, to allow control and monitoring of the trade. The Appendices are based on assessment of threat, but there may be heated debate – for example over whether elephants (i.e. ivory) should be in Appendix 1 or 2. CITES may prevent trade in products from endangered species raised in captivity – as with hawksbill turtle. Enforcement occurs at customs posts in the exporting and importing countries. Customs officers cannot be expected to be expert taxonomists, so whole groups of organisms, such as the cactus family, may be listed. Scientists must obtain permits to move specimens from listed species between countries. Over one million items of threatened wildlife were seized in Britain in the five years to 2002 – but much more slips undiscovered between countries. Wildlife products comprise the third biggest illegal trade in the world.

## 9.2.2   National and regional laws

National laws are vital in conservation, and enforcement is theoretically easier than for many international laws. Fines, prison sentences and other punishment acceptable to society is adjusted to suit the infringement. Despite this, there are frequent failures, owing to loopholes or failures of will in litigation or enforcement. Customs and quarantine help reduce imports of potential invasive species. Anti-pollution laws protect water and air quality. Legislation helps set up and protect the national protected areas networks, including National Parks, National Nature Reserves, and SSSIs. Examples of national and regional laws are given in Table 9.6.

Laws may have a bias to species or habitats. In the USA, two key conservation laws are the Endangered Species Act, and the National Forest Management Act. Both of these are species orientated, requiring populations of listed species to be maintained (including protection of their habitat, Section 8.5), and the ESA requires species to be recovered to non-threatened status. The Endangered Species Act also prevents the import of material from non-native listed species, such as beluga sturgeon caviar. In the USA, organisations such as Riverkeeper or the Natural Resources Defense Council take both developers and government to court if environmental laws are broken. In Britain, laws protect selected species, such as badgers, or groups of species such as birds, bats or reptiles. Selected species are also listed in appendices of the main conservation law, the Wildlife and Countryside Act.

Within nations, local plans and laws (such as bye-laws) may prohibit access, or activities such as driving vehicles, lighting fires, or dog walking. Local quota systems for harvest duration and quantities may be established – as with licensing to limit mushroom gathering in Epping Forest, England.

## 9.3   Education

Education is seen as an essential part of most conservation activities. It is important to explain to the general and local public – and politicians – why we need conservation, or why a particular management is needed. Education is often seen as a bright hope for conservation, since it has had some great successes. However, there is a limit to what education can do in the face of dogmatic cultural beliefs. Furthermore, it can take many years for education of young people to work through to changed attitudes in voters and workers, or improved funding, and in some cases this may happen too late to help.

Adult education is very important, despite the entrenched views adults may hold. There are numerous examples of poacher turned gamekeeper. Education may be far cheaper than enforcement.

Television and radio are massively important in conservation. They may raise consumption levels and expectations and damage local cultural values. Conversely, wildlife documentaries are very popular around the world. As with newspapers and the World Wide Web, it is difficult to assess the accuracy of reporting, or if it is coloured by political or environmental ideology, which might be counter-productive. The variety of scientific opinions needs to be considered, and the uncertainties stated. Consensus opinion and peer-reviewed publications should count for more than individual opinion – as the USA Administration's failure in 2001 to acknowledge climate change illustrates. Conversely, individual scientists should be taken more seriously by the scientific community – as James Lovelock has shown with the Gaia hypothesis.

Around the world, people have increasingly little direct experience of 'nature'. Field trips are fundamental to environmental education. Interpretation centres at nature reserves help explain the aims of the reserve, what visitors may see on a site, and the reasons for management. T-shirts and window stickers help to make people feel involved in a team effort. Posters and plays are helpful when literacy rates are low. A drama group has successfully raised environmental awareness around Hwange National Park, Zimbabwe. Celebrities can give powerful endorsement to projects.

Consumption patterns may be modified by education, as with the growing preferences for goods approved by 'environmental certification' schemes: for example the Forest Stewardship Council and the Marine Stewardship Council label products such as teak or Alaskan salmon as coming from apparently sustainably managed sources. Consumption of less damaging goods can be encouraged by linking them to status. Advertising which encourages *less* consumption, or responsible consumption, is needed to counter the barrage of enticement to consume. Advertisement of highly environmentally detrimental products might need to be banned, as with bans on advertising tobacco. Posters in schools can provide increased awareness of the conservation benefits of reef protection, low food-miles or less meat consumption. The advertising campaign suggesting people wearing furs were 'dumb animals' helped make furs less socially acceptable in the West. 'Ecological footprinting' can help demonstrate individual or corporate consumption (although the footprints are underestimates based mainly on energy use rather than extinction).

Unpopular groups such as sharks, crocodilians, snakes, fungi or 'creepy-crawlies' may need a public relations campaign – terms like 'shark-infested waters' are damaging. L. G. Frank found some white farmers in Kenya wanted fewer hyenas but more large cats: although cats do more economic damage to wildlife, hyenas have a lower perceived moral value.

Religion can be very influential in changing opinion, and many faiths have made statements on their environmental policy, particularly in relation to stewardship or the inter-linkage of nature. Appeal to Islamic teaching against wastage reduced dynamite fishing in Tanzania. Personal opinion may be firmly against some conservation activities, such as culling elephants or the invasive ruddy duck. However, it is possible to explain the welfare and conservation benefits of feral species control, as the conservation-minded public of New Zealand demonstrate.

Zoos, parks and botanic gardens can be a great force for education and are the main contact most people will be able to have with spectacular species. They may have large education divisions, as with Missouri Botanical Garden. In some zoos or gardens, selected species can be touched by visitors – adding to the intensity of the experience. Conservation work at Calgary Zoo is an examined part of the Alberta school curriculum. London Zoo has done much to promote invertebrate conservation. Over 90% of mammals and 70% of birds in North American zoos are captive bred. National pride has been fostered by exhibits of the breeding programmes for the Puerto Rican crested toad, the Aruba Island rattlesnake, or the giant panda. Species on stamps, money and the like can further increase public awareness and pride.

Training of professional conservationists includes training in zoos such as Jersey and Calgary, and may accompany technology transfer. The inclusion of an education component is a condition of some project grants. Diplomas, masters and doctoral degrees are proving increasingly useful to gain employment in conservation, as the level of skill required increases and as competition for jobs amongst motivated young people soars. More scholarships and exchange arrangements are required to train people from developing countries. Training in identification skills is fundamental for field conservationists.

It seems that education can work – although proof requires long-term studies and separation of confounding variables such as wealth. In a survey of attitudes to conservation in Tanzania, H. Pennington found that 44% of people with low scores for knowledge thought national parks should be used for agriculture, compared with only 24% of those with high education scores. In the USA, wolves are more popular amongst more highly educated people.

Awareness of the purpose and boundary of the Masaola National Park in Madagascar was inversely correlated with exploitation of the park.

More generally, literacy in women needs much more support, and has been shown to reduce population growth.


## 9.4   Politics and policy

There are a number of recurrent themes in conservation politics and policy. Enforcement of legislation may be weak – leading to so called 'paper parks' which are not really protected. Corruption may permit illegal exploitation or development, and sap scarce funds from conservation projects. Jobs and development may be seen as in conflict with wildlife – as with 'loggers versus the spotted owl' in the USA, or 'fishermen versus quotas' in Europe. Since the Endangered Species Act in the USA is very powerful, there is considerable pressure from developers against listing some species.

Sometimes the desire of conservationists in one country to influence policy in another is seen as 'conservation imperialism' or an assault on sovereignty. It may be impossible to dispel this impression, since an anti-colonial perspective has widespread appeal. Some counties fear 'internationalisation' of natural resources. However, everybody should have an interest in all parts of the world – nature is highly inter-linked. We all depend on shared resources such as the atmosphere and water, and other ecological services that are provided by biodiversity which has no relationship to national boundaries. The importance of the global heritage is recognised by the many sovereign nations that are party to the World Heritage Convention (Fig. 3.12). The value of biodiversity is recognised by the many countries which are signatory to the international conventions above. Unfortunately, the imperialistic interpretation may not be dispelled until there is a wider understanding of the inter-dependence of species and nations – and some people will probably always be suspicious of scientific opinion or international perspectives. However, I suggest that giving advice and assistance for conservation should be seen as no more imperialistic than giving advice and assistance for medical surgery.

For example, it is not hypocritical for somebody who lives in a county like Britain (which was deforested thousands of years ago) to suggest a developing country should conserve its forests. Mistakes made in one country should not be repeated. The loss of forest in a temperate region is usually far less serious and irreversible than loss in a tropical country, rich in endemic species (Section 3.4). Most temperate species have wide geographical ranges, whilst

93% of threatened forest birds are in the tropics. Many developed countries have responsibility for overseas territories, which in the case of European states are often their most important sites for endemic species. The policies of the 12 megadiverse countries (Section 3.2.3) will be pivotal to how many species can be seen by future generations, wherever they live.

I believe we should think globally and act globally, and help each other through international conservation programmes. Fortunately, there is increasing pressure from scientists, teachers, the public and leadership within many developing countries for stronger national conservation efforts. The growth of local NGOs is a positive sign; these include the BirdLife International partners in many countries, and National Trusts. There is pressure from groups such as the Alliance of Small Island States for the industrial countries to reduce greenhouse gas emissions. The solutions to many problems require international co-operation – and as described in Sections 1.3 and 1.4, all nations stand to lose if their conservation efforts fail.


## 9.4.1   National and international issues

National policy relating to conservation may be driven internally by politicians or the public, or by international agreements. Regulation (through laws) has proved more effective than voluntary agreements, as with stubble-burning in Britain. Environmental policy and law developed primarily for health or quality of life, including water quality and green belts round cities, may indirectly benefit wildlife. Parochialism in outlook (Section 3.1.2) is reduced by international agreements; for example, European Union legislation forced Britain to take great crested newts and bluebells more seriously.

National policy responses to the CBD vary. In Britain, the government published *Biodiversity: the UK Action Plan* in 1994, which led to the development of costed 'Biodiversity Action Plans' (BAPs) for species or habitats which are priorities for conservation action at national and local levels. These national and regional BAP 'priority' species and habitats have been identified based on population status and declines, and more will need to be designated. The 'globally threatened species' are the highest priority. As the Trap Grounds, Oxford, demonstrates (Section 8.6), priority species do not yet receive sufficient enforced legal protection. Performance indicators for local and national governments need to include more measures of wildlife conservation, with targets. The British government's Quality of Life indicator of 'sustainability' of lifestyles includes the Wild Bird Indicator: this summarises the status of nearly 140 species of breeding birds.

Conservation planning should be at as large a scale as possible: to protect species in viable populations (Section 5.4), to permit movement between habitats, and to reduce the impact if climate change shifts species ranges beyond isolated protected areas (Section 2.3.3). International co-operation is often required to maintain river quality and flow – ideally planning on a whole-catchment scale. Important habitats often cross national boundaries, as with Bialoweiza forest in Poland. The Meso-American Biological Corridor project is attempting to link protected areas throughout Central America.

International agreements are essential for protection of migratory species (including bats, birds and butterflies), which cross or reside in many countries. Special laws or agreements between countries in Europe, and between China and Japan, protect migrant birds. Migrant species are inadequately protected within many regions, and this can render national legislation almost worthless. Over five million birds are killed annually by collision with communications towers in the USA alone, whilst hunting and loss of stop-over habitats threaten many species globally.

Naturally dynamic ecosystems with large mobile herds of mammals, or shifting mosaics of habitat (Sections 5.1.1 and 6.1) require very large areas. These considerations required the linkage of the savannah systems in Kenya to those in Tanzania. The Great Limpopo Transfrontier Park links habitats in Zimbabwe, Mozambique, and South Africa; this 35 000 km$^2$ area is the core of the 'GKG Transfrontier Conservation Area', of about 100 000 km$^2$. Similarly, the large ranges and low densities of the Amur leopard and Siberian tiger require cross-frontier co-operation between China and Russia. A transboundary corridor is in development to link the Atlantic forests of South America. Many ecosystems cannot be protected without consideration of their natural boundaries. There are an increasing number of 'transboundary parks', which are also called 'peace parks' because they foster political goodwill and co-operation.

The international consequences of domestic economic policy should be considered by nations, or they may transfer environmental damage to poorer countries. For example, international trade and fishing agreements need to be carefully considered for their impact on wildlife. Fishing fleets from Europe are over-exploiting stocks off Africa and South America.

As with any development, conservation such as designation of protected areas may benefit or conflict with local people (Section 9.1.2). The interests of local, national and international stakeholders may clash over conservation – as with many development projects such as building railway lines. Not all stakeholders are legitimate, as with drug producers. Governments need to decide if the national (and international) social benefits outweigh the local objections, particularly in the case of displacement or exclusion of people from reserves. In Tanzania, the government protects the Mkomazi reserve from Maasai encroachment, despite lobbying from international pressure groups concerned with 'indigenous people', since this benefits the country as a whole. Numerous reserves have been created through displacement of local people, and attractive compensation schemes are required, as achieved with the Great Limpopo Transfrontier Park. Many large reserves have outreach programmes to benefit the local people around the reserve.

## 9.4.2  The commons

A recurrent theme in conservation is the abuse of 'common property resources' or 'open-access' resources. These are resources without private ownership. Classic examples include the atmosphere, and the international seas. G. Hardin identified 'the tragedy of the commons': in such systems, the short-term economic incentive is for each user to increase their use, since that gives a relatively large return to the individual at a small cost to every other user. There is thus a temptation for each individual to exploit as rapidly as possible (as evident with many fish stocks), or to dump pollution into a communal area (as with $CO_2$). History suggests the only ways to prevent a tragedy of the commons are either strong regulation by the state, or 'enclosure', meaning privatisation of the resource and strict policing of a sustainable quota. On privatised sites with fewer users but without adequate enforcement, there may be a tragedy on a smaller scale, as with overgrazing of Port Meadow SSSI, Oxford, by the 'commoners' entitled to use it. However, the smaller the number of people who use a resource, the more overexploitation can be seen to harm each user, their kin, and their descendants, and the greater the incentive to restrain short-term exploitation – unless discount rates are high and resource replacement low (Section 9.1.1).

Some authors have mistakenly applied the term 'commons' to savannah systems in Africa or Australia that are or were being exploited by indigenous people. However, tribes within these areas were territorial, and within their territories some tribes operated quota systems decided by elders with punishment for overuse: these are therefore privatised systems similar to some 'commons' in Britain.

Privatisation of resources has had some great successes: extension of Exclusive Economic Zones has permitted fish stocks to increase in the Atlantic's Georges bank, whilst New Zealand sets an overall quota for each fish species within which individuals hold 'tradeable individual quotas'. Quotas for $SO_2$ pollution are traded in the USA. Several of the 'community conservation' projects described in the next section, such as reef management in the Philippines, involve permitting or helping to maintain local control over resources. Many of the ancient protected areas described in Section 1.1.1 are effectively privatised.

## 9.4.3  Community conservation

Conservation projects which focus on providing benefits for local people are often described as 'community-based conservation', 'participatory conservation', or 'conservation with development'. Some conservationists see this as a 'new paradigm', essential for success as populations soar and the opportunity costs of setting land aside as reserves rise. Others see it as a dangerous, politically motivated dogma promoted by social scientists with little biological understanding of the vulnerability of species and ecosystems. Controversies have arisen – as can be found in the Further reading for this chapter. Whilst it is fair that benefits should come to local people from protection of wildlife in reserves, in the national or international interest these might best take the form of more effective compensation and subsidies (Section 9.1.2). The biological considerations of each case of exploitation near protected areas should ideally be considered individually using Environmental Impact Assessment (Section 4.7).

As discussed in Section 2.2 and Chapter 7, we should be very cautious of assuming sustainable resource use is occurring – or even possible. Few community-based schemes have detailed ecological monitoring. Reviews of community conservation schemes to date suggest very few achieve sustainability. Some examples of community conservation are given in Table 9.7. Many of these schemes effectively privatise resources for local people, in theory giving them a greater incentive to enforce restrained use. There is a risk of raising expectations of income from a resource or reserve above what is realistic, as happened in some forest parks in West Africa.

A famous example of community conservation is the Communal Areas Management Programme for Indigenous Resources, 'CAMPFIRE', in Zimbabwe. Here, local people reap the benefits of stewardship of wildlife on their lands (including big-game hunting, meat and skins); they therefore have a financial incentive to protect elephants and other species and their habitats – and also to support nearby protected areas. This scheme has been running since the 1980s, and despite some problems remains an important model.

Another success can be found in the release programme for the golden lion tamarin, a highly threatened primate of the Atlantic forests of Brazil. The Poco

Table 9.7 *Examples of community conservation projects*

| Project or location | Resources/exploitation |
|---|---|
| (a) *Projects which have achieved at least partial success; those too recently implemented to assess marked\** | |
| Handumon Village, Philippines | Seahorse fishing for medicine trade; handicrafts. |
| Apo Island, Philippines | Fisheries (prohibit outsiders and certain fishing methods); ecotourism |
| Taka Bone Rate, Indonesia | Marine resources; clam aquaculture |
| Tamshiyacu-Tahuayo, Peru | Bushmeat, non-timber products |
| Mamirauá Reserve, Brazil | Fish/forest |
| Kipepeo Project, Kenya | Forest butterfly farming |
| CAMPFIRE, Zimbabwe | Game animals/safari hunting, meat, etc. |
| Amboseli, Kenya | Ecotourism, game ranching, bushmeat |
| Kakadu, Australia | Ecotourism, hunting, gathering, cultural values |
| Bermudian landing, Belize | Forest primates, ecotourism, soil protection, etc. |
| Belize Barrier Reef\* | Ecotourism, etc. |
| Xcalak Peninsula, Mexico\* | Reef and wetland ecotourism and use |
| Cornwall, Britain | Mackerel hand-line fishing |

| Project or location | Resources/exploitation | Problem |
|---|---|---|
| (b) *Projects which have not prevented, or have led to, environmental degradation* | | |
| Ache, people, Paraguay | Forest produce/timber | Deforestation |
| Chachis people, coastal Ecuador | Forest rights | Deforestation, fragmentation |
| Korup Cameroon | Bushmeat; non-timber forest products | Overhunting |
| Luangwa Zambia | Safari hunting | Overhunting using snares |

Das Antas Biological Reserve employs local people, and education includes essay contests and press releases; local conservation groups have been formed, and some enthusiastic landowners have created private reserves. Notably, successful projects often involve ecotourism, which, unlike many extractive uses, can sometimes compete financially with alternative land use. Involvement of all legitimate stakeholders from the beginning of a planning process (including 'Stakeholder Decision Analysis') should help reduce the chances of subsequent conflicts over management. There are hopes that consultation to discover local knowledge and use will help retain cultural and biological diversity near Chiloé National Park in Chile, whilst at the New Forest in Britain there is active consultation with the community over management. The results of such projects should be examined with interest.

Community conservation is sometimes seen as a form of conflict resolution between conservationists and local people, without which conservation will fail owing to increased resentment and distrust. It is of course desirable to help development and local communities in poor countries. However, given the need to retain many areas of very natural habitat (Section 3.2 and Chapter 5), use and development is simply *not* always compatible with conservation of biodiversity. Community conservation may deplete high-quality species (which can not sustain even low harvest rates or disturbance, Section 3.1), and so degrade the value of a site just as much as deforestation or drainage. Wildlife outside reserves and in frequent contact with local people is often severely depleted of high-quality species (Section 3.1), as is so conspicuous in Europe, East Africa and southern Asia. How many rhino, elephants, hyenas or wild dogs survive outside protected areas?

A review by A. G. Bruner and colleagues in 2001 showed that protected areas are on the whole working well, with only 17% showing net land clearance since establishment and with 80% in better ecological condition than the surroundings; interestingly, local community involvement did *not* correlate with the success of parks, whilst the density of guards was the factor most strongly correlated with effectiveness. The effectiveness of protected areas is shown in Fig. 9.2. Many of the successes in conservation over hundreds of years have been in strictly enforced private reserves (Section 1.1.1).

Unfortunately, those who advocate community conservation have yet to demonstrate that it can be widely successful even *outside* reserves; given the irreversibility of loss of natural features this must be demonstrated in the same ecosystem before any encroachment of use into reserves in an area – or extinction rates will rise (Section 5.4). The fact that protected areas are often islands of wildlife in a sea of degraded land is effectively an experimental demonstration that human communities typically fail to conserve. Since the

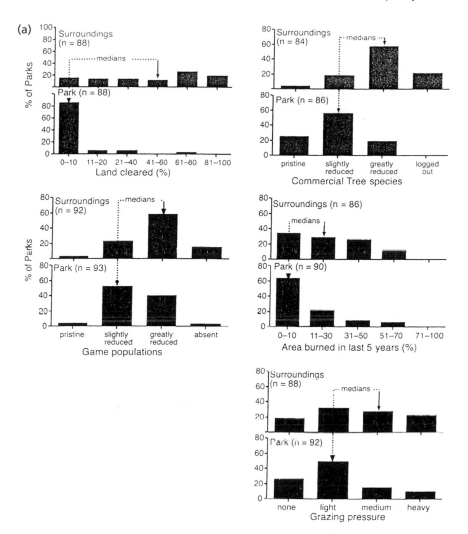

**Fig. 9.2.**   The success of protected areas internationally in reducing various pressures. (a) Indicators of degradation compared between the inside of protected areas and their surroundings. (b) Influence of establishment of a protected area on the subsequent condition of the vegetation.
*Source:* Reprinted with permission from Bruner, A. G. *et al. Science* **291** (2001), 125–128. Copyright 2001 American Association for the Advancement of Science.

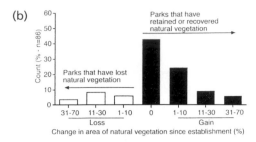

**Fig. 9.2.** *(cont.)*

limits to agricultural expansion will have to be addressed eventually even if all reserves were degazetted and used, it is better to face up to the problems now, and limit expansion whilst there is still some wildlife left. Conservation of wildlife will require a collaboration between the two approaches – strict protection ('fortress conservation') of high-quality core sites, and community conservation around them – as with the zoned Biosphere reserves (Section 5.5). Community conservation may be particularly appropriate where climatic change is predicted to require major shifts in the boundaries of protected areas, in which case the land around and between existing reserves needs to be retained in the nearest state to naturalness that is possible given local requirements for resources.

It should not be assumed that local people or indigenous people are superior at managing the environment: despite various traditional conservation activities (Section 1.1.1 and Table 9.8), indigenous peoples have had very substantial irreversible impact on wildlife (Sections 2.2, 5.1 and 7.3), and their recent impact may have been limited more by technology or coincidence than restraint. Indeed, reviews suggest there is very little hard evidence of harvesting restraint as opposed to constraint. Biological correctness, rather than 'political correctness', should make conservation more effective.

Even with highly traditional cultural practices, exploitation is often not sustainable (Sections 1.1, 2.2.1, 2.2.5, 5.1 and Chapter 7). In the best-documented area, Europe, traditional management evidently led to numerous local extirpations in the past few thousand years, including several mammals and forest insects in recent centuries. However, one of the main reasons why maintaining traditional use of resources in a protected area, and community conservation, may fail is that the local people are no longer traditional in several respects. They may seek and use more efficient technology (such as saws, torches, nets, hooks, axes, wire snares, diving masks, guns, or paraffin); they can be more mobile (using outboard motors, snowmobiles or cars, with

Table 9.8 *Possible examples of traditional practices which sustain some biodiversity – intentionally or incidentally*

| Resource | Tribe/(Region) | Practice which restrains exploitation |
|---|---|---|
| Deer | (Cachar, Assam) | Taboo on hunting pregnant females |
| Herons, egrets | (Assam) | Taboo on eating when nesting |
| Forest, bushmeat | (Central Africa) | Social pressure against wastage (clearing forest or killing but not using) |
| Forest plants | Kayapo (Amazonia) | Zoned and rotational management; plant forest islands <10 ha in savannah and grow plants to attract mammals |
| Minnow shoals | Kayapo (Amazonia) | Not harvested to prevent wrath of mythical serpent |
| African land snail | Ashanti (Ghana) | Closed season whilst egg laying |
| Forest | Indigenous tribes (NW America) | Forests near rivers not cleared or farmed, to protect fisheries |
| Timber and branches | Widespread | Coppicing and pollarding: rotational exploitation of trees and scrub |
| Megapode eggs | (Haruku, Molucca) | Closed season; collecting rights |

improved roads); they want money for goods such as batteries, and sell resources (including bushmeat) to very distant markets; they have new cultural values; and their population is no longer controlled by starvation, disease or warfare. In sum, they may be living beyond the carrying capacity of the system.

## 9.4.4  Population

Population growth is the single biggest conservation problem (Section 2.1). Although fuelled by many factors (including several religions), a principle cause is infant mortality, itself a function of poor water quality and sanitation. With improved survival of infants, and security for the elderly, children become expensive and couples choose to have fewer. Education and women's rights

Table 9.9 *Examples of differential annual per capita consumption of resources in various countries*

|  | Energy: kg oil equivalent | Domestic water from surface: $m^3$ | Paper: kg | Meat: kg | $CO_2$ production: tonnes |
|---|---|---|---|---|---|
| USA | 8000 | 134 | 290 | 120 | 20 |
| UK | 3900 | 104 | 200 | 80 | 9 |
| Australia | 5500 | 101 | 180 | 110 | 20 |
| Brazil | 1050 | 75 | 40 | 70 | 2 |
| China | 890 | 22 | 30 | 50 | 3 |
| India | 480 | 30 | 2 | 4 | 1 |
| Bangladesh | 200 | 16 | 1 | 3 | 0.2 |
| Madagascar | ? | 17 | 1 | 20 | 0.1 |

*Source:* Modified from *Human Development Report* 2001, UNDP, Oxford University Press, and *Word Resources 2000–2001. People and Ecosystems: the Fraying Web of Life* (World Resources Institute, Oxford University Press, 2000).
Figures are approximate, mostly from the 1990s.

help make this possible, but lack of contraceptives may limit their freedom to plan their families.

Already, hundreds of millions of people desire contraception but cannot get it. Meeting this simple human right would probably be the greatest and most cost-effective conservation action that could be taken – requiring about $6 billion per year. At the UN Conference on Population and Development, in 1994, many of the governments of the world acknowledged the need to slow their national population growth. The reasons contraception is not given priority and adequate funding include taboos, bad publicity following enforced population control, and the American anti-abortion lobby. Although the total impact is less, population growth in the developed countries is more damaging per person than in the developing world – owing to the high consumption per person in the 'developed' countries (Table 9.9 and Chapter 2). With more funds the World Health Organisation, and charities such as the International Planned Parenthood Federation (IPPF) and Population Concern, could play a leading role in conservation in *every* country. If we do not empower people to plan their families, then there is very little prospect of passing a rich diversity of species and ecosystems on to children in the future.

# 10

# Conclusions

What general themes emerge from the many facets of conservation? Firstly, although conservation is difficult, there is still much that can be achieved. Norman Myers points out the 'splendid opportunity' that faces us as we take decisions influencing uncountable trillions of people in the future. He reminds us that there is no greater mistake than to do nothing because we could only do a little. This is an essential point in conservation: individuals *can* make a difference. We will begin by looking at some conservation successes that highly motivated individuals or teams have brought about. I hope readers of this book will see how they too can make their own contributions to conservation. We shall then examine the future directions conservation may need to take.

## 10.1 Ideals and successes

In the 1980s, Mauritius was seen by many people as a hopeless case for conservation: 97% of its original habitat had been lost. Many species, including the dodo, giant tortoises, and several plants were known to have been exterminated – and untold others lost without trace. Its few remaining forests and several of its remaining endemic birds were highly endangered. Yet through co-operation between the Mauritian Government, Jersey and other zoos, and the dedication of conservationists in Mauritius, the situation is now far from bleak. The Mauritian pink pigeon, parakeet and kestrel and numerous plants have almost certainly been saved. Mauritius provides a model of the impact a committed government and a few dedicated people can have. If you are prepared to work hard for years and become expert on a species or habitat, you really can give it a chance. Similar notable successes can be found throughout the world. They include the conservation of the black robin and kakapo of New Zealand, and some of the great whales.

Individuals can make a difference in other ways, including the media: Gerald Durrell, David Attenborough and David Bellamy presented conservation to a wide public, inspiring very many people, young and old, to take up conservation. You too can make a difference by writing letters or articles, working on reserves, by teaching, or by the enthusiasm you display for wildlife.

## 10.2   Pragmatism, and limits to knowledge

Despite our best efforts, we will have to accept that very many species and habitats will be lost. It is our job to minimise the irreversible losses. This book has suggested the ideal management for many habitats and species, yet compromises will occur as population and consumption expand. We will have to do a better job of achieving conservation in the areas surrounding and beyond protected areas, as well as maintaining more of these precious fragments of nature for those species which are highly vulnerable. To reduce encroachment into important habitats, agriculture will have to be intensified carefully in many areas that are already degraded – as around Mananara in Madagascar. We will have to do a damage-limitation exercise, but not be swamped by depression at the scale of the destruction which will occur. There is as yet limited political will, and issues such as poverty, war and development will probably be seen as higher priorities for some time – perhaps until the environmental components of them are fully recognised.

Successful conservation will be helped by sound knowledge, and we need far more information, gleaned from research and natural history. Here again there is scope for public involvement. We should *always* be aware of the limits to our knowledge and the uncertainties in our estimates and conclusions. This does not weaken our case: we are less likely to make politically embarrassing mistakes if we make it clear what remains to be discovered – or what may be impossible to discover. Ecosystems contain uncounted species interacting in unknown ways with each other and with the abiotic environment, creating a complex system with 'emergent properties' we may never be able to comprehend or predict. We should expect many surprises, and sudden, nonlinear changes.

The precautionary principle of the Convention on Biological Diversity needs to be taken very seriously: 'Where there is a threat of significant reduction or loss of biological diversity, lack of full scientific certainty should not be used as a reason for postponing measures to avoid or minimise such a threat'.

## 10.3   Conservation in the future

As I showed in Chapter 1, many of the ideas of conservation are long established. In 1970, Prince Bernhard of the Netherlands indicated where we needed to go:

We have work to do – work in two directions: first, to stimulate and expedite the solutions to those main causal problems, and second to perform a 'holding operation', to save as much as we can of what is irreplaceable, while the solutions are being found and brought into effect. In the first area, It seems to me that conservationists must establish strong lines of communication with the organisations working on these basic solutions. For example, we should have close liaison with the various demographic bodies . . . In each case, conservation must be precise and specific. It must have well-defined, attainable objects, and because so much needs to be done and there are so few dedicated people and so little money to do it, conservation must have its priorities very carefully worked out and firmly based on scientific research.

It is revealing that although some progress has been made, this vision is equally valid today.

Conservation cannot be relied on to pay for itself, even in the long term. Fortunately, economic viability is *not* always paramount in human affairs: many expensive activities, such as wars, religion, building monuments, and saving works of art, are driven by factors other than economics. Massive (but realistic) funds will have to be raised, some through taxation and removal of perverse subsidies; redirecting only 2% of these subsidies would pay for a viable protected areas network. There must be a more positive and genuine involvement of the business community. Firm regulation will be required, for example to make polluters pay for externalities, and reduce deleterious trade. The success of the tax on plastic bags in Ireland illustrates that increasing the short-term financial costs will deter environmental damage – although regulation often requires international agreement to prevent harm to national industries.

Lifestyle changes will be inevitable. We will have to move towards a mentality more like that in war time – with the minimum of consumption and waste. I believe 'consumer confidence' is not sustainable. Decreased exploitation is better than attempts at recycling. We will have to look very at hard at our luxuries, including energy use and recreation. Unfortunately, polls in the 1990s suggest only 55% of Germans and 31% of the British public were willing to lower their standard of living to protect the environment. Conservation may not be much fun, but it will improve the quality of life for some people now, and many in the future.

Co-operation with local peoples will need to be improved, with better compensation and conflict resolution. We must consider the responsibilities and social benefits that conservation brings to everybody on Earth, and to the whole populace of a nation, and to future generations – and we must accept that these may often conflict with the short-term needs of the local people. There must be limitations on personal liberties to exploit or cause extinctions, just as there are limitations on liberty to pollute or murder. More park guards must be employed: their effectiveness has been clearly demonstrated. Costs and compensation will have to be shared fairly. Compensation with land, rather than cash, and improved political and financial stability, would help poor people plan ahead. There may be a need for inter-governmental organisations to take a fuller role in compensation, and in protection of the global heritage, including enforcement of legislation and the management of reserves.

Where will the science of conservation go in the future? I suggest some priorities:

- human population growth;
- energy production;
- taxonomy and phylogeny (to help protect diversity);
- field biology (to help map and manage habitats and species);
- examining the impact of 'sustainable' yields of one species on non-target species;
- remote sensing with ground-truthing (for verification of protection);
- large-scale and long-term planning;
- manipulation experiments and model ecosystems (to help unravel causality in patterns);
- examining changes to the evolutionary process (as through loss of high-quality species);
- palaeoecology and archaeology (to see what the past can tell us about the future);
- and Gaia (to understand the global ecosystem and its stability).

The word 'biodiversity' has been over-used: it should not encourage us to focus on diversity, but rather on extinctions and naturalness – perhaps 'biointegrity' would be better? I believe the words 'wildlife' and 'wilderness' should not go out of fashion.

More generally, what is the most important thing that can be done? An overall priority is to consider the personal value systems of the present and future generations. We must become less anthropocentric. Already, many people around the world value wildlife and wilderness. However, conservation will only succeed if respect for non-human nature and natural processes balances short-term self-interest. We must somehow help those billions of people who wish to conserve something – but cannot afford to do so.

# Further reading

## Chapter 1. Introduction to conservation

Ayensu, E. S., Haywood, V. H., Lucas, G. L. & Defilipps, R. A. *Our Green and Living World. The Wisdom to Save it* (Cambridge University Press, Cambridge, 1984).

Collar, N. J. Species are a measure of man's freedom: reflections after writing a Red Book on African Birds. *Oryx* **20** (1986), 15–19.

Hambler, C. & Speight, M. R. Extinction rates in British nonmarine invertebrates since 1900. *Conservation Biology* **10** (1996), 892–896.

Master, L. L., Stein, B. A., Kutner, L. S. & Hammerson, G. A. Vanishing assets. Conservation status of US species. In: B. A. Stein, L. S. Kutner, & J. S. Adams (Eds.) *Precious Heritage. The Status of Biodiversity in the United States* (Oxford University Press, New York, 2000, pp. 93–118).

May, R. M., Lawton, J. H. & Stork, N. E. Assessing extinction rates. In: J. H. Lawton & R. M. May (Eds.) *Extinction Rates* (Oxford University Press, Oxford, 1995, pp. 1–24).

May, R. M. The dimensions of life on earth. In: P. H. Raven (Ed.) *Nature and Human Society. The Quest for a Sustainable World* (National Academy Press, Washington, 2000, pp. 30–45).

Posey, D. A. (Ed.) *Cultural and Spiritual Values of Biodiversity* (Intermediate Technology Publications & UNEP, London & Nairobi, 1999).

## Chapter 2. Threats to biodiversity

Bibby, C. J. *et. al. Putting Biodiversity on the Map: Priority Areas for Global Conservation* (ICBP, Cambridge, 1992).

BirdLife International *Threatened Birds of the World* (Lynx Editions and BirdLife International, Barcelona and Cambridge UK, 2000).

Ehrlich, P. The scale of the human enterprise and biodiversity loss. In: J. H. Lawton & R. M. May (Eds.) *Extinction Rates* (Oxford University Press, Oxford, 1995, pp. 214–226).

Goudie, A. S. *The Human Impact on the Natural Environment*, 5th edition (Blackwell Publishing, Oxford, 2000).

Illius, A. W. & O'Connor, T. G. On the relevance of nonequilibrium concepts to arid and semiarid grazing systems. *Ecological Applications* **9** (1999), 798–813.

Jackson, J. C. B. *et al.* Historical overfishing and the recent collapse of coastal ecosystems. *Science* **293** (2001), 629–638.

Letourneau, D. K. & Burrows, B. E. (Eds.) *Genetically Engineered Organisms: Assessing Environmental and Human Health Effects* (CRC Press, Boca Raton, Florida, 2001).

Martin, P. S. & Klein, R. G. *Quaternary Extinctions* (University of Arizona Press, Tucson, 1984).

McCarty, J. P. Ecological consequences of recent climate change. *Conservation Biology* **15** (2001), 320–331.

Peres, C. A. Effects of subsistence hunting on vertebrate community structure in Amazonian fragments. *Conservation Biology* **14** (2000), 240–253.

Spencer, T. E., Teleki, K. A., Bradshaw, C. & Spalding, M. D. Coral bleaching in the southern Seychelles during the 1997–1998 Indian Ocean warm event. *Marine Pollution Bulletin* **40** (2000), 569–586.

Spellerberg, I. F. *Ecological Effects of Roads* (Science Publishers, Inc., Enfield, 2002).

Steadman, D. W. Prehistoric extinctions of Pacific island birds: biogeography meets zooarchaeology. *Science* **267** (1995), 1123–1131.

World Conservation Monitoring Centre (WCMC) *Global Biodiversity: Status of the Earth's Living Resources* (Chapman and Hall, London, 1992).

## Chapter 3. Evaluation of priorities for species and habitats

Bibby, C. J. *et al.* (1992): *see* Chapter 2.

Groombridge, B. & Jenkins, M. D. *World Atlas of Biodiversity: Earth's Living Resources in the 21st Century* (University of California Press, Berkeley, 2002).

Hunter, M. L. Jr. & Hutchinson, A. The virtues and shortcomings of parochialism: Conserving species that are locally rare but globally common. *Conservation Biology* **8** (1994), 1163–1165.

Myers, N., Mittermeier, R. A., Mittermeier, C. G., da Fonseca, G. A. B. & Kent, J. Biodiversity hotspots for conservation priorities. *Nature* **403** (2000), 853–858.

McNeely, J. A., Miller, K. R., Reid, W. V., Mittermeier, R. A. & Werner, T. B. *Conserving the World's Biological Diversity* (IUCN, Gland; WRI, CI, WWF-US, the World Bank, Washington, DC, 1990).

Ratcliffe, D. A. *A Nature Conservation Review* (Cambridge University Press, Cambridge, 1997).

Roberts, C. M. *et al.* Marine biodiversity hotspots and conservation priorities for tropical reefs. *Science* **295** (2002), 1280–1284.

Stattersfield, A. J., Crosby, M. J., Long, A. J. & Wege, D. C. *Endemic Bird Areas of the World. Priorities for Biodiversity Conservation* (Birdlife Conservation Series no 7, BirdLife International, Cambridge, 1998).

Usher, M. B. *Wildlife Conservation Evaluation* (Chapman & Hall, London, 1986). (Out of print.)

Vane-Wright, R. I., Humphries, C. J. & Williams, P. H. What to protect? Systematics and the agony of choice. *Biological Conservation* **55** (1991), 235–254.

## Chapter 4. Monitoring and Environmental Impact Assessment

Bibby, C. J., Burgess, N. D., Hill, D. A. & Mustoe, S. H. *Bird Census Techniques*, 2nd edition (Academic Press, London, 2000).

Henderson, P. A. *Practical Methods in Ecology* (Blackwell Publishing, Oxford, 2003).

Krebs, C. J. *Ecological Methodology*, 2nd edition (Benjamin Cummins, Menlo, California, 1999).

McCarthy, J. J. *et al.* (Eds.) *Climate Change 2001: Impacts, Adaptation and Vulnerability* (Cambridge University Press, Cambridge, 2001).

McGavin, G. C. *Insects and Other Terrestrial Invertebrates. Expedition Field Techniques* (Expedition Advisory Centre. Royal Geographical Society (with the Institute of British Geographers), London, 1997).

New, T. R. *Invertebrate Surveys for Conservation* (Oxford University Press, Oxford, 1998).

Ozanne, C. M. P. A comparison of the canopy arthropod communities of coniferous and broad-leaved trees in the United Kingdom. *Selbyana* **20** (1999), 290–298.

Southwood, T. R. E. & Henderson, P. A. *Ecological Methods* (Blackwell Science Ltd, Oxford, 2000).

Spellerberg, I. F. *Monitoring Ecological Change* (Cambridge University Press, Cambridge, 1991).

Sutherland, W. J. (Ed.) *Ecological Census Techniques: a Handbook* (Cambridge University Press, Cambridge, 1996).

Sykes, J. M. & Lane, A. M. J. (Eds.) *The United Kingdom Environmental Change Network: Protocols for Standard Measurements at Terrestrial Sites* (CEH Monks Wood Publications, Monks Wood, Huntingdon, 1997).

Treweek, J. *Ecological Impact Assessment* (Blackwell Science Ltd, Oxford, 1999).

## Chapter 5. Management of natural habitats

Beier, P. & Noss, R. F. Do habitat corridors provide connectivity? *Conservation Biology* **12** (1998), 1241–1252.

Brooks, T. M. *et al.* Habitat loss and extinction in the hotspots of biodiversity. *Conservation Biology* **16** (2002), 909–923.

Blake, J. G. & Karr, J. R. Species composition of bird communities and the conservation benefit of large versus small forests. *Biological Conservation* **30** (1984), 173–187.

Laurance, W. F., Vasconcelo, H. L. & Lovejoy, T. E. Forest loss and fragmentation in the Amazon: implications for wildlife conservation. *Oryx* **34** (1999), 39–45.

Laurance, W. F. Edge effects in tropical forest fragments: application of a model for the design of nature reserves. *Biological Conservation* **57** (1991), 205–219.

Lovejoy, T. E. *et al.* Edge and other effects of isolation on Amazon forest fragments. In: M. E. Soulé (Ed.) *Conservation Biology: the Science of Scarcity and Diversity* (Sinauer Assoc. Inc., Mass., 1986, pp. 257–285).

Ozanne, C. M. P., Hambler, C., Foggo, A. & Speight, M. R. The significance of edge effects in the management of forests for invertebrate biodiversity. In: N. E. Stork, J. Adis & R. Didham (Eds.) *Canopy Arthropods* (Chapman & Hall, London, 1997, pp. 534–550).

Roberts, C. M., Bohnsack, J. A., Gell, F., Hawkins, J. P. & Goodridge, R. Effects of marine reserves on adjacent fisheries. *Science* **294** (2001), 1920–1923.

Samways, M. J. *Insect Conservation Biology* (Chapman & Hall, London, 1994).

Whitmore, T. C. *An Introduction to Tropical Rain Forests*, 2nd edition (Oxford University Press, Oxford, 1998).

Woodroffe, R. & Ginsberg, J. F. Edge effects and the extinction of populations inside protected areas. *Science* **280** (1998), 2126–2128.

## Chapter 6. Management of species

For accounts of individual threatened species see the Red Data Books (published by IUCN and BirdLife or ICBP), and the Red List (on the IUCN website). For *ex situ* conservation of animals, see *The International Zoo Yearbook*, published by The Zoological Society of London.

Bowes, B. G. (Ed.) *A Colour Atlas of Plant Propagation and Conservation* (Manson Publishing Ltd, London, 1999).

Harrison, S. Metapopulations and conservation. In: P. J. Edwards, R. M. May & N. R. Webb (Eds.) *Large Scale Ecology and Conservation*. Blackwell Scientific Publications, Oxford, 1994, pp. 111–128.

Lacy, R. C. Importance of genetic variation to the viability of mammalian populations. *Journal of Mammology* **78** (1997), 320–335.

Lande, R. Mutation and conservation. *Conservation Biology* **9** (1995), 782–791.

## Chapter 7. Sustainability, and the management of semi-natural habitats

Gibson, C. W. D. & Brown, V. K. The nature and rate of development of calcareous grassland in southern Britain. *Biological Conservation* **58** (1991), 297–316.

Gibson, C. W. D., Brown, V. K., Losito, L. & McGavin, G. C. The response of invertebrate assemblies to grazing. *Ecography* **15** (1992), 166–176.

Hambler, C. & Speight, M. R. Biodiversity conservation in Britain: science replacing tradition. *British Wildlife* **6** (1995), 137–147.

Krebs, C. *Ecology: the Experimental Analysis of Distribution and Abundance*, 5th edition (Benjamin Cummings, San Francisco, 2001).

Lande, R. Threshold harvesting for sustainability of fluctuating resources. *Ecology* **78** (1997), 1341–1350.

Milner-Gulland, E. J. & Mace, R. *Conservation of Biological Resources* (Blackwell Science, Oxford, 1998).

Southwood, T. R. E., Brown, V. K. & Reader, P. M. The relationships of plant and insect diversities in succession. *Biological Journal of the Linnean Society* **12** (1979), 327–348.

## Chapter 8. Restoration, translocation and mitigation

Benstead, P. J., José, P. V., Joyce, C. B. & Wade, P. M. *European Wet Grassland. Guidelines for Management and Restoration* (RSPB, Sandy, 1999).

Gibson, C. W. D., Watt, T. A., & Brown, V. K. The use of sheep grazing to recreate species-rich grassland from abandoned arable land. *Biological Conservation* **42** (1987), 165–183.

Janzen, D. H. & Martin, P. S. Neotropical anachronisms: the fruits the Gomphotheres ate. *Science* **215** (1982), 19–27.

Jordan III, W. R., Gilpin, M. E. & Aber, J. D. (Eds.) *Restoration Ecology* (Cambridge University Press, Cambridge, 1987).

Macdonald, D. W., Mace, G. M. & Rushton, S. British mammals: is there a radical future? In: A. Entwistle & N. Dunstone (Eds.) *Priorities for the Conservation of Mammalian Diversity: Has the Panda had its Day?* (Cambridge University Press, Cambridge, 2000, pp. 175–205).

Maitland, P. S. & Morgan, N. C. *Conservation and Management of Freshwater Habitats. Lakes, Rivers and Wetlands* (Chapman & Hall, London, 1997).

Morris, M. G. The management of grassland for the conservation of invertebrate animals. In: E. Duffey & A. S. Watt (Eds.) *The Scientific Management of Animal and Plant Communities for Conservation* (Blackwell Scientific Publications, Oxford, 1971, pp. 527–552).

Perrow, M. R. & Davy, A. J. (Eds.) *Handbook of Ecological Restoration* (2 vols.) (Cambridge University Press, Cambridge, 2002).

## Chapter 9. Environmental economics, law and education

Alden Smith, E. & Wishnie, M. Conservation and subsistence in small-scale societies. *Annual Review of Anthropology* **29** (2000), 493–524.

Brandon, K., Redford, K. H. & Sanderson, S. E. (Eds.) *Parks in Peril: People, Politics and Protected Areas* (Island Press, Washington, DC, 1998).

Costanza, R. *et al.* The value of the world's ecosystem services and natural capital. *Nature* **387** (1997), 253–260.

Dasgupta, P. S. The economics of the environment. *Proceedings of the British Academy* **90** (1996), 165–221.

Ferraro, P. J. & Kiss, A. Direct payments to conserve biodiversity. *Science* **298** (2002), 1718–1719.

Glowka, L. *et al. A Guide to the Convention on Biological Diversity* (IUCN, Gland, Switzerland, 1994).

Haywood, V. H. (Ed.) *Global Biodiversity Assessment* (UNEP: Cambridge University Press, Cambridge, 1995).

Milner-Gulland, E. J. & Mace, R. (1998): *see* Chapter 7.

Simms, A. *An Environmental War Economy. The Lessons of Ecological Debt and Climate Change* (New Economics Foundation, London, 2001).

Western, D., Wright, R. M. & Strum, S. C. (Eds.) *Natural Connections: Perspectives in Community-Based Conservation* (Island Press, Washington, DC, 1994).

## Further information

The electronic media can be helpful for further information about conservation issues. The World Wide Web gives much information, but much is not peer-reviewed and is not necessarily very reliable. Websites for conservation non-governmental organisations (NGOs) such as BirdLife, FFI, IUCN, and WWF, and inter-governmental institutions such as UNESCO and UNEP, provide a gateway to find out about many publications and projects. Electronic databases (such as Biological Abstracts, Zoological Record, and TREE CD) can be used to search the scientific journals for specific topics or authors. Each database has its strengths and weaknesses, and several should be used for a fuller picture. Alternative spellings, such as 'reintroduction' and 're-introduction', should be checked when searching.

# List of species names

This list includes only the particular species (or group of species) which is referred to in the text; there may be other species with the same English name. Species often have more than one commonly used scientific or English name, and some such alternatives are denoted by '='. Taxonomy is changing fast in many groups, often because their DNA sequences have been investigated.

'Spp.' denotes more than one species in the genus. 'Agg.' denotes aggregate (a group of very similar species or varieties). 'Var.' denotes variety.

Not all species mentioned within the tables are included; for the scientific names of several extinct species see the source literature for the table.

| English name | | Scientific (Latin) name |
|---|---|---|
| acacia | | *Acacia* spp. |
| addax | | *Addax nasomaculatus* |
| African bugleweed | | *Ajuga remota* |
| African bush willow | | *Combretum caffrum* |
| African land snail | | *Achatina fulica* |
| African sausage tree | | *Kigelia pinnata* |
| afrormosia | | *Pericopsis elata* |
| albatross | – royal | *Diomedea epomophora* |
| albatrosses | | Family Diomedeidae |
| albizia species | | *Albizia* spp. |
| alerce | | *Fitzroya cupressoides* |
| alfalfa | | *Medicago sativa* |
| alligator | – American | *Alligator mississippiensis* |
| | – Chinese | *Alligator sinensis* |
| alligator flea beetle | | *Agasicles hygrophila* |
| alligator weed | | *Alternanthera philoxeroides* |
| Alpine pasque flower | | *Pulsatilla alpina* |
| American beachgrass | | *Ammophila breviligulata* |
| American redstart | | *Setophaga ruticilla* |
| ammi | | *Ammi visnaga* |
| anchovy | | *Engraulis* spp. |
| ant | – Argentine | *Iridomyrmex humilis* |
| | – crazy | *Anoplepis gracilipes* |
| | – fire | *Wasmannia auropunctata, Solenopsis geminata* |
| | – red fire | *Solenopsis invicta* |

| | | |
|---|---|---|
| ants/ant nests | | Family Formicidae |
| ancient murrelets | | *Synthliboramphus antiquus* |
| anole | – brown | *Anolis sagrei* |
| | – green | *Anolis carolinensis* |
| Apolinar's marsh wren | | *Cistothorus apolinari* |
| Arctic charr | | *Salvelinus alpinus* |
| Arctic lemming | | *Dicrostonyx torquatus* |
| arnicas | | *Arnica montana* |
| ash | | *Fraxinus excelsior* |
| Asiatic clam (= Asian clam) | | *Potamocorbula amurensis* and *Corbicula fluminea* |
| aspen | | *Populus tremula* |
| aurochs (= aurox) | | *Bos primigenius* |
| avocet | | *Recurvirostra avosetta* |
| aye-aye | | *Daubentonia madagascariensis* |
| Bactrian wild camel | | *Camelus bactrianus ferus* |
| badger | – Eurasian | *Meles meles* |
| | – American | *Taxidea taxus* |
| Bali starling (= Bali mynah) | | *Leucopsar rothschildi* |
| barley | | *Hordeum vulgarum* |
| barndoor skate | | *Raja laevis* |
| barred antshrike | | *Thamnophilus dolicatus* |
| bat | – fruit | Family Pteropodidae |
| | – vampire | *Desmodus rotundus* |
| bats | | Order Chiroptera |
| beach heather | | *Hudsonia tomentosa* |
| bear | – Asian black | *Ursus thibetanus* |
| | – brown | *Ursus arctos* |
| | polar | *Ursus maritimus* |
| beaver | – American | *Castor canadensis* |
| | – European | *Castor fiber* |
| beetles | – carabid | Family Carabidae |
| | – tiger | Family Cicindelidae (or Carabidae?) |
| beetles | | Order Coleoptera |
| beraliya | | *Shorea megistophylla* |
| bilbie | – greater | *Macrotis lagotis* |
| billfish | | Families Istiophoridae and Xiphiidae |
| birch | | *Betula* spp. |
| bison | – Caucasian | *Bison bison caucasicus* |
| | – European | *Bison bison bonasus* |
| | – Plains | *Bison bison bison* |
| | – Wood | *Bison bison athabascae* |
| bittern | | *Botaurus stellaris* |
| black colobus | | *Colobus satanas* |
| black locust | | *Robinia pseudoacacia* |
| black mangabey | | *Cercocebus aterrimus* |
| black myrobalan | | *Terminalia chebula* |
| black redstart | | *Phoenicurus ochruros* |
| black robin | | *Petroica traversi* |
| black-footed ferret | | *Mustela nigripes* |
| black-footed rock wallaby | | *Petrogale lateralis* |
| bladderpod | | *Lesquerella* spp. |
| bluebell | | *Endymion non-scriptus* |
| bracken | | *Pteridium aquilinum* |
| bramble | | *Rubus fruticosus* agg. |
| brazilwood | | *Caesalpina echinata* |

| | | |
|---|---|---|
| chimpanzee | | *Pan troglodytes* |
| | – pygmy (= bonobo) | *Pan paniscus* |
| Chinese grass carp | | *Ctenopharyngodon idella* |
| chipmunk | – eastern | *Tamias striatus* |
| chough | | *Pyrrhocorax pyrrhocorax* |
| chrysanthemum | | *Chrysanthemum cinerariaefolium* |
| cichlid fishes | | *Orthostoma* spp., and others |
| cinchona | | *Cinchona ledgeriana* |
| cinnamon | | *Cinnomomum zeylanicum* |
| cobra | | *Naja naja* |
| cochineal bug | | *Dactylopius coccus* |
| coco plum | | *Chrysobalanus icaco* |
| coconut | | *Cocos nucifera* |
| cod | – Atlantic | *Gadus morhua* |
| coelacanth | – African | *Latimaria chalumnae* |
| | – Indonesian | *Latimaria menadoensis* |
| Colorado Delta clam | | *Mulinia coloradoensis* |
| comb jelly | | *Mnemiopsis leidyi* |
| convolvulus | | *Convolvulus soldanella* |
| condor | – Andean | *Vultur gryphus* |
| | – California | *Gymnogyps californianus* |
| Cooke's kokio | | *Kokia cookei* |
| coral | – black | Family Antipathidae |
| | – brain | Family Faviidae |
| | – Caribbean gorgon | *Pseudogorgonia elisebethae* |
| | – staghorn | *Acropora* spp. |
| corkwood | | *Duboisia myoporoides* |
| cormorant | – European | *Phalacrocorax carbo* |
| | – pygmy | *Phalacrocorax pygmaeus* |
| corn buttercup | | *Ranunculus arvensis* |
| corn cockle | | *Agrostemma githago* |
| corn rootworm | | *Diabrotica barberi* |
| cornflower | | *Centaurea cyanus* |
| cotton | | *Gossypium* spp. |
| cotton-topped marmoset (= tamarin) | | *Saguinus oedipus* |
| cowslip | | *Primula veris* |
| coyote | | *Canis latrans* |
| coypu | | *Myocastor coypus* |
| crab | – Chinese mitten | *Eriocheir sinensis* |
| | – red land | *Gecacoidea natalis* |
| | – robber | *Birgus latro* |
| crab-eating macaque | | *Macaca fascicularis* |
| crambe | | *Crambe abyssinica* |
| crane | – demoiselle | *Anthropoides virgo* |
| | – white-naped | *Grus vipio* |
| | – sandhill | *Grus canadensis* |
| | – Siberian | *Grus leucogeranus* |
| crayfish | – European white-clawed | *Austropotamobius pallipes* |
| | – American signal | *Pacifastacus leniusculus* |
| crayfish plague | | *Aphanomyces astaci* |
| crocodilians | | Order Crocodylia |
| crocus | | *Crocus sativus* |
| crown-of-thorns starfish | | *Acanthaster planci* |
| Cuban tree frog | | *Osteopilus septentrionalis* |
| cycad | – bamboo | *Ceratozamia hildae* |
| cycads | | Division Cycadophyta |

| | | |
|---|---|---|
| darkling beetle | | *Stenocara* spp. |
| dawn redwood | | *Metasequoia glyptostroboides* |
| deadly nightshade | | *Atropas belladonna* |
| deer | – Fea's muntjac | *Muntiacus feae* |
| | – giant (= Irish elk) | *Megaloceros giganteus giganteus* |
| | – Pere David's | *Elaphurus davidianus* |
| | – red (possibly = elk) | *Cervus elaphus elaphus* |
| | – sika | *Cervus nippon nippon* |
| | – swamp | *Cervus duvauceli* |
| derbyshire feather-mosss | | *Thamnobryum angustifolium* |
| desert topminnows | | *Poeciliopsis* spp. |
| dhole | | *Cuon alpinus* |
| dingo | | *Canis familiaris dingo* |
| dipper | | *Cinclus cinclus* |
| dodo | | *Raphus cucullatus* |
| dog | – domestic and feral | *Canis familiaris* |
| dolphin | – Indus | *Platanista minor* |
| | – Yangtze | *Lipotes vexillifer* |
| dove | – Malagasy turtle | *Streptopelia pictata pictata* |
| | – turtle | *Streptopelia turtur* |
| downy gentian | | *Gentiana puberulenta* |
| dragonflies and damselflies | | Order Odonata |
| duck | – Hawaiian | *Anas wyvilliana* |
| | – Laysan | *Anas laysanensis* |
| | – mallard | *Anas platyrhynchos* |
| | – mandarin | *Aix galericulata* |
| | – ruddy | *Oxyura jamaicensis* |
| | – white-headed | *Oxyura leucocephala* |
| dugong | | *Dugong dugon* |
| dung beetles | | Sub-Family Scarabaeinae |
| dunlin | | *Calidris alpina* |
| eagle | – golden | *Aquila chrysaetos* |
| | – Philippines | *Pithecophaga jefferyi* |
| | – sea (= white-tailed eagle) | *Haliaeetus albicilla* |
| | – steppe | *Aquila nipalensis* |
| ebony | – Ceylon | *Diospyros ebenum* |
| ebonies | | *Diospyros* spp. |
| edelweiss | | *Leontopodium alpinum* |
| eel | – Asian | *Anguilla japonica* |
| | – European | *Anguilla anguilla* |
| eelgrass | | *Zostera marina* |
| egrets | | *Egretta* spp. |
| eland | – common | *Taurotragus oryx* |
| elephant | – African | *Loxodonta africana* |
| | – Asian | *Elephas maximus* |
| | – Cyprus pygmy | *Elephas cypriotes* |
| | – forest | *Loxodonta cyclotis* |
| elephant birds | | *Aepyornis* spp. |
| elk (Europe) = Moose | | *Alces alces* |
| elk (North America, possibly = red deer) | | *Cervus canadensis* (possibly = *Cervus elaphus*) |
| english sole | | *Pleuronectes vetulus* |
| ensign scale | | *Orhtezia insignis* |
| eucalyptus | | *Eucalyptus* spp. |
| European periwinkle | | *Littorina littorea* |
| Everglades snail kite | | *Rostrhamus sociabilis plumbeus* |

| | | |
|---|---|---|
| Falklands wolf (= Antarctic wolf) | | *Dusicyon australis* |
| fairy tern | | *Sterna nereis* |
| fathead minnow | | *Pimephales promelas* |
| ferns | | Division Pteridophyta |
| ferret | – black-footed | *Mustela nigripes* |
| | – European | *Mustela putorius* |
| Florida panther | | *Puma concolor coryi* (was *Felis*) |
| fox | – Arctic | *Alopex lagopus* |
| | – Catalina Island | *Urocyon littoralis catalinae* |
| | – red (= silver) | *Vulpes vulpes* |
| | – swift (= kit) | *Vulpes velox* |
| foxglove | – European | *Digitalis purpurea* |
| furbish lousewort | | *Pedicularis furbishae* |
| gadfly petrels (medium sized) | | *Pterodroma* spp. |
| garlic | | *Allium sativum* |
| gazelle | – goitred | *Gazella subgutturosa* |
| | – Tibetan | *Procapra picticaudata* |
| giant clam | | *Tridacna gigas* |
| giant panda | | *Ailuropoda melanoleuca* |
| ginger | | *Zingiber officinale* |
| ginkgo | | *Ginkgo biloba* |
| ginseng | | *Panax ginseng* |
| glowworm | | *Lampyris noctiluca* |
| goat | – domestic and feral | *Capra hircus* |
| | – Spanish (= bucardo) | *Capra pyrenaica pyrenaica* |
| golden lion tamarin | | *Leontopithecus rosalia* |
| golden monkey | | *Pygathrix roxellana* |
| goose | – Canada | *Branta canadensis* |
| | – Hawaiian (= ne ne) | *Branta sandvicensis* |
| gopher frog | | *Rana capito* |
| gorilla | – lowland | *Gorilla gorilla gorilla* and *G.g. graueri* |
| | – mountain | *Gorilla gorilla beringei* |
| gorse | | *Ulex europaeu* |
| goshawk | | *Acipiter gentilis* |
| gray catbird | | *Dumetella carolinensis* |
| great auk | | *Pinguinus impennis* |
| great blue lobelia | | *Lobelia siphilitica* |
| great crested newt | | *Triturus cristatus* |
| great kiskadee | | *Pitangus sulphuratus* |
| great tit | | *Parus major* |
| grebe | – Colombian | *Podiceps andinus* |
| | – Junin | *Podiceps taczanowskii* |
| green-bottle fly | | *Phaenicia sericata* |
| Greig's tulip | | *Tulipa greigii* |
| grey heron | | *Ardea cinerea* |
| grey partridge | | *Perdix perdix* |
| groupers | | *Epinephelus* spp. and others |
| grouse | – red | *Lagopus lagopus* |
| | – spruce | *Falcipennis canadensis* |
| Grevy's zebra | | *Equus grevyi* |
| ground hornbill | – southern | *Bucorvus leadbeateri* |
| guanacaste | | *Enterolobium cyclocarpum* |
| guanaco | | *Lama guanicoe* |
| guar | | *Bos guarus* |
| guava | | *Psidium* spp. |

| | | |
|---|---|---|
| guayule | | *Parthenium argentatum* |
| gypsy moth | | *Lymantria dispar* |
| haddock | | *Melanogrammus aeglefinus* |
| hairy spurge | | *Euphorbia villosa* |
| harelip sucker | | *Moxostoma lacerum* |
| hazel | | *Coryllus avellana* |
| hedgehog | | *Erinaceus europaeus* |
| hen harrier | | *Circus cyaneus* |
| herons | | Family Ardeidae |
| herring | – Pacific | *Clupea pallasi* |
| hippo | – common | *Hippopotamus amphibius* |
| | – Cyprus pygmy | *Phanourios minutus* |
| | – Madagascar pygmy | *Hippopotamus madagascariensis* and *H. lemerlei* |
| hornbeam | | *Carpinus betulus* |
| horse | – domestic | *Equus caballus* |
| | – wild (North America/Europe) | *Equus ferus* |
| | – Przewalski's (= takhi) | *Equus przewalskii* |
| hyena | – spotted | *Crocuta crocuta* |
| ibex | | *Capra ibex* |
| ibisbill | | *Ibidorhyncha struthersii* |
| Indian mynah | | *Acridotheres tristis* |
| indigo bunting | | *Passerina cyanea* |
| ipeca | | *Cephaelis ipecacnanta* |
| jaborandi | | *Pilocarpus jaborandi* |
| jaguar | | *Panthera onca* |
| Jameson's mamba | | *Dendroapsis jamesonii kaimosae* |
| Japanese oyster drill | | *Ocinebrellus inornatus* |
| jicaro | | *Crescentia alata* |
| jojoba | | *Simondsia chinensis* |
| Juan Fernandez sandalwood | | *Santalum fernanadezianum* |
| kakapo | | *Strigops habroptilus* |
| kelp | | *Laminaria* spp. |
| kokako | | *Callaeas cinerea wilsoni* |
| Korean pit viper | | *Agkistrodon brevicaudus* |
| krill | | *Euphausia superba* |
| lacepod | | *Lonchocarpus* spp. |
| Lake Tota fat fish | | *Rhizosomichthys totae* |
| lamprey | – European brook | *Lampetra planeri* |
| | – sea | *Petromyzon marinus* |
| lampreys (several species) | | Family Petromyzontidae |
| lantana | | *Lantana camara* |
| Lawson cypress | | *Chamaecyparis lawsoniana* |
| lemurs | | Families Lemuridae and Indriidae |
| leopard | – Amur | *Panthera pardus orientalis* |
| | – clouded | *Neofelis nebulosa* |
| | – snow | *Uncia uncia* |
| lesser duckweed | | *Lemna miniscula* |
| lesser florican | | *Sypheotides indica* |
| light orange underwing | | *Archiearis notha* |
| lime | – small-leaved | *Tilia cordata* |
| linseed | | *Linum usitatissimum* |
| lion | | *Panthera leo* |
| | – Barbary | *Panthera leo leo* |
| lipstick tree (= annatto) | | *Bixa orellana* |
| llama | | *Lama glama* |

| | | |
|---|---|---|
| lobsters | | *Homarus* spp. |
| lugworm | | *Arenicola marina* |
| Lundy cabbage | | *Coincya wrightii* (was *Rhynchosinapsis*) |
| lynx | – Canadian | *Lynx canadensis* |
| | – Eurasian | *Lynx lynx* (was *Felis*) |
| | – Iberian (= Spanish) | *Lynx pardinus* |
| macaw | – blue-throated | *Ara glaucogularis* |
| | – hyacinth | *Anodorhynchus hyacinthinus* |
| | – Illiger's (= blue-winged) | *Propyrrhura maracana* |
| | – Spix's | *Cyanopsitta spixii* |
| mackerel | | *Scomber scombrus* |
| Madagascar jumping rat | | *Hypogeomys antimena* |
| Madagascar rosy periwinkle | | *Catharanthus roseus* |
| Madeiran snail | | *Discus guerinianus* |
| magpie | | *Pica pica* |
| magpie robin | – Seychelles | *Copsychus sechellarum* |
| mahogany | – South American | *Swietenia mahagoni* |
| maize | | *Zea mays* |
| mammoths | | *Mammuthus* spp. |
| manatee | – Amazonian | *Trichechus inunguis* |
| | – Florida | *Trichechus manatus latirostris* |
| mandrinette | | *Hibiscus fragilis* |
| marmots | | *Marmota* spp. |
| Mauritius kestrel | | *Falco punctatus* |
| meadowfoam | | *Limnathes alba* |
| medicinal leech | | *Hirudo medicinalis* |
| meerkats | | *Suricata suricatta* |
| megapodes | | Family Megapodiidae |
| melaleuca tree | | *Melaleuca quinquenervia* |
| Mexican rosy boa | | *Lichanura trivirgata* |
| Mexican thorn bush | | *Prosopis juliflora* |
| Mexican yam | | *Dioscorea villosa* |
| mice | – house | *Mus musculus* |
| mink | – European | *Mustela lutreola* |
| | – American | *Mustela vison* |
| minnows | | various small schooling fish |
| moa species | | Order Dinorthiformes |
| mongoose | – Indian | *Herpestes auropunctatus* |
| mongooses | | *Herpestes* spp. |
| monkey puzzle tree | | *Araucaria araucana* |
| Moreton Bay chestnut | | *Castanospermum australe* |
| moss campion | | *Silene acaulis* |
| mosses | | Phylum Bryophyta |
| mountain bluebird | | *Sialia currucoides* |
| musk ox | | *Ovibos moschatus* |
| mussel | – Mediterranean | *Mytillus galloprovincialis* |
| | – zebra | *Dreissena polymorpha* |
| mussels | | Family Mytilidae |
| mynah | – Indian | *Acridotheres tristis* |
| mysore thorn | | *Caesalpina decapetala* |
| napier grass | | *Pennistum purpureum* |
| neem | | *Azadirachta indica* |
| nematode worms | | Phylum Nematoda |
| nettle | | *Urtica dioica* |
| New Zealand flatworm | | *Arthurdendyus triangulatus* |
| New Zealand grayling | | *Prototroctes oxyrhynchus* |

| | | |
|---|---|---|
| nigella | | *Nigella arvensis* |
| nightingale | | *Luscinia megarhynchos* |
| nile perch | | *Lates niloticus* |
| nine-banded armadillo | | *Dasypus novemcinatus* |
| North Island kokako | | *Callaeas cinerea wilsoni* |
| numbat | | *Myrmecobius fasciatus* |
| oak | | *Quercus* spp. |
| ocelot | | *Leopardus pardalis* (was *Felis*) |
| okapi | | *Okapia johnstoni* |
| opium poppy | | *Papaver somniferum* |
| orang-utang | – Bornean | *Pongo pygmaeus* |
| | – Sumatran | *Pongo abellii* |
| orchid | – eastern prairie fringed | *Platanthera leucophaea* |
| | – fen | *Liparis loeselii* |
| | – lady's slipper | *Cypripedium calceolus* |
| | – white nun | *Lycaste skinneri* |
| orchids | | Family Orchidaceae |
| oryx | – Arabian | *Oryx leucoryx* |
| | – scimitar-horned | *Oryx dammah* |
| otter | – European | *Lutra lutra* |
| | – sea | *Enhydra lutris* |
| owl | – barn | *Tyto alba* |
| | – eagle | *Bubo bubo* |
| | – elf | *Micranthene whitneyi* |
| | – northern spotted | *Strix occidentalis caurina* |
| oxpeckers | – yellow and red-billed | *Buphagus africanus* and *B. erythrorhynchus* |
| oysters | | *Pinctada* spp. |
| Pacific swallow | | *Hirundo tahitica* |
| palms | | Family Palmae |
| pampas grass | | *Cortaderia selloana* |
| pareira | | *Chrondrodendron tomentosum* |
| parakeet | – Carolina | *Conuropsis carolinensis* |
| | – echo (= Mauritian) | *Psittacula eques echo* |
| parrot | – Seychelles black | *Coracopsis niger barklyi* |
| parrots | | Family Psittacidae |
| partridge pea | | *Cassia fasiculata* |
| Partula snails | | *Partula* spp. |
| penguins | | Family Spheniscidae |
| peregrine falcon | | *Falco peregrinus* |
| petrel | – Barau's | *Pterodroma baraui* |
| petrels | | Family Procellariidae |
| pheasant | – cheer | *Catreus wallichii* |
| | – Reeves | *Syrmaticus reevesii* |
| | – Swinhoe's | *Lophura swinhoii* |
| pig | – domestic and feral | *Sus scrofa domestica* |
| | – Vietnamese warty | *Scrof bucculentus* |
| pigeon | – pink | *Columba mayeri* |
| | – passenger | *Ectopistes migratorius* |
| pika | | *Ochotona* spp. |
| pine | – Torrey | *Pinus torreyana* |
| piquia | | *Caryocar* spp. |
| plaice | | *Pleuronectes platessa* |
| plains-wanderer | | *Pedionomus torquatus* |
| pool frog | | *Rana lessonae* |
| poplar | | *Populus* spp. |

| | | |
|---|---|---|
| possum | – brush-tailed (= brushtail) | *Trichosurus vulpecula* |
| potato | | *Solanum tubrerosum* |
| prairie dog | – black tailed | *Cynomys ludovicianus* |
| primrose | | *Primula vulgaris* |
| | – bird's eye | *Primula farinosa* |
| | – Scottish | *Primula scotica* |
| privet (exotic on Mauritius) | | *Ligustrum robustum* var. *walkeri* |
| protists | | unicellular eukaryotes |
| ptarmigan | – rock | *Lagopus mutus* |
| puffer fish | | Family Tetrodontidae |
| puffin | – Atlantic | *Fratercula arctica* |
| puma (= cougar) | | *Puma concolor* (was *Felis*) |
| pupfish | – Commanche Springs | *Cyprinodon elegans* |
| | – desert | *Cyprinodon macularis* |
| | – Leon Springs | *Cyprinodon bovinus* |
| | – Parras | *Cyprinodon latifasciatus* |
| quagga | | *Equus quagga* |
| queen conch | | *Strombus gigas* |
| rabbit | | *Oryctolagus cuiculus* |
| raccoon | | *Procyon lotor* |
| ragwort | | *Senecio jacobaea* |
| rail | – Aldabra | *Dyrolimnas cuvieri aldabranus* |
| | – Bogota | *Rallus semiplumbeus* |
| | – Guam | *Rallus owstoni* (or *Gallirallus*) |
| | – light-footed clapper | *Rallus longirostris levipes* |
| Rarotonga flycatcher | | *Pomarea dimidiata* |
| rat | – black | *Rattus rattus* |
| | – brown | *Rattus norvegicus* |
| | – Polynesian (= Pacific) | *Rattus exulans* |
| rattlesnake | – Aruba Island | *Crotalus unicolor* |
| rattlesnakes | | *Crotalus* spp. |
| red-cockaded woodpecker | | *Picoides borealis* |
| red-whiskered bulbul | | *Pycnonotus jocosus* |
| redbreast sunfish | | *Lepomis auritus* |
| red kite | | *Milvus milvus* |
| red-tailed tropicbird | | *Phaethon rubicauda* |
| redwood | – giant | *Sequoia sempervirens* |
| reindeer (= Carribou) | | *Rangifer tarandus* |
| rhesus monkey | | *Maccaca mulatta* |
| rhododendron | | *Rhododendron ponticum* |
| rhino | – black | *Diceros bicornis* |
| | – white | *Ceratotherium simum* |
| rhinos | | Family Rhinocerotidae |
| rice | | *Oryza sativa* |
| rockfish | | *Sebastes* spp. |
| rockweed | | *Ascophyllum nodosum* |
| rosewoods | | *Dalbergia* spp. |
| round goby | | *Neogobius melanostomus* |
| royal catchfly | | *Silene regia* |
| rubber | | *Hevea brasiliensis* |
| ruff (bird) | | *Philomachus pugnax* |
| ruff (fish) | | *Gymnocephalus cernua* |
| sable | | *Martes zibellina* |
| sablefish | | *Anoplopoma fimbria* |
| saiga | | *Saiga tatarica* |

| | | |
|---|---|---|
| sailfish | | *Istiophorus platypterus* |
| St Helena gumwood | | *Commidendrum robustum* |
| St Helena redwood | | *Trochetiopis erythroxylon* |
| St John's wort | | *Hypericum* spp. |
| salmon | – Atlantic | *Salmo salar* |
| | – coho | *Onchorynchus kisutch* |
| saltcedar | | *Tamarix* spp. |
| sandpiper | – Henderson | *Prosobonia* sp. |
| | – upland | *Bartramia longicauda* |
| scarlet gilia | | *Ipomopsis aggregata* |
| Scottish crossbill (species status debated) | | *Loxia* sp., ? *scotica, curvirostra* or *pytyopsittacus* |
| seahorses | | Sub-Family Hippocampinae |
| sea bindweed | | *Convolvulus soldanella* |
| sea cucumbers | | Family Holothuriidae |
| sea holly | | *Eryngium maritimum* |
| sea plantain | | *Plantago maritima* |
| sea slug | | *Elysia subornata* |
| seal | – Caribbean monk | *Monachus tropicalis* |
| | – elephant (northern & southern) | *M. angustirostrus* and *M. leonia* |
| seals, sea lions and walruses | | Order Pinnipeda |
| Seychelles black paradise flycatcher | | *Terpsiphone corvina* |
| Seychelles scale insect | | *Icerya seychellarum* |
| Seychelles warbler | | *Acrocephalus sechellensis* |
| shad species | | *Alosa* spp. |
| shark | – basking | *Cetorhinus maximus* |
| | – great white | *Carcharodon carcharias* |
| | – hammerheads | *Sphyrna* spp. |
| | – whale | *Rhincodon typus* |
| sharks, skates and rays | | Class Chondrichthyes |
| shearwater | – Christmas | *Puffinus nativitatis* |
| | – Manx | *Puffinus puffinus* |
| | – sooty | *Puffinus griseus* |
| sheep | – blue | *Pseudois nayaur* |
| | – bighorn | *Ovis canadensis* |
| | – domestic | *Ovis aries* |
| sheepshead minnow | | *Cyprinodon variegatus* |
| shrew | – common | *Sorex araneus* |
| | – pygmy (Europe) | *Sorex minutus* |
| siam weed | | *Chromoleana odorata* |
| silkworm | | *Bombyx mori* |
| silver leaf | | *Desmodium uncinatum* |
| silversword | | *Brighamia rockii* and *B. insignis* |
| sisal | | *Agave sisalana* |
| snakeroot | | *Raouwolfia serpentina* |
| slow-worm | | *Anguis fragilis* |
| sole | | *Solea solea* |
| solitaire | | *Pezohaps solitaria* |
| sorghum | | *Sorghum bicolor* |
| sparrow | – house | *Passer domesticus* |
| | – song | *Melospiza melodia* |
| sparrowhawk | | *Accipiter nisus* |
| Spartina | | *Spartina* spp. |
| Sphagnum mosses | | *Sphagnum* spp. |
| spider monkey | – black | *Ateles paniscus* |

| | | |
|---|---|---|
| splendid toadfish | | *Sanopus splendidus* |
| squirrel | – grey | *Sciurus carolinensis* |
| | – red | *Sciurus vulgaris* |
| Steller's sea cow | | *Hydrodamalis gigas* |
| Stevens Island wren | | *Xenicus lyalli* |
| stickleback | – three spined | *Gasterosteus aculeatus* |
| stork | – white | *Ciconia ciconia* |
| | – wood | *Mycteria americana* |
| stumptooth minnow | | *Stypodon signifer* |
| sturgeon | – beluga | *Huso huso* |
| sturgeons | | Family Acipenseridae |
| sugar cane | | *Saccharum officinarum* |
| sunflower | | *Helianthus* spp. |
| swamp deer | | *Cervus duvauceli* |
| swan | – mute | *Cygnus olor* |
| swardfish | | *Xiphias gladius* |
| swiftlets | – birds nest (South-East Asia) | *Aerodramus* spp. |
| takahe | | *Porphyrio mantelli* |
| takamaka | | *Calophyllum inophyllum* |
| tambaqui | | *Colossoma macropomum* |
| tapirs | | *Tapirus* spp. |
| teasel | | *Dipsacus* spp. |
| tenebrionid beetle | | Family Tenebrionidae |
| teosinte | | *Zea diploperennis* |
| terrapins | | freshwater Chelonia |
| thistle | – musk | *Carduus nutans* |
| thistles | | *Cirsium* spp. and *Carduus* spp. |
| thistlehead feeding weevil | | *Rhinocyllus conicus* |
| thylacine | | *Thylacinus cynocephalus* |
| Tibetan antelope | | *Panthalops hodgsoni* |
| tiger | – Bali | *Panthera tigris balica* |
| | – Siberian | *Panthera tigris altaica* |
| tigers | | *Panthera tigris* |
| tilapia | | *Tilapia* spp. |
| toad | – cane (= marinc) | *Bufo marinus* |
| | – golden | *Bufo priglenes* |
| | – Puerto Rican crested | *Peltophryne lemur* |
| tobacco hornworm | | *Manduca sexta* |
| tomato | | *Lycopersicon esculentum* |
| toromiro | | *Sophora toromiro* |
| Torrey pine | | *Pinus torreyana* |
| tortoise | – Aldabran (= Seychelles) giant | *Geochelone gigantea* |
| | – desert | *Gopherus agassizii* |
| | – Galapagos giant | *Geochelone elephantopus* |
| | – gopher | *Gopherus polyphemus* |
| | – ploughshare | *Geochelone yniphora* |
| tortoises | | terrestrial Chelonia |
| totoaba | | *Totoaba macdonaldi* |
| triton | | *Charonia tritonis* |
| trout | – Apache | *Salmo apache* |
| | – brown | *Salmo trutta* |
| | – gila | *Salmo gilae* |
| | – rainbow | *Onchorhynchus mykiss* (was *Salmo gairdneri*) |
| tsetse fly | | *Glossina* spp. |
| tuatara | | *Sphenodon punctatus* and *S. guntheri* |
| tuna | – bluefin | *Thunnus thynnus* |

| | | |
|---|---|---|
| turmeric | | *Curcuma domestica* |
| turtle | – green | *Chelonia mydas* |
| | – hawksbill | *Eretmochelys imbricata* |
| | – leatherback | *Dermochelys coriacea* |
| turtles | – sea | marine Chelonia |
| turtles | – freshwater, *see* terrapins | |
| | – land, *see* tortoises | |
| vendace | | *Coregonus albula* |
| vicuna | | *Vicugna vicugna* |
| vine (= grape) | | *Vitis* spp. |
| violet click beetle | | *Limoniscus violaceus* |
| viper species | | *Vipera* spp. |
| Virgin Islands boa | | *Epicrates monensis granti* |
| vole | – red-backed | *Clethrionomys gapperi* |
| | – water | *Alticola terrestris* |
| wasp | – European | *Vespula* spp. |
| water hyacinth | | *Eichhornia crassipes* |
| water lettuce | | *Pistia stratiotes* |
| western barred bandicoot | | *Perameles bougainville* |
| weasel | | *Mustela nivalis* |
| weta | – Middle Island tusked | *Motuweta isolata* |
| whale | – blue | *Balaenoptera musculus* |
| | – grey | *Eschrichtius robustus* |
| | – killer | *Orcinus orca* |
| | – North Atlantic right | *Balaena glacialis glacialis* |
| whales and dolphins | | Order Cetacea |
| wheat | | *Triticum aestivum* |
| whelk | | *Murex* spp. |
| white abalone | | *Haliotis sorenseni* |
| white-breasted guineafowl | | *Agelastes meleagrides* |
| white forsythia | | *Abeliophyllum distichum* |
| white pelican | – eastern | *Pelecanus onocrotalus* |
| whitethroat | | *Sylvia communis* |
| whiting | | *Merlangius merlangus* |
| wild ass | – African | *Equus africanus* |
| | – Asiatic | *Equus hemionus* |
| wild boar | | *Sus scrofa* |
| wild dog (= painted hunting dog) | | *Lycaon pictus* |
| wildebeest | – blue | *Connochaetes taurinus* |
| willow | | *Salix* spp. |
| wolf | – Ethiopian | *Canis simensis* |
| | – grey (gray) | *Canis lupus* |
| | – red | *Canis rufus* |
| Wollemi pine | | *Wollemia nobilis* |
| wood anemone | | *Anemone nemorosa* |
| wood thrush | | *Hylocichla mustelina* |
| wolverine | | *Gulo gulo* |
| woylie (= brush-tailed bettong) | | *Bettongia penicillata* |
| wrasse | – humphead | *Cheilinus undulatus* |
| Wyalkatchem foxglove | | *Pityrodia scabra* |
| yellow-bellied glider | | *Petaurus australis* |
| yellow-eyed penguin | | *Megadyptes antipodes* |
| yellow rattle | | *Rhinanthus minor* |

| | |
|---|---|
| yellow swainson pea | *Swainsona laxa* |
| yellow-throated vireo | *Vireo flavifrons* |
| yellow-wort | *Blackstonia perfoliata* |
| yew | *Taxus baccata* |
| – Pacific | *Taxus brevifolia* |
| zander | *Stizostediaon lucioperca* |

# Index